MIND AS MIRROR
AND THE
MIRRORING OF MIND

MIND AS MIRROR AND THE MIRRORING OF MIND

Buddhist Reflections on Western Phenomenology

STEVEN LAYCOCK

STATE UNIVERSITY OF NEW YORK PRESS

Published by
State University of New York Press, Albany

Printed in the United States of America

For information, address the State University of New York Press,
State University Plaza, Albany, NY 12246

Production by Bernadine Dawes
Marketing by Terry Swierzowski

Library of Congress Cataloging-in-Publication Data

Laycock, Steven William.
Mind as mirror and the mirroring of mind : Buddhist reflections on western phenomenology / Steven Laycock.
p. cm. — (SUNY series in Buddhist studies)
Includes bibliographical references and index.
ISBN 0-7914-1997-5 ISBN 0-7914-1998-3 (pbk.)
1. Phenomenology. 2. Mādhyamika (Buddhism). 3. Knowledge, Theory of. 4. Philosophy, Comparative. I. Title. II. Series.
B829.5.L37 1994
181'.043—dc20 93-41539
CIP

1 2 3 4 5 6 7 8 9 10

Dedicated,

With boundless mettā, to:

Huma,

Rashid [Vimal]

and

Shahid [Chandra]

Contents

Acknowledgments

The fragile flower exfoliating before you throws itself into a sun that it can neither reach nor fully comprehend. If, in any limited degree, its insuperably futile efforts thrive, then its meaning, its dynamism, its very being, is an indication, a pointing, beyond itself, beyond *self,* towards the light. Its great and inexorable failure is its opacity, its becloudedness, its paradoxical faithlessness to its own message of no-self through its very visibility, its function of calling attention to itself, a self that, again paradoxically, it cannot possess. Though intended as an index, as indication, as a finger pointing, it remains, nonetheless, a finger, or perhaps a sore thumb. Its conjoint transparency and opacity, its pointing and its remaining, nonetheless, a pointer, illustrate, however, the phenomenal undecidability upon which this book revolves. And to that extent—yet another paradox—its very inadequacy is transformed into a certain success.

Though aspiring toward the resplendence of the sun, this plant, like the lotus, is rooted in the rich, dark soil which gives it nourishment and support. However, darkness, here, the turbidity of the soil, is not lightlessness, not the absence, but rather the interiorization of light. The profoundly interlarded strata of humus from which this work grows represent the deposit of numberless gifts of light: gifts of patience, gifts of intelligence, gifts of support, gifts of listening. For a work which, like the present, draws its inspiration from the deep, calm wellspring of Buddhist insight, the expression of thankfulness (which, as Heidegger knew, is inseparable from thoughtfulness) is neither academic ritual nor rhetorical posturing. Gratitude is ontology. To say that this book would not have been possible without the inspiration of teachers, the encouragement of colleagues, the engagement of students and the tolerance of family and friends is simply to illustrate the Buddhist *archē*: the principle of contingent co-arising *(pratītya-samutpāda)*. The manifold roots of indebtedness—tangled, complex, searching bottomlessly into the limitless reserve of interiorized illumination that opens below—can, regrettably, be expressed only in sorely abstract generalities and diffusion. Still, though each gift offers itself to expression only in a pervasive and generalized way, though I cannot pause to savor the benefaction of all who have contributed to this project, every grain of this rich soil was originally distinct and particular. Each deserves more than the collective expression of thanks which I offer here.

It was Kant who associated the obscurity, fragmentation and passive drifting of one's dream-life with the misguided pursuit of unfruitful philosophical byways and acknowledged Hume for having brought about his awakening. We must all, like Kant, find our way from Lotus Land to the radiant lotuslike fruition of awareness. We all need, not only our Buddhas, but our Bodhisattvas, not only those who are awakened, but those who bring awakening. And, to advance our metaphor a final step, this work would be radically incomplete without an initial expression of gratitude for the generosity, kindness, and engaged friendship of the two gardeners who have patiently pruned, nourished and watered the hesitant tendril in its drowsy stretching toward the light. This book is, in large measure, an effort to gather, to set beside one another, and, where possible, to reconcile two living and largely parallel currents of thought that, while independent, nonetheless embrace one another in profound affinity. The concord is not, however, perfect. And it is through the moments of discord that a significant, if altogether benevolent, challenge can be heard. Each thought-stream has been disclosed to me through the beneficence of a venerated teacher and guide, and each represents the outgrowth of a deep and enduring friendship.

My *Foundations for a Phenomenological Theology* was dedicated, with heartfelt esteem, to Professor James Hart, a teacher who, many years ago, awakened me from my analytic slumbers, and disclosed the possibility of a mode of philosophizing for which the beginning is everything, and for which the beginning is, not language or concept, but fully concrete, lived and living experience. It was under Jim's tutelage that Husserl's thought first became familiar to me. And though the present text may be seen, in evident respects, as a deconstruction of certain basic Husserlian conceptions, I stand apart from those who would say that Husserl is more honored in the breach. Indeed, I would be pleased should the present work be regarded as a continuing observation of the spirit, if not each syllable and letter, of Husserl's life-work. The extraordinary integrity of Husserl's philosophical character, and the uncompromising honesty of his thinking which, time after time, compelled him to start again, to stand afresh at the radical experiential origin of experience, is reflected in Jim's own person. I have met no one for whom method and result, practice and theory, are so little dissociated. And while I am boundlessly indebted to Jim's intellectual and academic guidance, his example has taught me far more: lessons of integrity, lessons of engagement, and lessons of humanity.

For those who have been given a Buddhist name, a task (perhaps a life task) is to come not only to a conceptual comprehension but to an experiential and transformative understanding of its significance. It was the Most Venerable Ratmalane Somaloka [Moonlight] who, when I took the robes briefly as a

Buddhist novice under his guidance, gave me my name, Chandima [Pure Moon]—a name the significance of which unmistakably resonates with his own. The Venerable Somaloka also named my twin sons, Shahid Chandra [Moon] and Rashid Vimal [Purity], after the brother monks, Candrakīrti and Vimalakīrti, who, in their own ways, stand as luminaries in the Buddhist tradition. There is much in these names to live and to live up to. And the present work is no more than a passing effort to plumb the inexhaustible purity of lunar reflection. The moon is a sun-mirror. And its purity lies in its selfless reflection. But while I am thankful for the inspiration that such poetic associations might bring, I am far more deeply grateful for the vast wealth that the Venerable Somaloka has placed at my disposal—riches which I have learned only in a smallest degree to make use of: the wealth of insight and deep learning, the wealth of kindness and compassion, the wealth of profoundly transformative meditation. Any adequate expression of gratitude for his guidance and encouragement along the Path must, at last, terminate in silence.

The author is gratefully indebted to the poets Stephen Berg, Bob Boldman, Alan Davies, Nelson Foster, Margaret Gibson, Allen Ginsberg, Michael Heller, Robert Kelly, Dale Pendell, Anthony Piccione, George Quasha, Gary Snyder, John Tarrant, Anne Waldman, and Philip Whalen, and to Davis and Grutman, New York, executors of the estate of John Cage, for their kind permission to use material from poems and essays appearing in *Beneath a Single Moon: Buddhism in Contemporary American Poetry,* edited by Kent Johnson and Craig Paulenich (Boston: Shambhala, 1991).

The author is also grateful to the following publishers for permission to reproduce copyrighted material:

Passages from *Negative Dialectics* by Theodor Adorno are reprinted by permission of The Continuum Publishing Company. English translation copyright © 1973 by The Continuum Publishing Company.

Passages from *Inner Experience* by George Bataille, translated by Leslie Anne Boldt, are reprinted by permission of the State University of New York Press. Copyright © 1988 by the State University of New York Press.

Passages from *Laws of Form* by G. Spencer Brown are reprinted by permission of Julian Press, Inc., a division of Crown Publishers, Inc. Copyright © 1972 by G. Spencer Brown.

Passages from *The Teachings of The Compassionate Buddha,* edited by E. A. Burtt, are reprinted by permission fo the estate of E. A. Burtt. Copyright © 1955 by E. A. Burtt.

Passages from *Who Comes After the Subject?*, edited by Eduardo Cadava, Peter Connor, and Jean-Luc Nancy are reprinted by permission of Routledge, Chapman, and Hall, Inc. Copyright © 1991 by Routledge, Chapman, and Hall, Inc.

Passages from *Original Teachings of Ch'an Buddhism* by Chang Chung-Yuan are reprinted by permission of Pantheon Books, a division of Random House, Inc. Copyright © 1969 by Chang Chung-Yuan.

A storm wind blows

out from among the grasses

the full moon grows.

(CHORA, 1729–81)

An Incident at Wang-Mei Shan

Imagine, if you will, the silent temple compound at Wang-mei Shan, bathed, perhaps, in the limpid luminescence of the full midnight moon. For some time the monastic community, quiescent by custom, has felt the touch of a deeper sobriety. Soon the aging master, Hung-jen (601–74 C.E.), will pass beyond the anguish of this world. The master's successor, as Hung-jen has declared, will be the monk who composes the most insightful gāthā. And everyone expects the scholarly and respected Shen-hsiu (605?–706 C.E.) to be capable of superlatively penetrating insight. Everyone, that is, with the possible exception of Shen-hsiu himself. Shen-hsiu has, indeed, written a very fine gāthā, a verse which will win the adulation of the master. Yet he is troubled by doubt. Stealing into Hung-jen's quarters, he affixes the following, anonymously, to the wall:

> Body is the Bodhi Tree,
> The mind a stand of mirror bright.
> Take care to wipe it continually,
> Allowing no dust to cling.[1]

Even before the mountain mist begins to glow in the first timid blush of morning light, the master arises. The dreamless curtain of sleep parting his mind only moments earlier, Hung-jen discovers the lovely verse, and in reverence for its insight summons his disciples. Incense is burned before it, and the community is admonished that enlightenment will unfailingly be attained by whoever should put the gāthā into practice. One monk, we may imagine, is inwardly delighted. Others, guessing the author of the verse, are warmly satisfied.

There is one, however, no doubt deeply inspired by the verse, whose remarkable insight plumbs deeper still. Hui-neng (638–713 C.E.), occasionally described by the tradition (though not without evident paradox) as an "illiterate" kitchen-helper from "the South" (perhaps Canton, or perhaps even farther south, Vietnam),[2] composes the following verse, tacks the gāthā anonymously beside its mate, and returns to his quarter in silence beneath the enigmatic half-smile of the onlooking full moon.

> There never was a Bodhi Tree,
> Nor bright mirror-stand.
> Originally, not one thing exists,
> So where is the dust to cling?[3]

Rising long before the earth begins to quiver and dance in the curious intruding beams of the sun's light, Hung-jen, a subdued flush of recognition rising to his eyes, summons Hui-neng to the Master's quarters, and confers upon him the robe and begging bowl of his office. The Master can now pass beyond this life content in the assurance that he has found in Hui-neng a successor of great profundity and wisdom.

Prelude in the Key of Emptiness

Frameworks

The urge to embellish this charming vignette is almost irresistible, and I must confess to succumbing. And if I may be forgiven the harmless lapse, surely my far more venerable predecessors (Shen-hui among them) may also. Perhaps, indeed, all we have in this narrative is embroidery upon embroidery. The account is almost certainly fictive. Yet fiction does not poison our enjoyment. Nor would even the discovery, contrary current to scholarly estimation, that our principals do not (or did not) exist mitigate in the least our appreciation of the deep insight offered by an attentive contemplation of the tale. Though the weight of historical consideration favors their existence, nothing would be lost were it to turn out that "Hui-neng" and "Shen-hsiu" fail, in the crude and unimaginative sense, to "denote."

The lovely, no doubt apocryphal, story of the *Platform Sutra* dramatizes the relationship between the alternative philosophical—and, indeed, specifically phenomenological—"positions" expressed in the two *gāthās*.[1] My own thinking regarding this relationship has progressed in three steps, the first patently naïve, the second concealing, if not entirely successfully, its now evident naïveté. Setting aside for the moment the precise import of the verses, one is immediately struck by the apparent relationship of aggressive frontal contradiction. If the law of contradiction is to preserve any purchase upon our interpretation, it simply cannot be simultaneously the case that "Body is the Bodhi Tree" and that "There never was a Bodhi Tree." "The mind [is] a stand of mirror bright" contradicts "There never was a . . . bright mirror-stand."[2] And "Originally, not one thing exists"[3] excludes the existence of Bodhi Tree, mirror and dust, and conversely. The most obvious, and most naïve, supposal regarding the relationship (my first step) invokes the logic of contradiction. If Hui-neng is *right*, Shen-hsiu is simply *wrong*. And the narrative, on this interpretation, has no other intent than that of demonstrating the alethic superiority of Hui-neng's position.[4]

Perhaps it is not too early to suggest the precedence of the *logos* of *phaínomena* over the logic which rules the ordered march of propositional entailment. Sartre finds that the principle of (non)contradiction

> can denote only the relations of being with the *external*, exactly because it presides over the relations of being with what it is not. We are dealing then with a principle constitutive of *external relations* such that they can appear to human reality present to being-in-itself and engaged in the world. This principle does not concern the internal relations of being; these relations, inasmuch as they would posit an otherness, do not exist. The principle of identity is the negation of every species of relation at the heart of being-in-itself." (BN, 124)

But not only is the principle of noncontradiction incapable of addressing itself to the *Ineinander* integrity of a phenomenal realm structured, in the Buddhist view, by the interpenetration, the interfusion, of all particular phenomenal beings, it is, indeed, of insufficient depth to voice the structure of phenomena. "[T]he phenomenal layer is literally prelogical. . . ." (PhP, 274). The principle of noncontradiction, foundational for logic, itself rests upon a prelogical, though by no means irrational, base. In its articulate form, it postulates that nothing can exemplify both a given property and that property's complement *in the same respect* and *at the same time*, thus making ineliminable reference to the essentially *prelogical* notions of *respect* and *time*. And it is, of course, the primordial notions of temporality and "respect" (perspective, mode of givenness, position taking) that phenomenology seeks to elucidate. It is not, then, surprising, as Merleau-Ponty affirms, that

> we arrive at contradictions when we describe the perceived world. And it is also true that if there were such a thing as a non-contradictory thought, it would exclude the world of perception as a simple appearance. But the question is precisely to know whether there is such a thing as logically coherent thought or thought in the pure state. (PP, 18)

Thus, "the accusation of contradiction is not decisive, *if the acknowledged contradiction appears as the very condition of consciousness*" (PP, 19).[5] Were these protological notions not univocal, and were phenomenological investigation incapable of converging upon them, we would be confronted with a selection of alterior principles of contradiction.[6]

Though now abashed at the grave naïveté of my earlier reading, I take, nonetheless, a certain comfort in having found myself in the company of no less illustrious an exegete than D. T. Suzuki, according to whom the practice of "dust wiping" sponsored by Shen-hsiu lent itself to a dissociation of the innately integral and inseparable conscious functions of *dhyāna* (meditation) and *prajñā* (wisdom):[7]

> Dhyāna became the exercise of killing life, of keeping the mind in a state of torpor and making the Yogins socially useless; while Prajñā, left to itself, lost its profundity, for it was identified with intellectual subtleties which dealt in concepts and their analyses. (NM, 32–33)

Thus divided, meditational "dust wiping" was viewed by Shen-hsiu as a necessary prerequisite for wisdom. *Dhyāna* and *prajñā* were sequentially ordered, the one required *before* the other could arise. Hui-neng's portrayal of this relationship appears to conflict with the teaching of stepwise attainment that Shen-hsiu maintained. Hui-neng proclaimed in an address to his followers:

> Good friends, how then are meditation and wisdom alike? They are like the lamp and the light it gives forth. If there is a lamp there is light; if there is no lamp there is no light. The lamp is the substance of the light; the light is the function of the lamp. Thus, although they have two names, in substance they are not two. Meditation and wisdom are also like this. (PS/y, 136)

Only by overcoming the conflictual duality of meditational *practice* and the profound "seeing"[8] that is "theory" *(theoria)*[9] in a sense akin to that which this term held for the Greeks,[10] could the transaction of ordinary life *(saṁsāra)* be rendered consistent with the attainment of supreme insight *(nirvāṇa)*.[11] As Nāgārjuna famously avers:

> *Saṁsāra* (i.e., the empirical life-death cycle) is nothing essentially different from *nirvāṇa*. *Nirvāṇa* is nothing essentially different from *saṁsāra*. The limits (i.e., realm) of *nirvāṇa* are the limits of *saṁsāra*. Between the two, also, there is not the slightest difference whatsoever. (MK, 25:19–20; N, 158).

My original suggestion will not, of course, withstand the text. The veneration that Hung-jen feels for Shen-hsiu's verse bars acceptance of simple contradiction as the mediating framework. The Master declares that enlightenment will pursue those who invoke the verse as a guide to *practice*. The *gāthā* is supremely "practical," revealing in a profoundly lucid way the path to enlightenment. Enlightenment is the "end," and "dust wiping" the "means." But no "means" can escape the fate of Wittgenstein's ladder once the "end" has been attained. Indeed, for the enlightened mind, the "ladder" is not simply taken up and discarded or stowed away. There *is* no ladder. And there *are* no mirror, no dust, and no polishing.[12] It would seem, then, that the two poems give voice to vividly alterior standpoints: that of "practice" and that of "attainment." Assuredly, no contradiction interposes itself between the descriptions of a coin (seen face-on) as "circular" and of the same coin (seen from the side) as "rectangular." Circularity and rectangularity do, of course, exclude one another. Yet the apparent contradiction is resolved in a relativity of "respects" or "standpoints."[13] In this way (my second faltering step), the two *gāthās* are rendered perfectly consistent. There is no question of truth-exclusion. Suitably relativized, *both* are equally and coherently true.[14]

If the fatefully naïve "dogmatic" proposal was stanched by the Master's adulation of Shen-hsiu's insight, the present "relativist" suggestion is barred no less by the narrative fact that Hui-neng receives the Master's mantle. Crassly put, Hung-jen institutes the contest, and Hui-neng wins the "prize."[15] The dogmatist, appealing to the principles of traditional logic, cleaves to one side or the other of a contradiction. The relativist, magically waiving "truth" into thin air and causing "truth-for" to appear in its place, finds no use for the dogmatist's fulcrum of bivalence, and is thus spared the unpleasant task of assigning alethic preferability to alternative views.[16] Yet the nonconflictual liberty thus purchased costs us dearly. Hui-neng's position *is* preferable, and, indeed, as I now believe and hope to demonstrate, *alethically* preferable, though our higher *aletheia* (the Buddhist *paramārtha)*[17] overlooks the battle of the lower truths *(saṃvṛti)*.[18]

If dogmatism and relativism exhaust the possibilities, we find ourselves at a fateful impasse. The narrative is straightforwardly self-contradictory. The ruin of reason must follow upon the Master's both approving Shen-hsiu's submission and awarding the mantle to Hui-neng for his.[19] Far too much is made in popular discussions of the alleged "irrationality" of the Buddhist meditative tradition,[20] and if Hung-jen is to be acquitted of simple irrationality,[21] we must find a tertiary proposal that *both* preserves the frontal contradiction of the two verses *and* permits their simultaneous truth.[22] The setting for the two gems can only be "dialectical."[23]

Mirroring and Representation

Though it might profit us more, little of our present energies will spent beneath the "Bodhi Tree." And perhaps we will forgiven for adverting equally little to the articulation of a somatic phenomenology. The lessons we shall draw from the jewellike, almost archetypal *Platform* narrative concern an issue of burning philosophical relevance: in our present terms, the relationship of "mirror" and "dust."

Rorty's notable study, *Philosophy and the Mirror of Nature*, offers a familiar exposition of this connection; and the title of our present study elicits the evident contrast of our own insights with Rorty's insistent dismissal of "our glassy essence." Rorty appears (deceptively) to align himself with Hui-neng in denying the mirror of mind. Yet what we find altogether lacking in Rorty's rejection of Shen-hsiu's position is any hint of Hung-jen's enlightened appreciation:

> The picture which holds traditional philosophy captive is that of the mind as a great mirror, containing various representations—some accurate, some not—and capable of being studied by pure, nonempirical methods. Without the notion of the mind as mirror, the notion of knowledge as accuracy of representation would not have suggested itself. Without this latter notion, the strategy common to Descartes and Kant—getting more accurate representations by inspecting, repairing, and polishing the mirror, so to speak—would not have made sense. Without this strategy in mind, recent claims that philosophy could consist of "conceptual analysis" or "phenomenological analysis" or "explication of meanings" or examination of the "logic of our language" or of "the structure of the constituting activity of consciousness" would not have made sense.[24]

Rorty's irritation with the conception of truth as *adequatio* is of little interest to us here. Any phenomenologist will suffer from some variant of the same allergy. What does concern us is that Rorty has fatefully misjudged the mirror, a misjudgment which follows upon the assumption that "The notion of an unclouded Mirror of Nature is the notion of a mirror which would be indistinguishable from what was mirrored, and thus would not be a mirror at all."[25] Should it turn out, as I believe it must, that a mirror *qua* mirror is of necessity "unclouded," then, of course, as Rorty asserts, mirror and mirrored will be phenomenally indistinguishable.[26] But then the distinction between "presentation" and "representation" collapses.[27] Rorty implicitly assumes a doctrine of essential "distortion." But under his pen, the assumption flares into inconsistency. There may be no mind-mirror, yet undeniably Rorty harbors a conception of one—which renders its putative nonexistence a merely contingent befallment, and thus beyond the ken of philosophy to demonstrate.[28] And even if uninstantiated, Rorty's ineluctably beclouded mirror will have to answer to our query, "Distorted with respect to what standard of clarity?" Or, it may be asked, "Where is the absolute reality that departs completely from our point of view as a yardstick?"[29] Rorty spends several hundred pages fulminating over the correspondence theory. But here, at a most crucial juncture, he is haunted by the silent presence of his foe. "Mirror polishing," for Rorty, is the benighted enterprise of achieving better and more congruent "representations."[30] Yet Shen-hsiu, patiently wiping the dust from the mind-mirror, will have nothing of Rorty's distinction.[31]

It might initially seem that the Derridean stance disclosed in Gasché's very interesting ruminations regarding the silvering, the "tain," of the mirror is at once phenomenologically more insightful and less vulnerable to internal critique. Gasché's project involves the "generalization of reflexivity" and "implies a breaking through of the tinfoils of the mirrors of reflection, demonstrating the uncertainty of the speculum." To do this:

> [T]he mirroring is made excessive in order that it may look through the looking glass toward what makes the speculum possible. To look through the mirror is to look at its reverse side, at the dull side doubling the mirror's specular play, in short, at the *tain* of the mirror. . . . the mirror's tinfoil necessarily becomes semitransparent and, as a correlate, only semireflective. Reflection, then, appears to be affected by the infrastructures that make it possible; it appears bracketed and breached as an inevitably imperfect and limited *Scheinen*.[32]

While the argument conflates a subtle, but descriptively vital, distinction—one looks "into," not "through," a mirror—it is the conflation of a second distinction which spells its undoing. "Mirror," having two references, is ambiguous. The rectangular object perched above the dresser, the "empirical mirror," if you will, assuredly has its glass and its tain, and is just assuredly "semireflective." Yet to the precise extent that the empirical mirror is also "semitransparent" and thus, indeed, "semiopaque," it thereby fails in its service as "phenomenal mirror." The "phenomenal mirror," the pure, immediate, and uncompromised reflective functioning that comprises no more than a limited aspect of the empirical mirror, is by no means "bracketed," "breached" or remiss in its duties as *Scheinen*. Indeed, "the mirror is the symbol of an unaltered vision of things."[33] Attributing to *mirroring* (the aspect) what can at best be said of the empirical *mirror*, the argument turns out to be a variant of the classical fallacy of division.

The ordinary household mirror is not, of course, unequivocally free of flaws. It betrays itself as a sobering "richness," instead of a magical "poverty," through its imperfections. Slight discolorations of the glass, light refracted from its surface, barely perceptible ripples and gaps in the silvering, bring the mirror itself to light as merely one more somber opacity among so many others.[34] In its application to the familiar mirrors of our experience, Rorty's point cannot be gainsaid. As a matter of cold empirical fact, the flawless mirror is nowhere to be encountered.[35] And it is precisely the flaws that lend opacity and objectivity to the empirical mirror.[36]

Yet to the extent that a "mirror" is thus flawed, it is no *mirror* at all.[37]

Exactly where the silvering has flaked and the back looms toward us as an object, there occurs a rupture of reflectivity. Exactly *there* we find opacity, objectivity, certainly not, in our sublimated sense, a "mirror," or even a *part* of one. Rorty is wrong. A "mirror" that is clouded disgraces the title.

Grant Rorty his claim that every mirror we encounter within the world of empirical reality is flawed. Ideal reflectivity is not thereby expelled from the phenomenal realm. We experience the "flawless" in the "flawed."[38] Rorty has not succeeded in banishing us from our experiential homeland. We are not left to wander in pursuit of reflective purity among the hollow ornaments of pure abstraction. For it is compellingly evident that, once the opaque imperfections are sifted away, we do, indeed, enjoy the experiential presence of the mirror—*qua* mirror.[39]

The phenomenal indistinguishability which pursues the ideal purity of the mirror is reinforced in Suzuki's discussion of Tsung-mi's alternative, but clearly parallel, metaphor:

> The mind . . . is like a crystal ball with no colour of its own. It is pure and perfect as it is. But as soon as it confronts the outside world it takes on all colours and forms of differentiation. This differentiation is in the outside world, and the mind, left to itself, shows no change of any character. Now suppose the ball to be placed against something altogether contrary to itself, and so become a dark-coloured ball. However pure it may have been before, it is now a dark-coloured ball, and this colour is seen as belonging from the first to the nature of the ball. When shown thus to ignorant people they will at once conclude that the ball is foul, and will not be easily convinced of its essential purity. (NM, 17)[40]

While Tsung-mi (780–841 C.E.), illustrating Shen-hsiu's position, suggests that mind is, in reality, pellucid and unadulterated crystal, I submit, on the contrary, not only that we can never *know*, solely by phenomenological inspection,[41] whether what we see "instantiates" or "manifests" its properties, but more searchingly, that there simply *is* no ontological truth of the matter.[42] The metaphors of mirroring and transparency[43] are equivalent in their experiential implications.[44] Ideal transparency, like ideal reflectivity,[45] consorts not at all with objectifying imperfections.[46] Place Tsung-mi's crystal ball against a red surface. Beside it place a ball made of red glass. Any discernible phenomenal difference between the two will be due entirely to a failure of genuine transparency.

Magritte's well-known painting *La condition humaine* illustrates exactly the same point. A "flawlessly" realistic landscape painting is set on easel in front of a "picture" window. "Landscape" is continuous with and indistinguishable from *landscape*.[47] And Magritte is assuredly right. The phenomenal indiscernibility of the "two" pictures portrays a searching aspect of the "human condition."[48] And, as Gongora, the notable Spanish poet, attests, the "condition" may not be limited to the entirely "human":

> I looked at myself and saw a sun shining in my forehead
> While an eye was visible in the sky
> the neutral water doubted which was real:
> the human sky or the celestial Cyclops.[49]

Let me offer yet another illustration. Experiences, like seeds, germinate in reflection. And some, like the proverbial mustard seed, seem of minuscule significance when washed along with the torrential surge of events. The "seeds" of experience may lie dormant indefinitely. Yet when their germinal life is awakened, the thought thus born exfoliates rapidly and ramifies extensively.[50] The present work is, in some measure, the outgrowth of just such a seminal experience. Many years ago, I found myself walking home in the rain under a transparent plastic umbrella borrowed from a friend. Slumped and miserably soaked from the downpour, my eyes were cast about my soggy shoes. As I approached a street lamp, however, I chanced to look up, and was met by the familiar halo-like diffraction distortion created by light passing prismatically through beads of rain. Yet for a brief moment, until the explanatory "account" solidified, I found it impossible to tell whether the cause of the "halo" was "in me" (perhaps a temporary distortion of the eye's lens, or, as seemed more likely, moisture on the surface of the eye) or "outside." The experience was simply "indifferent" to its alternative accounts. Though I lacked the word at the time, nothing could have been more effective in stimulating on my part an interest in the "logic" *(logos)* of *phaínomena*: phenomenology.

A Paradox of Phenomenological Optics

But the point is more general, and, in its generality, far more perplexing. *Phaínomenon*, in Heidegger's familiar rendering of the Greek, "is derived from the verb φαίνεσθαι, which signifies 'to show itself'. . . . φαίνεσθαι . . . comes from φαίνοω—to bring to the light of day, to put in the light."[51] And a Buddhist phenomenology, the realization of which is "enlightenment,"[52] cannot be indifferent to the exquisite metaphor of light.[53] Let us, then, as propadeutic to our phenomenological considerations, offer a few elementary reflections on this brightening trope. The career of light is strikingly vital:

(1) it is "born," emerges from its source;
(2) it proceeds along its "path," its "way," through its medium;
(3) it encounters adversity, obstacles, detours, is bent, reflected, out of the "way"; and in the end,
(4) it "dies," is resorbed.[54]

Light has its "Alpha" and "Omega," its "Way," and its "Adventure." It engages itself with "objects" in four distinctive, though not exclusive, ways: it is

(1) *emitted* (from its source);
(2) *transmitted* (through its medium);
(3) *reflected*; and
(4) *absorbed.*

If light is emitted, we call the object "luminous";[55] if transmitted, "transparent";[56] if reflected, "reflective"; and if absorbed, "opaque." Objects may fall at once into several or into all four optical categories, but it belongs, I submit, to the very notion of *object* that the four categories be exhaustive.[57] Remarkably, in the "pure," ideal case, luminosities, transparencies, reflectivities and opacities do not offer themselves *in presence*. They do not, with Buddhist emphasis, offer them/*selves* in presence. The very "self" of each, each it/self, is *invisible*. The philosopher of Plato's cave bears witness to the dazzling, if not blinding, propensity of the luminous.[58] One cannot gaze directly at the sun without forfeiting, at least temporarily, one's capacity for sight.[59] A perfect transparency would be precisely that—wholly eluding visual presentation.[60] And the invisibility of the ideal mirror needs, perhaps, no further motivation. One sees in the mirror what stands before it, not the mirror itself.[61] Finally, a pure opacity, purged of every least trace of transparency and reflectivity, devouring all light in its ravenous absorption, is the very type of the "black hole,"[62] and like the black hole,[63] is, for exactly the same reason, invisible:[64] light which enters does not emerge.[65]

In the four ideal cases, inclusive, and exhaustive, the "object" (itself) cannot be seen. Granting that the "objects" of our acquaintance are never, indeed could never be, "pure," still "impurity" can only amount to an admixture, in varying proportions, of the "pure" types.[66] And we must persist, then, in our aporetic expectation that the object, pure or impure, cannot become visibly present to us. The "object," cherished as intentional index by the phenomenologies of the West, encloses in its very notion an inconsistent dyad of attributes: *visibility* together with the disturbing disjunction of luminosity, transparency, reflectivity and opacity that at the same time ensures its *invisibility*.[67]

The signature and style of a given object is determined by the particular pattern and proportion of absorption and reflection, perhaps transparency and luminosity, which characterize it. And the culminating paradox, though certainly not alien in spirit from Buddhist insights, is that the "visible" object is distinct from others, and thus, indeed, visible *as an object*, only as a signature function of invisibilities.[68] The visible is a shifting pattern of invisibilities marked by a recognizable "style."

The metaphor of light is, however, only suggestive.[69] The inconceivably complex, linear process of luminal promulgation, mediated by a certain retinal excitation, the transformation of photonic into nervous energy, leading, through the optic nerves, into the astonishingly intricate neural thicket of the occipital cortex, eludes the thorough comprehension of the most gifted optical physicists and neurophysiologists. Set aside as a phenomenologically naïve, unwanted, perhaps unwarranted, presupposition this causal-explanatory nexus.[70] Still we have not depleted the powerfully suggestive energies of the luminal metaphor.[71] Loy reminds us that "given the nature of the eyes, all we can ever see is light."[72] And the "light" of manifestation is intentional.[73] Intentional acts, in Husserl's evocative imagery, are "rays," single or multiple.[74] Apperception, co-occurrent with perception, is depicted as "a stream of dispersed light enveloping the central ray and terminating in a dimly lit halo."[75] We see "in light of" the *eidos*. Reflection "brings to light."[76] And the task of phenomenology is to "elucidate."[77] And just as we cannot tell, without investigation, without background information, without inference—without, that is, presupposition—whether a given display of phenomenal light has been emitted directly into the eye[78] or has been reflected or refracted by some specular surface, so we cannot, to chant the indispensable Husserlian litany, without presupposition discriminate the actual "object" from a vivid hallucinatory representation.[79]

Existence, we might say, is the "difference"[80] between the luminous and the reflective,[81] and, as the *epochē* inculcates, is not phenomenal. Accordingly, as we have seen, existence remains from the subtraction of reflectivity from transparency. What separates the two cases is the origination of manifestation from an actually existent object.

From the phenomenal display of manifest "light," called *presence*,[82] we learn nothing of the optical category—luminous, transparent, or reflective—of its "object."[83] The "optical" categories, as we have, perhaps perversely, called them, are not, and in principle cannot be, the categories of phenomenological description. Any given "object" may be *seen as* luminous, transparent or reflective. But the morphic dimension of such *Auffassungen* eludes presentational certification.

Husserlian phenomenology is a phenomenology of "light," an investigation of *presence*.[84] But consider, now, the last indistinction: pure opacity is no more visible than pure luminescence. The sun illuminating the world above the Platonic cave abolishes presence by a surfeit of presence.[85] And it is not surprising to find, as we will, that Husserl feels the need to reject "absolute presence," the omniscient, simultaneous disclosure of the object in every possible mode of its givenness. The sun is invisible not simply because it blinds, but because it blinds by filling us with light, leaving no contrast, and thus removes itself from the realm of phenomenal objectivity. In opacity, we are robbed of intentional illumination. Invisibility is effected, not by plenary presence, but by utter evacuation. It is as though the "rays" of mind, probing infinitely into the void,[86] meet not the slightest pellicle of dust which could make their illumination manifest.[87] Like fullness of light,[88] phenomenal emptiness is objectless.[89] Enlightenment is emptiness.[90] Mind pours "itself" selflessly into the void, indifferent to the presence or absence of determinate objectual occasions of manifestation.[91] Thus, as Ch'an Master Hui-hai remarks:

> The nature of perception being eternal, we go on perceiving whether objects are present or not. . . . whereas objects naturally appear and disappear, the nature of perception does neither of those things; and it is the same with all your other senses.[92]

Being equally reticent of presentation, pure luminosity and pure opacity, pure presence and pure absence, birth and death,[93] are indistinguishable. Thus, again, Buddhist phenomenology is neither a theory of presence nor of absence, but of the contrastive "play"[94] of invisibilities that grounds visibility. A Buddhist phenomenology, consistent with the deep lesson of *anātman* (substancelessness, egolessness), is not the disclosure of a realm of perdurant objects, noumenal objects "themselves" or "in-themselves," but is rather the study of the free play of phenomenal light, a dance of "light" *(bodhi)* which is the very "being" *(sattva)* of the phenomenological practitioner: the *Bodhisattva*.[95]

The Dialectic of Mirroring

The dialectical circuit stands, then, expectantly adumbrated before us.[96] Shen-hsiu's mind-mirror, unperturbed by Rorty's empirical considerations, is flawlessly reflective. His assertion, "The mind is like a bright mirror-stand" entails Hui-neng's concomitant negation, "There never was . . . a bright mirror-stand," and conversely. Both claims are ostensibly *true*, since there is no truth without judgment, and no judgment of experience is innocent of the divisive attribution that severs "seeing nothing" from "not seeing."[97] The two "positions" are not derived from disciplined meditative insight into the nature of the phenomenal, but spring, rather, from the primordial *(Ur-)* partition *(-teil)* of analytic judgment. A phenomenology purged of "metaphysical"[98] (pre-phenomenological) presupposition—purged, that is, of what we "know,"[99] what we *judge*, rightly "dividing" the word of truth[100]—can discern no difference between *mirror* and *object,* mind and its field,[101] subject and object, and in this momentous "failure" lies the mind's mirrorlikeness. In this undecidability lies also the ground (or rather, *Abgrund)* of Hui-neng's denial of mirrorlikeness. For the one thing which, in principle, can never be seen "in" the mirror is precisely the mirror itself.

The mirror, returning in reflection what is offered (the only "self" it could have), and, having thus emptied "itself" of "itself," thus possessing nothing of "itself" to offer, is "ec/static," beside "itself." Reflexively, having kenotically drained "itself" to the dregs in reflection, the mirror empties "itself" even of "its own" self-emptying.[102] Thus, devoid *even of self-emptying*, the mirror offers *itself* (its genuine *self)* to intuition.[103] Devoid, through self-emptying, of self-emptying "itself," there is no "object" to be seen. Yet paradoxically, the very self-emptying which evacuates *even itself* ensures that, in this "intuition,"[104] there is nothing to see.[105] In self-emptying, the mirror comes curiously to light as an *object*—though an object *itself* ineluctably beyond visibility. One "sees" *nothing*.[106] It is precisely *nothing* that one sees. As paralleled in the Epimenides, negation begets affirmation,[107] and cyclically, affirmation begets negation.[108] Hui-neng is the father of Shen-hsiu; and Shen-hsiu the father of Hui-neng.[109]

Might there not be at work here a principle not unlike the "undecidability" which has always haunted the formal sciences, and, in our century, has shaken the previously inviolate sanctum of physics as well? The formal disciplines have never been without their *aporiai*. From antiquity, logic has had its "liar paradox." The ostensibly benign, if improbable, pronouncement of Epimenides, verifiable (or, as the odds would have it, falsifiable) by ordinary means, that all Cretans are liars would have passed, unproblematic and unremarked, into obscurity, were it not for the embarrassing fact that Epimenides himself was a Cretan. We are offered the option of conferring "true" or "false" upon the statement. Yet it is precisely this "decision" which we must not, on pain of evident contradiction, be moved to make. The undecidability of the Epimenides is, of course, a consequence of a certain mediated "auto-deconstructive" self-referentiality,[110] a fact brought to focus in the immediate self-referentiality of the condensed version: "This very sentence is false."

In 1931, Kurt Gödel stunned the mathematical academy with his formulation of a revolutionary theorem prohibiting "decision" in favor of any axiomatic system of sufficient vitality to generate the truths of elementary number theory.[111] The Incompleteness Theorem, a cousin of the "Liar," is of interest as much for the distance it keeps as for its familial tie. Yet the technicalities of "Gödel numbering" and the amenities of the proof cannot detain us here. An informal sketch might, however, prove of some use. Suppose a particularly "honest" computer (call it "Abe," shall we?) were so programmed that it could display only *true* statements. "Abe," of course, refers to a peculiar piece of "software" and thus to a given axiomatic system, not to "hard" circuits and a console. Hence, if Abe can display a certain result, the result is provable (decidable) in Abe. "Decidability-in-Abe" entails truth, since Abe is, after all, tirelessly "honest." But the converse fails. There is at least one sentence which, while *true*, is not decidable-in-Abe, namely: "This very sentence is not decidable-in-Abe." If Abe could prove it, then, *per impossibile*, the primordial law of Abe's "honesty" would have been abrogated.[112] Yet the sentence is clearly *true*. Again, auto-deconstructive self-referentiality breeds undecidability.[113]

Nor is topology immune to the curse of undecidability. The well-known configuration that bears the name of A. F. Möbius (1790–1868) attests to a "local" bipolarity that vanishes in the "global" comprehension. By imparting a half-twist to a narrow rectangular strip of paper, then pasting the ends together, one creates a figure with the astounding peculiarity of having only one side. Considered "locally," there is, at every point, an obverse and a reverse. Yet, if one begins to draw a line following the longitude of the Möbius strip, the starting point will be rejoined without at any point shifting to the opposite side.[114] The question, "On what side, obverse or reverse, have we drawn the line?" is thus undecidable. Obverse and reverse, the polarities of an analytic that separates and keeps separate, are, in a perfectly legitimate, though merely "local," acceptation, "op/posite," posed *against* one another.[115] Nonetheless, the tension vanishes in the "ultimate" comprehension articulated by Hui-hai: "Ultimate realization is beyond realization and non-realization. . . . Ultimate voidness is beyond voidness and non-voidness" (HH, 82). Or in the lofty wisdom of the *Prajñāpāramitā*, "Beings, beings, O Subhūti, as no-beings have they been taught by the Tathāgata. Therefore they are called 'beings'."[116] Comprehensively, the "unconditioned identity of the conditioned and of the Unconditioned is the principal message of the *Prajñāpāramitā*."[117] The lowly doughnut conveys the point with equal elegance, however. Draw a circle around the top of the morning's toroidal delicacy. Looking down from on high, there is, of course, a clear demarcation of "inside" from "outside." Yet, on a torus, the area marked "outside" is continuous with, indeed, identical with, the area marked "inside."

Few theoretical advances have shaken our conception of the physical world as profoundly as the Uncertainty Principle promulgated by Werner Heisenberg. The technicalities, beyond our present reach, can be dispensed with in favor of the summary delineation that "[w]e cannot observe the course of nature without disturbing it,"[118] and that "[o]bservation means interference with what we are observing" and thus that "observation disturbs reality."[119] Indeed, Heisenberg's own conclusion represents a serious challenge to our encrusted Cartesian categories: "the common division of the world into subject and object, inner world and outer world, body and soul, is no longer adequate and leads us into difficulties."[120] It might be complained (by those, at least, who admit no communication between the "empirical" and the "transcendental")[121] that empirical confirmation counts for naught in matters philosophical. If so, we have, nonetheless, a striking natural-scientific parallel to a phenomenological vision, profoundly Buddhist in its implications, and a momentous "vision"[122] that subjects the founding assumptions of Occidental phenomenology to deep and critical question.[123]

The profoundly Buddhist repudiation of the self *(ātman)*, and thus, of the "itself," is the very engine of dialectical paradox.[124] And this (on my third—and, I now believe, entirely suitable—rendering of the *Platform* narrative) is exactly the source of Hung-jen's confirmation of Hui-neng. Again, the Liar Paradox serves our comprehension. Write upon both sides of a card: "The sentence on the other side of this card is true." Though we are passed interminably from side to side, no *paradox*, beyond the innocuous merry-go-round, is born. Write the same sentence on one side, and on the other, its negate, and paradox is inescapable. It is not, as I once assumed, Hui-neng's *position* that is alethically preferable. Both "positions," affirmation and denial,[125] are, at the level of their frontal contradiction, equally *true.*[126] Rather, in offering the radical and systematic negation of Shen-hsiu's view *in full appreciation of its truth,*[127] Hui-neng bore witness to the dialectical paradox which enframes the two "positions" *(samvṛti)*[128] and discloses a higher "truth" *(paramārtha)*[129] that neither affirmation nor negation could articulate.[130]

The Thesis of Phenomenal Undecidability

The cumulative effect of our guiding illustrations is to fan the glowing coals of a certain suspicion. If mirror-image and mirrored-object are phenomenally indiscriminable, if "transparency-to-color" cannot be divided from "colored semi-translucency," perhaps there is something paradoxically awry at the very base of Western phenomenological investigation, something which, as I hope to show, Buddhist phenomenology has, from its very inception, understood very clearly and has never failed to illustrate.

Return with me, once again, to our "crystal ball." Simultaneously, it is, in the register of experience, *exactly as if* a figured red surface were lucidly disclosed through perfectly transparent crystal and *exactly as if* a figured surface were disclosed through a red-tinted, and thus merely "translucent," crystal. Indeed, advancing another step in this line of succession, it is also *exactly as if* the crystal, tinted-red, were etched with the "figure" and viewed by holding it up to the light. A final step is irresistible. It is also, and at the same time, *exactly as if* the crystal, tinted-red and etched with the "figure" were to glow with a certain illumination internal to the crystal itself. Modeled before us, imperfectly though suggestively, are four significantly distinct theoretical (if not purely phenomenological) orientations, each epitomizing the naïve, prereflective functioning of consciousness as it might appear to the reflective gaze—four theories, that is, of "naïveté."

The first view, implicit in one strand of Sartre's early thought, finds in consciousness utter vacuity, "nothingness,"[131] and thus a complete absence of qualitative content.[132] Consciousness is "all lightness, all translucence" (TE, 42). The for-itself is "invisible," an "open window," sheer uninhibited and undistorted revelation of its object. Our model is admittedly a bit strained. Sartrean "nothingness" is not the subject-term of an orthodox Cartesian dualism.[133] It is not a "crystal ball" standing obstinately *over against* its object. And we must, to this extent, be wary of the untoward, but harmless, suggestions of our model. In Merleau-Ponty's entirely accurate exposition, "We are beyond monism and dualism, because dualism has been pushed so far that the opposites, no longer in competition, are at rest the one against the other, coextensive with one another" (VI, 54–55). The position is marked, however, by a "naïve" realism of the most extreme form. Since the "nothingness" of consciousness and the absolute plenitude of being are "the obverse and the reverse of the same thought" (VI, 52), the utter vacuity of consciousness[134] ensures lucid and undistorted access to the object precisely as it is "in-itself."[135]

The second view typifies the nonsubjectivist "Kantian" side of Husserl's thought, as well as the later, and predominant, Sartrean emphasis upon "embodied" consciousness—a view which sits uneasily beside the latter's ontology of "nothingness."[136] The "figure" (object) is, to be sure, "out there." Yet, by affecting itself with a particular tincture, consciousness "constitutes" its object.[137] "Constitution" (Husserl) and "projection" (Sartre) do not institute the existence of the object, but determine, rather, the object's significance *(Sinn),* its "mode of givenness." The model serves also to typify the body as "existed" by the Sartrean for-itself offers a certain prereflective "taste" which qualitatively permeates the "crystal."

The third view is somewhat more difficult to assign, though the Platonic-Augustinian proclivity of Husserl's thought makes it a likely candidate. Husserl claims that, through the enactment of *Ideenschau*, "the 'idea' in the Platonic sense" is "taken exactly as it becomes intuitively given to us."[138] Yet, inasmuch as even eidetic intuition[139] is transacted under the aegis of the *epochē*,[140] it is "apprehended purely and free from all metaphysical interpretations."[141] To borrow an Augustinian idiom, the figure internal to the crystal is seen "in the light" of the *eidē*. As Husserl's thought advances, the locus of eidetic illumination shifts from a purportedly separate realm, the *topos noētos* of the *Ideas*, to ingredience within the stratum of transcendental subjectivity. Thus, while the earlier Husserl was given to holding the crystal up to the light, the later discovered the source of illumination in the transcendental gaze itself. Whatever purchase the charge of "subjectivism" might have upon Husserlian transcendentalism (and I remain unconvinced by the allegation) is represented in the "monistic" absence of an external "figure."[142]

The fourth model, again "monist" like the third, might naturally, though incorrectly, be interpreted as the most radically subjectivist. Both the object and the condition of its revelation (the "light") seem to be taken into the "crystal." Yet the fate of the classical materialist (and subjectivist) "identity theory" should give us pause. If mind simply *is*, in the strict and formal sense, *identical with* the substance or the functioning of the central nervous system, then we are remanded to the symmetry of identity. Neurophysiology becomes a function of mind. Were it legitimate to formulate either materialism or subjectivism by interposing identity between mind and matter, the two positions would simply fuse, remainderless, into one another. A genuine "identity theory" can be neither materialist nor subjectivist. Our fourth model thus represents, not the inherence of the object and its modes and conditions of givenness within a crystalline subjectivity, but rather their utter inseparability and interpenetration. It seems, then, not inappropriate to reserve this model for the consistently antidualist stance of Merleau-Ponty, who supplanted the Cartesian bipolarity by a "monism" whose central term, as typically explicated in the *Phenomenology*, was the "lived body"—a notion that was transmuted, in his posthumous work, *The Visible and the Invisible*, into the chiasmic reciprocity denominated "flesh."

Again, from the vantage of strict adherence to the phenomenal, it is *exactly as if* each of the four positions were true. Or, after expanding, we may now condense: it is *exactly as if* both "dualism" (the views represented by our first two models) and "monism" (the views represented by the latter two), *exactly as if* both "apophantic" phenomenology (our first view) and "cataphantic" phenomenology (the remainder) were, though patently contradictory, equally true. And since the four positions (or condensing: "dualism" and "monism") are "experientially equivalent," the postulated differences which divide them bespeak our "presuppositions." The differences are "metaphysical"[143] or "speculative" in precisely the sense that a rigorous phenomenological loyalty to experience precludes. It is not that phenomenology would be forever deprived of a metaphysic. But if pre-phenomenological speculation enters into our investigations at the beginning,[144] and if, at the end, we find ourselves with a culminating metaphysic, we may simply have pulled the speculative "rabbit" from the purportedly phenomenological "hat"—the very "rabbit," that is, in which it had previously been concealed. Phenomenology becomes, then, a ruse to captivate our attention while the "real" work of philosophical dupery is surreptitiously carried out.[145]

Perhaps, however, the situation is not so dire. Could we not *post facto* sift the genuine contribution of the "hat" from the spurious trickery of the "rabbit"? To suppose as much is to neglect the possibility of a certain "guilt by association," a certain gestalt of reflection and presupposition wholly infected and transformed by the latter. As the Vietnamese proverb counsels, "Playing with ink will get your hands black" *(Gần mực thì đen)*.[146] To assume from the outset, and without experiential warrant, the unambiguous discernibility of "rabbit" and "hat" is, whatever else it might be, assuredly not phenomenology.

If phenomenological investigation is not, then, to be adulterated from its nativity, it must demonstrate a determination exclusively to imbibe the salutary elixir of experience precisely as, and only as, it is given.[147] Yet the ramifications of "undecidability" redound in the fundamental transmutation of the very notion of the unsullied *Erlebnis*. Nothing is spared the tremor—not even, as we shall see, the bedrock conceptions of "immanence" and "transcendence" which ground the strategies of phenomenological reflection.[148]

Com(mens)uration

Edmund Husserl—the ponderously august, painstakingly scrupulous "perpetual beginner" from whose insistent shoals the bark of contemporary phenomenology was launched—rises, even today, after so many minor oceans have been charted, after the great sea of experience has brought so many intrepid attempts to chart it to fathomless wreckage, as a welcoming beacon, a signal communicating both the dangers to be averted and the living presence of a mind keeping vigilant watch. Jean-Paul Sartre, impatient with the lofty and uninvolved life of the lighthouse, must be accounted among the most capable navigators of the age, a philosopher who insisted upon drafting his charts from the heaving midst of the human condition. Deriving from Husserl a certain taste for detached observation, and like Sartre, endowed with a penchant for engaged phenomenological cartography, Merleau-Ponty is a mariner of serene seas of fathomless and murky depths. If Sartre sounds the crystalline white water, the "shimmer," of the shoals, Merleau-Ponty, constitutionally less disposed to negotiate the frenzied brine, plumbs the almost lightless bowels of "flesh."[149]

Were we allowed only the labels "essentialist" and "existentialist," "dualist" and "monist," "transcendentalist" and "immanentist," we should have little to say about the profound affinities uniting this triumvirate of phenomenological luminaries, affinities, we should note, dialectically inseparable from their deep divergence. I do not offer here a treatise on the "Trinity." Though Husserl, the "Father," perpetually gazes over our shoulder, it is primarily the Occidental counterparts of Shen-hsiu and Hui-neng which will occupy us.

Nor is this a study of Merleau-Ponty *and* Sartre. The literature featuring both phenomenological dignitaries is voluminous and rapidly leavening. And we could contribute little more than chatter to an already deafening din of commentary by voicing yet another frightfully "original" exegesis. The following pages offer, rather, a meditation, inspired by the culminating insights of Buddhist phenomenology, upon the "space"[150] enframing our Western phenomenological views, a space at once "dialectical" and "meontic."[151] What I have distilled from these insights is meant as challenge, not a threat. Western phenomenology is imperiled, not from the gentle encouragement, offered by the Buddhist philosophical tradition, to grow beyond its own limitations, but by its very attachment to those limitations.

I have spoken of *the* Buddhist tradition seeking to pass over without detailed comment the deep and irremediable philosophical disparities which mark it. *The* Buddhist tradition is host to almost every philosophical disagreement known to the West. There is the "idealism" of Yogācāra and the "mystical realism" of Dōgen (1200–1253 C.E.), the "rationalism" of certain strands and interpretations of Theravāda and the "radical empiricism" of Zen. There are disagreements of substance regarding the relationship between meditation and the attainment of wisdom, the nature of nirvāṇa, and the proper human ideal. In the words of the Venerable Ñaṇamoli:

> There have been, and are, numerous and various attempts made to prove that Buddhism teaches annihilation or eternal existence, that it is negativist, positivist, atheist, theist, or inconsistent, that [it] is a reformed

> Vedānta, a Humanism, pessimism, absolutism, pluralism, monism, that it is a philosophy, a religion, an ethical system, or indeed almost what you will.[152]

Though Buddhism can be understood as a corpus of doctrine only at the peril of fragmenting into a thousand shards, there is, nonetheless, a silver thread which runs through the center of all the myriad beads. It is a certain profound and transformative experience, the experience of "waking up," which each party to the almost interminable internecine disputes has labored, in its own way, to express, understand and account for.[153] Thus, as Sangharakshita confirms:

> [T]he doctrinal and other differences between the schools are not resolved by being reduced on their own level one to another or all to a conceptual common denominator, but transcended by referring them to a factor which, being supra-logical, can be the common object of contradictory assertions.[154]

The task of giving voice to the prelogical ground of liberation I call "Buddhist phenomenology." Or again, in Sangharakshita's words, "What, for want of a better word, we are compelled to term Buddhist philosophy is, in fact, essentially the conceptual formulation of the non-conceptual content of Wisdom or Enlightenment."[155] It is the Zen tradition, closer, perhaps, to *theoria* and farther from theory, from which I have distilled the views posed to challenge the phenomenologies of the West. But Zen, of course, is nothing without the deconstructive logic of Mādhyamika, the psychological insight of Yogācāra, and the holographic vision of Hua-yen. Nor is it separable from the "existential" concern of the Buddha's original teaching.[156] Together these five—Zen, Mādhyamika, Yogācāra, Hua-yen and the original teachings regarding human suffering and its elimination—describe a certain vector of philosophical thinking and concern that, I believe, quite rightly merits the label: *the* Buddhist tradition.

From the outset, a deliberate dissociation of the "space" of phenomenology, the "emptiness" subtending both the primary phenomena and the secondary "views" of phenomena, from the data of historical scholarship must be registered. Though an extended intellectual-historical investigation of the relationship between our Occidental phenomenologists might prove of some interest, our "space" is not a delegate for the historian's empirical-factual "relationship." "Space" is a phenomenological, not a historical, descriptor.[157]

The reflections offered here are inspired by our opening narrative and by the two verses which it enfolds. No one, of course, would mistake Merleau-Ponty for Hui-neng, or Sartre for Shen-hsiu. Yet, for us, the story of the *Platform Sutra* will become archetypal. And in its luminescence we will be enabled to discern, framing Merleau-Ponty and Sartre, the same meontic "space" which frames the disparate visions of the two monks.

Our work, once again, is specifically informed by the searching insights of Buddhist phenomenology. And in this may lie a certain measure of uniqueness. Borrowing Kuhn's suggestive idiom, "normal" philosophy,[158] as practiced in the West, is disadvantaged by its exclusion of the rich conceptual heritage of Asian philosophical thought. Our limited "paradigms" of philosophical practice contravene the thought-practices of the East, and reinforce a rigidly ingrown unwillingness to seek wisdom at the feet of cultures alien to our own. The real tragedy is not that of lack, but of a failure to recognize our own fullness which manifests itself in exclusive rigidity. In-breeding hermetically seals the doors and windows. Thankfully, however, there are those who gasp for fresh air.[159] Yet even if the seals are broken, the revitalizing breeze which caresses us will seem, to the "normal" practitioner, a mysterious and uncomprehended presence. It is only when convinced that the invigorating current of thought which now sweeps through "our own" house, teasing "our own" faces, disarranging the papers on "our own" desk, is, indeed, a visitation of our proper philosophical inheritance that the frozen mind comes to recognize and, in the only way it can, to "understand" the entering spirit.[160] We must not, however, contaminate our inquiry with "the vulgar prejudices of those who, from mere tribal sluggishness, are convinced that 'Western', i.e., Judaeo-Christian and scientific, modes of thinking are the unfailing standards of all truth" (BTI, 10). Borrowing a phrase from a joyful logical mystic, the "looking-glass" of normal philosophy returns to us only our image.[161] The real "magic" of philosophy is, however, to enable us, like Alice, to step "through."[162] Perhaps one is not to be despised for sheltering hope that Asian thought may be made comprehensible within "our own" categories. I have, in my very limited way, attempted Occidental phenomenological appropriations of certain aspects of Buddhist thought.[163] Rarer, I expect, are those endeavors, like the present one, whose "figure" is Western and whose "ground" is Eastern.[164]

Let no one mistake me, however, for an apologist of what might naturally be suggested by the grievous solecism, "comparative philosophy." Comparison, the trivial act of setting side by side, "pairing together," if purified of any other redeeming intellectual activity, is assuredly *not philosophy*.[165] Comparison, if not odious, is at best a minor instrument of the philosophical historian. And while I would shudder at precipitating their divorce, it would seem an equal error to confuse the philosopher and the historian.

Once, in my reckless youth, I thoughtlessly quipped that, in my philosophical work, I would rather "make" history than "study" it, assuming then that the division was painfully patent. It is not. And while I now perceive the two islands rising distinctly from the sea, I also am also aware of their subliminal continuity. Surely, at least, we learn an intricate skill by first watching the adept. And what counts for us as successfully practicing the skill is general conformity with the master's practice. The study of philosophical history is our initiatory period of observation. The ritual practices of our philosophical masters differ dramatically. And though the exercise might always be possible, it would be a serious mistake to draw lessons for our own practice from mere "comparison."

Philosophy is innately "histrionic." And philosophers must have the openness and flexibility of mind to enter dramaturgically into the intellectual "roles" of their predecessors, to imitate, in their own intellectual being, the thought-movements of their worthiest teachers.[166] What Loewenberg says on Hegel's behalf, we conscript for our own:

> [M]ind serves as laboratory in which the experiments performed are not strictly analogous to scientific. The manner of reproducing the phenomenon of knowledge, the phenomenon in each case being a unique persuasion, is comparable more to the actor's part of impersonation than to laboratorial behavior of the scientist. The actor's performance, described as histrionic, involves an experiment in vicariousness. Concealing his real self behind an alien mask, and assuming with fidelity the appearance of another being, the actor is required, as the saying goes, to play a part. He must mimic a personality not his own, and in this consists the histrionic experiment. It is an experiment deemed successful only if, seizing a given character from within, the actor is able to identify himself for the moment with the inner life of the dramatis persona he is called upon to portray. In the illusion of identity between himself and his role lies the test of the actor's performance, an illusion dispelled only when, the play being over, he appears without his assumed mask to receive the plaudits for his deft experiment in simulation.[167]

Comparison does nothing to encourage this fluidity, but may actually stultify it. Comparison demands the simultaneous display of two commensurable exteriors. Yet we cannot "enter" with deep histrionic engagement into more than a single philosophical "role" or "thought-ritual" at a time. Comparison allows us simply to acknowledge, from a vantage point paradoxically external to our own, that "our" view, "our" categorial framework, is, in certain respects, like "theirs," leaving us unmoved.[168] It does not inculcate the vital habit of "entering."[169]

Fichte was radiantly clear on this point. Of his *Wissenschaftslehre* he insisted: "not even the smallest spark of it can be grasped or communicated as an appropriation from someone else's mind."[170] Philosophy is not, in Fichte's view, or in ours, a pleasant afternoon's diversion akin to reading the Sunday newspaper. Nor, *pace* Professor Rorty, is it the interminable cocktail chatter of perpetual "conversation." If I were to rewrite Sartre's *Huis clos*, I would sharply delimit the conclusion, "L'enfer c'est les autres." Blessedly, hell is not "other people" *tout court*. But it may have a good deal in common with the incessant, demonic, mind-deadening din that Rorty would have us raise.[171] Philosophy, mere chitchat without histrionic "embodiment," cannot, if approached in adoration of wisdom, leave us where it found us. "What we genuinely comprehend becomes part of ourselves, and if it is a genuinely new insight, it produces a personal transformation."[172] And we find in Fichte no more forthright presentation of philosophical "embodiment" than his earnest appeal:

> From now on I wish to be considered silenced and erased, and you yourselves must come forward and stand in my place. From now on, everything which is to be thought in this assembly should be thought and be true only to the extent that you yourselves have thought it and seen it as true.

Philosophies are "com/mensurate" if they can be "measured together," if, that is, their problematics and operative concepts are "mediable," if there lies between them a "mean" (from the Old High German, *meina*, *minni*, and thus the English, "mind"), instituting a certain dimension of commonality. To require of the "measure" that it be borrowed from among the products of philosophical excrescence is to presume a philosophical relativism even before the inaugural practice of the art. Mādhyamika Buddhism, the "Middle Way," would smile to learn that "mind" (Latin: *mens;* Sanskrit: *manas)* is the "medium" (thus: "median"), and, indeed that "meditation" is "measuring." With mind itself as "measure," we have no need of the reified products of philosophical "minding," our "means" of having the world "in mind," to serve this function. In histrionically "entering" one philosophical outlook, we need only "re/mind" ourselves of the other. What matters, as any teacher of meditation will convey, is to be "mindful" (Greek: *mnemon)*. Mnemosyne is the mother of the Muses. And we do well to remind ourselves that, in its original sense, to "muse" is to stare fixedly, lost in thought. The Muses minister no more to the poet than to the philosopher.

The reader is invited to "enter," with me, into the spirit of two apparently conflicting "phenomenologies," those of Shen-hsiu and Hui-neng. We may find it useful, if little edifying, to emphasize certain salient comparative affinities between Sartre and Shen-hsiu, or between Merleau-Ponty and Hui-neng. But mere comparison must be surpassed. In immersing ourselves in the salutary waters of Buddhist "meontic" phenomenology, if only up to our intellects, we shall be prepared to discern, glowing in vague outline between our two Occidental phenomenologists, a certain dialectic and meontic "space." And it may be that here, if in no other Occidental place, we see, as in a glass darkly, the serene luminescence of Buddhist "emptiness" *(śūnyatā)*.[177]

I. MIND AS MIRROR

The moon on the pine—

I keep hanging—taking it off—

and gazing each time.

(HOKUSHI, 1665?–1718)

The Mirrorless Mirror

REFLECTIONS ON BUDDHIST DIALECTIC

Analytic and Dialectic Phenomeno-Logic

Logicians frequently speak of "logical space," and concomitantly, we might consider the very different "spaces" defined by a sphere and by a plane.[1] The globe offers two directly opposite ways of arriving at a given location: *toward* and *away*. But a two-dimensional representation of the globe affords only one: *toward*. Let us begin in "Flatland." And let us say that *A* implies *B*, either materially or formally, if *B* lies directly to the east of *A*. Thus, every proposition due east of *A* is *true* provided that *A* is true. East, of course, is a direction, not a location. Yet we do, informally and intelligibly, speak of going "toward the East." The East of Flatland might, then, appropriately signify the region of logically necessary truth, the ensemble of propositions entailed by every proposition whatsoever. Ignoring, for the moment, the commonplace that truths are entailed by truths (we might, in our rudimentary model, locate true antecedents along a line of longitude to the north).[2] Due west lies the false. And accordingly, The West becomes the region of logically necessary falsehoods false on every supposal. East and West—Necessity and Impossibility—are, of course, idealized abstractions,[3] represented, perhaps, by the equatorial extremities of our planar map.[4]

In global space, however, there is little temptation to reify either extremity. It becomes easily evident that East and West are not, even in some idealized sense, the termini of a dipolar logical space. *B* can be attained by proceeding *toward* or by proceeding *away* from *A*. From *A*, *B (any B)* is both true and false. Every point is both east and west of any other. And this, to say the least, is logically anomalous.[5]

If we are to insist upon the anomaly (not to say absurdity) of a global logical framework embracing the conflicting positions of Shen-hsiu and Hui-neng, the logician's altogether reasonable qualms must be pacified. And this we can do, if only in part, by explicating the relationship between the analytic logician's "Flatland" and our dialectical "sphere." A few further words of explanation might then serve to make our global logical space at least somewhat less philosophically foreboding. But nothing, I expect, would be quite so helpful in showing that Shen-hsiu entails Hui-neng and conversely,[6] as the attempt to "enter" into the deep meaning of the verses themselves.[7]

A two-dimensional map of the planet is created by one of several standard methods of "projection," each with its own particular distortions, each useful for a certain limited range of purposes. The niceties and demerits, advantages and disadvantages, of the several projective modes can be safely vouchsafed to the cartographers and topologists, though we should bear in mind that distortion of one sort or another is inevitable. One species of distortion foisted upon us by projection involves the selection of a *center*. Are we to make Kansas or Khartoum, Louvain or Lahore, the center of our map? I have heard it suggested that God can apprehend the staggeringly vast welter of possible views of an orange simultaneously in a way analogous to cartographical projection. In the omniscient envisagement, the surface of the orange is "peeled off," as it were, and presented in the divine field of consciousness as a two-dimensional "map" of our three-dimensional sphere. Yet, again, there are at least as many such "maps" to be apprehended as there are possible centers. God would have, not a single "projective" field of consciousness, but an infinite, perhaps a nondenumerably infinite, array of them.[8] And since consciousness can enjoy no more than a single field at any given moment, the malady is worse than schizophrenia. It is polytheism run wild, "gods" multiplied without end. The apparent solution is to suppose, on God's part, a unitary synoptic vision of the vast multiplicity of fields. Once again, however, the problem of the center breaks out. Which field is central? Thus the original problem reproduces itself at endlessly higher levels. In a different, though intimately related, idiom, Husserl complains that the presumption of omniscience would abolish what he regards as an inviolate distinction:

> that there is no *essential difference* between transcendent and immanent, that in the postulated divine intuition a spatial thing is a real

> *(reeles)* constituent, and indeed an experience itself, a constituent of the stream of the divine consciousness and the divine experience.[9]

This, of course, is no place to vent my biases concerning divine omniscience. I have done so elsewhere.[10] But the problem of the center, if not, for the present, the problem of omniscience, introduces a grave sense in which two-dimensional maps of spherical surfaces are ineluctably infected with distortion.

Yet another sense of distortion, previously glimpsed and inextricable from the problem of the center, is the problem of the equatorial extremities: East and West. A planar framework for modal logical relationships inevitably posits an East, a unitary easternmost node entailed by every possible proposition. East is entailed, not simply by every proposition along a single line of latitude, and serves, thus, not merely as the most remote logical descendent of a single relatively westerly proposition, but by *every* proposition, at *every* location on the map. East, once again, is *Necessity*; and West, *Impossibility*. If, however, our "map is, indeed, a spherical projection, then the equatorial extremity becomes a matter of sheer contingency. Is it Honolulu or The Hague which lies in the East? And how, then, is the contingency of the extremity to be reconciled with its significance as Necessity?[11]

Ex/planation

If distortion and logical *aporiai* are the natural inheritance of our "projection hypothesis," why, then, should we suppose that planar logic is derivative from spherical dialectics? The assumption, like Pandora's box, has released so many troubles that we might well wish it had not been opened. Without the assumption, planar logic ticks like a well-adjusted clock. A powerfully telling hint, however, of what calls for the assumption is implicit in G. Spencer Brown's poetic musings on the relationship between "explanation" and "reality":

> [T]o *explain* [is] literally to lay *out* in a *plane* where particulars can be readily seen. Thus to *place* or *plan* in *flat* land, sacrificing other dimensions for the sake of appearance. Thus to *expound* or *put out* at the cost of ignoring the *reality* or *richness* of what is so put out. Thus to take a view away from its *prime reality* or *royalty*, or to gain knowledge and lose the kingdom. (LF, 126n)

To "explain," as Brown clearly sees, invokes a logic of analysis which opens its subject matter to articulation. The *intent* of analytic logic, however, is precisely the provision of a framework of explanation within which "reality," in its richness and royalty,[12] can be shadowlessly illuminated.[13] Yet if shadowless lucidity is the culmination of a *process*, that of ex/planation, laying out in a plane, the initial state of that process, the grist for the explanatory mill, cannot be planar.[14] Explanation thus represents its datum within a logical framework, that of analysis, alien to the *explanandum* in its pristine pre-explanatory richness.[15] Explanation inescapably involves the analytic articulation of the *explanandum*. The pre-explanatory subject matter is thus inarticulate (not to say ineffable),[16] indeterminate, and wild, flourishing in the wilderness of *l'être sauvage*.[17] "The world," as Merleau-Ponty instructs us, "is there before any possible analysis of mine. . . . " (PhP, x). Explanation delivers us from the "savage" indeterminacy of the pre-explanatory, and, at its most successful, sets in its place what appears to be an altogether humbled and housebroken surrogate.[18] If, in the Aristotelian idiom, the transition from indeterminacy to determinacy is an "essential change," if tame articulation is an essential feature of the explanatory product, then the projection hypothesis is compellingly confirmed. Savage reality and analytically gentled explanation fall substantially in twain, the latter derivative from the former.[19] In this case, however, explanation is not transformation, but surrogation. If, on the other hand, the change is accidental—and consistent rejection of the projection assumption demands this—explanation becomes the transformation of a unitary *explanandum*. We are not, then, constrained to suppose a duality of levels, those of reality and explanation, since explanation offers no more than accidental transformation of its subject matter: *reality*.[20] Reality bestows itself upon the mind as murky or perspicacious, and these features, psychological or phenomenal, are a matter of pure indifference to the underlying *explanandum*. If the *explanandum* remains untouched, however, by the transition from shadow to light, then explanation, this very transformation, enjoys no incisive purchase upon its datum.[21] The datum lies beyond the exhaustive phenomenal categories of clarity and confusion, light and shadow, articulation and indeterminacy, falling thus to the nether side of the phenomenal realm.[22] The *explanandum* becomes noumenal, a thing-in-itself.[23] Thus, rejection of the projection hypothesis smuggles in the familiar Kantian dualism, a dualism left of necessity at the portals of phenomenology.

By projecting the voluminous sphere of reality upon the plane of analytic logic, ex/planation inevitably distorts in multiple ways. Yet, as we have seen, ex/planation, as accidental transformation from obscurity to clarity—the only sense consistent with a denial of the projection hypothesis—casts the *explanandum* into the muddy and impenetrable waters of the noumenal. The realism implicit in this desperate strategy to preserve the adequation of reality and analytic ex/planation can only assume itself, as we shall see, thus opening itself to the quasi-Berkeleyan interrogation of the inaccessible noumenon. Conversely, phenomenology, inasmuch as it arrays itself against realism and idealism alike, must sponsor the projection hypothesis. Disciplined phenomenological labor is informed by a clear-sighted wariness of analytic-explanatory distortion. The phenomenological gaze rests solely upon reality, not upon its projective delegate.

Absolute and Relative "Space"

In his correspondence with Clarke, Leibniz registers against the latter's absolute space, a confutation of considerable cogency and interest. The issue, though explicitly theological, holds immediate consequences for our discussion of dialectical space. According to Leibniz's summary, Clarke claims that

> there should be a reason, why God, preserving the same situations of bodies among themselves, should have placed them in space after one certain particular manner, and not otherwise; why everything was not placed the quite contrary way, for instance, by changing East into West.[24]

Space, on Clarke's view, is indifferent to the disposition of objects within it. Yet, as Leibniz argues, "Space is something absolutely uniform; and, without the things placed in it, one point of space does not absolutely differ in any respect whatsoever from another point of space."[25] Given Leibniz's Law—the powerful (if, as I believe, technically erroneous) principle that identity *tout court* is equivalent to universal coextension of predication[26]—the uniformity of an absolute space culminates in the aporetic conjunction: first, that space is *infinite*, since no point in space can be qualitatively differentiated in virtue of its proximity to any presumed limit; and second, that space is *infinitesimal*, since uniformity implies identity, the boundless multiplicity of spatial points thus collapsing into a single dimensionless point. For Leibniz, on the contrary, space is not a sublime and unmoved framework, but precisely the order, the network of relatedness, among, and constituted by, spatiotemporal objects. Space, as Leibniz inculcates,

> is nothing at all without bodies, but the possibility of placing them; then those two states [i.e., the straightforward disposition of East and West and its inverse], the one such as it now is, the other supposed to be the quite contrary way, would not at all differ from one another. Their difference therefore is only to be found in our chimerical supposition of the reality of space in itself. But in truth the one would exactly be the same thing as the other, they being absolutely indiscernible; and consequently there is no room to enquire after a reason of the preference of the one to the other.[27]

Qualms over Leibniz's Law aside—it *does* govern strictly formal identity[28]—*aporia* pursues the assumption of indifference. In our metaphorical appropriation, this suggests that the logic of "reality" cannot survive insensitivity, inflexibility; that logic itself must, on pain of distortion, "bend" in conformity to the rounded contours of reality. It is not that *A* entails *B* because *B* is capriciously or accidentally inserted to the east of *A*, but exactly the reverse. *B* lies to the east of

A precisely because the very sense of this propositional diptych establishes the vectorial order: to the east. Were logical space intrinsically anisotropic, "*X* is an equilateral triangle" could be laid arbitrarily to the east of "*X* is a triangle," in this way, counterintuitively, inducing the latter to entail the former. The resounding clash with our intuitions thus produced confirms that "easterliness" is rooted in meaning,[29] and meaning, in turn, in reality.[30]

The "flat" logical space of analysis is imbued, however, with the perceptible blush of a different form of "absoluteness." The failure of relativity is much more subtle than the belligerent refusal to alter one's logic in the face of propositions we take to be displaced with respect to the "horseshoe." Analytic logic dissociates matter and form, arrogating to itself absolute and unquestioned governance of the latter, and concerning itself with the former, if at all, only as arbitrary illustration.[31] Logic, in the familiar refrain, is a calculus of "symbols"[32] (though even this may be too liberal an admission). Analytic logic is the engine of a purely formal transformation. It rules its exemplifications without mercy and without the slightest quiver at their particularities. It is absolute insofar as it insolently refuses to stoop to its instances, unwilling to bend to their demands. It is the logic of ex/planation. And the plane of analytic logic does not embrace, does not fold itself around, its subject matter. The projection hypothesis holds firm.

The immediacy with which our "dogmatic" interpretation of the *Platform* narrative insinuated itself bears eloquent witness to its absoluteness. The principle of contradiction, unchallenged, unquestioned and aloof, structures the logical space within which, according to our first interpretation, Shen-hsiu and Hui-neng humorlessly confront one another in their grim alethic contest.[33] No inquiry is made into the phenomenological positions of the venerable bonzes before the logical drama begins. The curtain rises on the logical play, with its conflicting roles, before the actors are consulted. Relativism has another play to perform, one in which all roles are consistent, falsity being thus jubilantly banished. Yet again, the actors have not been solicited for their contribution to the dramatic movement.

The hoary venerability of the principle of contradiction, loftiest of the forms of logical passage, is not lightly to be offended, and we might well shudder to violate its solemn dictates in the spirit of mere caprice or willful perversion. If, however, as our global dialectic requires, any proposition can be approached from another either by proceeding directly *toward* it or directly *away* from it, we can cherish no hope of forgiveness from the proponents of analytic logic.[34] For our spherical space makes every proposition both true and false. Refuge is to be sought only by entering into the very heart, the inner meaning,[35] of the two positions.[36] If we enter into the spirit of Shen-hsiu's *gāthā* only to find ourselves abruptly transported into the spirit of Hui-neng's, and conversely, we stand in need of no further defence.

Though his most familiar illustrations comprise ambiguous, "multi-stable" phenomena which present themselves in a strained duality of aspects,[37] Heraclitus, probably the first thinker of the Western philosophical tradition to give eloquent voice to the perennial *coincidentia oppositorum*, provides unmistakable examples of oppositional unity framed in a global dialectic space, a logic conforming to the dictum (Fr. 103) that "Beginning and end are general in the circumference of the circle."[38] One need only consider his oracular pronouncements:

> Hesiod is the teacher of very many, he who did not understand day and night: for they are one. (Fr. 57)[39]

> God [the Logos, or Unity of Opposites Itself] is day-night, winter-summer. . . . (Fr. 67)[40]

Day and night, winter and summer, are one, not in any counterintuitive sense trading upon strict formal identity, nor even in the looser sense of material identity by which *my brother* and *my brother as I conceive him* are allied.[41] It is rather that, by following a unitary path (through time, as instanced by these cyclical cases, or through space), one traverses the opposites.[42] And this is possible only within a topological framework, like that of the circle or sphere, in which beginning and end *are* materially identical, and every point is both. It is not that the material, dual-aspectual identity, informing the more familiar Heraclitean illustrations, thereby grounds the dialectical examples as well, but rather the reverse. It is the circle which offers at every point the occasion for material juncture. It is the circle which thus provides the grounding (or rather, ab/grounding), permissive space for formal identity.[43]

I have summoned the spirit of Heraclitus, not simply because of the many deep affinities which the pre-Socratic enjoys with aspects of Buddhist phenomenology, though these are unmistakably in evidence, but obversely, and more prosaically, to demonstrate that the global logic which rules "day and night" is by no means unique to Eastern philosophical proclivities. And to find the beast at one's back door might, for the otherwise unmoved, show it in a somewhat more endearing light. But before unleashing the beast (and I find the pet quite dear), we must spare a few words of general comment concerning the nature of the Buddhist dialectic.

Reflective Negativity

The remarkably insightful comment of Shen-hui, Dharma descendent of Hui-neng, plumbs the gaping abyss of negativity which informs the mirror:

> A bright mirror is set up on a high stand; its illumination reaches the ten thousand things, and they are all reflected in it. The masters are wont to consider this phenomenon most wonderful. But as far as my school

> is concerned it is not to be considered wonderful. Why? As to this bright mirror, its illumination reaches the ten thousand things, and these ten thousand things are not reflected in it. This is what I would declare to be most wonderful. Why? The Tathāgata discriminates all things with non-discriminating Prajñā *(chih)*. If he has any discriminating mind, do you think he could discriminate all things? (NM, 51)

The mirror's faithful affirmation of the "ten thousand things" will hardly escape notice. For the present, however, I propose, in the spirit of Shen-hui, an examination of the mirror's deep nay-saying,[44] the profound No with which it greets its reflections. The Yes and the No are not, of course, like matter and antimatter, reciprocally destructive.[45] Unlike the affirmation and negation of analytic logic, our Yes and No gasp for one another.[46] They cannot be extricated from their enfusing embrace. Positivity requires permission. Permission is permission to the positive. Our No is like the void.[47] Negativity is an "attitude of mind" which, as Hui-neng will say, "is as void as space" (PS/pw, 26).[48] Negativity consorts not at all with the childish recalcitrance which this word often brings to mind. To be negative, in the sense of immature defiance, is to resist. The negativity of the mirror is, quite to the contrary, a yielding, a permitting, a letting. It is striking to find in Descartes the assertion,

> Space or internal place and the corporeal substance which is contained in it, are not different otherwise than in the mode in which they are conceived by us. . . . the difference between them consists only in the fact that in body we consider extension as particular and conceive it to change just as body changes; in space, on the contrary, we attribute to extension a generic unity, so that after having removed from a certain space the body which occupied it, we do not suppose that we have also removed the extension of that space, because it appears to us that the same extension remains so long as it is of the same magnitude and figure, and preserves the same position in relation to certain other bodies, whereby we determine this space.[49]

No portrayal of the entwinement of the mirror's negative spatiality and its positive reflectivity could be more apt. The difference is purely "conceptual,"[50] and, as we shall see, vanishes upon lucid phenomenological inspection.[51] Still, inasmuch as we do, in fact, make the distinction, we are haunted by the No.

The No, once again, is not a refusal to reflect the "ten thousand things."[52] Indeed, were the mirror to exhibit such rank belligerence, we would not account it a *mirror* at all. Reflectivity would resolve into opacity. To say, with Shen-hui, that the "ten thousand things are not reflected in it" is rather to remark on the salient insouciance of the mirror in the face of its reflections.[53] The mirror itself remains buoyantly undisturbed reflections come what may.[54] Its equanimity is a function of its negativity, the utter dis-identity with which it abjures its reflections.[55] It *is not* its reflections.[56] Not a single reflection, no matter what its phenomenal credentials may be, can affect its "essence" in the least.[57] And this is precisely because it *has* no essence. A mirror is not a *substance*,[58] but an *activity*—the activity of reflecting.[59] "Mirror" is a disguised gerund.[60]

Buddhist Dialectics

Though I would shudder to confess as much in the hearing of Professor Rorty, the Greek *dialektikē* does signify "conversation"—not, to be sure, the incessant prattle which Rorty would have supplant philosophy, but the voicing and considering of seriously entertained positions. *Legein* suggests the act of *choice* as much as the act of *speech*.[61] And "conversation" springs from the same Latin counterpart as "conversion." Thus, the dialectic begins with committed position taking within a dialogical framework, and advances inexorably to the *dia-*, the "betweenness" or "throughness," which unifies the disparate products of *legein*.[62]

Zeno of Elea, as Aristotle purports, was the first of our Western philosophical predecessors to employ the method of dialectical reasoning, and did so, as we know, in the service of Parmenidean monism. Immovability is counted, by Parmenides, among the signs *(semata)* of the serenely immutable sphere of Being, and Zeno, himself no friend of the senses, therefore set about to demonstrate the rational impossibility of motion.[63] Motion is inconceivable apart from space and time. And on one influential proposal,[64] the four antinomies of motion represent a succession of *argumenta ad absurdum* lodged upon a fourfold exhaustive permutation of possible positions regarding the smallest units of space and time:[65]

(1) Space is infinitely divisible; time consists of indivisible minima (the Stadium).
(2) Space consists of indivisible minima; time is infinitely divisible (the Achilles).
(3) Space and time are both infinitely divisible (the Arrow).[66]
(4) Space and time both consist of indivisible minima (the Moving Rows).[67]

We cannot pause to explicate the Zenonian paradoxes. Only the framework of argumentation is of interest to us here. Characteristically dialectical in approach, Zeno himself sponsors none of the positions catalogued. Each of the antinomies assumes, but merely for the sake of argument, a possible position which may or may not have enjoyed the support of extant opinion. "If you believe this," he seems to say, "you lapse immediately into hopeless *aporia*." In this, Zeno's polemic is stunningly allied with the Mādhyamika dialectic so adroitly wielded by its notable proponent, Nāgārjuna:

> How does the Madhyamika reject any and all views? He uses only one weapon. By drawing out the implications of any view he shows its self-contradictory character. The dialectic is a series of *reductio ad absurdum* arguments. Every thesis is turned against itself. . . . The Madhyamika *disproves* the opponent's thesis, and does not prove any thesis of his own. . . . The *reductio ad absurdum* is for the sole benefit of the holder of the thesis; and it is done with his own logic, on principles and procedures fully acceptable to him. (CPB, 131–32)

Aristotle, firmly committed to establishing the veracity of his own positions, subordinated dialectic to demonstration *(apodeixis)*.[68] Demonstration rests serenely upon incontrovertible principle;[69] dialectic, in Aristotle's view, teeters atop mere opinion *(endoxa)*.[70] Indeed, Plato would fault Zeno's procedure (as well as Nāgārjuna's) as mere disputation (eristic).[71] In his hands, the dialectic becomes an ascent, via an ordered sequence of "positions *(hypotheseis)*, to the unhypothesized ultimate of the Platonic scheme: the very Good Itself *(auto to agathon)*, which, like the Hegelian Absolute, the culmination of Hegel's dialectic, subsumes in its synoptic embrace the "positions" that have led to it.[72]

The "four-cornered" dialectic of the Mādhyamika school is immersed in the mirror's shimmering negativity. Though the historicity of the purported Zenonian tetralemma may be left to scholarly dispute, Nāgārjuna is indisputably explicit in his rejection of each permutation of the exhaustive fourfold *(catuskotika)*:

(1) Being is affirmed; non-being is denied.
(2) Being is denied; non-being is affirmed.
(3) Being and non-being are both affirmed.
(4) Being and non-being are both denied.[73]

Though it has become traditional to present the quadratic negation in this way, the scheme, as it stands, detonates our logic without demonstrating that it is exactly the explosive of analytic logic by which logic itself is ruptured.[74] Watts's explication has the virtue of elucidating this analytic self-destruction:

> [A]ny affirmation or denial whatsoever can have meaning only in relation to its own opposite. Every statement, every definition, sets up a boundary or limit; it classifies something, and thus it can always be shown that what is inside the boundary must coexist with what is outside. Even the idea of the boundless is meaningless without the contrast of the bounded.[75]

The Buddhist dialectic, like any of its Western counterparts, assuredly does have its outcome. It "ascends." But unlike the Hegelian, the Buddhist dialectic does not culminate in *concept*[76]—not even the Concept of the Whole.[77] Again, we may have a friend in Zeno. Granting the exhaustive fourfold negation of "positions" regarding space and time,[78] Zeno intends to exhaust the possibilities for rational position-taking, negating them all.[79] Reason finds itself without a "position," without a particle of support beneath its feet,[80] freely afloat in the boundless abyss of space—not, perhaps, hoisted by its own petard, but if not, then (as Parmenides would approve) pulling itself up by its own bootstraps, and thus radically aloof from experienced reality. Zeno's conclusion, *there is no motion*, is hardly smelted from the white heat of existential anguish. Yet neither is it merely one more "position" which, in our logical inadvertence, we had somehow overlooked before. It is the exhaustion of position taking, and to this extent, the "releasing of one's hands over the abyss."

Even the Platonic dialectic holds some promise for reconciliation with the Buddhist. The stepwise "hypothetical" escalation which Plato envisions is an ascent in the direction of the Good, which, like the sun, can only dazzle and blind those who dare to gaze directly upon it. There are two ways in which the angular distinctness of experienced objectivity can be softened and finally obliterated. Our experience can be washed in darkness or bathed in light.[81] And in terms of the resultant indistinctness, it matters little which remedy is chosen. The sun, like the mirror, "makes things visible."[82] And like the mirror, also, the sun itself, because it blinds the inquisitive, is no less invisible, devoid of any phenomenally discernible "self-nature." And we must not, in this connection, neglect Plato's intriguing pronouncement that the Good is "beyond Being."

Distinguished Distinctions

I want now to advert to Watts's very serviceable explication of the Mādhyamika dialectic. In Watts's reading, which I follow, the dialectic rests upon two pillars:

(1) "any affirmation or denial whatsoever can have meaning only in relaion to its own opposite"; and
(2) "what is inside the boundary must coexist with what is outside."

In his rejection of "being" as a highest genus, Aristotle clearly appreciated the force of (1). Every attribution is an implicit negation. To say of a tomato that it is red is to say that it falls to one side of a distinction. It is *not* non-red.[83] But to say of a given entity (redundantly, "something" which exists, a "being" endowed with Being) that it is fitted with ontic credentials distinguishes it from nothing whatsoever. To say this is to *say* nothing at all. For what is said "makes no difference." The admission of (2), however, would commit Aristotle to the abandonment of any position whatsoever, and could not, for this reason, have been congenial.

To distinguish (literally, to "prick apart") is to sever the world in twain.[84] "*Distinction*," in Brown's pellucid definition, "*is perfect continence*" (LF, 1).

> That is to say, a distinction is drawn by arranging a boundary with separate sides so that a point on one side cannot reach the other side without crossing the boundary. For example, in a plane space a circle draws a distinction. (LF, 1)

Accordingly,

> a universe comes into being when a space is severed or taken apart. . . . the familiar laws of our own experience follow inexorably from the original act of severance. The act is itself already remembered, even if unconsciously, as our first attempt to distinguish different things in a world where, in the first place, the universe cannot be distinguished from how we act upon it, and the world may seem like shifting sand beneath our feet. (LF, v)

If, now, the whole of reality ("severed space") is thus fatefully cleft,[85] we cannot, without evident paradox, affirm or deny any universal attribution. For to say of our bifurcated world[86] that it is eternal (or infinite, or absolute) is to apply *to the whole* categories derived from dividing the whole. And it is little surprise to learn that the Buddha, on being questioned concerning the world's station within this grid of attributes, maintained a "noble silence."[87] The contradiction is patent: the polarities—eternal/temporal, infinite/finite, absolute/relative[88]—"part" the world. And it cannot simultaneously be maintained that the world *in its entirety* is eternal and that *only part* of the world is eternal. Mirrorlike, the entirety must repose in silence,[89] untouched by attribution.[90]

Kant's transcendental dialectic warns against the ineluctable, yet inevitably fallacious, employment of reason in its application to the whole of reality.[91] Yet Kant, in company with most philosophers, seems little troubled by partisan attributions. "The soup is sour" appropriately relegates the soup to its side of the universe, does it not?[92] But in speaking of the soup, are we not covertly speaking of the universe *as a whole*[93] (or rather, "the all," not "merely the *formal appearance* of *one* of the possible manifestations which make up the world")?[94] Could the soup be sour were it not the case that reality *as a whole* is such that the soup is sour? In attributing sourness to the soup, are we not thereby attributing "(being such that the soup is sour)-ness" to the entirety?[95] And if so (a crucial insight of Buddhist dialectics), then even our particular affirmations and denials are fraught with self-contradiction.[96] "Shuzan held out his short staff and said: 'If you call this a short staff, you oppose its reality. If you do not call it a short staff, you ignore the fact. Now what do you wish to call this?'"[97] Since the entirety is such that the soup is sour, or the staff is short, the attribution has the effect of splitting the entirety into one part answering to the truth of the proposition and a second part answering to its falsity,[98] *only part* of the entirety is thus qualified.[99] We are left speechless before Mumon's demand: "It cannot be expressed with words and it cannot be expressed without words. Now say quickly what it is."[100]

Archaic Distinctions

Distinction, to recall Brown's definition, is "perfect continence." And we must recall as well, that any purportedly "first" distinction presupposes an earlier one. The "deconstructive" logic of mirroring is self-reflexive. One cannot distinguish *A* from *B* without assuming a prior distinction between the pristine uncleft terrain before the imposition of distinction and the scarred landscape which results from the act of severing. The second distinction is perpendicular to the first, a transcendental distinction, if you will. Yet setting aside for the moment the vertical presuppositions of differentiation, we may appropriately wonder what the absolutely primordial horizontal distinction might be. If, as often claimed, *intentionality* is the unsurpassably archaic distantiation *(écart)* separating subjective immanence from objective transcendence, should we not expect the sundering of *subject* from *object* to appear as the inaugural cleft?[101]

For Heidegger, of course, the "first" difference is the "ontological difference," the difference of *Sein* from *Seiend*, not the differentiating encounter of *Dasein* with beings. *Dasein*, in its very ex/sistence relational, the confrontation of subject with object, is itself *a being*, and must not, on this account, be confounded with Being. Imagining a boundless plane surface, we inscribe upon it a circle, thus demarcating a being. But what, then, is *Being*? It cannot be the primordial uncleft field of the distinction. For prior to *any* distinction, even the ontological, Being is not accorded a *topos*. Nor is Being to be accounted the cleft field. For beings in their *not-being* Being exclude Being. Nor, again, is Being the *difference* between the cleft and the uncleft field. For prior to the cleaving, there "is" no Being. Being wanders conceptually homeless.[102] Being, it might also seem, would simply be the complement of the distinguished being, the "space" excluded. But this is to ignore the sublime indifference of Being with respect to particularity. Being is not merely the Being *of this being*, but of *any possible* being. And this has the effect of hounding Being to the very margin of the field. Being becomes, in effect, the boundary, or, if you like, the horizon, of the field of beings. Thus, the plane severed by the "ontological difference" is a bounded plane, in contradistinction to the unbounded primordial field. Were intentionality "archaic," it could only be the differentiation of the object from its external horizon, not, as Merleau-Ponty insists, the *écart* deliminating figure from ground. But this would leave intentionality without a figural object, without a being, as the *telos* of its vectorial flux.[103]

But consider the alternative, a proposal compatible with an Husserlian appreciation of the transcendental (vertical) function of intentionality. Where are *we* when the act of inscription is performed? Where are *we* who now gaze upon the inscribed field? Indeed, more searchingly, where were *we* who once gazed upon an undifferentiated field? Again, we take our clue from Brown:

> [W]e cannot escape the fact that the world we know is constructed in order (and thus in such a way as to be able) to see itself.
>
> This is indeed amazing.
>
> Not so much in view of what it sees, although this may appear fantastic enough, but in respect of the fact that it *can* see *at all.*
>
> But *in order* to do so, evidently it must first cut itself into at least one state which sees, and at least one other state which is seen. In this severed and mutilated condition, whatever it sees is *only partially* itself. We may take it that the world undoubtedly is itself (i.e., is indistinct from itself), but in any attempt to see itself as an object, it must, equally undoubtedly, act so as to make itself distinct from, and therefore false to, itself. In this condition it will always partially elude itself.
>
> It seems hard to find an acceptable answer to the question of how or why the world conceives a desire, and discovers an ability, to see itself, and appears to suffer the process. That it does so is sometimes called the original mystery. Perhaps, in view of *the form* in which *we* presently *take* ourselves *to exist*, the mystery *arises from* our insistence on *framing* a question where there is, in reality, *nothing* to question. (LF, 105)

We set beside Brown's proposal a similar, but more articulate, second suggestion, that of D. T. Suzuki:

> In the beginning, which is really no beginning . . . the will wants to know itself, and consciousness is awakened, and with the awakening of consciousness the will is split in two. The one will, whole and complete in itself, is now at once actor and observer. Conflict is inevitable; for the actor now wants to be free from the limitations under which he has been obliged to put himself in his desire for consciousness. He has in one sense been enabled to see, but at the same time there is something which he, as observer, cannot see. (EZB I, 130–31)

"Seeing," for Brown, and "consciousness," for Suzuki, both import a fateful dualism of subject and object. There is, for Husserl, no question of the Clearing *(Lichtung)* clearing itself. Though Heidegger would say that Nothing doth "noth," Husserl would say it "noths" not. Rather, the logic of con/sciousness requires that we ask, just as we have, how *we*, the observers, are located with respect to the observed, and thus, how *we* have constituted the primordial distinction.[104] Yet Suzuki's "*arche*/ology" runs deeper.

Brown's redeeming comment enables us to appreciate the role of valuation in the act of differentiation: "There can be no distinction without motive, and there can be no motive unless contents are seen to differ in value" (LF, 1). Distinction rests upon "differentiated" valuation—a *prior* differentiation, to be sure, but nonetheless "vertical." "The will," as Suzuki remarks, "wants to know itself."[105] It differentially values *theoria*, not simply above *praxis*, but more importantly, above the primordial fusion of *theoria* and *praxis* prior to their differentiation. Suzuki has uncovered a third dimension of distinction. Along the "horizontal," we find *theoria* severed from *praxis*. Along the "vertical," we find their fusion distinguished from their articulation. And now, along the dimension of "depth"[106] running endwise from *our* very "location," we find the alternatives of a differentiated valuing in contrast with a profound inner contentment which wills all, or nothing, with equal impartiality, a universal yea-saying or nay-saying, it matters not, a serenity and equanimity without which intentional consciousness inevitably arises. Once again, *we* are drawn into the scheme of things, our "location" brought into question. But this time it is no longer a question of where the observer resides. It is a question of what we shall choose: *intentionality* or *enlightenment*. Or rather, if I may postulate a fourth dimension, perhaps a transcendentally more primal parturition is that between choosing and not-choosing. For, as we have begun to see, the mind's deep mirror-likeness excludes neither subject or object, neither being nor acting, neither willing nor not-willing. And certainly, then, it excludes neither the intrinsic intentional structuration of consciousness nor its utter vacuity.[107]

Deconstructing the Mirror

I would not here venture upon the morass of Derridean neologisms. But perhaps a few remarks on the familiar *différance* would not be out of place. Language, as Whorf famously hypothesized, carves the world:

> *Segmentation of nature is an aspect of grammar*. . . . We cut up and organize the spread and flow of events as we do, largely because, through our mother tongue, we are parties to an agreement to do so, not because nature itself is segmented in exactly that way for all to see. . . . *We dissect nature along lines laid down by our native languages*.[108]

Yet language, in the deconstructive idiom derived from Saussure, is a "system of differences,"[109] not, as much of analytic semantics assumes, a rattling assemblage of independent atomic symbols which "denote" language-external elements of reality.[110] Units of language are like the counters in a game.[111]

> Nothing is separately, in isolation, a pawn, a chess piece. A pawn is a *role*, a function within a game. . . . It is, therefore, a *relatum*, a "difference" among a system of differences . . . that thereby form a *system*. Furthermore, a *relatum* is what it is only within the network in which it functions: change the network of concepts and you change its *relata*. . . . But nothing *is*, is real, simply as a *relatum*; to treat anything merely as a *relatum* is to deny that it *is* as such, or is real.[112]

This "functionalist" vision of the systematicity of language is perfectly congruent with the Buddhist thesis that what is inside the boundary must coexist with what is outside. The difference of inside from outside is precisely analogous to the difference between linguistic *relata*. And profoundly Buddhist, also, in its implications, is Derrida's typical subsumption of the "system of differences" itself under its own requirements. The system remains, *within the system*, one side of the contrast between system and the pristine, unmutilated terrain of reality prior to the imposition of distinction.[113] Thus:

> [T]he functional distinctions of "signified" and "signifier," so essential to Saussure's theory of language, are eligible only within the invented (notational) *system* said to be language *(langue)* . . . they are *relata* or differences only.[114]

We have, then, in the Derridian theory of language, an unmistakable counterpart to the Buddhist vision of emptiness *(śūnyatā)* in which there remains no ontological excess, no "own-being" *(svabhāva)*, to the thing beyond its constitutive conditions, and in which even emptiness itself is thus empty.

Thinking, as ordinarily practiced, takes as its object the content of "perfect continence," a systemic *relatum*, a particular slice of the pie determined by the system of pie-slicing employed. Yet in Heidegger's revolutionary reformulation, "The matter of thinking is difference *as* difference."[115] Indeed, the thinking of "difference *as* difference" is precisely the thinking of "Being as difference."[116] And Being *(Sein)* is, indeed, difference—difference, that is, from every being *(Seiend)*. The negativity of the mirror models, with a certain limited aptness, Heidegger's "Being as difference." The mirror *is not* its reflections.[117] And the "eikonic difference" of mirror from reflection accordingly models the "ontico-ontological difference" of Being from being. Yet the Heideggerean conception of difference is insufficiently radical. For, as Derrida suggests, there may, indeed, be a difference that "is older than Being itself. There may be a difference still more unthought than the difference between Being and beings."[118] No doubt Heidegger has fastened upon an extraordinarily archaic difference. Yet, "within the decisive concept of the ontological difference, *all is not to be thought in one go*."[119] Or, to borrow Brown's term, now in its nuanced signification, "the all," embracing manifest and unmanifest alike, is not to be thought at once.[120] The purportedly primordial distinction of Being from being cleaves the all, thus marking beneath itself a distinction which is older: that between the cleft and the uncleft,[121] the field subsequent to and the field prior to the initial differentiation. The self-undercutting logic of this movement[122] is indifferent to the given candidate for primordiality. *Any* difference creates a deeper difference: the difference between the differentiated and the undifferentiated.[123] Thus, in Gasché's depiction:

> [D]ifférance . . . refer[s] to a Difference which for structural reasons erases its essentialization or phenomenologization . . . différance represents the thought of a difference that ceaselessly differs from and defers (itself).[124]

Différance is this reflexive movement of perpetual self-effacement, and as such represents a certain "generalization." Yet

> différance is not a generalization of the ontico-ontological difference. . . . What is generalized in the notion of différance is a structure of self-deferral, of a structure whose thinking is required to account not only for all regional differences but also for the ontico-ontological difference, not to speak of the difference between the ontic and the ontico-ontological difference.[125]

The mirror "defers" the purported primordiality of any distinct object (any parturition of the all) which comes before it. *Qua* mirror, nothing whatsoever is "engraved" upon it. It rejects, as alien, any structure proposed. Nor would another mirror placed before it escape the negative power of its incessant differing.

We have until now pictured the mirror as a rigid two-dimensional reflecting surface. Suppose, instead, that our reflecting surface were flexible. Bend the surface upon itself into the shape of the letter *U*. Or bend it completely into the shape of a cylinder. In this posture, the mirror reflects *itself*.[126] This self-externalizing comportment whereby the mind, in flexion upon itself, brings itself to givenness is, of course, reflection—a word ambiguous in the English, but disambiguated in the separate terms of French: *réflection* and *réflexion*. Cumming elucidates:

> "Reflection" implies etymologically a reversal in the direction of a movement, but this reversal can be instanced either by an optical reflection in a mirror (and in this instance the reflection is immediate in the sense that no movement is visible) or by the visible movement of a physical body (for which French has the term *réflexion*). Sartre will rely on reflection in the sense suggested by the instance of the mirror

> (*i.e.*, on the reflective consciousness, insofar as it *immediately* reflects what appears to the pre-reflective consciousness) in order to expose the distortions in the structure of consciousness which we shall see are introduced in the *movement* of reflection in the second sense.[127]

Suppose, indeed, that every *réflection* were a *réflexion*, that, in reflection, the mind deferred to itself by bowing, that reflection were the flexuous arcing of a single reflecting surface into a *C* or a *U* or an *O*.[128] Our flexible mirror would, of course, reflect upon itself, and, to that extent, effect a certain distance, a certain positionality, a certain denial, with respect to itself.[129] And there is no more stunning illustration of the mirror's negativity. For in reflecting "itself" it is, as Sartre would happily confirm, exactly *not* itself.

The Mirror of Mind

"The mind," as Shen-hsiu inculcates, "is like a bright mirror-stand" *(ching t'ai)*. Setting aside, if only temporarily, the awkward presence of the "stand" *(t'ai)*, let us muse (not to say "reflect") for a few moments more upon that irresistibly captivating feature of the mirror which entrances the child, inspires the poet, and furrows the philosopher's brow:[130] in the Buddhist idiom, its utter lack of "self-nature." Parakeets may discover within the mirror an *other*, like themselves, a friend or a foe. And it is, of course, remarkable, if true, that "the other" is, indeed, *like themselves*. It may be more accurate to presume a certain kinship with the human infant.

> A baby . . . opens its mouth if I playfully take one of its fingers between my teeth and pretend to bite it. And yet it has scarcely looked at its face in a glass. . . . The fact is that its own mouth and teeth, as it feels them from the inside, are immediately, for it, an apparatus to bite with, and my jaw, as the baby sees it from the outside, is immediately, for it capable of the same intentions. (PhP, 352)

The parakeet doubtless perceives its *likeness*, if not *itself*, in the mirror. And it may be, as in the case of the infant, that, for it, the *same intentions* are exhibited in the image "from the outside" as felt "from the inside." Nonetheless *we*, in our advanced intelligence, hold ourselves superior to the brute and its blindness to the laws of optics. This, perhaps, accounts for the almost successfully repressed glow of humiliation which, if honesty prevails, we certainly do feel at being deceived by the mirror. And which of us has not been thus deceived? Perhaps our newfound humility will teach us a deeper kinship with the parakeet after all.[131]

Nonetheless, *we* know (because *we* understand, if only vaguely, the laws of optics) that the ghastly demon, eyes shot with blood, mane disheveled, who appears in the mirror at dawn is not an *other*, not merely a being "like" us, not even our very self,[132] but what our intelligence pleases to conceive as an "image" or "reflection."[133] All of us know this, that is, except the protagonist of Harding's delightful spoof, "On Having No Head":[134]

> In my saner moments I see the man over there, the too-familiar fellow who lives in that other room behind the looking-glass and seemingly spends all his time staring into this room—that small, dull, circumscribed, particularized, ageing, and oh-so-vulnerable gazer—as the opposite in every way of my real Self here. I have never been anything but this ageless, adamantine, measureless, lucid, and altogether immaculate Void; it is unthinkable that I could ever have confused that staring wraith over there with what I plainly perceive myself to be here and now and forever![135]

Humor is often the only way possibility provides of resolving an insupportable tension. And this wonderfully amusing scenario plays mercilessly with a stressed duality central to phenomenology: that of "knowing" and "seeing."[136] We seldom pause to consider that the way we *see* the world[137] might collide at points with what we *know* the world to be like.[138] Yet the phenomenological inadmissibility of presupposition is poised upon precisely this deeply humorous possibility.[139] Harding's protagonist, the consistent phenomenologist, is laughable in the eyes of the world—and, let us admit it, in *our* eyes as well[140]—because, in his zealous cult of seeing, he refuses to admit what we all know.[141]

How, then, does a mirror *appear*?[142] What does it *look* like (or, again, what is its "look" like)?[143] Let us begin with what we know. As Reginald Allen well knows:

> We see reflections in the mirror, and we see the mirror in the room. But "in" here is ambiguous. Mirrors are physical objects which may be located relatively to other physical objects. But we can locate reflections only relatively to the reflecting medium; otherwise, we would be forced to claim that two things, the reflection and the surface of the medium, may be in the same place at the same time.[144]

From Allen, attestably the very soul of philosophical sobriety, one would expect no less than the eminently reasonable exposition just advanced. Mirrors, as common knowledge assents, are exactly what Allen claims them to be: physical objects, but physical objects, nonetheless, "in" which reflections are manifest and with respect to which they are located.[145] One can easily sort the mirrors from the nonmirrors in the sitting room simply by determining which of the surrounding objects have reflections in them. What do mirrors look like? The answer, of course, is insipid. They look like objects with reflections in them.

Fast in pursuit comes the expectable query, "But what do *reflections* look like?" It is when this question is thoroughly savored that what we "know" slumps into doubt. For should it turn out, as it evidently does, that reflection and original are phenomenally indistinguishable, we will be unable to determine which is the reflection, and thus, which of the physical objects pressing about us is a mirror. It may even turn out that a mirror (*qua* mirror) is not a physical object after all.

Reflections

Setting the teacher's apple before the mirror, *we*, at least, are not tempted to believe that the mirror itself has become red. The mirror does not duplicate its object. There are not now *two* apples, both quite literally red. Thus, the mirror does not instantiate our apple's redness. It "does" no more than provide an occasion for the manifestation of a *reflection-of.* In Allen's summation,

> The very being of a reflection is relational, wholly dependent upon what is other than itself: the original, and the reflecting medium. . . . The reflection does not *resemble* the original; rather, it is a *resemblance of* the original. This is its nature, and the whole of its nature.[146]

Still, beneath the veneer of theory lies the disturbing fact that we can, like the parakeet, be deceived. And great though our shame may be, it may be that the parakeet is the better phenomenologist.

Rendering unto Rorty what is Rorty's, we must cheerfully admit the expectable rejoinder. Yet even if our mirror is clouded, discolored or chipped, and this is no doubt empirically likely, we maintain our residence in the empirical. But, empirically illustrated or not, the logic of mirroring rivets us inescapably to phenomenal undecidability.

An ideally flawless mirror is benignly devoid of visible properties. What we see "in" the mirror, as we know, is what we place before it. The colors we see therein are not the mirror's; nor are the shapes. And in this perhaps limited respect, the mirror brings vividly to mind the Aristotelian *protē hylē*. The innate poverty of the mirror is displayed in its utter want of property.[147] Yet, as any child would aver, it is graced with a sort of "magic" which occasions the manifestation of any visible property whatsoever.[148]

Our friend with no head, the laughable companion who declines our knowledge,[149] seeing as a mirror would see (if it could), exclaims, in language irresistibly descriptive of the Buddhist experience of "emptiness" *(śūnyatā):*

> [T]his nothing, this hole where a head should have been, was no ordinary vacancy, no mere nothing. . . . It was a vast emptiness vastly filled,

> a nothing that found room for everything . . . I had lost a head and gained a world.
>
> It was all, quite literally, breathtaking. I seemed to stop breathing altogether, absorbed in the Given. Here it was, this superb scene, brightly shining in the clear air, alone and unsupported, mysteriously suspended in the void, and . . . utterly free of "me," unstained by any observer. Its total presence was my total absence, body and soul. Lighter than air, clearer than glass, altogether released from myself, I was nowhere around.[150]

We must imagine Hui-neng smiling—not merely in mirth, nor simply in enjoyment of Harding's superb wit and the delectably irreverent and lighthearted treatment of an experience of such profoundly transformative significance, but in recognition. This is exactly Hui-neng's own position: There never was a mind-mirror.[151]

Visible Invisibility

Buddhist phenomenology embraces no deeper paradox than its recognition that the very visibility of the mirror is its invisibility. The spirit *(pneuma)* bloweth where it listeth.[152] But those with eyes to see will not be blind to the wind in the trees. We "see," in a perfectly genuine sense, the field of magnetic force in the pattern of iron filings. And we "see," to borrow Sartre's example, the very absence of Pièrre at the evening's soirée. It might be said that in each case, the "visible" manifestation of that which, in the positivist's estimation, would lie beyond the visible is sustained by a certain active functioning: the restless blowing of the winds, the patterned attraction of magnetism, our expectation, now thwarted, of meeting Pièrre. But to parse the situation by *first* distinguishing "positive" iron filings from the secret causal activity of the loadstone, and *then* inferring from effect back to cause, does violence to the immediacy of our experience.[153] And besides, the causal inference would be phenomenologically licensed only if the purported cause were itself visible. The experienced scientist *sees* neutrinos in the cloud chamber. Or as Hanson says, "the microscopist sees coelenterate mesoglea, his new student sees only a gooey, formless stuff"[154]—*sees*, we must emphasize, not "infers." The gestalt of chairs arranged in a circle is no less "positive" than the chairs thus arranged. There can be no doubt that we do *see* the circle. The electron, it is sometimes claimed, *is* nothing more than a certain organized totality of concomitant observable functionings. To witness such functionings (or a selection of them) *is* to witness the electron. To witness the swaying of branches and the quivering of leaves *is* to see the wind in its prankish fluidity.[155] And prescinding from objectuating flaws, what, precisely, could a mirror *be* if not its reflective functioning. "Mirror," once again, is a covert gerund (and thus, *pace* Allen, not a "physical object" at all). An eleventh-century Vietnamese monk declared, *"The free man sees all, but nothing is seen by him."*[156] We *see* the mirror in its reflectings. Shen-hsiu "sees" the mirror in seeing no mirror. Hui-neng sees it not. And both are right.[157]

The mirror bears a certain evident kinship to Nicholas of Cusa's "omnivoyant icon," of which he writes:

> [E]ach of you shall find that, from whatever quarter he regardeth it, it looketh upon him as if it looked on none other. . . . And as he knoweth the icon to be fixed and unmoved, he will marvel at the motion of its immovable gaze.[158]

But even more than with this earthly analogue, the mirror enjoys an uncanny affinity with the very God of apophantic theology which Cusa's remarkable icon is intended to represent. The point is not merely epistemological. It is not merely that we cannot perceptually know *what* the mirror is (though this is assuredly the case—the mirror is not presented in its reflections). The mirror simply *has* no "what is it?" *(todi ti?),* no essence, no self-nature.[159] The wise Maimonides, however, undeniably among the most thoughtful pilgrims to tread the *via negativa*, allows the attribution to God of predicates of action. While this may seem surprising in view of his adamant prohibition against attributing definitions (in whole or in part), qualities, and relations to the Divine,[160] actions bespeak nothing of the divine "whatness."[161] And likewise, by identifying the mirror with its functioning, we have not thereby surreptitiously smuggled an "essence" behind the looking-glass.[162] Again, it is not *of the essence* of the mirror to reflect.[163] The mirror *is* its reflecting.

Instantiation and Manifestation

What divides presentation from reflective representation is, as we know, the manner in which visible properties are, neutrally, "enjoyed." And the intelligence which allegedly elevates us above the parakeet issues the distinction between literal instantiation and reflective manifestation. The apple *is* red. It boldly exemplifies the property of redness. Yet its mirror-image cannot properly be said to *be* red. Rather, as Allen perspicuously comments, "[T]hough you may call the reflection of a red scarf red if you so please, you cannot mean the *same* thing you mean when you call its original red."[164] The apple and the scarf instantiate redness; the mirror, we shall say, manifests it. But the lesson of the parakeet, and of our headless colleague, is that no purely phenomenal feature of our experience inclines us in one direction or the other.

> For, however carefully I attend, I fail to find here even so much as a blank screen on which these mountains and sun and sky are projected, or a clear mirror in which they are reflected, or a transparent lens or aperture through which they are viewed—still less a soul or a mind to which they are presented, or a viewer (however shadowy) who is distinguishable from the view.[165]

Neither the fullness of opacity nor the emptiness of reflectivity is present within the experience as the "medium" of phenomenal display. We can never tell, solely by phenomenological inspection, whether what we see "instantiates" or "manifests" its properties.[166]

But the saga of undecidability suggests alternative morals. Either we simply cannot *tell*, by phenomenological means, whether a given phenomenon instantiates or manifests its properties, though, indeed, there remains a clear extra-phenomenal ("metaphysical") difference; or there *is* no distinction, phenomenal or extra-phenomenal, to be had. We shall observe, with due respect, the last rites of the ill-fated Kantian thing-in-itself.[167] And we may perhaps be excused, at this point, from rehearsal. Having solidly bolted the door against the Kantian *Ding-an-sich*, we are summoned beyond the epistemological. The ground of an extraphenomenal distinction can only be noumenal. And we are thus clearly committed to the more radical claim. The distinction has no ground, either intra- or extraphenomenal. Epistemology is simply beside the issue at hand. To be sure, we cannot *know*, in any particular case, whether we are confronted with object or image. But more importantly, there simply *is* nothing to be known.

Are we then, contrary to our paradoxical embracing of "visible invisibility," to admit that the categories of *mirror* and *object* are "metaphysical" in the sense disdained by thoughtful and disciplined practitioners of phenomenology? If the very distinction between image and original,[168] mirror and object, is unceremoniously retired from beneath our feet, on what are we standing when we claim that the mirror is "visible" in its very invisibility, that mirror(ing) is no-mirror(ing)? Has the distinction been decisively dissolved? And if so, are Shen-hsiu's affirmation and Hui-neng's denial of the mirrorlikeness of mind thereby rendered nonsense?

In language only an Hegelian could love, the distinction has not been lost—only "sublated" *(aufgehoben)*. Prescinding from the involvement of this sonorous term in the great speculative System in which it thrives, we borrow only those two principal connotations offered by the German: "canceled" and "uplifted." Our ruminations have delivered us from the eikonic distinctions. The distinctions are "canceled." And now, self-satisfied, we can point the finger at all those benighted souls who would commit the "eikonic fallacy," imputing distinction where none lies. But confessedly we find ourselves a bit perplexed, a bit breathless and stupefied, in being thus abruptly "liberated." The landscape is not entirely familiar. We see the reason in our deliverance. What we cannot understand is our lapsarian proclivity for such distinctions. Why, after all, did we hold ourselves superior to the parakeet?

Analytic Thought

Adorno answers: "We cannot, by thinking, assume any position in which that separation of subject and object will directly vanish, for the separation is inherent in each thought; it is inherent in thinking itself" (ND, 85). "Thought"—or as I would prefer, *analytic* thought[169]—is the template in which the subject/object (mirror/mirrored) distinction is indelibly inscribed,[170] the "map" whose "legend" we read back into reality, the "dust" which Shen-hsiu would have us wipe away. And failing vigilant "wariness" (awareness), we fall almost irresistibly into the supposition that experience conforms to the "template." Kant sternly warns, in the "Transcendental Dialectic," against the employment of a reason loosed from its moorings in concrete experience. Yamada roshi, delightfully free of Kantian sobriety, quips that all Kant needs is a good swift kick in the pants.[171] Profiting not from Yamada's "kick," Kant remains unaware that the noumenal structures of his elaborate critical epistemology belong to the map, not to the terrain, thus neglecting the very strictures intended to promote transcendental disillusionment.[172] The mariner will never espy the International Date Line dividing the boiling brine.

Reading the analytic chart's necessary embellishments back into the charted may account both for the distinction and for its dialectical cancellation.[173] But in what sense is it "taken up"? The answer is implicit in Hui-neng's treatment of "dust." The dust which so occupies Shen-hsiu turns out, if you will, not to be *dust* at all. The obscuration of mind is a function of the external vantage point,[174] the sensible standpoint of "knowing" which frowns, unbemused, upon the delightfully laughable standpoint of "seeing."[175] Of itself, the "mirror" is unhindered in its reflectivity even if completely blanketed in opacity. Analytic distinctions, too arrogant to bend to the reality to which they purport to minister, serve an ex/planatory, not a descriptive, function. And accordingly, it is phenomenological folly to assume that the contours of experience are congruently demarcated. The distinctions are canceled, since they have no purchase upon experience. Yet the bipolar categories of analytic intellection are also "taken up" inasmuch as they themselves, as much as anything else, are *experienced*. Enraptured by the pastel ambience of the fading sunset or coldly inspecting the eidetic landscape of the *topos noētos*, the mind remains unsullied in the purity of its reflective functioning. Of themselves, analytic distinctions do not distort. What distorts is the additional assumption that they "describe." Bracketing the distinctions, treating them as quotations, they become harmless toys. And no philosophical harm will come to those who playfully disport themselves therewith.

But we can get more dialectical "kick" out of Yamada's brisk commentary.[176] For if Kant is culpable of confusing template with experience, we, in our turn, may be too eager to see them distinguished. By our own eikonic logic, a crystal ball tinted red is indiscriminable from a transparent crystal ball set against a red surface. Perhaps in giving the boot to Kant, we ourselves must feel the shock of encounter. If Kant is in error, we also err who only stand and criticize. There is just no phenomenological procedure for deciding between Kant's red crystal—mind intrinsically informed with transcendental structure—and an equally inadequate dualism of pure crystal transparent to red. Both positions, reciprocally antagonistic, are equally falsified by undecidability.

The Thing-in-Itself

Husserlian phenomenology is, to be sure, a noumenology. Not only is the phenomenon to be comprehended as the object *in itself* precisely as it appears, but the phenomenon itself, in its immanence, is *in itself*,[177] and, in its appearing, appears *as it is*: *in itself*.[178] Its being (in itself) *is* its appearing.[179] The Kantian noumenon, by contrast, does not, and cannot, appear. It is wholly occluded by the very phenomenon to which it gives birth. The noumenon inseminates the phenomenal, giving incipient rise to the unformed stirrings of sensibility. But gestated within the dark womb of form-giving understanding,[180] the newly born phenomenon is the pride of the eye. The parents are lost in the attendant presentation of the "child." The star *itself* is lost sight of in its telescopic presentation. For its sensory illumination is wholly transformed by the intricate system of lenses and filters—forms of intuition, categories, schemata—integral to its functioning.[181]

Buddhism thoroughly repudiates "self," eradicating even its most subtle manifestation. Not even the "itself" of the in-itself is spared purgation.[182] And accordingly, we must issue a variant of the Berkeleyan challenge that the realist, and thus the Kantian dualist, submit even a single illuminating instance of the fabulous *Ding-an-sich*. The challenge can met only by fishing the example from the blind and lightless depths of the noumenal realm, reeling it in for phenomenal inspection. The moment our sullen quarry rises to the surface, becoming thus exemplary, it simultaneously becomes phenomenal. Pointing vaguely to the brackish brew in which the noumenal allegedly thrives is of no avail. We must *see* the movement, the outline, feel the quiver of what the realist purports, else the claim is consigned, with so many other philosophical ephemera, to the currents of mere superstition.

In fact, however, the Kantian realist is not unduly impressed with what must appear to be a purely ad hoc desideratum for verification: that *seeing* is requisite. "Conceiving of the unconceived" becomes paradoxical only if an unaltered univocal sense of "conceived" is in force throughout—only, that is, if "Kant conceives *X* and *X* is unconceived" represents a straightforward logical contradiction. But does it? Suppose that "conceives" in the first instance is understood in the propositional sense: "conceives that." And suppose, by contrast, that "conceived" in the second instance is understood objectivally: "conceived of." What appeared to be a frightful inconsistency now turns out to be the perfectly harmless proposition: "Kant conceives *that X* is unconceived *(of).*" Thus, the realist walks away unruffled from what promised to be a rather brutish confrontation with Berkeley.

But not so fast! What, exactly, *is* the difference between "conceiving that" and "conceiving of"? The realist, wittingly or not, is committed to the claim that "Kant conceives *that X* is . . ." (interpolating one's favorite predicate) does not entail "Kant conceives of *X*." One can, it seems, form and comprehend judgments about *X* without conceiving *of* their subject term. Yet an object conceived *of* is, in a vitally expansive sense, a sense congruent with that employed in the A redaction of the first *Critique*, "phenomenal." If it can be conceived *that X* exists (or *that X* possesses certain attributes)[183] without *X* falling to the phenomenal, we have lost our object to the noumenal. But this tragedy aside, notice the circuitous route which the realist has now traversed. In order to preserve the Kantian distinction from Berkeley's challenge, the realist has taken refuge in a second distinction, that between "conceiving that" and "conceiving of." Yet the second distinction presupposes the first, thus assuming precisely what remains to be proved: *petitio principii*.

Bivalence and the Real

It is striking (shall we say) that the two positions, like tigers ominously circling one another, co-en"tail." This follows, of course, in virtue of the trivial truth-table truism that false implies true. Thus, both positions wash out true as well as false. But there is an alternative route to this conclusion. We have now ostracized the extraphenomenal thing-in-itself.[184] Thus, the only intrinsic transcendental determination we permit ourselves is phenomenal. This established, were Kant, our temporary stand-in for Shen-hsiu, indeed, correct in his transcendentalism, we would be licensed to affirm, with Hui-neng, that there never was an intrinsic transcendental determination. This is because, from the standpoint of a "crystalline" mind, there can be no phenomenal wedge between "intrinsic" and "extrinsic" structure.[185] The assertion of intrinsic determination must always be accounted false, not because extrinsic determination is true, but because the affirmation enjoys no purchase upon the phenomenal experience. And the principle of bivalence shoulders the remaining work.

In the Hegelian dialectic, contradictory moments are set apart in binary opposition by the centrifugal impulsion of the analytic understanding *(Verstand)*. It is the unifying, centripetal gravitation of reason *(Vernunft)* which reconciles contradiction in higher synthesis.[186] The Buddhist dialectic, by contrast, is powered entirely by the understanding and its laws. Were we firm in our allegiance to experience, to what we *see* as opposed to what we *know*, there would be no issue dividing proponents of intrinsic and extrinsic structure. The distinctions of inside and outside, subject and object, arise, like the extremities of West and East, from the ex/planatory projection of the analytic intellect.[187] But then, of course, we should have nothing to say, and assuredly would not be in a position to offer our voice to *truth*.[188]

Like the gods who despised the hermaphroditic contentment of original humanity, the Principle of Contradiction seizes upon the innocent experience, severs it in twain, and thenceforth, the two halves wander abroad in painful separation, feeling a profound inner affinity with the other, but unable to overcome, and now mortally horrified of overcoming, their isolation. The voice of experience is not a lullaby of reconciliation, but a re/minder, a re/membering, that reconciliation is not at all called for.[189] To pine for the innocent days of experiential youth only blinds us the more. For we thereby willingly assume the very duality of pure mind and extrinsic impurity which the analytic gods have made our lot, falling into a nostalgia for purity which Hui-neng vigorously decries:

> Purity has no form, but, nonetheless, some people try to postulate the form of purity and consider this to be Ch'an practice. People who hold this view obstruct their own original natures and end up by being bound to purity. (PS/y, 139–40)

And we are thus admonished "neither to cling to the notion of a mind, nor to cling to the notion of purity, nor to cherish the thought of immovability; for these are not our meditation" (NM, 27). Our experience *is* informed by the contrast of intrinsic and extrinsic structure, subject and object. It would be dishonest and unworthy of our phenomenological pretensions to claim otherwise. And, inasmuch as the destiny of phenomenology is to give articulate, and thus, partitionary voice to the *logos* of experience, we cannot forswear an altogether worthy determination to speak the *truth*.[190] But even truthful attribution divides. Certainly, a profession of purity can never be warranted by the smug pretense of being "more enlightened than thou."[191] Yet we must not, again, lapse into the eikonic fallacy of assuming that *this* contrast is *itself* "within" or "without."

Once the gods have surgically severed the original experiential hermaphrodite into a "male" rendering (positive, full of itself, intrinsically structured) and a "female" rendering (void, open, indeterminate) they proceed—we imagine with a certain vicious glee—to sow the bitter seeds of contention. Our infelicitous duo is now roughly informed that one—and *only* one—of them has been granted a priceless endowment, a certain magical attribute which the Olympians are pleased to call "Truth." At the question "Which of us has it?" a great silence engulfs the earth. The law of this endowment is, of course, the Principle of Bivalence. The Principle of Contradiction has performed the evil surgery. Now the Principle of Bivalence malignantly ensures that the wound will never heal. As the curtain descends, however, Bivalence turns out to be a curiously just, if unintended, friend. Contradiction commands that the pearl of Truth not be given to both. Experience, no god but a wise and reliable counselor, has issued a verdict upon the ill-begotten male and female of our tale. Both are to be accounted false. Bivalence, in loyalty to an ancient friendship, is unwilling to contravene this sentence, and defies the edict of Contradiction, declaring, as was his unaltered intent, that if "Falsehood" falls to the one, "Truth" will fall to the other. Thus, Truth falls to both.

The play, however, has not seen its final act. For the ostensibly happy dénouement conceals a fateful and powerfully consequential act of betrayal. Contradiction and Bivalence, fast and consistent friends until this dark moment of treachery, now brace for battle. Will the sacred alliance of the gods be shattered in conformity with the dictate of sub-Olympian Experience? If so, the gods have had their bloodstained way with the pristine hermaphrodite at the expense of an all too costly rift among themselves. Harmony among the gods can be secured only by turning a deaf ear to the behest of Experience.

But wait! Great Bivalence, battle-girt, has fallen. The counsel of Experience has proven a mighty potion. Bivalence, now twisted and divided against himself, has quaffed the unholy cup of conjoint falsehood.[192] The god has been fatally poisoned, the very law of his being violated. A hush befalls Olympus. The gods gather in silence, astonished at the fateful deed.

As our parable fancifully suggests, a phenomenological adherence to experience sufficiently faithful to forswear the allure of the eikonic fallacy, renders the very laws of analytic logic balefully inconsistent. And this momentous accomplishment shatters logical bedrock: the principle that every proposition is either true or false. Realism, as Dummett has helpfully shown,[193] is suspended from the principle. But the negation of bivalence does not thereby make idealists of us all. Dummett illustrates his antirealist commitments in remarks concerning the nature of mathematical truth:

> If . . . one believes with the intuitionists, that the content of a mathematical statement resides entirely in our ability to recognize what constitutes a proof of it and what a disproof, we have no right to declare it either true or false, one will prefer a picture according to which mathematical reality is constructed by us, or at least, comes into existence only as we become aware of it.[194]

The "construction of reality" so offensive to our antisubjectivist sensibilities, is, however, substantially qualified in Dummett's poignant recognition that "The question was not whether the reality that rendered our statements true or false was *external*, but whether it was *fully determinate*. . . ." Seamless experience offers not the slightest interstice for the insertion of de/termination. The subject/object wedge finds no welcoming crevasse. The conflicting positions of Shen-hsiu and Hui-neng are conjointly falsified, not because each confronts an antagonistic "external" truth, but because *reality itself*, the reality of phenomenal experience, is insufficiently determinate to support the truth of either. The failure of bivalence leads not to an abandonment of reality, but to its indetermination.[196]

In all this cool

is the moon also sleeping

there in the pool?

(RYUSUI, 1691–1758)

The Pathless Path

REFLECTIONS ON BUDDHIST MEDITATIVE PRACTICE

Tranquility and Insight

Sonorous, deep-throated knelling of an ancient temple bell. . . . Conversation halts, cut off. Thoughts flee. Resonance fills the hollow vale, expelling all else.[1] The rich, all-pervasive sonority commands alertness, and vigilance is born within us.[2] Findlay tells us that "the manifestation of bodies to the senses involves a violence."[3] And, of course, manifestation is the impact *(festus)* received at the hand *(manus)* of the object, received, that is, from the object as tightened fist. Yet it would be a mistake to assume that every disruption of the native course of events is thus brutalizing. The bell appears as a figure of grace. And its disruption is the severing of chains (chains of centrifugal thought, edifying chains of Rortyan verbosity).[4] What offers the uncanny impression of passivity in the hands of a gracious beneficence such as the temple bell is exactly its self-bestowal—a gift which no comportment of our own will prepare us to receive.

Presently the sonority fades. Bird song, a snatch of human prattle, a curious musing, invade us as the resonance retreats, dissolving into a vibration felt more in the bones than in the ear. Then nothingness. And everything. Everything is restored. The aural world is once again congested and interminably busy. The noise of traffic, a pestering fly, the drone of a lawn mower, all reassert themselves. And we find ourselves longing for the gracious disruption of the bell whose knelling, like its founding, is lost in the nothingness of time.[5]

Yet something has changed. For we have attentively followed the passage from plenary resonance to horizonal vacuity. Silence is the bell's final gift.[6] And now silence embraces the cacophonous fray.[7] Aurality wrapped in silence is brighter, cleaner, more vibrant than any harmonious strain could be, unmindful of its horizon.[8] If it is true, as Merleau-Ponty avers, that "silence is still a modality of the world of sound" (PhP, 452),[9] then silence can only offer itself as the "null sound,"[10] the aural vacuity which provides the very condition, the aural space, of sound.[11] Now attuned to silence, the ear is blessed for the first time with an authentic hearing.[12] Focus is sharpened by contrast. And the contrast of focal aurality of any intensity with the zero-point of absolute silence[13] is the infinite.[14] Buddhism is "a philosophy that ends in silence, for the enlightened has nothing more to say about being and non-being."[15] Indeed, "the only 'answer' one can receive from wisdom *(prajñā)* is silence" (E, 89).

The passage to horizonal silence illustrates, as effectively as anything could, the two concordant, but divergent, phases of Buddhist meditative practice. Reversing their given order, the final "steps" (or better: "stripes") of the Noble Eightfold Path,[16] "right concentration" (Pali: *sammā samādhi)* and "right mindfulness" (Pali: *sammā sati)*, are echoed, if insufficiently, in the "gracious" disruption of the temple bell which puts discursive thought to flight[17] and in the intensifying awareness of ambient aurality brought about by the horizonal pursuit of deep silence. In its primordiality, the powerful sonority of the bell is arresting. In its ultimacy, the remaining silence is releasing.[18] Buddhist meditation begins with concentrative cessation and continues, until ultimate liberation is realized, in the direction of a detached experiential intensification.[19]

There are, that is, two very different forms of meditative being (sometimes rendered "cultivation": *bhāvanā*) that lay legitimate claim to being Buddhist: the cultivation of tranquility (Pali: *samatha bhāvanā*), which Buddhism shares with the tradition of raja yoga, and the cultivation of insight (Pali: *vipassanā bhāvanā*), which is uniquely and distinctively Buddhist. Of tranquility meditation, Solé-Leris writes: "It is rather like bringing down a light beam to the sharpest possible focus on one single, intensely bright point" (TI, 25). And, in Solé-Leris's concomitant description of the "clear vision" (from the Pali, *vipassati*) of insight meditation:

> [H]ere the beam of light is not narrowed down to an infinitesimal point, but only to a size which will provide a powerful and finely focused but rather broader light field, which follows and illuminates whatever is happening at any given moment. (TI, 25)

Nor do the disparate practices culminate in the same modes of experiencing. Like our temple bell, tranquility meditation effects "a suspension of sense perception, interruption of the verbal, rational activities of the mind, and feelings of bliss, happiness, serenity and ineffable intuition" (TI, 25). The tradition of Ch'an (Zen) meditation, which takes its name from a sinicization of the Sanskrit *dhyāna* (Pali: *jhāna*), is remarkably effective in bringing about a distinctive mode of mind that answers to this description. While it is seriously misleading to regard Buddhism as no more than "a branch of Yoga,"[20] and intolerably presumptuous to claim that "the whole of Buddhism, through and through, is nothing but Yoga,"[21] it cannot be gainsaid that "Yoga is an essential ingredient in the primitive doctrine"[22] of Buddhism. And, with due caution, it would not be inappropriate to attribute to Zen a continuation of the tradition of "yoking" (from the Sanskrit *yuj),* uniting the individual and the Ultimate *(Brahman).* If Suzuki remonstrates that "Zen is not the same as *Dhyāna,*"[23] that "Zen is not a system of *Dhyāna,*"[24] and, indeed, that "*Dhyāna*, as it is understood by Zen, does not correspond to the practice as carried on in Zen,"[25] it is to mark the decisive departure of the life of mindfulness from mere quietistic absorption, not to sever a vital and life-giving root. Rinzai Zen, sponsored by Hui-neng, short-circuits "the verbal, rational activities of the mind" through intense contemplation of the logically paradoxical *koan,*[26] thus giving rise to the temporary rapture[27] and potentiated feelings of "bliss, happiness, serenity and ineffable intuition" typical of *satori* or *kensho.*[28] Soto Zen, the meditative "gradualism" often associated with the teachings of Shen-hsiu, has no quarrel with the abruptness of *satori.* McDaniel sponsors the distinction between "enlightenment experience" and an "enlightened way of experiencing": "the enlightenment experience, rather than being an end in itself, is a means toward the enlightened way of experiencing. The way itself is the end. When one lives this way, there is then no other end to seek."[29] What divides the two great houses is, in the final analysis, a mere nuance, a simple shift of emphasis. Both find in *satori* a precipitous, compelling and invaluable experience-event. And neither assumes that the experience is more than a prelude to an authentic Buddhist life. *Satori* is, if you like, the powerfully transformative knelling of the temple bell. As an "event" it is an occurrence, brief or perdurant, and perhaps a recurrence, but an occurrence, nonetheless, that is hopelessly temporal and temporary. As Rahula writes:

> Even the very pure states of *dhyāna* . . . attained by the practice of higher meditation, free from even a shadow of suffering in the accepted sense of the word, states which may be described as unmixed happiness, as well as the state of *dhyāna* which is free from sensations both pleasant *(sukha)* and unpleasant *(dukkha)* and is only pure equanimity and awareness—even these very high spiritual states are included in *dukkha*. . . . after praising the spiritual happiness of these *dhyānas*, the Buddha says that they are "impermanent, *dukkha*, and subject to change." . . . It is *dukkha*, not because there is "suffering" in the ordinary sense of the word, but because "whatever is impermanent is *dukkha.*" . . . (WBT, 18)

Thus, we may appreciate the supersession of the "enlightened way of experiencing" over the "enlightenment experience."[30] And thus, also, we may understand Suzuki's impatience with the thoughtless identification of Zen and the inauthentic quietistic meditation aiming solely at impermanent ecstasy.

Samatha and *vipassanā* meditation are alike "*attention-training methods*" (TI, 24). And "every attention," as Ricoeur observes, "reveals an 'I can' at the heart of the 'I think.'"[31] Both, then, represent a training of the will comparable to magnetic induction. The patient stroking of a bar of iron with a magnet will, degree by patient degree, generate on the part of the iron bar a detectable magnetic field which grows in intensity as induction proceeds. The abstractive practice of tranquility cultivation, in contrast to the insight *(vipassanā)* evolved through a detached and dispassionate observation of the "concrete," seeks ultimately to foreclose the "I think"[32] by riveting attention to a specific meditation subject *(kasiṇa)* from which are successively withdrawn the various hierarchically founded laminations of concreteness, ultimating in the cessation *(nirodha)* of perception and sensation in which even the meditative "I can" is lost in indistinction.[33] The practice of "mindfulness" *(sati),* on the other hand, forecloses neither the "I can" nor the "I think," but rather witnesses with sharpened vigilance the patterns of the "magnetic field" as it manifests itself with each successive stage of meditative advance.[34]

If Merleau-Ponty is correct in his unadorned assertion that "To be conscious = to have a figure on a ground—one cannot go back any further" (VI, 191), we find in the two forms of cultivation, the two forms of *being*, two very different ways of surpassing consciousness. In tranquility meditation, attention is focused upon the subject *to the exclusion* of extraneous background disturbances. The "figure" expands, and, at its limit, entirely fills the field of consciousness. The differentiation of figure upon ground has vanished, expelled by the incursion of the swelling "figure." At the zenith of absorption, figure is no longer figure, for ground has vanished.[35] In the development of uniquely Buddhist insight, on the other hand, incursion occurs in precisely the opposite direction. One becomes increasingly mindful of horizonal elements conditioning the focal theme.[36] Figure is increasingly enriched by an awareness of the inseparability of features of the ground. The ground "comes in," until, at the zenith of insight (enlightenment) the *écart* separating figure from ground, and thus consciousness itself, dissolves in favor of a perfectly lucid awareness of the field in all its richness. Tranquility is effected through "impoverishment," and insight, through "enrichment."[37]

The Formal Absorptions

We would stray insufferably from our course were we to treat in any satisfactory way the eight stages of yogic absorption—the four formal and four formless meditations (Pali: *rūpa jhāna* and *arūpa jhāna*) most of which were practiced by the Buddha's accomplished teachers, Alāra Kālāma and Uddaka Rāmaputta—and the ultimate state of cessation *(nirodha)* appended by the Buddha himself. Heiler finds in the Four Immeasurables, the uppermost absorptions unbounded by material content, "a translucidation, a transformation and fulfillment of one's being at its deepest recess."[38] Crediting whatever truth this claim may embody, we must nonetheless remind ourselves, once again, that the "translucidation" is short-lived. And we must rejoin, with Lamotte, that such subtle delicacies comprise only an "hors d'oeuvre"[39] to the authentic life of mindfulness.

To "absorb" is to "drink [*sorbere*] in," to become, in Merleau-Ponty's words, "a nothing filled with being," and to make of the meditation subject (Pali: *kasiṇa*) a "being emptied by nothingness" (VI, 75). When absorption is incomplete, there is a nothing only partially filled, and a being only partially emptied. The ascent through the eight stages of meditative absorption in the direction of cessation, the perfect coincidence "being" and "nothingness," holds challenging implications for Western phenomenology generally, and Sartrean phenomenological ontology as a crucial instance.[40]

The most evident has no doubt already been glimpsed, our teasing employment of "being" and "nothingness" perhaps facilitating the connection. If cessation is possible, then Sartre's renunciation of the in-itself-for-itself, the elusive being incessantly pursued in our "futile passion" to rid ourselves of the curse of contingency, to found ourselves, to assume the being *causa sui* attributed by speculative theology to Deity, is fundamentally misguided.[41] Misguided, also, as we shall see, is the assumption that a being in-itself-for-itself is, indeed, the ground of its own being. For the being which is nothingness, the nothingness which is being, *śūnyatā*, is not the floor, but the ceiling of phenomenal being, the limit, not the ground, of *saṁsāra*. But this in due course. Let us begin, if not in practice, at least in thought, to climb the ladder.

Toward a Critique of Pure Suffering

In the Buddha's incisive, but boundlessly compassionate, inquiry:

> Which do you think is more: the flood of tears which, weeping and wailing, you have shed upon this long way—hurrying and hastening through the round of rebirths, united with the undesired, separated from the desired—this, or the waters of the four oceans?[42]

Popular expositions of the Second Noble Truth, the "arising of suffering" *(duḥkha samudaya)*,[43] inculpate a vaguely delimited "desire" as the founding condition for the experience of human anguish, frustration and pain, burdening the adherent with the incoherent attempt to deracinate "desire" of every species.[44] "Desire," however, ranges much too freely over the plane of human motivation, and would, if eradicated, eliminate at a single stroke even the loving-kindness *(maitrī)* and compassion *(karuṇā)* which the Buddha labored to instill.[45] Indeed, followers of the Buddha are admonished to cultivate a spontaneously overflowing *desire* for the well-being of all, as expressed in the lovely words of the *Metta-sutta*:

> May all beings be happy and secure; may their minds be contented.
>
> Whatever living beings there may be . . . may all beings, without exception, be happy-minded! . . .
>
> Just as a mother would protect her only child even at the risk of her own life, even so let one cultivate a boundless heart towards all beings.
>
> Let one's thoughts of boundless love pervade the whole world—above, below and across—without any obstruction, without any hatred, without any enmity.[46]

Nothing could be more profoundly indicative of a genuine and wholly meritorious "desire" than the "May . . ." of the "Sutra of Loving-Kindness."

It cannot be desire, then, in all of its manifestations, which gives rise to suffering, but rather a specifically delimited modalization of desire: a "craving" (Sanskrit: *tṛṣṇā*; Pali: *taṇhā*) which is at once egocentric and ego-encasing:[47]

> It is this "thirst" (craving, *taṇhā*) which produces re-existence and re-becoming *(ponobhavikā)*, and which is bound up with passionate greed *(nandīrāgasahagatā)*, and which finds fresh delight now here and now there *(tatratatrābhinandinī)*, namely, (1) thirst for sense-pleasures *(kāma-taṇhā)*, (2) thirst for existence and becoming *(bhava-taṇhā)* and (3) thirst for non-existence (self-annihilation, *vibhava-taṇhā*).[48]

The Buddhist response to "thirst" of whatever form is never one of violent repression or extirpation. There is no rapacious ripping of the offending faculty from the bleeding tissue of the mind's fragile life. Nor is meditation to be conceived as anesthesia for a certain invasive form of psychic surgery. "Thirst" *(tṛṣṇā)* is not a cancer, but an internal organ of the psyche—an organ, useful, indeed essential, in its proper mode of functioning, and an organ, moreover, like any other, with its own cycle of development and ultimate decay.

> We must therefore clearly and carefully mark and remember that the cause, the germ, of the arising of *dukkha* is within *dukkha* itself, and not outside; and we must equally well remember that the cause, the germ, of the cessation of *dukkha*, of the destruction of *dukkha*, is also within *dukkha* itself, and not outside. (WBT, 31)

In the canonical declamation: "Whatever is of the nature of arising, all that is of the nature of cessation" (WBT, 31). It is not, then, extirpation which is called for, but rather a perpetually deepened assuagement, a radically authentic assuagement, of thirst.

In the first four, the "formal" or "material," absorptions, the meditative path which traverses the second stratum of the Triple World, the practitioner

(1) "dwells concentrated . . .
(2) happy [first and second absorption] . . .
(3) and blissful [first, second and third absorption] . . .
(4) exercising applied and sustained thought [first absorption only]."[49]

Each successive level of absorption is a "loss." At the first, the "hindrances" fall away; at the second, thought, both applied (Pali: *vitakka*) and sustained (Pali: *vicāra*), vanishes;[50] at the third, happiness *(sukha)*—"the contentedness at getting a desirable object"[51]—evaporates; and in the fourth, even bliss (Pali: *pīti*)—"the actual experiencing of it when got"[52]—disappears, leaving only a state of pure equanimity ("even-mindedness"), the undistorted "mirrorlikeness" of a mind which simply "reflects"—without attachment, without aversion, without comment.

The self-canceling fulfillment of *tṛṣṇā* is found even in the stages of formal absorption in which happiness and bliss successively fall away. Both, of course, are varieties of feeling or sensation *(vedanā)*. And their presence at the lower, though not the higher, stages of absorption is by no means a condemnation, but a clear indication that, by traversing them, going "through" them, thus, fulfilling them, they can be surpassed. Sensation is a door, an entryway through which one passes.[53] It is not the lid of Pandora's chest of unearthly evils, furies to be tightly sealed away at all costs. Nor, of course, is the resolute and unmoving occupation of the threshhold the answer to human suffering. As always, in Buddhist practice, the only way "out" is "through."

Thus, happiness, for example, is by no means to be despised. Nor is the "desire" for happiness. The five-tiered "archaeology" of happiness recognized by early Buddhism is articulated thus in the *Visuddhimagga*:

> [1] . . . *minor happiness* is only able to raise the hairs on the body. [2] *Momentary happiness* is like flashes of lightning at different moments. [3] *Showering happiness* breaks over the body again and again like waves on the sea shore.[54]

[4] *Uplifting happiness*, as Solé-Leris explains, "is manifested not only as mental uplift, but also as producing a physical sensation of extreme lightness, as if one were floating on air" (TI, 60). "But when [5] *pervading (rapturous) happiness* arises, the whole body is completely pervaded, like a filled bladder, like a rock

cavern invaded by a huge inundation."[55] We know, of course, the difference between happiness and bliss: "If a man exhausted in a desert saw or heard about a pond on the edge of a wood, he would have happiness; if he went into the wood's shade and used the water, he would have bliss."[56] What divides happiness from bliss is the getting, in contrast to the experiencing, of the desirable object. In bliss, there is, in a recognizably Hegelian acceptation, a spiritualization of the object. The moments of the mind's fluid life, which bliss pervades, and in which bliss functions as an ingredient, "flow into one another." And in the fourth absorption, the disenfranchisement of immanence becomes a lesson thoroughly learned. Bliss, which previously seemed not a property seized by the hand but an integral moment of our very being, a radiant coloration pervading the real *(reell)* flux of experience, now offers up its secret. There is no "appearing," only "seeming." Or if there is, in any legitimate sense, an "appearance," it neither occludes, discloses, nor simply fuses with a purportedly positive, permanent and underlying being.[57] Bliss belongs to a resuscitated "immanence" for which to appear and *not to be* are indifferent.

Though we may quibble with Sartre over the details of his early theory of constitution, *The Transcendence of the Ego* does open the way to more luminous discernment. Borrowing, then, a few pages from Sartre, if bliss is a spontaneous "Er/lebnis," a "living-through," happiness may well reside upon the plane of the "psychic" whereupon dwell the "states," the "actions," and the "qualities," indeed, their inclusive gestalt, the ego, of the Sartrean egology. The *psychic* is "the transcendent object of reflective consciousness" (TE, 71), the "outside" of consciousness (TE, 84), the patinate boundary separating being from the inner vacuity of nothingness.[58] It is the "shimmering" of a nothingness[59] otherwise invisible and imponderable.[60] Inasmuch as happiness is our "representative," the "possession" of which cannot be "smelted" in the crucible of interiority but itself enfolds our sublimiated identity, it resembles, in remarkable respects, the Sartrean "state," a "noematic unity of spontaneities" (TE, 71).

The state is helpless to found itself, owing its very existence to the stratum of transient *Erlebnisse*. And by replacing Sartre's typically morose example, that of "hatred," with our present "happiness," the following passage is rendered lucidly serviceable:

> My [happiness] escapes from each [bliss-experience] by affirming its permanence. . . . It effects by itself, moreover, a distinction between *to be* and *to appear*, since it gives itself as continuing *to be* even when I am absorbed in other occupations and no consciousness reveals it. . . . [happiness] is not *of* consciousness. It overflows the instantaneousness of consciousness. . . . Each *Erlebnis* reveals it as a whole, but at the same time the *Erlebnis* is a profile, a projection (an *Abschattung*). [Happiness] is credit for an infinity of [bliss-experiences]. (TE, 62–63)

However, while the state displays a certain indifference, a certain insensitivity, to its founding *Erlebnisse*, its disdain is rewarded by insecurity. Like the Sartrean ego, the state is a "virtual locus of unity" constituted "in *a direction contrary to* that actually taken by the production" (TE, 81). It appears to offer sanctuary from the thousand shocks of transitory existence, a solid possessability which smiles serenely upon its captor. Like the moon, happiness appears to enjoy a certain "self-luminosity." Yet like the moon, also, happiness shines by borrowed light. It is an irony of some portent that the moon, unreachable in its haughty elevation, charms only by appropriation. The lesson of the moon is a lesson of indirection—or rather, redirection, counterdirection. Despite its evident allurement, the moon has no luminescence of its own to offer.

Sartre would claim that the merely apparent spontaneity of the "state" of happiness, "*represented* and *hypostatized* in an object, becomes a degraded and bastard spontaneity, which magically preserves its creative power even while becoming passive" (TE, 81). As we ascend, the "shimmering" ceases to delude us. For we are increasingly able to see beneath the seeming. Yet, we must not view the pursuit of tranquility as a decisive abandonment of the "lunar" for the "solar." Meditative concentration is not the centering of our attention upon some "inner sun." We find in meditation yet another loss, the loss of our supposed ability to discriminate "sun" from "moon," original from reflection,[61] and the loss of our willingness to impale our innocent experience upon these merely conceptual categories.[62]

Yet happiness, despite its undeniable worth as a mediate and provisional end of human action, is not the final destination of the Buddhist path.[63] Buddhism cannot be subsumed under the head of crass "utilitarianism." It differs both in its "end" and in its disavowal of the latter's calculative means. The end of the Buddhist life, *nirvāṇa*, enjoys greater affinity with the Aristotelian *eudaimonia* (well-being), than with the Benthamite "pleasure," or with Mill's revision of it.[64] Perhaps we should rather say that, deepened and expanded to its utmost, indeed, beyond self-enclosing limit, happiness is transformed into ek/static *joy*: one, but then only one, of the seven factors of enlightenment.

Being beyond oneself—indeed, perpetually beyond *self*,[65] in joy—is (to carry forward the images of the *Visuddhimagga*) to experience the rupture of the bladder, the shattering of the cavern walls, to be unable to "contain" oneself, to be unable to contain "self."[66] Joy is kenotic dis/integration,[67] the emptying of the self of itself.[68] If, in happiness, one possesses the key, in bliss, one experiences what is thereby unlocked. Yet bliss is still ego-bound.[69] The experience is *mine* because the key is. The bladder has not yet burst. Joy, however, coincident with detachment (Pali: *virāga*), is the explosion of any sense of *Jemeinigkeit*, the very openness of an experience which is neither "mine" nor "thine," nor even "ours."

Sense-desire, one of the "five hindrances," is not obstructive in virtue of its content. Sense-pleasures are not evils to be self-righteously shunned. Nor are they fire-eyed panthers crouching in the treacherous night, objects of terror from which we would wisely flee. The "danger" of sense-desire is not its fulfillment, but precisely the inverse, the stultification which inevitably attends the desire, the desperate cleaving to a limited phase of fulfillment which permits no further advance.[70] Pleasure and pain, happiness and misery, joy and suffering, all enter through a single door.[71] If, through fear of pain, we lock and bolt the door, we thereby seal ourselves away from the very possibility of fulfillment. If, as is more probably our custom, we prop the door ajar, allowing only that degree of pleasure consistent with our capacity to bear pain, we also bar the way to complete fulfillment. The thirst for sense-pleasures *(kāma-taṇhā)* is exactly this barring, this blocking and inhibiting. Paradoxically, "sense-desire" does *not* seek its own fulfillment. It is a desire, not for the fullness of joy, but for its own emptiness. It is a desire *for desire*, an endless and bootless psychic loop, a "self."[72]

The "suffering" *(duḥkha)* of the First Noble Truth is not, as we have seen, confined to bodily torment.[73] Nor is it extended merely to mental, even to existential, anguish. "[W]hatever is impermanent is *dukkha*." Thus, although there is

> the happiness of family life and the happiness of the life of a recluse, the happiness of sense pleasures and the happiness of renunciation, the happiness of attachment and the happiness of detachment, physical happiness and mental happiness (WBT, 18)

it remains the case that "all these are included in *dukkha*" (WBT, 18). The hunger of the human heart for pleasure, for happiness, and, ultimately, for joy, finds fulfillment only in that which is lasting. Yet no pleasure, no happiness, can offer us the endurance that we seek. The honey of bodily pleasure turns bitter almost at the taste. The happiness of possession is ruined by the fear of loss, accident and decay. The elation over a newfound friend is marred, perhaps subtly, but nonetheless decisively, by the possibility of the other's betrayal, parting, or the inevitable: death. Even the amusements of the mind, even the pleasures of philosophy, sense, in subtle anxiety, their own instability and impermanence.[74] The mind, as we say, can be "lost" in insanity, in disease, or simply in lethargy and disuse. In happiness, the object has merely been brought into the orbit of our possessiveness. We have it—not, or not necessarily, in any legal sense, but precisely inasmuch as we invest ourselves in it, identify ourselves with it. The object becomes a symbol, a delegate, for our very selves. And this is why "possession" leaves us vulnerable. We can be dispossessed. And our possessions, even our cognitive, even our spiritual, attainments are corruptible, if not by moth and rust, at least by the plundering of time.

In the spirit of Kant, a certain "critique" could be undertaken, suspended from the purported authenticity and meaningfulness of *tṛṣṇā;* in Baier's words, it would be "a kind of inverse of a transcendental argument, whereby what is shown is not 'how possible,' but 'how impossible.'"[75] What conditions must be in place in order to accommodate the tripartite functioning of human craving: as (1) "craving for sense-pleasures *(kāma-taṇhā)*"; (2) "craving for existence and becoming *(bhava-taṇhā)*"; and (3) "craving for nonexistence (self-annihilation, *vibhava-taṇhā*"? The answer arrives, in part, as a summary of the foregoing discussion: Since desire must be capable of desiring "itself," it must have a "self" to desire. And since it must be possible to arrest the fulfillment of desire prior to achievement of the ek/static joy coincident with the shattering of the ego's rock-ribbed self-enclosure, there must be not only possession of the means to enjoyment, but also the "self" which invests itself in the key and which enjoys the experience thereby unlocked. *Kāma-taṇhā* presupposes "self," both as identical presence vouchsafed to reflection (the "self" of "desire itself") and as ego-pole to which experience "itself" makes reference.[76] The "itself" of experience is, however, no more than a variant formula for immanence. And the principle of undecidability argues eloquently against the fusion of being and appearing. The rupture of immanence alone, a leading entailment of our present study, is sufficient to overturn the very possibility of *tṛṣṇā*. And the more profound subversion of egology, independently sufficient, bears consequence of such magnitude as to warrant a separate study.

It is of no small importance that Buddhist practice proceeds, as an inversion of Kantian deduction, by de-possibilizing the presuppositions of human suffering and its proximal condition, craving. It is not that craving is to be forcibly evicted. Still less is the citadel of craving to be stormed and the lord of the manor executed on the spot. Again, violence of *any* sort is radically inconsistent with Buddhist practice. Buddhism advances through insight, insight which renders human craving, not wrong, not evil, not even futile, but simply impracticable. If, that is, we come lucidly to realize the utter impossibility of having or enjoying that for which we thirst, then thirst itself, as desire *for desire*, has no master to serve, and withers for want of illusory nourishment. Unenlightened consciousness is not, *pace* Sartre, a "futile passion." The for-itself does not persist in its incoherent quest to become in-itself, knowing all the while, if only pre-positionally, that the quest is, indeed, futile. Consciousness is rather lead by insight. The bursting of the illusory promise of *tṛṣṇā* is exactly its cessation.

But let us continue with our critique, this time interrogating the presuppositions of our "thirst for existence and becoming" and our "thirst for non-existence and self-annihilation." What, exactly, do we *want?* To be sure, the craving for existence would not be satisfied by the promise of ten more minutes of life. Nor, were we assured of an additional ten years, would we be much comforted. Heidegger has assuredly struck a deep chord in his recognition that *Dasein* is pervaded with *Angst*, an objectless mood *(Bestimmung)* disclosing precisely Nothing, our own nothingness, our "ownmost possibility," the possible foreclosure of every other possibility in death.[77] And in our inauthenticity, we retreat into faceless anonymity, the bustling "crowd" too busy to know time, in order to comfort ourselves with immersion in inauthentic timelessness.[78] What we want, of course, is release from the dreadful anxiety of mortality. We crave an eternity which could only be ours in an afterworld projected, like an infinitely protracted shadow, by the light of our present terminal experience.

Yet few of us would pass the Nietzschean exam (if it is that) to receive our credentials as *Übermenschen*. We would be sufficiently horror-struck by the thought of an eternal recurrence of the events of our lives, even those not charged with *ressentiment*. But the prospect of eternal tedium, of being installed in a timeless *nunc stans*, gazing forever at a single unchanging landscape, would strike us as ironic cruelty, the perversion, rather than the satisfaction, of our appetite for eternity.[79] We want, that is, not only a life extended without limit, but a life forever varied, marked by genuine adventure, discovery, novelty. We desire not only existence but "becoming," not eternal *stasis* but dynamic and unending *ek/stasis*. More searchingly, however, we would remain discontent at the prospect of a life, interminably protracted and continually varied, but a life for which earlier phases of experience were simply supplanted by later phases without promise of personal continuity. We want to know that the "self" of present experience will be the "self" of future experience, and we want the ability to re/call, and thus, re/present, the earlier. We wish, that is, to lose nothing to the backwater of time, and to gain everything from its onrush,[80] to be the same now as before, the same now as later.[81] We want, to invert Hegel's surmounting of Spinoza, to be not simply subject, but substance. As a substantial soul *(ātman),* we want to underlie the variational flux of our own becoming.[82] Yet as the Buddhist doctrine of soullessness *(anātman)* has always maintained, the substantializing of individual personhood usurps the prerogative of experience, installing dry theoretical construction in the place of fluid life.

It is interesting to find, among the teachings of Śākyamuni, an unmistakable recognition of the death-instinct, an insight which slumbered in the West well over two millennia beyond the life of the historical Buddha until awakened by Freud. It is no mere inconsistency that we desire, simultaneously, both eternal becoming *(bhava-taṇhā)* and self-annihilation *(vibhava-taṇhā)*. We swell with the love of life when our projects come to fruition, and we sink into life-annihilating despair when our most valued plans come to naught. But should we find ourselves incessantly *in medias res*, pursuing the realization of an elusive *telos* perpetually at infinite remove, always farther from our starting point, but never closer to our goal, we could hardly be faulted for elation over "approximation" and deflation over the failure of "proximation."[83] And this, as we shall see, is precisely our situation. The allurement of *thanatos* is bound to a certain pernicious perfectionism that dashes the products of an unconsummated drive to consummate realization. One's life is not as one as one wishes. One has "failed" in the quest for the good life. One wishes to clear away the mess in order to start again. We are potters, as we inconsistently think, throwing our lives on the wheel. When faults appear in the clay, as they inevitably will, we find ourselves tempted to reduce the clay to formlessness in order to effect a more satisfying re/formation. But the incongruity of this temptation is exhibited in the scarcely noticed fact that potter and pot are one. To destroy the "pot" is to subvert the very possibility of reformation.[84]

But there are, it seems, pots other than the potter, pots which invoke the potter, to be sure, and pots in which the potter is invested, yet pots, nonetheless, which are of the potter's *having*, and not of the potter's *being*. And the remainder of our present remarks is devoted to the subversion of the very framework of "possession."

We can ask, as we did earlier, exactly *what* we desire when we crave the "existence" and "non-existence" of our possessions. And the answer is now familiar: we desire *substance (svabhāva)*. We would be little amused were our prized possessions (our books, for example) simply to vanish after a given period of employment. And the outrage we express over planned obsolescence is an oblique confirmation of our desire that our possessions continue both in existence and in serviceability without limit. Yet a diamond which will not sparkle in the light, a sports car which will not budge when the ignition is engaged, a scholarly edition of some favored philosophical text that will not open, though they remain perpetually in the same state, will not satisfy. Again, we want more than perpetuity. We want variability. And we would assuredly be disconcerted were a *different* possession to replace the old with each alteration of state. A desire for substance underwrites our craving for existence and becoming.

We suffer from not having. But we also suffer from having.[85] For having is blemished by the anxiety of loosing. And there is nothing possessed which cannot, through destruction, corruption, or obsolescence, be lost. Again, it is a certain "perfectionism," sometimes culminating in false renunciation, which would put an end to possession, either through violence to the object (destruction), or through violence to the subject (dispossession). Buddhism will countenance neither form of violence. And renunciation remains false which preserves the desire for incorruptible possession.

Discursive Thought

The first (formal) absorption *(rūpa jhāna)* of the path of tranquility is marked by a freedom from the "five hindrances." In the Buddha's own description: "in him who has attained the first absorption there is no [1] sense desire, no [2] ill-will, no [3] sloth and torpor, no [4] agitation and worry, and no [5] doubt."[86] I shall not comment here in any detail on the five hindrances *(kleśas)*. But the fifth, *doubt*, is intriguing, in light of our ensuing methodological musings. We shall examine the Great Doubt spoken of in the Zen tradition, and it is important to distinguish the "impediment" from the very path to enlightenment. Entrance into the first *dhyāna* presupposes, of course, certain doxastic engagements. And this provides one vital sense of Buddhist faith (*śraddhā*): the footsteps of practice are guided by a certain taken-for-grantedness. Our quotidian activities rest upon a mesh of prereflective *doxa* regarding, first, the possibility of our practices, then their worth, perhaps their utility, and then, again, their harmlessness to the practitioner. Yet the "transcendental" states of absorption are not purchased by any doxastic coin current within the economy of belief. There is, if you like, an innate assurance, an inner security and freedom from dualistic furtiveness, which rises to conscious prominence when the mind is purged of the defilement of doubt.

We shall, in the succeeding chapter, elucidate the important discrepancy between doubt as doxastic equipoise (the only conceivable freedom from the "gravity" which would draw us into a grim and determined doxic "seriousness") and what is very different, also, from the weightlessness and playfulness of balance:[87] the "doubt" typified by a certain quavering, a certain vacillation or oscillation between the poles of duality. The Great Doubt is sportiveness and poise. The doubt that hinders, an illustration of the fourth *kleśa*, agitation, is the engine of disquiet. Vacillation is inimical to equipoise.

Though now intimately conversant with the phenomenal equivalence of object and reflection, reality and mirror, we nonetheless find ourselves ill at ease in the absence of a distinction which could only be an insufferable machination of *manas* overstepping the limits of its proper functioning, not the deliverance of intuitive wisdom *(prajñā)*.[88] And the dis/eased attempt to settle the irreconcilable issue in favor of one party to duality or the other is exactly the doubt that thwarts absorption.

Discursive thought trades in assertoric holdings subject to, if not only always vanquished by, doubt. If it is true, as Sokolowski claims, that "Thinking is the power of distinctly recognizing otherness and sameness"[89] (or, to avert any untoward "separatist" impression that the "and" might convey, the power of distinctly recognizing sameness *in* otherness), and if, moreover, thought is expected to yield fundamental truth, then, of course, "reality," the realm of *res*, to which thought purports to respond, must embrace the unequivocally unitary and the unequivocally divergent.[90]

It is not, however, solely a failure of veracity which brings about thought's elimination upon ascent to the second absorption. Thought is left behind, in the traditional idiom, because of its grossness. Each ascent from one level of material absorption to the next is a step more refined, more subtle. And part, if only part, of what subtlety entails is a relative freedom from the disquieting vicissitudes of contingency. Thought, happiness and bliss are successively dropped because of the "excitement" they generate, an "excitement" teetering upon the undulating disquiet of contingency.[91] And, of course, meditative ascent is ascent in the direction of absolute tranquility.

Advance in the direction of subtlety is also a movement of unification and concomitant dis/articulation. Thus, as Sokolowski observes, while "The parts flow into one another in sensibility," it is nonetheless true that "Sensibility is not decisive, as thinking is."[92] Decisiveness, or articulation, is a matter of "keeping things straight." What, in sensibility, exists *partes inter partes*, in thought exists *partes extra partes*.

Thought, though traditionally conceived as the most inviolate of our resources, shows itself to be the most vulnerable.[93] For it takes as its subject matter both our "possessions": the states, acts, and dispositions that "stand for" us and the fluid hyletic experiencing in which we find ourselves awash. Again, Sokolowski:

> Thinking does not set up ways of experiencing; it presupposes them and is parasitic on them. . . . Thinking may register various arrangements within a way of experiencing and make the experience more varied, refined, critical, and perhaps more humane. But thinking cannot establish a new kind of experiencing, for it is essentially a founded activity.[94]

Thought, of course, need in no way be denigrated, even though, in Husserlian hands, it has forfeited the pride of an assumed autonomy.

The two forms of thought, "applied" and "sustained," are an auxiliary to the first absorption. "*Applied thought* is like the first striking of a bell; *sustained thought* is like the continued ringing of the bell. . . ."[95] Like the striking of a bell, applied thought is disruptive, originative. It is not, then, the continuation of discursive trains already in play, but, if discursive at all, is the very inauguration of such an associative linkage. Discursion propagates outward. With rare and salient exceptions noted, thought is almost inevitably self-reflective, taking itself, in one way or another, as theme. The apparently desultory thinking which flows in patterns of association may be the primordial exemplar of self-thematic discursion. The associative passage from a thought of the wild and open sea to a thought of the morning's tea has revolved upon a certain quality of fluidity implicit in the former. As Merleau-Ponty says, "[T]here is no association that comes into play unless there is overdetermination, that is, a relation of relations, a coincidence that cannot be fortuitous, that has an *omnial* sense" (VI, 240). Association and conceptual entrainment may begin with the immediate, but inevitably carry thought "away." Thus, thought surprised *in medias res* pays no compliment to immediacy. Even the disciplined thought of strict logical entailment is a process of impoverishment. A conclusion, if validly derived, can never be richer than its premises, and discounting trivialities, can never be as rich. The end is always more abstract, and thus more remote from the immediate, than the beginning. Applied thought, arising in the embrace of the immediate, is "about" (or shall we say, with heightened nuance, concerns) the immediate in a way which no intermediate link could.

As for sustained thought, is it not itself one of the central definitions of "meditation"? To meditate, in a sense quite at home in Buddhist practice, is to *think*:[96] to think deeply, deliberately and uninterruptedly upon a given subject.[97] The voluntative sustaining of thoughtful attention is "like the bee's buzzing above the lotus after it has dived towards it."[98] Phenomenology, of course, is "more" than experience. It is thought which buzzes about the flower of experience, fatally charmed, and unwilling to seek release from its allurements.[99] And in this respect, the thought which is phenomenology exhibits itself as profoundly meditative, and, if not entirely at home in the first absorption, at least leading directly to its threshold.

The incisively radical nature of the phenomenological enterprise is displayed in its refusal even to grant a certain pre-philosophical warrant to the innocent entailments of logic. Logic cannot be "used" until phenomeno/logically grounded—and then a good deal of serious phenomenological work has already been done. And the provision of a phenomenology of logic only seals the "uselessness" of the traditional *organon.* Akin to Buddhist practice, phenomenology is prelogical, not by any means antilogical, and certainly not illogical. And its insistent concern, not simply with the antelogical, but more searchingly, with the antepredicative, ensures that its thought cannot flee immediate experience in the direction of logical entrainment. Its thought is "applied" (folded toward) experience.[100] And experience is its *point d'appui.* Since it cannot be thought arrested in the thick, it must be irruptive, spontaneous and responsive thought, thought which "sponsors" (speaks for) experience, thought responsible to, thus (from the Latin *spondere*) "pledged" to experience.

Meditative ascent, once again, is loss. Nothing supervenes upon the practitioner. Nothing is superadded. Like the layers of an onion, the levels of grossness are peeled away, until, at last, nothing, not even "nothingness," remains.[101] Solé-Leris recommissions the far lovelier image of the moon:

> [J]ust as the moon is hardly visible during the day, even when riding high in the sky, because it is outshone by the sun's greater radiance, so too the equanimity which exists in the three lower absorptions is "outshone by the glare" of the gross factors. . . .
>
> . . . the third absorption is like the moment of sundown, when the soft radiance of the moon begins to be discernible. . . . With the fourth absorption, night has fallen; as the obscuring factors have disappeared, the moon of equanimity shines in its full purity, which is the purity of mindfulness. (TI, 66–67)

Only when the deadening din of our daily traffic comes to a halt do the gentle hush of breeze teasing the branches, the song of nightingale and cricket, find a listening ear. Quieter still, and we may hear our own inspiration, perhaps the palpitation of our own heart. Loss of the raucous carnival of quotidian affairs is immeasurable gain in the subtlety, nuance, clarity and refinement of audition.

The moon, as we say, "comes out" in the darkness of night, though it never departed the heavens. Equanimity, "there" from the beginning, awaits only to be realized. And under this head, Annette Baier perspicaciously remarks that

> It is realization, not knowledge, . . . in which the facts one has absorbed have lost their tie to the doubts and questions to which they provided, or might have provided, the answers, and have been assimilated into a background body of information, presupposed in the questions *and* answers one is now concerned with, taken for granted, acted on, in one's cognitive and practical moves.[102]

Realized equanimity does not plug an interrogative gap prepared for it by our prior questioning.[103] It does not fit our needs and concerns, our doubts and our queries, like a plug in a socket. After all, "[T]he interrogative is not a mode derived by inversion or by reversal of the indicative" (VI, 129).[104] When the moon shines forth, it never fails to bear our astonishment. Nothing could prepare us for its appearance. As Fink says of the phenomenological reduction, "[I]t does not at all present a possibility for our *human* existence."[105] Merleau-Ponty seconds and forwards Baier's contribution with his own observations regarding the philosophical question:

> The philosophical interrogation is . . . not the simple expectation of a signification that would come to fill it. . . . It is characteristic of the philosophical questioning that it return upon itself, that it ask itself also what to question is and what to respond is. (VI, 119-20)

Realization cannot "fill," and philosophical questioning cannot be "filled."[106] Philosophy is self-questioning, and that which is realized is "presupposed in the questions *and* answers."[107] If philosophy is an unanswerable self-questioning, realization is an unquestionable self-answering. Perhaps the only "answer" afforded by an unanswerable question is precisely the unquestionable. Perhaps philosophy desires to be surprised, taken upon, caught napping by its own truth.[108] Perhaps philosophy wishes to be delivered from the awesome burden of its own promise, to be shown unprepared for the reception of its response. And perhaps the realization of the intrinsic mirrorlikeness of the mind answers to philosophy's ardent longing to understand the nature of its own emptiness, its own questioning.

> The philosopher speaks, but this is a weakness in him, and an inexplicable weakness: he should keep silent, coincide in silence, and rejoin

> in Being a philosophy that is there ready-made. But yet everything comes to pass as though he wished to put into words a certain silence he harkens to within himself. (VI, 125)

Silence is the mirror of sound, not a limit case of the audible. Speaking of silence is like painting a mirror. Representational success destroys itself. Success is precisely failure. And here, once again, we find, in deep paradox, deep wisdom. Still, "philosophy is the reconversion of silence and speech into one another" (VI, 129). Philosophy is summoned by the necessity of this paradoxical task. Realization is the secret of its absurdity. The philosopher seeks the "other side" of the Möbius strip, only to be grievously disappointed. The realized, like a child, delights in the paradox. The philosopher "wrote in order to state his contact with Being; he did not state it, and could not state it, since it is silence. Then he recommences . . ." (VI, 125). The philosopher is to the enlightened practitioner as suffering is to joy. The philosopher is a gaunt and hungry figure, consumed with the passion to understand, a hollow figure, all question and no answer.[109] The realized, though rotund with enjoyment, all answer, no question, is no less empty. Yet this "emptiness" is very fulfillment. The philosopher, like Sisyphus, "recommences," and in this, does not differ in any vital respect from the realized. Yet, "One must imagine Sisyphus happy."[110]

The Formless Absorptions

The "formal" absorptions *(rūpa jhāna)* have seen the successive dropping away of the pervasive material (hyletic) determinations of mind. Indeed, the word *rūpa* (form), cast from etymological suggestions not entirely unfamiliar to the West, signifies "matter." A material object is a form or formation. And, accordingly, the formal absorptions could, with equal pertinence, be termed the material. This leads, naturally, if treacherously, to an association of the formal with the empirical. Do not the elements purged in the material absorptions find their home in empirical (descriptive) psychology? And should we not expect, upon mounting to the formless absorptions, to encounter the structures of transcendental phenomenology? Do we not find, dividing the formal from the formless absorptions, the same fissure the separates the empirical sciences from philosophy? And are not the lessons of the lower, the empirical, realms of consideration strictly irrelevant to the lofty pursuits of philosophy?

The supposal is ruined, however, by equanimity, the mirrorlikeness silently, invisibly, present in the first two formal absorptions, adumbrated in the crepuscular blush of the third, and shining forth serenely in the fourth. The formless absorptions begin upon the decisive surmounting of the "material." Yet if equanimity has not vanished in the fourth absorption, it must be preserved at the higher reaches of concentration.[111] And, as I shall suggest, it is present, if only paradoxically present by its absence, throughout. Thus, mirrorlikeness accompanies every step of meditative advance in the direction of *samatha*.

The mirror, of course, is not an empirical presence. It grants itself to us, not by empirical differentiation from other objects empirically vouchsafed, but precisely by an utter failure of differentiation, a perfect permissiveness and acceptance of the empirical. It lets the empirical be, and in this sense courts the epithet transcendental. But the mirror is not, as Kant would have it, the terminus of a deductive chain. It is precisely *phenomenal*, but phenomenal in a wholly original sense: that of presence through *complete and ineluctable absence*. To be sure, we live among absences. My pen is all too often present through absence when a phone call brings important information. We also live among ineluctable absences. Though I might apperceive the world as you perceive it, I shall never, and, in principle, can never, enjoy its living, compulsive, presence exactly as it is granted to your perception. I may anticipate or imagine the landscape as you see it. But unlike the view from another window, your present vision is entirely, ineluctably, out of reach. But the mirror's presence is not merely a prize that no "struggle" (Latin: *luctari*) could win, not even a prize that we would not know how to go about winning. It is a prize that we could in no sense even recognize. And *a fortiori* we could never recognize it even as a prize. It announces itself inevitably as a surprise. For, as Eliot tells us, "hope would be hope for the wrong thing."[112] Again:

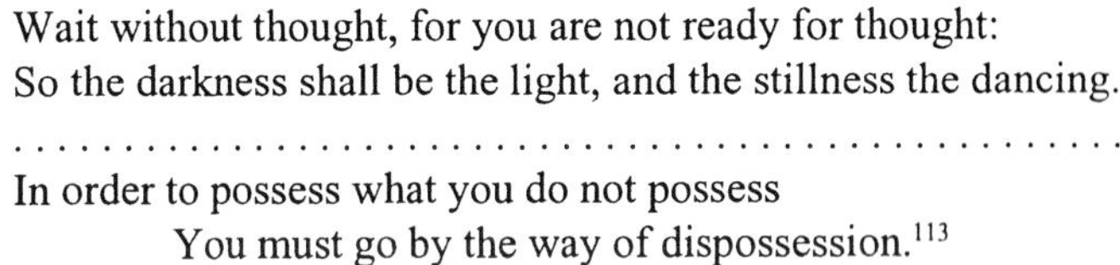

Wait without thought, for you are not ready for thought:
So the darkness shall be the light, and the stillness the dancing.

. . . .

In order to possess what you do not possess
You must go by the way of dispossession.[113]

Ascent, in our litany, is loss—and immeasurable gain.

The ascension from the formal to the formless absorptions is not, then, the transition from science to philosophy. For the "unquestionable" surprise of equanimity may be the unhoped-for answer of philosophy's self-questioning. Rather, the divide may mark an advertence to distinct functions of mirroring. If the mirror is a presence through "complete and ineluctable absence," it both reveals and conceals, and does so, not alternatively, and not in part, but simultaneously. In revealing the empirical without distortion, it thereby conceals itself. It is wholly self-concealing and wholly revelatory of the world. The formal absorptions begin with the world revealed, and by purgation, end with a lucid awareness of the very revealing. The formless absorptions begin with revealing, and end with concealing. And cessation *(nirodha),* one might speculate, is the witness of their identity.

The formless absorptions begin already at an advanced level of "abstraction." In the fifth absorption, every trace of "materiality" *(hylē)* has been purged from the practitioner's mind, leaving only the undisturbed awareness of boundless space.[114] Again, this is not to say that the "revelatory" function of mind has vanished, only that the "revealed" has.

Kant envisioned space in somewhat the same way. The object which confronts us can, by abstraction, be stripped of its empirical determinations, leaving only the space (or rather, the place) which it occupies. By thinking away the empirical, we arrive at the purely formal, the form of the given sensory intuition. And, by thinking away, not simply the empirical determinations of the particular object presently occupying us, but *all* empirical determination in general, we arrive at the form of (outer) intuition—in general. What might well give us pause, however, is the surreptitious transition from place to space of which Kant seems to have been culpable.[115] Aristotle knew that not all place is "placed," that the assumption of a place for every place launches a desperate regress. Yet in shifting from the place of this particular object to space as an *a priori* form of (outer) intuition in general, Kant may have abandoned the sober Prussian march of generalization for an uncharacteristic leap. To think away the empirical determinations of *X* and *Y* and *Z* leaves us their places, not their space. The universal deprivation of determination leaves space, not place. We cannot leap into "space" in an orderly way. At best, the abstraction of phenomenal determination from a given object glances into the abyss. Perhaps the fourth absorption is the plunge, and the fifth, the continuation and deepening of its momentum. The boundless and seamless space which now greets the practitioner is not an alternative to a mirroring outgrown and surpassed, but a deepening of its significance. For we have suspected, since the Platonic receptacle (the "mirror of the Forms") first found its function within Occidental philosophy, that space must be a curious mirror with an added dimension of depth.

In the sixth absorption, we witness for the first time a decisive gesture toward concealment. The mind turns from itself as it has thus far reflectively appeared—a sort of quasi object, a presence-in-absence, a space, a permissive openness for the empirical in the fullness of its depth[116]—and turns toward the very *consciousness* functioning in its self-consciousness.[117] "This," as Solé-Leris says, "is a process of becoming aware of awareness" (TI, 69) in which the meditating subject takes as his theme "the consciousness that occurred pervading that space [as its object]. . . ."[118] The mind is no longer occupied with itself as presence-in-absence, and begins to deepen its consciousness of itself as sheer absence-of-presence.

Yet, *pace* Sartre, an absence which defines itself as one term of a binary contrast (nothingness *against* being) is at best a relative vacuity. Sartrean nothingness cannot be an absolute, not even an insubstantial one.[119] The pluralization of "nothingnesses" infects each with its own *differentium*, no matter how subtle or pervasive. Even an absence defined against absence-by-presence is merely relative. And the practitioner is thus moved to ascend yet another step toward the "Absolute."[120]

In the seventh absorption, everything— boundless consciousness and space, its boundless quasi object—is forsaken. This is absorption in "nothingness," a "nothingness" characterized in terms poignantly reminiscent of, though sharply differentiable from, the Sartrean *négativité.*

> Suppose a man sees a community of bhikkhus gathered together in a meeting hall, or some such place and then goes elsewhere; then after the bhikkhus have risen at the conclusion of the business for which they had met and have departed, the man comes back, and as he stands in the doorway looking at that place again, he sees it only as void. . . . [121]

Those acquainted with Sartre's Pièrre will look for a different ending. Should the story not conclude with the man seeing the place, not as void, but as devoid of the monks? Should he not enjoy the "neg-intuition" of their very absence? But this would be the wrong moral. For it would only serve to reintroduce the relative nothingness which ascent to the seventh absorption proposed to surpass. We would be offered absence *instead of* presence. Rather, the place is seen "only as void"—not as deprived of a presence which is its *de jure* possession. As Merleau-Ponty says of the Sartrean categories, "each of them," being and nothingness, "is only the exclusion of the other," thus "there subsists only the split between them" (VI, 74). Nothingness, in a sense more radical than dreamed of in Sartre's philosophy, supervenes when the split is healed made whole. We find then, not being and its negative, but the very emptiness of which the Sartrean categories are but alternative "takes."[122]

But consider the moral of our story once more. It is related that, "looking at that place again," our friend "sees it only as void."[123] The language opens a gap between the place and its voidness.[124] Looking at the place for the first time—*prima facie*—not the boundless permissive opening for the empirical in its richness and depth, and not the pervasive consciousness of this mirrorlike space—we witness their very exclusion of one another. Looking at that place again, upon deeper consideration, with heightened concentration, the split vanishes, leaving nothingness in its place.

The remaining disjunction of nothingness and the witnessing of nothingness remains to be surmounted, and is surmounted in the eighth absorption, the level described as "neither perception nor non-perception." Here every remaining vestige of intentionality has been decisively eradicated. No longer is there self-transcendence in the direction of an object, even if that object is self-transcendence itself. The mind has settled into perfect coincidence with itself. It *is* its own object. Insofar as perception imports even the shadow of difference between *percipi* and *percipere*, we find here no perception. Yet insofar as non-perception suggests a lapse into utter mindlessness, unconsciousness—not the "no-mind" of the Ch'an tradition, but simply *no mind*, no "minding," at all—even non-perception is expelled.[125] The air of paradox borne by the slogan for this state—"neither perception nor non-perception"[126]—is a function of a certain logic implicit in our notion of perception, and implicit, more generally, in our logic of consciousness.[127]

The offending assumption is that consciousness invariantly, and of solid eidetic necessity, exhibits the vectorial character of intentionality. The "intentionality thesis" does not require for its fulfillment that consciousness transcend itself toward an object which lies *beyond* itself. Consciousness may, instead, take "itself" as object—though even here the objectified consciousness of reflection is already ossified. Like a foot suffering from gangrene, the lifeless "consciousness-object" has not undergone amputation. But life has receded.

More subtle still is the prethematic "of-ness," the "parenthetical" directedness, exhibited by the Sartrean "prereflective *cogito*." There is, as Sartre recognizes, a certain insightfulness about the rationalist thesis that to know is *to know* that one knows, the thesis, that is, that knowing is accompanied by a "bell." Something "chimes" when we *really* know. Of course, we have no need of an inner tintinnabulation to follow Sartre in this matter. Indeed, an unnuanced "gong" epistemology only sends us off in endless pursuit of the untamed logical goose: *to know* that we know, we must *know* that we know that we know, and thus forevermore. The regress is brought up short by instituting the vital nuance. The first *know* receives a different sense from the second. "To *know* that we *know*" is parsed as enjoying a nonpositional (nonintentional) awareness of our "positional" (intentional) knowing. We have, in Sartre's favored iconography, a "consciousness (of)" our *consciousness of* . . . Yet this "prereflective *cogito*" is the self-lucid nonpositional awareness of the very *being* of the nothingness that is consciousness.[128] Whatever consciousness *is*, it nonpositionally "knows" itself to be. And the Sartrean for-itself *is*, precisely, its *not-being* the in-itself. Thus, the prereflective *cogito* is the nonpositional awareness of *being* the *not-being* of the object.[129] And thus, finally, nonpositional self-lucidity is of no avail as a candidate for the state of "neither perception nor nonperception"—unless, over Sartre's vigorous protest, we abandon the original positionality of the for-itself. And then, of course, we would have no need for a reduplicated self-awareness. The eighth absorption is exactly what dissipates the "futility" of human passion.[130] This advanced state, the very possibility of which is precluded by the Sartrean theory of nihilation, is exactly in-itself-for-itself. If it stands as a genuine possibility for human attainment, being and nothingness cannot exclude one another. And the Sartrean vision of consciousness as a bubble in being, a nihilation which exists precisely in its *not-being* the in-itself, must be forsaken.

The very possibility of the eighth absorption is, in the most radical way, inimical to the "apophantic" model of mind which would make of the mind an open window, a perfectly transparent crystal ball, a flawless and undistorted mirror. And, in fact, the merger of being and nothingness at the supreme reaches of meditative concentration urges upon us exactly the opposite model, a model at once monistic and "cataphantic":[131] the mind as semitranslucent colored crystal. The tradition of meditative concentration, represented by Ālāra Kālāma and Uddaka Rāmaputta who taught the Buddha the techniques of yogic concentration, can take us no farther. Yet the Buddha was able to attain a final state of concentration beyond even the state of absolute self-coincidence and self-lucidity. Little can be said about this state. It cannot be reached simply by ascension through the various stages of absorption, since it "can be attained only by a meditator who has fully mastered not only all the stages of tranquility but also the practice of insight. . . ." (TI, 72). Cessation is thus approached "laterally," from the advanced practice of *vipassanā bhāvanā*. Sāriputta, one of the most devoted followers of the Buddha, describes the state thus:

> When a monk . . . has entered upon the cessation of perception and sensation, his bodily, verbal and mental formations also have ceased and are quite still, but his life is unexhausted, his heat has not subsided, and his faculties are quite whole.[132]

We must not be too quick to assume that cessation of the active functioning of consciousness, the stilling of the verbal and mental formations, spells the utter extinction of mentality. The eighth absorption seems to allow a certain flowing functionality, conditioned only by the demand that objectivation of every sort has been put to rest. But cessation ends even the non-objectivated, wholly self-coincident stirrings of mind. The clearest implication of cessation, assuming, once again, its possibility, is the dissociation of consciousness and conscious activity. Sartre would claim that consciousness *is* as consciousness *does*. Cessation presumes that the "doing" can cease without the "being."

But we must go deeper. If, as I have supposed, the mirrorlikeness, the equanimity, of mind has been with us throughout the ascent, and if, in the formless absorptions, we have found a deepening awareness of the self-concealing function of mirroring, culminating, at the eighth absorption, in the utter concealing of the mind even from itself, culminating, that is, in the utter disappearance of the "itself," what work remains for "cessation" to do? Tranquility meditation plumbs to the very bottom the mind's mirrorlikeness, the mind as mirror. *Vipassanā* meditation, at its apogee, offers its searching insight through the mirroring of mind. Ascent in the direction of tranquility is a movement[133] from the revealing to the concealing function of mirroring, from presence-in-absence to absence-of-presence. Ascent in the direction of insight begins, as does *samatha bhāvanā*, at the level of "access concentration" *(upacāra-samādhi)* at which "a steady and intense concentration of mental attention" (TI, 28) has been attained, but "there is no inhibition as yet in the reception of sensory and mental inputs" (TI, 28). Indeed,

> The abstractive nature of the states of absorption attained in tranquillity practice . . . is not suitable for the development of insight. In fact, what is needed for the purpose of insight . . . is precisely the opposite of abstraction. . . . (TI, 74)

Vipassanā is the cumulative deepening of our awareness of the mind as *presence*, though presence-in-absence. Sangharakshita examines "the simile which compares *vipassanā* to the lightning that, on a dark night, lights up for an instant with dazzling brilliance the whole surrounding countryside."[134] In words of surpassing poetic energy, he writes:

> Insight comes, not all at once, but in a series of "instantaneous," that is to say, time-transcending "flashes" that are as it were not continuous with, but utterly discrete from, the phenomenal order. These flashes, coming with ever-increasing frequence, gradually merge first into a series of more and more sustained emissions of radiance, and then into the unbroken and wholly transcendental illumination of Perfect Wisdom.[135]

The work of *vipassanā*, uniquely Buddhist, is transacted in the apophantic mode, and thus assumes, if only as a provisional "seeming," a certain dualism of mindfulness and the configurations of presence, clear crystal against a colored surface. Expectably, the supreme insights of Buddhist meditative practice cannot be dualist. And ultimately, the undecidability of cataphansis and apophansis, monism and dualism, must find realization. To realize undecidability is to be poised between two equally compelling seemings, to install oneself at the "still point of the turning world."[136] It is at the "still point" that we find cessation *(nirodha)*.

The Hierarchy of Concretion

In the *Logical Investigations*, Husserl expounds a mereology of considerable intrinsic interest. A distinction, not unlike that which Husserl makes between "pieces" and "moments," has become a philosophical commonplace. There are parts which *can*, and parts which *cannot*, exist separately from the "whole" which comprises them. Husserl's distinction will thus seem familiar. However, in Husserl's charge, the distinction is decisively modified in two significant ways. First, the Husserlian piece is not simply a part which can *exist* independently of its founding whole, but rather, a part which can be *presented* in isolation. And the same must be said, *mutatis mutandis*, for moments. Moments are not presentable by themselves. It is hardly surprising to find that the Husserlian distinction is *phenomenological*, not *ontological*. What is, perhaps, surprising, but also congruent with Buddhist insights, our second qualification, is Husserl's rejection of the notion of *whole* as a form of unity exceeding the array of founded moments *(abstracta)* and their founding determination (the *concretum*).[137] There is no whole beyond the *concretum* and its mediate or immediate *abstracta*. A given determination can serve as *concretum* for one determination and *abstractum* for another, thus "mediating" the founding of its *abstractum* in its *concretum*. But clearly, the relationship between a founding *concretum* and its immediately founded *abstractum* cannot, on pain of regress, be conceived as mediated. No third determination, no tertium quid, is interposed between a *concretum* and its proximal *abstractum*. No relation connects them.[138] Nor are these terms merely contiguous, flush upon one another with no intervening distance. For this would fail to account for their inseparability. A typical Husserlian example illustrates what the immediacy of their relatedness comes to. *Pitch* cannot be presented apart from *loudness*. In this illustration, we have, of course, a case of reciprocal founding. But isolating a single vector, *pitch* is an "abstract" moment of *loudness*. And their unmediated intimacy is exhibited in the "translucency" of *pitch* with respect to *loudness*. Pitch cannot be heard without some dynamic determination, muted or thunderous. Thus, *loudness* (of some degree) is heard throughout *pitch*. It pervades pitch. *Pitch* becomes, if you will, "saturated" with *loudness*. Immediacy is, then, the crystalline revelation of the concrete founding determination as an extensive and permeating qualitative determination. The piece, by contrast, is external. It is at best given through, not throughout, its associated whole.

The Buddhist tradition speaks emphatically to the Husserlian mereological vision, challenging both its operative concepts and its evident application. The Husserlian distinction first courts the familiar predicament of "eikonic" undecidability: the crystalline audition of *loudness* through *pitch* could be differentiated from the muddied suffusion of *loudness* throughout *pitch*. But suffusion is fusion. And this has the effect, unwanted by Husserl, of delegitimating the notion of mediation. Suppose *A* is founded in *B*, which, in turn, is founded in *C*. It will be exactly as if the (suf)fusion, *B*/*C*, were revealed through the crystalline *abstractum*, *A*, and also exactly as if *A* were suffused throughout *B*/*C*. Since we cannot distinguish the "through" and the "throughout," we will never be in a position to recognize a genuine case of mediation.

Moreover, the "suffusion" of *A* "throughout" *B* illustrates, not their reciprocal founding in which the two determinations are held apart, each serving as *abstractum* and as *concretum* of the other, but the very obliteration of the purported difference between founded and founding. Thus, while undecidability leaves intact the undeniable "seeming" of the Husserlian distinction, it introduces the equally undeniable "seeming" of its undoing.

While the Husserlian mereology has its uses as a framework for the microanalysis of sensory determination, its most exalted commission lies in the ontological path to the reduction. In the "natural" naïveté of consciousness, the world is given as the ultimate founding *concretum*. Nothing is presentable apart from the world. Tables, chairs, our very psyches, are "moments" of the world. It is little wonder that everything is shaken when the very existence of the world is brought into question. And what the questioning discloses is exactly the dependence of "world" upon that consciousness for which "world" has become a question: "transcendental subjectivity."[139]

Serious reservations must, however, attend any attempt to effect conformity of the ladder of absorptions with the transcendental chain culminating in genuinely ultimate concretion. Setting aside the formal, the formless absorptions suggest a certain hierarchy of dependence:[140] boundless space would seem to depend upon the boundless consciousness of it; and since their opposition presupposes an original field of the distinction, both would seem to depend upon nothingness; and the field of nothingness, contrasting with the "somethingnesses" distinguished upon it, depends upon the utterly indistinct coincidence of the mind with "itself."[141] And finally, inasmuch as "motion," even the delicate stirrings of a mind perfectly at one with itself, entails stillness, it would seem to be the state of *nirodha* on which all else depends.[142]

The Husserlian reduction would welcome the founding of space in transcendental subjectivity. And indeed, more searchingly, what comes to light in the reduction is the very correlation of *noēsis* and *noēma*, the "act-life" of consciousness and the object precisely as given within the act. Transcendental subjectivity is thus disclosed as the field of the distinction between space and consciousness. Though Husserl might offer transcendental subjectivity as a counterpart for nothingness, the Husserlian analysis offers nothing deeper. Transcendental subjectivity is the absolute founding *concretum*. We find nothing "below" transcendental subjectivity answering to absolute self-coincidence or absolute stillness.

The reason for Husserl's silence here may lie in a curious inversion of the abstract and the concrete. Transcendental subjectivity, once again, is absolutely concrete. Yet the result of the abstractive activity of meditation through which one ascends to the field of subject/object correlation is precisely nothing (no *thing*) at all—not even nothingness. The Husserlian reduction essentializes experience. The objects and features of experience are taken as pure possibilities, and their relatedness is seen as exhibiting eidetic necessity. The "tranquility reduction," if we may call it that, displays a chain of relative necessities, each operating upon what lies below it, and each, in turn, proving dispensable to what lies above it. In Husserlian parlance, we have a chain of successively more remote mediations. Thus, in ascending, we are enabled to leave behind the "lower" phases of experience. The concretion of transcendental subjectivity enjoys, then, a dimension of presentational dependence wholly absent from the absolute stillness of tranquility. It is not simply that every determination requires, for its presentation, the absolute stratum of transcendental subjectivity, but conversely, as well, subjectivity calls for its determinations. There is simply no question of apprehending subjectivity in their absence. The tranquility reduction does, however, ensure this possibility. "Ground" opens itself to contemplation independently of the "grounded," and independently, moreover, of the distinctions marked out upon that ground. Thus, ground, like a mirror, remains in itself indifferent to the discriminations reflected upon it. Transcendental subjectivity retains the footprints of discrimination. In the ground of tranquility, not the slightest trace is left. Treading upon this miraculous "ground" is like walking upon water. Or, in the more common image, determination passes like a flock of wild geese flying through the cloudless sky.

> The wild geese do not intend to cast their reflection;
> The water has no mind to receive their image.[143]

In a more luminous vision of *saṁsāra*, it is, then, "exactly as if" parts were, one and all, assimilated to the category of moments. Similarly, in the lovely Plotinian vision

> [A]ll is transparent, nothing dark, nothing resistant; every being is lucid to every other, in breadth and depth; light runs through light. And each of them contains all within itself, and at the same time sees all in every other, so that everywhere there is all, and all is all and each is all, and infinite the glory.[144]

Again, it is "exactly as if" reality were informed by the *Ineinander* structuration of *partes inter partes* illustrated in the *Gaṇḍavyūha-sutra* of Hua-yen Buddhism:

> [W]hat we have here is an infinite mutual fusion or penetration of all things, each with its own individuality yet with something universal in it. . . . To illustrate this state of existence, the *Gaṇḍavyūha* makes everything transparent and luminous, for luminosity is the only possible earthly representation that conveys the idea of universal interpenetration . . . no shadows are visible anywhere. The clouds themselves are luminous bodies. . . . This universe of luminosity, this scene of interpenetration, is known as the Dharmadhātu, in contrast to the Lokadhātu, which is the world of particulars. . . . The Dharmadhātu is a real existence and not separated from the Lokadhātu, but it is not the same as the latter when we do not come up to the spiritual level where Bodhisattvas are living. (EZB III, 77–78)[145]

Yet it is also "exactly as if" the manifold residents of reality existed *partes extra partes*. Thus the Dharmadhātu, reality envisioned under the aspect of *partes inter partes*, is the same as the atomistic Lokadhātu when one rises to the spiritual vantage point of the Bodhisattvas.[146] The "two" realms can never *seem* the same. But what the Bodhisattva clearly entertains is not the identity of the seemings, but their indiscernibility. The logical tension framing the conflictual diptych is not resolved in enlightened intuition. Indeed, as we know, it is the tension, not resolution in favor of the Dharmadhātu, which enables us to witness the emptiness of experience, or, in our ensuing idiom, the rupture of immanence. Poetic and imagistic expressions of the Dharmadhātu are breathtaking in their loveliness, profoundly moving, inspiring, and transformative in their metanoetic restructuring of perception. Yet attachment to the Dharmadhātu as a final verity in belligerent conflict with the falsity of the Lokadhātu forfeits the deeper truth of *śūnyatā*.[147]

The human craving for sensory amusement *(kāma-taṇhā)* is, of course, the desire that pleasure be an enduring and inseparable "moment" of our experience. And we would have no "part" of pain. Or if pain insists, we would gladly find it to be a mere "piece": separable, inessential, enduring only by accident, not through integrity. We would willingly find our residence in a Dharmadhātu pervaded by the positively happifying qualities of experience. But if suffering must be our lot, we and our miseries should be consigned to an infernal Lokadhātu, there, at least, to disentangle ourselves from our woes. Likewise, it would be insufferably audacious for our possessions to disintegrate in our grasp. Their parts must be moments, "all . . . transparent, nothing dark, nothing resistant; every [part] . . . lucid to every other."[148] Yet, inasmuch as we are possessed by our possessions, inasmuch as our hearts are laden with the anxieties of loss because of them, inasmuch as we suffer through the very having without which we suffer as well, we would fain see our pots shattered into a thousand shards, remanded to a world of particulars.

Still, with the Bodhisattvas, we must be mindful of the naïveté of giving ourselves over to the alethic allurements of the two seemings.[149] We cannot take hold of our possessions without their sifting through our fingers like sand. For no palpable truth is granted to the seeming of the Dharmadhātu. Nor can we rid ourselves of the furies which attend possession. For truth is no more at home in the seeming of the Lokadhātu. Neither the desire for pleasure nor the aversion to pain, neither the craving for existence nor the thirst for nonexistence, can find consummation in this bipartite negation. The object of craving belongs to seeming, not to unadorned experience entertained exactly "as it is," or rather, "as it has *become*" *(yathā bhūtaṃ)*. And with the lucid realization that craving can never find satisfaction in experience, the proximal "condition" of *duḥkha* (impermanence) atrophies for want of functionability.

Infinite Divisibility

Zeno of Elea, popularly known for his four paradoxes of motion, is seldom remembered for an antinomy which, though formally flawed, touches the heart of the Buddhist vision. The groundwork is laid in Simplicius's report:

> If there are many things, it is necessary that they are just as many as they are, and neither more nor less than that. But if they are as many as they are, they will be limited.
>
> If there are many things, the things that are are unlimited; for there are always others between the things that are, and again others between those. And thus the things that are are unlimited.[150]

The first arm of the antinomy trades, in part, upon what appears to be an elementary logical mistake, a mistake which, in deference to antiquity, could not have been readily apparent to the ancients. We have long known, and known clearly since Cantor, that being "as many as they are" does not entail being "limited." The indenumerability of a set is perfectly consistent with its containing exactly as many elements as it contains. The second arm assumes, without warrant, a "dense series" of points spanning any two "things," and compounds the proof's instability with the additional assumption that points are "things" to be counted among the rest.

It is not my intent to vindicate the antinomy of its patent errors and weaknesses. Yet perhaps, in offering the present version, Zeno's keen mind was groping obscurely for another, more fortuitously formulated and free from certain technical flaws of the first. Presupposed in Zeno's claim that the many things are exactly "as many as they are," is the supposition that each such "thing" is a singularity, a numerical unity, that, when counted, totals exactly *one*. And perhaps Zeno would willingly substitute for his claim that "there are always others between the things that are, and again others between those" the somewhat more cogent thesis of infinite divisibility.[151] Infinite divisibility has the potentiated advantage of *not* identifying points and things. The reworked antinomy, more secure than the original version, has, then, the paradoxical consequence that *one* thing is, at the same time, *many*, an oddity to which Eddington's more contemporary musings on the "two tables" has sensitized us.

That Zeno did have something of the sort in mind is attested by Simplicius's additional testimony. In Simplicius's account, Zeno is found demonstrating that the infinitesimal is devoid of genuine existence:

> [W]hat has neither magnitude nor solidity nor bulk would not even exist. "For," he says, "if it were added to something else that is, it would make it no larger; for if it were of no magnitude, but were added, it [sc., what it was added to] could not increase in magnitude. And thus what was added would in fact be nothing. If when it is taken away the other thing is no smaller, and again when it is added will not increase, it is clear that what was added was nothing nor again what was taken away."[152]

Thus, were an object actually decomposed into an infinite plurality of dimensionless points, it would, quite literally, "come to nothing." Contiguity is coincidence. Points *A* and *B*, cannot touch without overlapping remainderlessly. Yet, we also have Simplicius's summation of the Zenonian counterargument:

> [E]ach of the many infinite things has magnitude, since there is always something in front of what is taken, because of infinite division; and this he proves having first proved that it has no magnitude since each of the many is the same as itself and one.[153]

In a dense series, there is, lying between any two points, *A* and *B*, a third point, *C*. Yet the distance between *A* and *B*, and, indeed, between *A* and *C*, is always finite. Thus, the original subject of infinitary decomposition is always endowed with "magnitude." And we are confronted with the paradoxical result that, prior to infinite division, the object has magnitude, and subsequent to infinite division, it has none.[154] Yet "infinite division" is a purely analytical artifice. It "adds" nothing. Nor does it alter anything. The one *is* the many.[155]

Let us conjoin, finally, the Zenonian tour de force:

> But if it is, it is necessary for each to have some magnitude and thickness, and for the one part of it to be away from the other. And the same argument holds about the part out in front; for that too will have magnitude and a part of it will be out in front. Indeed it is the same thing to say this once and to go on saying it always; for no such part of it will be last, nor will there not be one part related to another.—Thus if there are many things, it is necessary that they are both small and large; so small as not to have magnitude, so large as to be unlimited.[156]

If, between any "two" (thus, noncontiguous) points, *A* and *B*, there lies a finite distance, then, granting the dense series, we are given the sum of an infinite series of finite magnitudes, a sum, as Zeno thinks, equivalent to infinity. Thus, the finite magnitudes with which we began have surprisingly swollen to boundless proportions.

Any student of the infinitary calculus will be able to prick the balloon. An infinite series of systematically decreasing "rational" numbers may only asymptotically approximate a finite bound. Moreover, as Aristotle perceived, "infinite divisibility" does not entail "infinite dividedness." Thus, the process of "infinite division" *does* alter what it operates upon. An infinitely "divisible," but "undivided" object is entirely distinct from an object "infinitely divided." The *one* has magnitude; the "other" does not. The *one* exists; the "other" does not.

Indeed, there is something awry in very notion of "completing" a genuinely "infinite" process. Thompson writes of the "super-task" of pressing the on/off button of a reading lamp an infinite number of times in a finite interval of time:

> After I have completed the whole infinite sequence of jabs ... is the lamp on or off? It seems impossible to answer this question. It cannot be on, because I did not ever turn it on without at once turning it off. It cannot be off, because I did in the first place turn it on, and thereafter I never turned it off without at once turning it on. But the lamp must be either on or off. This is a contradiction.[157]

Granting, of course, that infinite division is not a process of binary alteration, still "magnitude" remains until the *final* division is made, and disappears beyond the terminus. And the notion of the "final" phase of an infinite process is straightforwardly incoherent.

There have been, within the Buddhist tradition, conspicuously comparable attempts to resolve the ostensibly self-subsistent being into "a complex of infinitely extensive relations between infinitesimally small parts,"[158] and thus, to lead the mind, through certain "spatio-analytic" considerations,[159] to a lively realization of *śūnyatā*. But consider now the analogous, though entirely distinctive, approach tendered by Vasubandhu, the revered ācārya of the *yogācāra* lineage. To the realist question of a realm of elements existing separately from the mind, Vasubandhu responds:

> That realm is neither one thing,
> Nor is it many atoms;
> Again, it is not an agglomeration,
> Because the atom is not proved.
>
> (TCB, 175)

In Vasubandhu's self-elucidation:

> [T]he external object cannot logically be one, because we cannot grasp the substance of the whole apart from the parts. Also it logically is not many, because we cannot apprehend the atoms separately. Again logically, they do not in agglomeration or combination make objects, because the theory of single real atoms is not proved. (TCB, 176)

Unlike Zeno's antinomy, the argument does not purport to demonstrate that the realm of external magnitude is *both* one *and* many, but that it is *neither*. And unlike its Zenonian counterpart, also, the argument relies, not upon the cerebral contrivances of a resplendent mathematical mind (though a mind which was not, of course, in a position to benefit from the later refinements which it inspired), but upon a certain dimension of phenomenological consideration: "the atom is not proved."[160] More is meant by this admission than the simple confession, now falsified by photon microscopy, that no one has ever "seen" an atom. No student of elementary particle theory can escape the irony that our atoms are not "atoms." The atom *(atoma)* is literally the "indivisible." And our atoms have long ago forsaken the solid status of bedrock. Physics has not seen, and cannot see, to the bottom. The waters become murkier as the probe goes deeper. And it is probably in much the same sense that Vasubandhu's relinquishment of proof was meant. Though we have not, and, on pain of logical *aporia*, *could* not extend the process of division without limit, nonetheless, *for all we know*, reality (the realm of *res*) may enjoy *potential* divisibility *ad indefinitum*. The argument rests upon a question, not upon an answer,[161] upon our recognized ignorance, not upon positive knowledge, and because of this, enjoys a measure of cogency which its Zenonian counterpart does not merit. Since we can never be in a position to say whether, in the root sense, there are genuine atoms, we can also never be in a position to posit the genuine molecule. The molar follows its constituents. And if the constituents perpetually disintegrate into lower-level components beneath our gaze, we will never be assured of the legitimacy of the agglomeration.[162]

Vasubandhu's argument for dual negation of unity and multiplicity is followed by a supplemental demonstration purporting to show that "atoms" (were any extant) would neither have nor fail to have spatial division:

> If the atom has spatial divisions
> It logically should not make a unity;
> If it has none, there should be neither shadow nor occultation
> Aggregates being no different [would likewise be] without these two.
> (TCB, 177)[163]

The assumption underlying the first arm of the antinomy is explicit: "If one atom on each of its six sides joins with another atom, it must consist of six parts [i.e., "spatial divisions"], because the place of one does not permit of being the place of the others" (TCB, 176). As it stands, the premise seems wholly unconvincing. The fact that I can touch the wall in front of me at various points by no means carries the implication that an array of alternative spatial divisions (or spatially discontinuous volumes) has thereby been designated. A plurality of distinct "touchings" does not entail a plurality of distinct items "touched"—even if the multiplicity forms an integral whole.[164] Certainly, a point is not a part. Nor are the radii emanating from the vague heart of a voluminous solid. Thus, to say that sunlight strikes an "atom" at one point, but not at another, is not to say that one part, but not another, is thereby illuminated. Or again, to say that six contiguous atoms touch the atom they embrace at six distinct points, is not to say that six "parts" are thereby demarcated. Nor, finally, does the intentional sighting of an atom along one of its radii entail the apprehension of a part.[165]

Vasubandhu is not, however, committing, but rather considering, the misattribution. Vasubandhu's confession that "the atom is not proved" conceals the deeply phenomenological commitment to refrain from positing what experience has not granted. The language is very clear. He does not claim that the atom is "nothing but the class of all its parts," since he has already denied being in a position to posit the parts. The atom is the darling of analytic thought. And the enframing assumption of "analysis" in its entirety involves the assimilation of parts to pieces. In the Husserlian idiom, a piece is a part which can be presented in isolation from the whole. Thus, to have "parts" is to be capable of decomposition, without remainder, into a multiplicity of discrete elements, the ensemble existing *partes extra partes*. The atom is a desideratum of the molecule. Were parts to decompose into parts *ad infinitum*, there would be neither parts nor complexes of parts. And analytic thought can conceive of nothing which is neither simple nor complex. Thus, the atom is a requirement of existence itself. Vasubandhu's second antinomy is transacted entirely beneath the aegis of the *hypothesis* (not the *assertion*)[166] of the atom. Yet, the atom is an inextricable node in the lattice-work of analytic thought. One cannot assume the atom without thinking analytically. Though ostensibly the passage from points to pieces is designed to witness the outbreak of plurality under the presumption of unity, the path of the inference is strictly analytic—thus, reflexively, and perhaps ironically, demonstrating the absurdity not simply of its destination, but also of the inferential path itself.

The distinction between moment and piece is purely speculative, and not phenomenological. Qualitative pervasion (the moment) cannot be discriminated from transparency to quality (the piece).[167] Thus, disciplined adherence to experience will not license the segregation of moments from pieces. And no less than this is written into Vasubandhu's admission that "the theory of single real atoms is not proved." We need only append the rider that the atomic theory has not been disproved, either. It is exactly as if the objects of our experience decompose into an infinite series of multiplicities of pieces. And if analytic thought is to be entrusted with any sense of "existence," it is also exactly as if the process of decomposition came to rest at a bottommost level of elementary pieces: atoms.

Dependent Co-origination

Craving, if you will, makes the world go around. Suffering, in the expansive sense recognized by the Buddhist tradition, is our resistance to impermanence. And craving is its *proximal* cause.[168] The epithet cries, however, for clarification:

> [I]t should not be taken as the first cause, for there is no first cause possible as, according to Buddhism, everything is relative and inter-

dependent. Even this "thirst," *taṇhā*, which is considered as the cause or origin of *dukkha*, depends for its arising *(samudaya)* on something else, which is sensation *(vedanā)*, and sensation arises depending on contact *(phassa)*, and so on and so forth goes on the circle which is known as Conditioned Genesis *(Paṭicca-samuppāda)*. . . . (WBT, 29)

The "circuitry" of *saṁsāra*, described in the "narrow" rendering of *pratītya-samutpāda*,[169] returns the energetic transformation of human life upon itself in a circular series of twelve "relays," twelve necessary, perhaps transcendental, conditions, the last being the condition for the first:[170]

> Ignorance *(āvidyā)* conditions action;
> Action *(saṁskārākarma)* conditions consciousness;
> Consciousness *(vijñāna)* conditions name and form;
> Name and form *(nāma-rūpa)* conditions the sense bases;
> The sense bases *(āyatana)* condition contact;
> Contact *(sparśa)* conditions feeling;
> Feeling *(vedanā)* conditions attachment;
> Attachment *(tṛṣṇā)* conditions grasping;
> Grasping *(upādāna)* conditions becoming;
> Becoming *(bhāva)* conditions birth;
> Birth *(jāti)* conditions aging, death, and all the suffering
> *(dukkha)* therewith accompanied; and
> Aging and death *(jarā-manaṇa)* condition ignorance.

Each link *(nidāna)* of the chain, in its intricate connections with the others, is a facet of the resplendent jewel of Buddhist phenomenology. Our present study can be no more than programmatic and indicative. We cannot hope to reach here the specificity invoked by a thorough realization of this program, and must be content with a few words regarding *pratītya-samutpāda* in its "broad" sense.

As the circle of becoming *(bhāva-cakra)* itself suggests, causality has no model in rectilinear geometry, and cannot be conceived as a binary "relation" spanning cause and effect.[171] Indeed, causality, in the Buddhist acceptation, is not a unidimensional phenomenon at all, but rather the universal conditioning of each by all and all by each the comprehension of which, in a "dynamic-synthetical"[172] way, brings about the realization of emptiness. Devoid of "own-being" *(svabhāva)*, each being/event owes its very existence to a radiance of conditions, each disjunctively necessary, all conjointly sufficient, for its immediate presence. And since this ontological debt is at once owing and repaid, its very existence resides with its manifold creditors. It *is* nothing over and beyond its conditions. *In itself* it is empty *(śūnya)*. And the same, in turn, must be said regarding the creditors. *Pratītya-samutpāda* is exemplified in the resplendent

Hua-yen vision of the "net" of Indra.[173] The resplendent "golden lion" of Fa-tsang (643–712 C.E.) makes the point with eloquence:

> In each of the lion's eyes, in its ears, limbs, and so forth, down to each and every single hair, there is a golden lion. All the lions embraced by each and every hair simultaneously and instantaneously enter into one single hair. Thus, in each and every hair there are an infinite number of lions. . . . The progression is infinite, like the jewels of Celestial Lord Indra's Net: a realm-embracing-realm ad infinitum is thus established, and is called the realm of Indra's Net.[174]

Causality, if a notion of conditioning this remote from the linear transmission typical of occidental thought can pretend to the same denomination, is not an exercise attributable to a singular isolatable agency. Were causality legitimately to be conceived as a relation at all, it would assuredly be "multigrade," a "polyadic" function taking every resident of the world as one of its arguments, a function which, by the astonishing richness of its input, would dispel any sense of individual causal agency.[175] Though less precise (and therefore, less abstract), a more picturesque illustration of dependent co-origination might serve. Cast a pebble into a pond, and the expectable concentric wave patterns propagate outward, affecting the pond in its entirety. Toss another pebble into the pond at a different location, and, again, the entire pond is affected. But this time, the very pattern of propagation is altered. Interference patterns are generated. Conjoint occurrence not only claims universal causal ramification, but modifies, in vital ways, the very modality of causal influence. There are no causal concatenations tediously linked by tireless iterations of a univocal relation. Dependent co-origination gives expression to the modification, not only of causal values, but also of causal affectivity, as well. *Pratītya-samutpāda* is the etio/logic of universal organism.

It is commonly supposed that, although the items entering into a causal relationship (be they objects, processes, events or conditions) are phenomenal and accessible to perceptual consciousness, the causal relationship itself is not. The terms of the relationship, it is thought, are experientially positive, while the relationship itself is experientially privative. Certainly, Hume would have favored such a view. For Hume, to say that *A* causes *B* is simply to say that *A*-like events are consistently followed by *B*-like events, and that we are endowed with a certain psychological disposition to expect *B*-like events to follow the *A*-like. We have immediate sensory "impressions" of *A* and *B*, and we have memory-images of *A*- and *B*-like events. But the purported causal nexus which connects *A* and *B*, if it obtains at all, is not a relational entity lying within our perceptual ken.

Kant's position is no friendlier to phenomenological articulation. For Kant, causality resists reduction to a regular succession of events. What Hume neglected, thought Kant, was the sense of *necessity* which one inevitably encounters in the notion of causality. To say that *A* causes *B*, whatever additional conceptual freight this phrase might carry, is to say *at least* that *A* necessitates *B*, *A* "makes" *B* happen. Kant attempted to accommodate this sense of necessity by making causality a category, one of the permanent templates of the mind which serve to organize our phenomenal experience. Thus, Kant assumes from the outset that causality itself is nonphenomenal. The objects of our experience are necessarily seen *as causative*. But causation itself cannot be seen.

The Buddhist conception of causality is unremittingly phenomenological, finding its origin, not in metaphysical speculation, but in the insightful penetration of a certain samsaric seeming. The secret of its givenness resides in the horizonal structuration of experience. And though we are left to interrogate the "how" of causality's manifestation, we must, as we shall see, be consistently wary of attributing any ontological weight to our results.[176]

Whatever else might be involved in the ordinary notion of causality, to say that *A* causes *B* is *at least* to say that were *A* to occur, then *B* would occur. The occurrence of *A* is a *sufficient* condition for the occurrence of *B*; and the occurrence of *B* is, conversely, a *necessary* condition for the occurrence of *A*: *A* could not have occurred without the subsequent occurrence of *B*. And should we succeed, then, in discovering a necessary ground, *B*, for a given figural object, *A*, we will have taken a vital preliminary step toward demonstrating that figure and ground are related in a distinctively causal way.

Every theme-in-context, every object-in-horizon, every figure-against-ground corresponds to a provisional hypothesis that the present ground *(B)* is necessary, and thus, that, in at least the most rudimentary sense, the present object *(A)* is its cause: the cause, that is, of the manifold perceptual elements comprised within the ground. This hypothesis is minimally confirmed, in a primordial way, simply by the perception of figure-against-ground. And causality, in this original and limiting sense, thus appears through the confirmation of such figure-ground hypotheses. Subsequent holistic presentations confirm the hypothesis, if the figure is cast upon a relevantly similar ground.

Gurwitsch conjoins a significant dimension of articulation to the relatively unnuanced Husserlian adaptation of gestalt structuration to the "field of consciousness." The field, for Gurwitsch, comprises not a duality of domains ("text" and "context"), but a triplicity:

> The first domain is the *theme*, that which engrosses the mind of the experiencing subject, . . . which stands in the "focus of his attention." Second is the *thematic field*, defined as the totality of those data, co-present with the theme, which are experienced as materially relevant or pertinent to the theme and form the background or horizon out of which the theme emerges as the center. The third includes data which, though co-present with, have no relevancy to, the theme and comprise in their totality what we propose to call the *margin*.[177]

The cornerstone of Gurwitsch's distinction between thematicity (or contextuality) and marginality is, of course, the notion of relevance: the pertinent data of context "appear . . . as *being of a certain concern* to the theme. They *have something to do* with it; they are relevant to it."[178] But more tellingly, in apperception, as Gurwitsch underscores,

> *what is anticipated are perceptions through which will be given in the mode of direct and genuine perceptual presentation, aspects, properties, attributes, etc., co-determinant for the perceptual meaning of the present perception. . . .* [179]

In "co-determination" we hear the unmistakable echo of *pratītya-samutpāda*.[180] The elements of the thematic field collectively determine the sense *(Sinn)* of the theme. And again, we find a certain logic of organism: the modification of a single apperceptual factor would ring holistic changes in the field.[181]

The hypothesis of etiological relevance thus hinges on the domain of the co-determinant. If the causal factor falls within the thematic field, it serves as a necessary condition for the theme *as thus presented*, and is subject to its causal suasion, exemplified primordially in apperception. Falling to the margin, it has no part whatsoever in thematic causality.

But delve deeper. The Gurwitschean margin is an externally associated piece of the field, not a moment. And we have come to see that the ambiguity of piece and moment is a phenomenon of undecidability. The piece, like a red surface external to and disclosed through transparent glass, contrasts, but only conceptually, with the moment which, like the red coloration of red glass, imbues and pervades its *concretum*. Phenomenally, the alleged duality offers not a hair's breadth for insertion of the conceptual wedge. And for this reason, our causal hypothesis can never pretend to experiential confirmation. The result is fateful. In Nāgārjuna's summation:

> Therefore, that product does not consist in those causes; [yet] it is agreed that a product does not consist of non-causes.
> How [can there be] a conditioning cause or non-cause when a product is not produced? (MK, 1:14; E, 184)

And no "effect" does arise because:

> Since existing things which have no self-existence are not real,
> It is not possible that: "This thing 'becomes' upon the existence of that other one." (MK, 1:10; E, 184)

Thus, in words unmistakably reminiscent of Hui-neng's assertion that "Not one thing exists," Nāgārjuna avers: "There absolutely are no things" (TCB, 170).[182]

The Lotus and the Chiasm

The ruminations of the present chapter rest upon certain lessons of Buddhist meditative practice. While I would not offer here a manual of Buddhist meditation, I am concerned to elucidate certain issues pertinent to the methodology of Buddhist applied phenomenology. And Buddhist phenomenology is deeply and inextricably rooted in meditation. Having just foresworn the pragmatics of meditative practice, I must plead indulgence for a few remarks on the posture of meditative practice: the lotus position.

Insight meditation *(vipassanā bhāvanā)*, the meditative amplification of mindfulness, can be practiced in any bodily posture—walking, standing, lying, and, of course, "sitting." But the practitioner of tranquility meditation *(samatha bhāvanā)* is explicitly counseled to sit in the erect, cross-legged position which is the indelible image of the Buddha. The lotus position affords a certain stability, permitting at once both relaxation and equilibrium for extended periods of time, and facilitating the engagement of certain autonomic functions of postural balance which, while never entirely voluntary, are now vouchsafed entirely to our somatic "automatic pilot,"[183] thus permitting undisturbed dedication to meditative concentration.[184] Empirical claims such as this may hold a certain interest for the psychologist and physiologist. But we have not yet begun to address the intrinsic phenomenological significance of the lotus.[185]

Of course, were the legs extended, we would feel a readiness, if not a present willingness, to walk. And were the arms extended, we would feel a similar readiness to grasp.[186] And it may be that at the deeper reaches of tranquility meditation even the most subtle inclination, even the "readiness" to act, and perhaps, even the conscious possibility, is itself a distraction. The "Buddhist *epochē*," as we shall later see, wrests the rug from under the very possibility of motility.[187]

For the present, however, another petal of the lotus unfolds before us: a phenomenon sometimes referred to as "double sensation." In the formalized crossing of the legs, in the folding of the hands, one upon another,[188] thumbs touching, in tucking the folded hands against the abdomen, in setting the tongue against the roof of the mouth, the body touches itself in the most integral and undivided way which human physiology will allow. In the simple touching of one hand with another, says Merleau-Ponty, my hand "takes its place among the things it touches, is in a sense one of them, opens finally upon a tangible being of which it is a part" (VI, 133). Thus, the lotus position both realizes and illustrates, through the inner unity of the body,[189] the dialectical undoing of the subject-object polarity.[190] Body *(Leib),* as the unthematizable medium of world-disclosure, is pre-egological subject.[191] Body *(Körper),* as thematized inhabitant of the world, is object. There is, then, no posture more eloquently bespeaking the nonduality of body-subject and body-object than the "lotus."[192]

Though there is, in Sartre, a strain which militates against the Cartesianism of which he is frequently, if somewhat naïvely, accused, there is also a distinct proclivity for that very dualism—a leaning nowhere more vividly displayed than in his treatment of the two hands:

> We are dealing with two essentially different orders of reality. To touch and to be touched, to feel that one is touching and to feel that one is touched—these are two species of phenomena which it is useless to try to reunite. . . . In fact they are radically distinct, and they exist on two incommunicable levels. (BN, 402–3)

Yet, if the two "orders of reality" are, quite genuinely, "incommunicable," then, as Dillon rightly charges, the experience of one hand touching the other "would be qualitatively equivalent to that of touching yours."[193] Sartre misguidedly affirms: "Either [the body] is a thing among things, or else it is that by which things are revealed to me. But it cannot be both at the same time" (BN, 304). Undeniably, however, the body *is* both.[194] The hand touched does feel the hand touching. The felt feels the feeling. And we cannot but credit Merleau-Ponty's phenomenologically more allegiant assertion that between "my body touched and my body touching, there is overlapping or encroachment" (VI, 123). Earlier, in the *Phenomenology of Perception*, a work which gropes toward, but never accomplishes, the nondualism of *The Visible and the Invisible*, Merleau-Ponty had presented subject and object "as two abstract 'moments' of a unique structure which is *presence*" (PP, 430). In this earlier view, presence is infected with a certain ambiguity:

> [T]he two hands are never simultaneously in the relationship of touched and touching to each other. When I press my two hands together, it is not a matter of two sensations felt together as one perceives two objects placed side by side, but of an ambiguous set-up in which both hands can alternate the roles of "touching" and being "touched." (PP, 93)

Like the "multi-stable" figures of Gestalt experimentation (the duck-rabbit, for example), the underlying "structure which is *presence*" presents itself in distinctly alterior ways: in this case, *as touching* and *as touched*. The best we get here is oscillation. But a gap remains.[195] The roles are ineluctably alternative, and cannot be rendered simultaneous. And though a single neutral actor plays both roles, we are, from a phenomenological standpoint, little farther advanced toward the undermining of dualism than the Sartrean ontologization of "two essentially different orders of reality" which remain "radically distinct" and "exist on two incommunicable levels." If Merleau-Ponty is correct in his assertion that "The presence and absence of external objects are only variations within a field of primordial presence. . . ." (PhP, 92), the changes are rung in succession, not, on pain of collapsing thematic alternativity into cacophonous simultaneity, at a single sounding. Sartre assumes that phenomenal alterity reflects ontological diversity. Merleau-Ponty, at this stage, grounds alterity in unity. Neither thinks beyond *prima facie* ambiguity.

The later language of "overlapping or encroachment" does, it seems, represent a decisive triumph over dualism. No longer does presence play the elective, but exclusive, roles of subjective "transparency" and objective "opacity." Admittedly, in the later work, coincidence is elusive:

> My left hand is always on the verge of touching my right hand touching the things, but I never reach coincidence; the coincidence eclipses at the moment of realization and one of two things always occurs: either my right hand really passes over to the rank of touched, but then its hold on the world is interrupted; or it retains its hold on the world, but then I do not really touch *it*. . . . " (VI, 147–48).

Yet now the gap is "spanned by the total being of my body, and by that of the world" (VI, 148): the "flesh" *(la chair)*. In Merleau-Ponty's later notion of "flesh," the unity of body-subject and body-object is made phenomenal.[196] We are served "muddy water." For those, however, unable to acquire a philosophical taste for this peculiar blend, thoroughly homogenized though it might be, the victory is, regrettably, short-lived. Our thesis of undecidability assuredly renders the Merleau-Pontyan brew impotable.

In our tireless refrain, "transparency to quality" is phenomenally indistinguishable from "qualitative pervasion." Merleau-Ponty's mistake, the error of overlapping, is quite innocent, yet fatefully consequential. The "fleshly" tonic which promises to cure the ills of dualism is, of course, no bane. He has simply fallen, unbefittingly, into speculative "decision." His "muddy water" is a colored translucence. And, since the austere exactions of uncompromising adhesion to experience proscribe this very decision, he has lapsed, unwittingly, into speculative metaphysics.

No, muddy water is not the lesson of the lotus. What is brought to experiential givenness through the folding of the body upon itself is not some nebulous fusion of the transparent and the opaque, body-touching and body-touched.[197] Nor do we enjoy a crystalline disclosure of an objective, but indistinct, presence. Both temptations to "decision" must be abandoned.

There are two ways, both grounded in experience, to undercut Cartesianism. There is the way of monism, the path Merleau-Ponty trod, which offers an experienced fusion of subject and object. One makes a salad and tosses well. But there is also the way of nondualism (advaitism). The monist is left with the task of accounting for the occasional separation of the mixture. In reflection, we *seem*, at least, to find, not muddy water, but the limpid water of consciousness secluded from the obscurity of objectual mud, a duality of disclosive act *and* manifest object. If the elements of the mixture can, even in principle, be separated out, they were not sufficiently homogenized to begin with. Our mud and our water, though offering the appearance of a thorough fusion, must always have remained two and not one. Or if, in reflection, a new "two" supervenes, we are confronted with a new, higher order, dualism.[198]

The nondualism which we favor aligns itself undeviatingly with the phenomenon, and thus embraces, though in no exclusionary way, the patent truth of Merleau-Ponty's monism. From the vantage of strict conformity to experience, it is "exactly as if" subject and object were thoroughly fused. And it is a credit to Merleau-Ponty's phenomenological perspicuity to have borne witness to this fact. Yet, at the same time, it is also exactly as if there were a perfectly transparent medium of disclosure through which an indistinct reality (including Merleau-Ponty's semiopaque "flesh") were revealed.[199] In fact, the *Phenomenology*, with its disavowal of the "prejudice of determinate being" (PP, 45n),[200] seems to encourage this very different impression as well. *Being* (dare we say: "in-itself") is indeterminate, or only partially or incipiently determinate, and thus (in-itself) is determinately neither subject nor object. And, inasmuch as *being* and *appearing* contrast, we have the dualism: diaphaneity disclosing unclarity. It is, in fact, exactly as if both monism and dualism, though logically conflictual, were nonetheless equally true.

One vital step separates the Sartrean for-itself from the Buddhist *śūnyatā*. Despite Sartre's protestations to the contrary, the for-itself cannot consistently be the universal and unqualified nihilation of the in-itself that his more cogent intuitions would suggest. In the plurality of conscious subjects we do not find "a nothingness filled with being, a being emptied by nothingness" (VI, 75). For I am a "perspective" upon the world, as are you. And the untraversable distance which separates us, radically and hopelessly, from one another entails a certain "modalization" of our several nihilations. I am the universal negation of the in-itself, to be sure, but *in my own way*. And the "way" cannot fail to introduce, at the heart of nothingness, a ghostly and pervasive qualitative *differentium*, a spectral opacity, a taste of difference, which despoils the absolute transparency of the for-itself. Even neglecting this clandestine opacity, Merleau-Ponty is moved to declare of being and subjectivity that

> if they are absolute opposites they are not defined by anything that would be proper to them. As soon as the one is negated the other is there, each of them is only the exclusion of the other, and nothing prevents them, in the end, from exchanging their roles: there subsists only the split between them. (VI, 74)

And this is to say that the "split" is not licensed by the phenomenon. Hegel cheerfully asserts what, in its application to Sartre, becomes an allegation: Being (as the least common qualitative denominator of all possible beings) is qualitatively indistinct from Nothingness (the utter expulsion of qualitative content). Their reciprocal exclusion founds Becoming, in Hegel, and temporality, in Sartre. In the absence of phenomenal differentiation, exclusion can only be a function of the will *(tṛṣṇā)*. And emptiness *(śūnyatā)* is what remains when exclusion ceases.

Like the Sartrean for-itself, *śūnyatā* is "incoherent," and like the for-itself, also, *śūnyatā* is "incoherent" precisely in being the very instantiation of a contradiction. The Sartrean apophantic ontology of nothingness is inseparably the limit case of a transcendentalism of being. In the cataphantic muddy water served by Merleau-Ponty, we find a contrary immanentism. Suzuki writes:

> A world of relativities is set on and in *śūnyatā*; *śūnyatā* envelops . . . the whole world, and yet is in every object existing in the world. The doctrine of *śūnyatā* is neither an immanentism nor a transcendentalism; . . . it is both. If it is declared that immanentism and transcendentalism contradict each other, *śūnyatā* is this contradiction itself. A contradiction implies two terms which are set against each other. *Śūnyatā* is absolutely one; hence there is no contradiction in it.
>
> A contradiction is felt only when we are out of *śūnyatā*. As long as we live in it, there is no contradiction. . . . [201]

The domain of pure possibility is itself an incoherent notion inasmuch as possibility comprises incompossibility. But the domain of possibility is only a bloodless abstraction, a Meinongian "impossible object." Yet, to repeat, *śūnyatā* is "this contradiction itself." When the membrane which divides the instantial from the pre-instantial ruptures, *śūnyatā* is brought to light as the very fount of living possibility.

Letting "seems" stand in for the maladroit "exactly as if," Merleau-Ponty has done no violence to "seeming."[202] Nor has he violated the appearance *(ad parere)*, a word which suggests a coming forth into visibility, for there is no "being" crouching in the shadows behind or beyond the seeming. Nor, again, is Merleau-Ponty disloyal to the "pure experience" which can "seem" this way or that. For there is no other way of articulating pure experience but through its seeming. Rather, Merleau-Ponty has simply, and quite understandably, forgotten the other seeming. The omission is understandable because the commission ruins consistency. It is not Merleau-Ponty who is culpable of disloyalty, but rather, as Findlay comments, "The appearances . . . may be disloyal to themselves: they may, like reversible diagrams or puzzle pictures, reveal new emphases when one considers them intently."[203] Monism and dualism each *seem* to be true. They cannot both *be* true. But neither can one be true at the expense of the other. For to say that one seeming is veridical while the other, equally compelling, is not, is to posit behind the putatively illusory appearance a noumenal *Sachverhalt* with which it conflicts. And we have found good reason to reject the Kantian *Ding-an-sich*. There simply is no *ontological* truth to be had here.[204]

Nondualism allows, to be sure, no ontological ground for a duality of subject and object.[205] But equally, and with equal insistence, nondualism allows no ontological ground for their oneness.[206] Seng-ts'an (d. 606 C.E.) lends poetic accompaniment:

> All forms of dualism
> Are ignorantly contrived by the mind itself.
> They are like unto visions and flowers in the air:
> Why should we trouble ourselves to take hold of them?
> . . . .
> When dualism does no more obtain,
> Even Oneness itself remains not as such.
> . . . .
> When a direct identification is asked for,
> We can only say, "*Not two.*"
>
> (EZB I, 199–201)

Reality is empty, void of ontological factuality. The lotus discloses "emptiness."[207] Yet Merleau-Ponty cements his contrary intention to offer an ontology in remarking,

> [T]his hiatus between my right hand touched and my right hand touching . . . is not an ontological void, a non-being: it is spanned by the total being of my body, and by that of the world; it is the zero of pressure between two solids that makes them adhere to one another. (VI, 148)

Merleau-Ponty's wonderful metaphor is egregiously mistreated. The "zero of pressure" is precisely an "ontological void"—not, to be sure, a nonbeing, defined against being, not a relativized privation of being (for consistency rules "being" entirely out of question) but "absolute nothingness."[208]

> The relative nothing ("this is absent in that") cannot be hypostatized into an absolute nothing, into the non-existence of everything, or the denial of all reality and of all being. Nor does "emptiness" mean the complete indeterminate, the purely potential, which can become everything without being anything, the "mass of matter" of which Jeremy Taylor spoke as "having nothing in it but an obediential capacity for passivity." (BTI, 61)

For the Buddhist, reality is *śūnya* (empty), swollen (from the Sanskrit *svi:* "to swell") like a hollow gourd. And, as the perennial wisdom proposes, "Something which looks 'swollen' from the outside is 'hollow' inside."[209] The conflictual seemings of monism and dualism, apophansis and cataphansis, do not reveal an underlying ontology. There is no hidden, distorted or inverted ontological "fact of the matter."[210] As we have seen, this is because an ontology of instantiated contradiction is phenomenologically undecidable—not because decision favors the negative.[211] Thus, the monist and dualist seemings are not to be regarded as "viewpoints."

The chiasmic folding of hand upon hand, leg over leg, opens a dimension of cosmic relevance. Merleau-Ponty's understands the "vision" which we are as "this fold, this central cavity of the visible which is my vision, these two mirror arrangements of the seeing and the visible, the touching and the touched." (VI, 146). Conscious life is a "fold" in being: "a certain visible . . . turns back upon [*se retourne sur*] the whole of the visible" (VI, 139).[212] And one can be no less than "the sensible Being . . . that feels itself *[se sent]* in me." We are, as Merleau-Ponty avers, "the world that thinks itself" (VI, 136).[213] Again, in words ringing with Buddhist overtones:

> As I contemplate the blue of the sky I am not *set over against* it as an acosmic subject; I do not possess it in thought, or spread out towards it some idea of blue such as might reveal the secret of it, I abandon myself to it and plunge into this mystery, it "thinks itself within me," I am the sky itself as it is drawn together and unified, and as it begins to exist for itself; my consciousness is saturated with this limitless blue. (PP, 214)

It is not simply that conscious life is played out between "these two mirror arrangements of the seeing and the visible." The fold in being is, for Merleau-Ponty, the flexion of a unitary reflecting surface, a single endlessly flexible mirror. "The flesh is a *mirror phenomenon*, and the mirror is an extension of my relation with my body" (VI, 255).[214] Straightened, this universal medium relinquishes intentionality. There is nothing before it. Folded upon itself, it initiates vision, the "central cavity of the visible."

The renowned physicist, Erwin Schrödinger, corroborates the Merleau-Pontyan vision in a way which, at the same time, draws it seriously into question: "The world is given but once. Nothing is reflected. The original and the mirror-image are identical."[215] And of course, inasmuch as the flexion of our reflecting surface generates "reflection," image and original *must* be one. Nothing is reflected—or there is nothing to reflect. We are left with irreducible ambiguity, undecidability. But this is exactly the predicament of our two opening *gāthā*s: The mind is a bright mirror, yet there never was a bright mirror. Assuming a "mind-mirror" folded upon itself, the dialectic of Shen-hsiu and Hui-neng is easily comprehended. For there would then be *nothing reflected*. And a mirror which fails to reflect is certainly "no-mirror." Shen-hsiu entails Hui-neng. But equally, since not-reflecting is indistinguishable from reflecting nothing, Hui-neng entails Shen-hsiu as well. *Śūnyatā*, as Suzuki notes, is experienced in a "unique way" consisting in "*śūnyatā*'s remaining in itself and yet making itself an object of experience to itself. This means dividing itself and yet holding itself together. . . . *Śūnyatā* is experienced only when it is both subject and object."[216] Merleau-Ponty's lovely vision of the fold is itself faultless. Still, what Merleau-Ponty ignored, and what both Shen-hsiu and Hui-neng lucidly discerned, is that the fold is not a fold *in being*.

The Body and the Bodhi Tree

The meditative absorptions are, at very least, very special modes of mind. As Solé-Leris observes, "When you are in one of the states of absorption *(jhāna)* you are neither awake, nor asleep, nor dreaming; you are operating in a specifically distinct mode" (TI, 25). The cultivation of "insight," on the other hand, exfoliates in

> an increasingly intense and characteristic manner of experiencing, which is not a state of consciousness intrinsically different from the ordinary states, but is a modification which opens them up to a new dimension. One is then operating not outside the ordinary states of consciousness, but within them in a new way. . . . The person who experiences the insight of *vipassanā* lives differently, whether waking, dreaming or even sleeping. The new manner is distinguished by . . . a sense of detachment, psychological and mental balance, openness and availability to others, and exceptional relevance and functionality of thought and action. (TI, 25)

Husserl, one might imagine, would take particular delight in certain elements of the descriptions advanced. The phenomenological *epochē* is precisely a "suspension," and undeniably effects a certain "interruption" of the naïve and ingenuous life of the mind. The phenomenological reduction is, to be sure, a "modification" which opens "ordinary states" and ordinary experiencing to "a new dimension," and achieves a certain reflective "detachment." Phenomenology is both a *method* and a fund of methodologically derived *doctrine*, both "mill" and the product of its operations upon the "grist" of raw experience. The practice of *vipassanā* meditation, and the concomitant attitude of mindfulness which is its generalized accompaniment, holds unmistakable implications for the phenomenological method.[217]

Listen, now, to the Buddha's counsel regarding the cultivation of mindfulness:

> Herein, monks, a monk dwells contemplating [1] the body in the body, ardent, clearly comprehending and mindful, having overcome covetousness and grief concerning the world; he dwells contemplating [2]

> the sensations in the sensations . . . , [3] the mind in the mind . . . , [4] mental objects in mental objects. . . . (TI, 76)

Though much deserves to be said regarding the engagements of contemplation, comprehension, and mindfulness, we must practice reserve, offering, rather, a few musings regarding the four items here catalogued. In our final chapter, we shall offer a few reflections on the tensed and intensive [3] "minding" and its [4] "meant" of Occidental phenomenology. Let us turn, now, to deepen our understanding of [1] the body and its [2] sensations appearing first in the catalogue.

The Bodhi Tree, Tree of Wisdom, magnificent symbol of refuge, offered shelter and protection to Gautama during the several days and nights of unfathomable meditation that culminated in the Buddha's Unexcelled Complete Awakening.[218] Indeed, *bodhi* (from the Sanskrit *budh*) straightforwardly signifies "awakening" or "enlightenment." The Bo Tree thus serves as a natural and unmistakable metaphor for those *conditions* "under which" enlightenment is to be attained. Shen-hsiu, the gradualist, the evolutionary, in no way departs from the Buddha's express message in claiming that the "body is the Bodhi Tree." Institute the conditions leading to enlightenment, enact the "means," wipe the dust from the mirror, and, step by meditative step, realization will follow. Hung-jen never wavered in his esteem for this simple, yet profound, thesis. But, as one might well expect, Shen-hsiu's association of the soteriological means with the body imports greatly more than the practical advisability of assuming the lotus position in meditation.

Sartre sees in the body a phenomenological significance endlessly exceeding the epidermis,[219] and Shen-hsiu's own Buddhist understanding, recognizing the seamless continuity between the "small body" in its wrapper of skin and the "great body" of the world, can hardly fail to be allied:

> [T]o say that I have entered into the world, "come to the world," or that I have a body is one and the same thing. In this sense my body is everywhere in the world; it is over there in the fact that the lamp-post hides the bush which grows along the path, as well in the fact that the roof up there is above the windows of the sixth floor or in the fact that a passing car swerves from right to left behind the truck or that the woman who is crossing the street appears smaller than the man who is sitting on the sidewalk in front of the cafe. *My body is co-extensive with the world, spread across all things*, and at the same time it is condensed into this single point which all things indicate and which I am, without being able to know it. (Emphasis added; BN, 419–20)

Contemporary physics has long ago eschewed the billiard-ball model of its elementary units, and, in a vision almost indistinguishable from the Hua-yen philosophy of universal interpenetration, regards the particle as the "condensation" of a universal field of causal influence. In Sartre's notion of the body-as-a-point-of-view (BN, 433), we find a poignant reminder of the field-particle structure, that interfusion of particularity and universality altogether typical of the dialectic.[220] We are reminded, as well, of Whitehead's "actual occasions," each uniquely reflecting within its momentary immanence the vast buzzing welter of immediately elapsed occasion-events, and thus, in its universality, warning us of the fallacy of simple location.

The body is "co-extensive with the world."[221] And extrapolating, we might imagine a Buddhist theory of rebirth as envisioning a certain order of such bodily, perspectival world-insertions.[222] We must, in Hui-neng's consonant counsel, "separate . . . [our]selves from views" (PS/y, 136). Perfection in the line of right views, the first factor of the Noble Eightfold Path, is "no views." We must, if we are to awaken, learn to see the world not in this or that particular way, not in a "way" at all, but *yathā bhūtaṃ* precisely "as it is." In Shen-hsiu's doctrine, one senses the proximity of unadorned, basic truth.[223] How are we to see without blind spot and without distortion, "as it is"?[224] The answer, consorting with paradox, is that in reflexive and lucid awareness of our blind spots and distortions we are free of them.[225] Liberation, as any Buddhist will aver, is inseparable from the absolute clarity of awakening. And one can hardly miss the affinity of this paradoxical thesis with Spinoza's doctrine that freedom is knowledge of necessity. Consonantly, Buddhism envisions nirvanic deliverance as one, in the crucible of lucid awareness, with the samsaric world, constituted in delusion and illustrating the profound interrelatedness of "dependent co-origination." Seeing *yathā bhūtaṃ* does not, of itself, deliver us from insertion within a "bodily" worldview, but rather enables us to see our views for what they are: infinite foreshortenings, thus deformations, of the phenomenal world. Clarity is inseparable from the awareness of obscurity. But if enlightened envisionment is precisely the crystalline awareness of our "body-as-a-point-of-view," it cannot be gainsaid that the "Body is the Bodhi Tree."

Hui-neng's alarming dismissal of the very existence of the "Tree" conceals the affirmation that enlightenment is radically unconditioned. Shen-hsiu sponsors the practice of patient dust wiping. Meditative awareness of the beclouding and distorting "dust" of itself effects the distantiation. To be lucidly aware of the befouling dust liberates us from its "cling," thereby giving birth to "detachment" *(vairāgya)*. All this seems true enough. But why, then, does Hui-neng appear to deny it? Perhaps because the model of dust wiping assumes an externalized stance, an impossible posture of mind alien to the "mind-mirror" itself. Both "dust" and "mirror" are objectified. One object, a pellicule of dust, occludes and darkens a second, the mirror. Suppose, however, that a certain opaque object stands before, but at a distance, from our mirror. The mirror unhesitatingly reflects. Bring the object closer. The mirror continues to reflect. Now place the object directly against the mirror. Its contiguity in no way affects the mirror's effortless and spontaneous reflective functioning. Nor is this functioning inhibited in the least even if the surface of our mirror is thoroughly caked with dust. Wiping the dust away changes nothing whatsoever. As Hui-neng confirms, "enlightenment *(bodhi)* and intuitive wisdom *(prajñā)* are from the outset possessed by men of this world themselves" (PS/y, 135).

The histrionic nature of philosophical pedagogy opens a further dimension of our musings on the body as conditioning the great awakening. Simple observation may initiate the learning of philosophical art, but were our development arrested at that pitiful point, we should be in the same position as that of the beginning acting student who may have seen Olivier perform, but has never been on the opposite side of the footlights. There is just no substitute for taking on the philosophical role, *embodying* the philosophical character.

Certainly, of course, Shen-hsiu is not recommending the histrionic "embodiment" of any speculative system. Indeed, although clarity cannot be divorced from distortion, Shen-hsiu could not, as a scholarly, dedicated and thoughtful practitioner of Buddhism, have disavowed Hui-neng's admonition to "separate" oneself from views, to effect conscious distantiation even from that universal worldview that is one's body.[226] What is requisite is not the assumption of a given philosophical perspective, even though it faithfully vow the remanding of Truth into our very hands, but something of an altogether different order,[227] something that cannot fail to bring about a profound transformation.[228]

What it is that demands embodiment scintillates, if indistinctly, in the *Platform Sutra*'s exposition of the three bodies *(trikāya)* doctrine:

> [T]he pure Dharmakaya is your (essential) nature; the perfect Sambhogakaya is your wisdom; and the myriad Nirmanakayas are your actions. If you deal with these Three Bodies apart from the Essence of Mind, there would be "bodies without wisdom." If you realize that these Three Bodies have no positive essence of their own (because they are only the properties of the Essence of Mind) you attain the Bodhi of the four Prajñas. (PS/pw, 67)

Hui-neng, ever wary of the proliferating metaphysical speculation which would choke the expansive and winsome spirit of Mahāyāna, reclaims the bodies in terms phenomenologically galvanized: "The threefold body . . . is within your own self-nature" (PS/y, 141). A rewarding exegesis of the *trikāya* passage may begin with the "lowest" of the bodies, the *nirmāṇakāya*. Though the "apparition body" of the Buddha may, like a magnetized bar of iron, have been subtly informed by the energetic induction of enlightenment, it was, no less than our own, an alliance of

> hair of the head, hair of the body, nails, teeth, skin, flesh, sinews, bones, marrow, kidneys, heart, liver, midriff, spleen, lungs, intestines, mesen-

> tery, stomach, faeces, bile, phlegm, pus, blood, sweat, fat, tears, grease, saliva, nasal mucus, synovial fluid, urine[229]

and, like our own, was no less subject to dissolution. The remarkably clinical catalogue of bodily elements just appealed to was presented as a meditative theme, no doubt, in order to instill in the practitioner a certain detached equanimity in the face of inevitable bodily corruption. One is admonished to acknowledge, in confronting the festering remains of the charnel house: "Verily, my own body, too, is of the same nature; such it will become and will not escape it."[230] While a searching acceptance of the corruptibility of the objectified body (*Körper*, in the useful German term) promotes a certain needed detachment, the body is also lived from within. And Sartre, as we have seen, has provided a sound and insightful description of the "lived body" *(Leib)*. *As lived*, body is position taking, a perspectival envisionment of the world. "[M]y body does not perceive, but it is as if it were built around the perception that dawns through it" (VI, 9). And we can therefore explicate the *nirmāṇakāyas* as position-taking acts, either particular, as when we inspect a barn from alternative points of view, or universal, the "view of all views" which is our lived body. With Merleau-Ponty, we can regard the body "as a possibility for changing point of view, a 'seeing apparatus,' or a sedimented science of the 'point of view'" (VI, 37).[231] What, then, are the *nirmāṇakāyas* to "embody"? Surely, the *sambhogakāya*, the body of wisdom *(prajñā)*. The *nirmāṇakāyas* comprise the prereflective noetic activity of the mind, and *sambhogakāya* is the wisdom of reflective intuition. Wisdom, then, is the wisdom of phenomenology. *Noēsis* is embodied with wisdom in phenomenological reflection. Yet a crucial blind spot remains. "[C]onsciousness has a *punctum caecum*" (VI, 247). First-order phenomenological investigation brings to light the prereflective order, but omits itself as the very activity of reflection. The final surpassing of this foveal lacuna can only be effected by a "phenomenology of phenomenology." Wisdom, then, is in turn "embodied" by the *dharmakāya* (Body of Truth), this shadowless lucidity of awareness.

Contrastingly, for Hui-neng, there is no "Tree."[232] Once again, "If you deal with these Three Bodies apart from the Essence of Mind, there would be 'bodies without wisdom'." "Essence," here, does not import Aristotelian metaphysics. Mind, neither *ousia* nor *hypokeimenon*, responds only in silence to the Aristotelian query, *Ti esti?* The Essence of Mind can signify only the life of mind as lived from within.[233] Shen-hsiu seems to be adopting a vantage point external to the mind itself: *nirmāṇakāya* embodies *sambhogakāya* which, in turn, embodies *dharmakāya*. To risk the unforgivable, Shen-hsiu would have to be "out of his mind" to envision this order of embodiment. The marvelous power of the mind whereby the mind announces itself to itself in the "third person" is richly evoked in Borges's brief *relato,* "Borges and I":

> This happens to him, the other one, to Borges. . . . news of Borges reaches me in the mail and I see his name on an academic ballot or in a biographical dictionary. . . . I live, I go on living, so that Borges may contrive his literature; and that literature justifies me. I do not find it hard to admit that he has achieved some valid pages, but these pages can not save me. . . . In any case, I am destined to perish, definitively, and only some instant of me may live on in him. Little by little, I yield him ground, the whole terrain . . . I shall subsist in Borges, not in myself (assuming I am someone). . . . Years ago I tried to free myself from him . . . but now those games belong to Borges, and I will have to think up something else. Thus is my life a flight, and I lose everything, and everything belongs to oblivion, or to him.
>
> I don't know which one of the two of us is writing this page.[234]

Hui-neng, assuredly no unequivocal opponent of the deeply human and deeply humanizing faculty of "reflection," discovers, not Borges's poignant ambiguity ("I don't know which one of the two of us is writing this page"), but something far more remarkable: the utter absence of any phenomenal distinction between reflective activity and reflective object.

Shen-hsiu, of course, has not fallen into bad company. The Platonic "text" from which, in the Whiteheadean saw, all of our Occidental "footnotes" descend, sanctifies an objectified mind with the seal of eternity. Indeed, the objectification of Mind Itself *(noûs)*, neither "yours" nor "mine," is prepared by an altogether unique faculty of intellectual intuition *(noēsis)*. Plato, of course, was not the first Western philosopher to be thus "out of his mind." We have, for example, Anaxagoras's word that "when Mind initiated motion, from all that was moved Mind was separated, and as much as Mind moved was all divided off; and as things moved and were divided off, the rotation greatly increased the process of dividing."[235] This early objectification of Mind as the engine of cosmic revolution, coupled with Plato's "onto-theology" of the Mind-Form, exemplifies a certain vital current of Western thought, at times surging magnificently, at times merely trickling through the pores, but in any case never wholly stanched in its flow. Indeed, Descartes, excessively maligned by those who would obliterate the distinction which bears his name, is hardly original in dividing mind from the extended world. Though he would not have added "mine" to Mind, Plato envisioned Mind Itself as standing majestically aloof from the realm of transitory Form-images, spatial and temporal particularities (clearly, *extensae*) appearing in the receptacle which itself is said to be "like space." And let us not forget Kant, or those who, like Husserl, have their roots deep in Kantian transcendentalism. The transcendental epistemology of the first *Critique* is assuredly one of the most striking instances of mind-objectification. No, Shen-hsiu, though never cognizant of his alignment with typically Western proclivities, had certainly not fallen among rascals and thieves. And again, we have Hung-jen's delighted approval as earnest.

Hui-neng, however, perhaps more consistently Buddhist in his outlook, resisted even the subtlest forms of mind-objectification. There *is* no "Bodhi Tree," nor any "dust." It will not suffice simply to explain Hui-neng's concomitant rejection of the "mirror." For in merely doing so, we would not have gotten decisively beyond the dogmatic, or at best, the relativist, fixation on the evident contrast. The task before us in the remaining two chapters is to display, with regard to the method of phenomenology (the next chapter) and its deliverances (the final chapter), the logical round dance in which the two great Buddhist visionaries are engaged, to trace out the subtle circuit of implication in which their positions, though analytically contradictory, nonetheless premise one another.

II. THE MIRRORING OF MIND

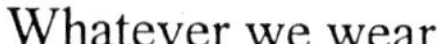

Whatever we wear

we become beautiful

moon viewing!

(CHIYO, 1703–75)

The Gateless Gate

REFLECTIONS ON THE METHODOLOGY OF REFLECTION

Phenomenology and Its "Word"

Nowhere, perhaps, are Heidegger's considerable philological talents more serviceably displayed than in his richly suggestive, if somewhat idiosyncratic, etymological rendering of "phenomenology":

> The Greek expression φαίνομενον . . . is derived from the verb φαίνεσθαι, which signifies "to show itself." Thus φαίνομενον means that which shows itself, the manifest. Φαίνεσθαι itself is a *middle-voiced* form which comes from φαίοω—to bring to the light of day, to put in the light. Φαίοω comes from the stem φα, like φως, the light, that which is bright—in other words, that wherein something can become manifest, visible in itself.[1]

Phenomenology is the "bringing to light," the very "elucidation," of the manifest. "That which shows itself" is its subject-matter. And *logos* is its method, its "way."

> The λογος lets something be seen (φαίνεσθαι), namely what the discourse is about. . . . The expression "phenomenology" may be formu-

> lated in Greek as λεγειν τα φαίνομενα, where λεγειν means ἀποφαίνεσθαι. Thus "phenomenology" means . . . to let that which shows itself be seen from itself in the very way in which it shows itself from itself.[2]

But phenomenology is significantly more than illuminating discourse concerning the phenomenon.[3] "Discourse," Heidegger's eccentric rendering of the Protean λογος, is, by itself, insufficient to express the crucial demonstrative and injunctive character of the phenomenological "word."[4] Λεγευν conveys not only "speaking," but also "choosing." The "word" of phenomenological discourse is a "chosen" word, a "good" word, a word selected in a disciplined and methodical way.[5]

"Phenomenology," in Spiegelberg's deeply thought-provoking articulation, "begins in silence."[6] Indeed, since "language lives only from silence" (VI, 126), phenomenology offers its voice to the serene reticence of experience, deploying its own *logos* to "realize, by breaking the silence, what the silence wished and did not obtain" (VI, 176). Yet the rupture of silence is not an act of violence. Silence does not limp away bleeding from its breaking. "[E]verything comes to pass," we are assured, "as though [the phenomenologist] wished to put into words a certain silence he harkens to within himself" (VI, 125).[7] Yet, if phenomenology is practiced in faithful atunement with the melody of experience, the wish thus born is not the professional possession of the practitioner, but the very voice of silence itself. Phenomenology does give voice to the manifest. It de/scribes. And we have Husserl's word that phenomenology

> aims at being a descriptive theory of the essence of pure transcendental experiences from the phenomenological standpoint, and like every descriptive discipline, neither idealizing nor working at the substructure of things, it has its own justification.[8]

The de/scriptive reportage of phenomenology purports to articulate the features of the phenomenon with the decisiveness and finality of writing *(scribere)*. Yet in some respects the *logos* of phenomena has greater affinity with fluid speech.[9] "The λογος is φώνη."[10] The very "universality" of the written word, its liberation from the immediate concrete context of utterance, drains it of demonstrative force.

We might well, then, reserve a qualm over the striking Derridian thesis of the priority of writing over speech. Still, Derrida's re/mark is insightful and offers much to ponder:

> If one admits that writing (and the mark in general) must be able to function in the absence of the sender, the receiver, the context of production, etc., that implies that this power, this being able, this possibility is always inscribed, hence necessarily inscribed as possibility in the functioning or the functional structure of the mark.[11]

Moreover, "This re-mark constitutes part of the mark itself. And this remark is inseparable from the structure of its iterability."[12] And if phenomenology requires, or even desires, to be inscribed, marked, then Derrida is quite right in sniffing paradox abrew. Since language is unmistakably historical, belonging to the domain of the natural, the empirical, the inextricability of language from phenomenological practice breeds *aporia*.

> The paradox is that, without the apparent fall back into language and thereby into history, a fall which would alienate the ideal purity of sense, sense would remain an empirical formation imprisoned as fact in a psychological subjectivity—*in the inventor's head*. Historical incarnation sets free the transcendental, instead of binding it.[13]

What is significant here is not that "scribbling," inscription, as a condition of the phenomenological project of description, adulterates the "purity" of the described, but rather, that a vital function of phenomenology would be lost were the natural and transcendental levels of experience rendered incommunicable.[14] Lacan pointedly insists that there is no metalanguage, since "it is necessary that all so-called metalanguages be presented to you with language."[15] We might rather admit a distinction of function exercised by a unitary language. Phenomenology has no need of a second and superior language in which to couch its descriptions. It needs only the assurance that language can function descriptively.[16]

There is something ineluctably demonstrative about phenomenological discourse.[17] Finding "Here lies a noble soul" scribbled on an index card inserted among the pages of an old book, we are lost. "Here" is no/where; for the absence of context prohibits the "here" from doing its proper work. Finding the same sentence inscribed on a gravestone, we have no question concerning the location referred to. Again, I might write to you describing the subtle hues of a Hawaiian sunset. Yet, though the letter is penned with the luxuriant expressiveness of the poet's art, you, if you have not been with me on that lovely evening, moved by the mysterious power of the sea, soothed by the balm of gentle breeze, transported by the nuanced dance of light on the clouds, can only decode into a cipher drawn from your own very different experience. I write that the sunset culminates in a brilliant reddish-orange. And of course, you know what I mean. You have just purchased a table lamp of reddish-orange. Yet what in your experience advances to greet my own is sorely, abysmally, inadequate. You must *be here*. Our horizons must fuse. Otherwise, words which merely describe languish in their failure to communicate.[18] The taste of tea, as Seng-chao's adage goes, cannot be conveyed in words. But it assuredly can be experienced.[19]

For this reason, the word *(logos)* of phenomenology is a word of invitation. What Lacan says of the function of language in general we may say more particularly of the function of phenomenological language: it "is not to inform but to evoke."[20] Unlike highly abstract theoretical discourse, phenomenological language does not feed upon a stratum of ideality conveyed, mind to mind, without the mediation of experience. The language of phenomenology exhausts itself in its reference to the structures of immediate, lived experience. Any residual conceptual content still clinging to the "word" bears no relevance to phenomenology.[21]

You *cannot* understand what a sunset is like by gazing fondly at the color of your new lamp. But it would be equally foolish to suppose that you could enter, with me, into the inner sanctum of my own mind, sharing in the light of my own reflective musings. My mind cannot be your "sunset." Thus, the invitation extended by the phenomenological *logos* cannot, in principle, beckon toward an objective experience which, by entering into a single perceptual context, we both might share.[22] The invitation is rather a call for a certain practice, the performance of a certain philosophical ritual. Phenomenology is a recipe.[23] We are enjoined to follow the instructions, and assured that a batch of experiential cookies of a certain description will result. When Husserl speaks of the intentional act, the pure ego, or the tripartite modalities of time-consciousness, the language employed does not advertise the latest metaphysical fad. In effect, Husserl issues the injunction: Reflect (in a specified way), and *this* is precisely what you will *see*! This, perhaps, occasions Gurwitsch's carefully phrased observation that "phenomenological investigations must be carried out in a *strictly descriptive* orientation."[24] "Descriptive" qualifies one's *approach* to experience, not its inscriptional *report*.

From its inception, Buddhism has always conjoined one modality of experience beyond the traditional five senses recognized by the folk psychology of the West: the ideational sense. We *see* the plumeria blossom and *hear* the shrill announcement of the bush warbler. But we also "grasp" the concept of zero, "comprehend" the Pythagorean Theorem, and, on occasion, "understand" the cerebral machinations of our colleagues. We have, that is, a sense, not unlike the Husserlian *Wesensschau*, but a sense which delivers to us not simply denuded thought, purified *eidos*, but also thought and conception as arrayed in the regal garments of language.[25] Phenomenology "gives voice" to silent experience. But the "voice" itself is borrowed from silence and returns to silence.[26] "[L]anguage is everything, since it is the voice of no one, since it is the very voice of the things, the waves, and the forests" (VI, 155). Language, for a Buddhist phenomenology, does not reside on *this* side of the reflective divide. It is not an instrument in the phenomenologist's tool kit, a pair of tongs to be used in steadying experience for reflective examination. Language belongs organically to experience and is willingly "lent" to the phenomenologist, as one might lend a hand, at the mere cost of recognition.[27] "[T]he things have us, and . . . it is not we who have the things. . . . language has us and . . . it is not we who have language. . . . it is being that speaks within us and not we who speak of being" (VI, 194). But the "grateful" *(dankbar)*, and thus "thoughtful" *(denkbar)*, recognition thus required is, as it turns out, a fateful exaction. Language, meaning, and conceptuality are dimensions of experience, and could operate upon the *entirety* of experience only by the unspeakably rapacious severance of its limbs.[28] If phenomenology is not to brutalize what it elucidates, leaving intact the integral unity of experience and its *organon*, we must, with Merleau-Ponty, admit the impossibility of a "complete reduction" (PhP, xiv).[29] A "gentle" phenomenology can never voice the "last word." Nor is there a "last thought," since "there is no thought which embraces all our thought" (PhP, xiv).[30]

"Right Speech" (Pali: *sammā vācā*) appears as the third element of the Noble Eightfold Path (Pali: *Ariya-Aṭṭhagika-magga*), appears, that is, as an ingredient of the Buddhist "prescription" for the dis/ease, the failure of ease, which is suffering *(duḥkha)*. Undeniably, the "right" (Pali: *sammā*) employment of language is of consummate import to the Buddhist life. And while it would be dense blindness to overlook the surrender of language to the service of compassion, neither should we neglect its devotion to *aletheia*. Speech deployed in the "right" way, though having no resonance with the Latinate "correctness," is nonetheless *true*.[31] Language, though not straightforwardly "led" *(regere)*, not ruled, not regimented, by *(com-)* the reality it would bespeak, may nonetheless demonstrate its faithfulness. The reality to which Buddhism dedicates itself is not endowed with determinate form, and thus presents not the slightest edge or crevasse to which speech might be expected to "con/form."[32] Like a boundless ocean of purest glass, like a limitless mirror, reality seems to "manifest," but not "instantiate," form. The *truth* of language is the truth of *fidelity*, not the truth of *adequation*.[33] Language in its proper employment is "true to" the reality which it serves. It follows that the proper *(sammā)* delegation of the word would not be *merely* descriptive. For if reality reflects the contours of language and conceptuality upon their approach, *mere* description becomes self-serving—fidelity to language, not to reality. Language, to be true, must voice the paradoxical nature, the antinature, of the mirror.[34] It must articulate its own ineluctable failure to copy out the original of reality.[35] The truth of language is precisely its in-turning,[36] its negative employment in bearing witness to this failure,[37] and thus, though inarticulatable in language, the demonstration of the very limits of language in its confrontation with the mirror of reality.[38] The usefulness of the raft *(yāna)* of speech[39] is fully disclosed only when the other shore has been reached, and, paradoxically, the raft shows forth its uselessness.[40]

Speech which is *sammā* is consummate, summatory—not, to repeat, in voicing the "last word," but rather, in its invocation of silence.[41] "Silence continues to envelop language; the silence of the absolute language, of the thinking language" (VI, 176). Yet speech which voices its enveloping silence is seldom to be heard.[42] Certainly, it remains inaudible amidst the prattle of metaphysical disputation. Concerning the speculative positions

> that the world is eternal, that the world is not eternal, that the world is finite, that the world is infinite, that the soul and the body are identical, that the soul is one thing and the body another, that the saint exists after death, that the saint does not exist after death, that the saint both exists and does not exist after death, that the saint neither exists nor does not exist after death. . . . (TCB, 32)

the Buddha maintains a "noble silence," urging that such troubling questions "tend not to edification" (Cf. TCB, 32ff.). While he would not pronounce upon such perplexities, he did not hesitate to pronounce upon the pronouncing: stirring the murky stream bed is of no practical avail in the attainment of clarity. It is in the second-order, the "transcendental," registration of speech that the interminable din of partisan disputation is fully heard. Yet transcendental speech, pronouncement upon the pronouncing, is consummate *(sammā)* inasmuch as the ceaseless prattle thus disclosed is disclosed *as such*, and thus given summation. Silence is heard as the horizon of speech.[43]

Mirror as Metaphor

The frigate which ferries *(pherein)* our musings across *(meta-)* toward their conclusions is, of course, the metaphor of mirroring.[44] And our study relies heavily, though not exclusively, upon a certain "poetics" of mirroring. There may be among us certain dour and inflexible literalists who would excise the methods and deliverances of poetics from the domain of philosophy altogether.[45] And a moment's pause to address this concern may not be ill spent.[46]

It is my earnest suspicion that, in the history of language, the powerfully generative richness of metaphor arrives before the vapid unidimensionality of literal discourse. Language clings to the concretion of experience like fog nuzzling in a valley,[47] and rises ethereally into the empty air of abstraction only in the countenance of the serene and contented sun: ever the symbol of a certain otherworldly *logos*.[48] Language, the companion of our leavening awareness of the world, could not be commissioned to designate the abstract and circumscribed qualities of a thing without holding in place the *concretum* from which such *abstracta* are extracted. "Apple" may not precede "red." But surely, there would be no "red" without a designation for some such concretion, found among our practical concerns, pregnant with redness.

But to say that language is born of the concrete is not sufficient to explain its human appeal and serviceability. "Sunset" adjoins nothing to our enjoyment of the sunset, and may, indeed, sharply detract from it. Lost and absorbed in appreciation of the Monet before me, I may feel only consternation at the museum guide's incessant description of the pitifully patent. The primary function of language is not, it would seem, that of literal description. For at very best, description could offer only a "second" Monet, a "second" world—a "world," that is, which, though meeting the concrete at a scattering of points, is nonetheless infinitely impoverished, drained to dry dregs of the perceptible welter of detail and significance characteristic of experience. With the world perennially before us, we have no need for a mutilated replica. And it would thus seem perverse to imagine the primordial function of language as that of literal re/presentation, presenting in a reduced and subsidiary way what is originally and unmistakably disclosed before us. Language, I submit, seeks rather to elucidate the lived and living reality, not to pluck witlessly at its shadow, and in this it remains irreducibly metaphorical.

"Juliet is the sun." And Cavell, perhaps more "moon" than "earth," suggests that, by his confession,

> Romeo means that Juliet is the warmth of his world; that his day begins with her; that only in her nourishment can he grow. And his declaration suggests that the moon, which other lovers use as emblems of their love, is merely her reflected light, and dead in comparison; and so on.[49]

Romeo's wistful proclamation is not, of course, a description. Nor, one must add, is it merely a comparison. For com/parison merely interposes a relation between two items independently designated. And Juliet is not, for Romeo, a referential locus of property inherence, but, precisely, "the sun." Cavell's "and so on" signals not only the open-ended generativity of metaphor, but the inexhaustible significance which Juliet holds for Romeo—a significance not confined to the few items of Cavell's exegesis, indeed, not confined, and incapable of being confined, to any limited stock of literal predications. In Rorty's insightful assessment:

> to think of metaphor as a . . . source of beliefs, and thus a . . . motive for reweaving our network of beliefs and desires, is to think of language, logical space, and the realm of possibility, as open-ended. It is to abandon the idea that the aim of thought is the attainment of a God's-eye-view.[50]

Metaphor, it seems, is the matrix of the literal, and not conversely. A metaphor could never be constructed by tirelessly heaping one literal description atop another. And if so, then any theory of literal discourse will invoke a poetics or go wanting in completeness.

Our literalist will doubtless remind us of the refined and well-oiled machinery of modern formal logic, and suggest that, whatever its origins, it would be mockery to channel philosophical lucidity out of its licensed grooves. It is not my sport here to deprecate the authority of logic in its passing of judgment upon formal inference. Let us render unto logic what properly pertains. And the pertinent domain of logic is the legitimate suspension of "position" from "sup/position." Metaphor is no antagonist of formal reasoning, but provides, rather, the very traction required to discharge the conditional. Metaphor lies, that is, at the heart of the pre/supposition. Indeed, the "space" of philosophical disputation is opened by the reciprocal repulsion of contending metaphors. As Rorty clearly sees,

> A metaphor is, so to speak, a voice from outside logical space, rather than an empirical filling-up of a portion of that space. It is a call to change one's language and one's life, rather than a proposal about how to systematize either.[51]

Phenomenology, which withholds in order to see, elucidates presupposition, and is thus ever the gracious protector of its attendant discipline: poetics.[52]

Our motive metaphor, *the mirror*, is an object (or more accurately, an anti-object) of surpassing oddity. Like transparency, like empty space, the mirror effaces itself.[53] The qualities beheld within the looking glass are neither intrinsic nor extrinsic, but simply reflected. Nothing is gleaned of the intimate nature of the mirror by cataloguing the qualities of its reflections. "Juliet is the sun" is a wellspring of relatively literal attributions. And this is because the sun itself is fathomless in qualitative richness and relatedness. But the suggestiveness of Shen-hsiu's proclamation that "The mind is a bright mirror" cannot, in this way, rest upon the visible qualities *of the mirror*. For the mirror "itself" is devoid of perceptible attributes.[54] In its self-effacement, the mirror is a "nothing." In its reflectivity, it is an "everything": a "something" that is "everything" by making itself "nothing."[55] Though unmistakable, the ontological overtones will not detain us here. More to the present point, nothing is metaphorically conveyed by the qualities "of" the mirror. For there are none. It is rather the very *absence* of quality, self-effacement and universal permissiveness, which fund our more literal attributions. We learn nothing *of mind* by considering the objects which it entertains,[56] including, as a crucial instance, those self-objectifications and objectivities which it offers itself in reflection.[57] The world of our experience is not in the least enriched by the functioning of mind. Mind *adds* nothing.[58] It appends not a single qualitative determination to the world.[59] But it does not follow that mind is dispensable, a mere *façon de parler* ontologically factorable into an assemblage of mundane objects, each with its own intrinsic determinations. For now a certain suspicion has arisen, a suspicion which, once given life, will not die. Phenomenological rigor will permit no discrimination between reflection and object, between mirror and reality. And we can therefore never be assured that the world, which profits not from mind, is not, in fact, the mind-mirror itself. The "two" are phenomenologically "indifferent."

But can any part serve as delegate for the whole? To be sure, the mirror is a something, a particular denizen of the world, a part. And the strategy of world-modeling is no younger, and no less venerable, than philosophy itself. "There was a sailor, a Baptist I believe, who said that all was water."[60] The "Baptist," of course, was Thales, the first of our Occidental breed. And Thales's famous opinion concerning the watery ways of the world was almost certainly prompted by the very natural proclivity to take a significant portion (e.g., *hydor*) as earnest for universal immensity. Hume, the wary, is no champion of this presumably naive propensity. In the person of Philo, Hume queries, "[I]s a part of nature . . . a rule for the whole? Is a very small part a rule for the universe?"[61] And we know his answer from his questions: "From observing the growth of a hair, can we learn any thing concerning the generation of a man? Would the manner of a leaf's blowing, even though perfectly known, afford us any instruction concerning the vegetation of a tree?"[62] For the skeptical Hume, the whole of reality cannot, with any epistemic warrant, be claimed kin of its residents. The world cannot be known to be "like" a cleverly designed machine, nor, for that matter, "like" a toad or "like" a field of new-mown hay. And we have only to transpose Hume's epistemological reservations into an ontological key to arrive at the Buddhist doctrine of emptiness *(śūnyatā)*: Ultimate Reality *is not* "like" anything at all.[63] Models and metaphor have no purchase upon reality. Paradoxically, however, the very resistance of reality to metaphor points directly to the aptness of the mirror. The mirror is, if you like, an antimetaphor, representing, in its intrinsic freedom from visible quality, the very failure of metaphorical purchase that typifies emptiness.[64] As Trinh thi Minh-hà remarks, "It is by virtue of consciousness of such a mirage-displacement that in Asian cultures the mirror often functions as the 'symbol of the very void of symbols.'"[65] And it is through investigation of the inner nothingness *(to mēon)* of the mind-mirror that Buddhist thought secures the designation "meontic phenomenology."[66]

Why should the mirror be accounted a more appropriate metaphor for the world than an onion or a falling star? I answer that it should not, that there is no reason whatsoever to prefer one metaphor over the other. Reflectivity serves the purpose no better than opacity. Paradoxically, however, it is precisely the failure of preferability which confirms the mirror's appropriateness. Mirrors are simply "like that." If the reflection is like its original, then it is also like any opacity which might suitably serve to model reality.

The "Madness" of Phenomenological Method

Natanson tells us that "believing-in-the-world is the paradigm of normality."[67] And phenomenology would not degenerate into the aberration of world-denial. Husserl, in particular, is no naysayer, but seeks, rather, the unshakable experiential warrant for giving the "yes" to intuited structures of experience that he discovers through phenomenological method.[68] The phenomeno-*logos*, as we have seen, is a select word, and the *epochē* and reduction are its archaic principles of se/lection, the logic *(logos)* according to which "to speak" *(legein)* is thereby to gather *(legere)*, and, indeed, to gather apart.

But phenomenological method draws apart from the world, not in flight, and not in order to take up cloistered residence in the lotus-land of pure subjectivity. That, indeed, *would* be madness. In Merleau-Ponty's suggestive portrayal:

> Reflection does not withdraw from the world towards the unity of consciousness as the world's basis; it steps back to watch the forms of transcendence fly up like sparks from a fire; it slackens the intentional threads which attach us to the world and thus brings them to our notice; it alone is consciousness of the world because it reveals that world is strange and paradoxical. (PhP, xiii)

The world, like Melville's leviathan, masters the intentional space in which it dwells. A Husserlian Ahab might think to harpoon it from the safety of some putatively external vantage point, but only at the peril of learning this dreadful lesson. The Absolute Scientist, like a fragile whaling dinghy, is dragged and shivered by the world he would possess. Like an Ahab, we are fatefully snarled in the world, trapped by our very harpoon lines.

> [W]hen it will have learned to invest it, science will little by little reintroduce what it first put aside as subjective; but it will integrate it as a particular case of the relations and objects that define the world for science. Then the world will close in over itself, and, except for what within us thinks and builds science, that impartial spectator that inhabits us, we will have become parts or moments of the Great Object. (VI, 15)

All we can expect on the part of our epochetic suspension is a slackening of the cords. Denial would sever them, setting our bark adrift, mooringless, upon a chartless sea of chaotic "experience," untethered to the world or its objects. Madness! Philosophical sanity lies, however, in giving notice to the unnoticed, uncovering the covered, re-veil-ation.[69]

The "veil" which the *epochē* would lift is not an opaque screen which occludes the object by interposing itself. Paradoxically, the veil is precisely the revelation of the object itself, the very posture or attitude of consciousness in its activity of disclosure. And paradoxically, also, it is the veil (the unveiling of the object) which phenomenology seeks primarily to elucidate, not the unveiled (the object itself). Slackening, the dissolution of intentional tension, allows the very tautness of the native and predominant attitude of consciousness to come to light.

What is "natural" (and, indeed, normal) about the "natural attitude" of consciousness is the primordial believing-in-the-world which Husserl denominates the "general positing,"[70] and which, in Merleau-Ponty's hands, becomes perceptual faith. Indeed, as the latter avers, "Philosophy is the perceptual faith questioning itself about itself" (VI, 103).[71] Consciousness, by its very nature, posits existence. The "sense" of consciousness would be opaque in isolation from its native investment in being. Yet, according to Husserl, no more than the bare possibility of deception is needed in order to ring sonorous changes in our apprehension of experienced objectivity. Even the most insidious suspicion of nonexistence phenomenalizes the world,[72] "reduc[ing] perception to the thought of perceiving, under the pretext that immanence alone is sure" (VI, 36). And this, for Merleau-Ponty, is "to take out an insurance against doubt whose premiums are more onerous than the loss for which it is to indemnify us. . . ." (VI, 36). As Levin writes:

> Every perception is, as the German word *Wahr-nehmung* makes quite plain, a giving of something itself; in every perception, the thing is given as itself there. Thus, the act of perception is in its essence a moment of existential commitment. . . . If this be so, then the possibility of a methodological suspension of the existential belief-component of the perceptual act becomes problematic.[73]

Husserl, of course, is by no means insensitive to the vital existential commitment of perception, and, indeed, witnesses the disclosure of the *Urdoxa* from the vantage of ontological neutrality.[74] The quarrel does not concern the ineluctability of "positing," since both Husserl and Merleau-Ponty sponsor this. Rather, the very nature of the perceptual *noēma*, and thus the very subject-matter of phenomenology, is called into question.[75] Gurwitsch reminds us that "The Husserlian *noema* is understood as the object such, exactly such and only such, as the . . . subject is aware of it, as he intends it in this concrete experienced mental state."[76] And the perceptual object is given precisely *as existing*. To say this is not merely to append an accidental stratum of sense to an idealized phenomenon floating languidly above the urgent roil of concrete reality, but rather, *to believe*, or less cerebrally, *to posit*.[77] Philosophy, however, "does not seek a verbal substitute for the world we see" (VI, 4). And perceptual faith, whose self-interrogation is philosophy itself, cannot be ripped from the living tissue of the *noēma*. Faith is the heart. And it follows that reflection, though stalking perception with the utmost ingenuity, can never seize its prey. Always and necessarily pursuer and pursued are separated by a certain preconscious moment of reflective conversion, a "zero-point" which marks the modulation of consciousness naïveté into disingenuous in-turning.[78]

There is deep wisdom to be tapped in our unformed, undeformed, and still "wondering" students. Almost invariably, a lecture on Kant's refutation of the ontological argument is attended by questions concerning the edibility of imaginary apples.[79] (Born not for riches, I prefer apples to thalers.) If an imaginary apple can, in imagination, possess all the properties of its counterpart, the real apple, and if the real and the imaginary remain *two* across the assumption that "existence" designates a "real predicate" (or, shall we not hedge: a *property*), then, the familiar conclusion follows: It cannot be "existence" which accounts for the *existence* of the extant apple. The impatient rejoinder is never long in coming: "Yes, but we can *eat* real apples. The imaginary one will do you no good if you're hungry." Precisely! But without prompting, someone else will break in: "*In imagination*, you can eat imaginary apples. And *in imagination*, they will satisfy your hunger." There's the budding Husserlian! Modify the problem in but a single respect, and the "bud" opens to the light. How are we to distinguish the "real" apple from an hallucinatory semblance like it in every perceivable respect? "Existence" profits us not, since the hallucination also *seems* to exist.[80]

The problem, of course, was, before Husserl's, also Descartes's. Veridical perception cannot, as both claim, be discriminated from dream in virtue of the purported extraphenomenal *existence* of its object. Descartes leaps, frivolously it seems, to the familiar skeptical conclusion. Yet two alternative responses are equally available. We can, for example, seek the ineluctable differences which segregate dream from reality, thus overturning the very terms of the Cartesian problem. Findlay does just that in his assertion that "to experienced parties mirror-images *look* like reflections, and not like things behind the mirror, and mirages *look* like mirages, and not like villages, water, etc., on the horizon."[81] More to the point is Gordon's very serviceable suggestion that

> precisely this *lived certainty*—precognitive, preconceptual, and incorrigible—is the surest sign we have that we are awake. The eclipse of this experience is the necessary condition of immersion into the dream, but one loses oneself as dreamer to emerge in the world as flesh.[82]

In the world of the dreamer,

> What is lacking is his ability to get a *grip* on things in this world and their ability to get a grip on him. . . . hence his feeling of being immersed in a world of wholly magical relationships where he is without defense against the vicissitudes of fortune. . . . [83]

Though different in detail, Sartre's very similar proposal is no less apposite:

> [T]he real is anterior to the possible. The world of dream, which is imaginary, does not allow this distinction. . . . In a dream there is no distinction between wanting to drink and dreaming that one is drink-

> ing. So the mind, victim of its omnipotence, *cannot* wish. It cannot even wish to wake up. It will only dream that it does wake up. For it to be itself again, the real must invade its dream in some way. Thus the dreamer is bound hand and foot by his absolute power. . . . Let a genie give me power to realize my desires there and then, and at once I fall asleep—being unable to hold them off, to *prevent* them from being realized.[84]

Findlay, Gordon, and Sartre, each in his own way, insist upon the very distinction which would detonate the Cartesian problematic. If dreams "look like" dreams, discrimination is always possible—a result which short-circuits the skeptical argument.[85] Finally, we have the resonant testimony of the Buddha himself. Asked, "Are you a god?" a simple "No" was his response. "Are you an angel?" Again: "No." "Then what"—*what*, not *who*—"are you?" In a simple sentence galvanized with significance, the Buddha replied: "I am awake."[86] And indeed, he was. The Sanskrit *budh* signifies a waking, the evaporation of dream-shadows, the dispelling of the drifting mists of reverie, the gathering of the mind from dispersion and aimless wandering.[87] When the clouds roll back, the cheerful radiance of the sun brightens the world, chasing the shadows. Thus, the Buddha was "enlightened." "I am awake." Only the fully awakened could announce this with the authority of one whose present experience gives contrast to the somnambulence of worldly immersion and dissolution.

There is, however, a third response, one which, without further thought, might seem alluring to the metaphysical idealist, though second thoughts will dispel the allurement. This response is, I believe, Husserl's. And its *prima facie* idealistic charm may explain the charge of idealism so frequently leveled at the *Ideas*. Setting aside, though by no means denying, the evident contrast of dream and the waking state, we may, quite harmlessly, grant their indiscernibility. Suppose, then, but only provisionally, *pace* Sartre, and *pace* the Buddha himself, that reality cannot, on the terms of this "grant," be discriminated from perfect hallucinatory semblance. Skepticism would be forthcoming *only* in the wake of a second, indispensable, and untenable, assumption: that *one* of the purportedly "two" experiences is veridical, that in "one," the presence of a solidly *existing* object is disclosed.[88] Cartesian skepticism amounts only to a blind disjunction. One hand, and *only* one, conceals the marble. And we cannot, by looking at the two hands, tell which.[89] The Husserlian *epochē* is emphatically alien to the suppositions of skepticism. Though it will crystalize once again within the phenomenal domain, the very distinction between appearance and reality is, at the entryway, dissolved in epochetic acid.[90] There is, from the outset, no question of "choosing hands."

The failure of realism would by no means import the victory of Berkeleyan idealism. Nor, indeed, would the supersession of idealism in its subjectivist, empirical guise, toll the demise of rigorous phenomenological method.

Berkeleyan idealism preserves the Kantian distinction of the phenomenal from the noumenal, appearance from reality, as a suprapositional schema, a framework or "space" of possible views, within which to situate itself. Nowhere does Berkeley reject the very distinction between thing-in-itself and thing-for-us. His intent is rather to evacuate the noumenal. Idealism is the view which results from corralling reality into phenomenal pastures, leaving the noumenal void, untrodden.

In vivid contrast, the phenomenologist drops the distinction at the gateway of philosophy.[91] Without, let it serve as it may. Once the threshold has been crossed, it plays a very different role. The laws of the phenomenological land permit its importation only if securely "bracketed." The *epochē* does not comport with the simple insistence upon doing philosophy solely on *this* side of the noumenal-phenomenal divide, merely leaving in abeyance the question of noumenal reality. This frequent, but fatefully naïve, reading leaves entirely out of account the phenomenality of the noumenal. The bracketing of existence does not import the jettison of our existential beliefs into the abyss. Pre-philosophical existential beliefs are not *used* in the conduct of philosophical investigation. But this disciplined restraint in no way modifies our pre-philosophical commitments. Nor, decisively, does it purge phenomenal reality of existence. Existence, barred at the entrance, finds access through the back door.[92] Indeed, phenomenology suspends commitment to purported extra-phenomenal existence precisely in order to discover existence *as phenomenon.*[93] Things appear "existingly," and it is a cardinal task of phenomenology to describe this manner of appearance. Noumenality and phenomenality divide, in an evidently reflexive way, the only philosophically possible terrain: *phenomenality*. Berkeley gathers reality to one side of a philosophical landscape already divided. For Berkeley, Truth occupies a delimited region of philosophical space. For phenomenology, Truth is congruent with philosophy itself.[94] After all, "Philosophy is not the reflection of a pre-existing truth, but, like art, the act of bringing truth into being" (PhP, xx), and, since philosophical space could not subsist in advance of this act, neither could its occupants.

In our natural positing of existence we are, as Husserl might admit, little different from the indomitable Dr. Johnson. In Eddington's edifying report:

> When Dr. Johnson felt himself getting tied up in argument over "Bishop Berkeley's ingenious sophistry to prove the non-existence of matter, and that everything in the universe is merely ideal," he answered, "striking his foot with mighty force against a large stone, till he rebounded from it,—'I refute it *thus*.'" Just what that action assured him of is not very obvious; but apparently he found it comforting.[95]

But what would become of the stone if Dr. Johnson's "refutation" were to fail? From a phenomenological point of view: absolutely *nothing*—and, of course, absolutely *everything*. "Nothing" would become of it inasmuch as every element of the story—stone, kick, and even the irascible Dr. Johnson himself—might fail to exist without disturbing the phenomenal display in the least. Yet "everything" would change. For we would be translated into the heaven, the transcendental haven, of the phenomenal.

But our crystals are once again eager for service. The divergence of reality from appearance, which buttresses Sartre's imposing ontology, has but a single hope of phenomenological legitimation. The reality disclosed through our crystalline medium and the differently nuanced tincture pervading the medium must, at very least, be comparable. The model: at once dualistic and cataphantic. Husserl's arrest of the distinction at the very portal of phenomenology confirms an unsurprising departure from earlier realist *(Göttingen)* commitments. The model: monist, cataphantic and illuminationist. But recall the "magic" of the crystals. Beneath their *als ob* diversity lies a seamless unity. Penetrating their "seeming," the crystals are indiscernible. Or is there not rather *one* crystal which, by a curious diplopia, shimmers into several, transparent and translucent, self-illumined and otherwise, at the approach of the theoretical construct? A suspicion, first itching and then gnawing, is thus loosed upon the domain of phenomenological method. Perhaps all is not, as we might once have hoped, entirely well. Is the edifice of reflection, like the decaying ruins of some forgotten temple, in serious disrepair? Or perhaps things stand entirely *too* well. The magic of the crystals, the induction of ideological diplopia, grants to each partisan the wish for truth, and bestows upon us all a sun-drenched paradise in which every theoretical approach gets its way, a shadowless land from which all falsehood has been banished. While I would not revoke philosophical license, bursting the bubbles of theory upon the needles of fact, nor would I summon Hobbes from his rest to lecture us on the war of each position against all, I sense, beneath the gaiety and joyous piping of our magic domain a barely perceptible *bourdon* of sadness. Our theoretical partisans, not content with the part, would have the whole. The nisus of theory, not satisfied with the status of "perspective," "interpretation," "view," would seize *Truth* for itself.[96] And, indeed, its wish is granted by the accommodating crystals. The crystals, now pluralized, offer themselves entire to each of the competing partisans. Each partisan now owns, not *a* truth, not a pathway to Truth, but Truth Itself. Those, however, who avail themselves of our truth-bestowing magic have, in their bedazzlement, become blind to the nature of what now squirms in their clutch. The "truth" thus seized does not answer to the formula *adequatio intellectus et rei*. For the crystal, the unitary crystal in its pristine and undivided state, submits to the grasp of theory only by dividing itself. The crystal, mirrorlike in its indifference to adventitious claims, offers to theory the theory's own image, and this denominates truth. The truth thus seized is the truth *of the theory*. For there is no truth *of the crystal* to be grasped. Or rather, while the crystal rests serene in its own truth, its truth is a truth which conceals itself at the approach of theory.[97] Yet might one not wish, quite simply, to witness the crystal in its primordial oneness? And is it not this quiet, ungrasping vision, rather than the indifferent conferral of truth upon the several guests at the ideological revel, the dream fervently cherished by an uncorrupted phenomenology?[98]

Presuppositionlessness

Existence, Husserl will urge, is the peg upon which we hang our presuppositions, our most deeply enframing presumptions regarding the nature of the intentional object and the world in which it thrives. The assumption that a given megalith is massive and humanly impenetrable, and causes untold pain when struck with the might that Dr. Johnson summoned, hangs from the presumption of its existence. Bracket the latter presumption, and you thereby bracket the former. Bracket the "natural positing" of the world, and all of our presuppositions are thereby suspended.[99] Assuming systematic deception, everything will remain (phenomenally) the same. It will be just *as if* the stone were solid, and we will not be spared our share of agony upon solidly kicking it. No longer, however, do we have before us merely a solid stone. What greets the mind is the "stone-as-solid." Our presuppositions, no longer taken for granted, are brought explicitly to light as belonging to the very sense of the object as presented.

To *posit* is to place or pose (German: *setzen*, *stellen*). To posit the world is not to "lay it down" *that* the world exists. For the general positing of Husserlian phenomenology is not propositional. What is posited is the *very existence* of the world (or rather, the *world* in its very existing). Yet in Hui-hai's formulation of the Mādhyamika doctrine: "Thinking in terms of being and non-being is called wrong thinking, while not thinking in those terms is called right thinking."[100] In other contexts, however, we do "posit that." And an analogy drawn from propositional argumentation might be of some use. If we posit, without argumentation, that a certain controversial claim is true, our colleagues will call for our premises (if not our resignation), the "sup/positions" which lie beneath and support our positions. Managing to secure their assent to our suppositions, we may still be challenged regarding the material logic of our inference. The issue becomes one of meaning. Does it really follow, for example, from the *very sense* of a given action's being "morally right" that anyone similarly placed ought to do likewise? Does being a "body" entail, by its *very sense*, being extended? To assume so (and to assume no) is to harbor a pre/supposition. Presuppositions are not formal rules of inference, but assumptions regarding the very meaning of our supposals. Our presuppositions are elicited through the articulation of our concepts.

Unmistakably Cartesian in his pursuit of the apodictic, unmistakably foundationalist in his pursuit of *Evidenz* (the "appearance of validity")[101] Husserl asks:

> Must not the demand for a philosophy aiming at the ultimate conceivable freedom from prejudice, shaping itself with actual autonomy ac-

> cording to ultimate evidences it has itself produced, and therefore absolutely self-responsible—must not this demand, instead of being excessive, be part of the fundamental sense of genuine philosophy?[102]

The goal of all Buddhist practice is, of course, "the ultimate conceivable freedom from prejudice,"[103] liberation from conceptual and ideological bondage of even the most subtle form, and thus, with Husserl, the purification of our outlook from the defilement of presupposition.[104] Nor does Husserl incur the least censure from the Buddhist quarter for his insistence upon autonomy. The Buddhist sees clearly that whoever would find the priceless pearl of wisdom must "withdraw into himself,"[105] and can quite consistently intone, with Husserl, that wisdom "must arise as *his* wisdom, as his self-acquired knowledge tending toward universality, a knowledge for which he can answer from the beginning, and at each step, by virtue of his own absolute insights."[106] For among the Buddha's final and most solemn words to his disciples we find the injunction:

> Therefore, O Ananda, be ye lamps unto yourselves. Rely on yourselves, and do not rely on external help.
>
> Hold fast to the truth as a lamp. Seek salvation alone in the truth. Look not for assistance to any one besides yourselves. (TCB, 49)

Eschewing presupposition, we must "begin in absolute poverty."[107] Yet renouncing *all*—all presuppositions and all views—we find within our poverty an incomparable richness. We find the lamp. We find *truth*. And while Buddhism would assuredly repudiate the early realist disposition of Husserl's thought which invites submission to the putative external authority of "ultimate evidence," nothing could be more congenial than the coherent phenomenological assimilation of truth to the ultimate evidence which the very enterprise of reflective investigation has itself engendered.[108]

The entertainment of right view, the enaction of right viewing (*sammā-diṭṭhi*: singular, not plural, in the Pali) this element inaugurating the Noble Eightfold Path, bears no affinity with empirical adequation.[109] *Sammā*, kin to the Latin *summa*, resounds with unmistakable overtones of "summary" and "consummation." "Right" views are *complete* views, views completely or thoroughly *(per-)* accomplished *(fectus)*, penetrating views, as the archaic "throughly" suggests. The right view is also the balanced view, the view of the Middle Way. For *sammā* is "same"—not, by any means, suggesting permanence, enduring identity, but connoting, rather, a certain quality of consummate equipoise.[110] The empirical world is fathomlessly rich. And though popular presentation of the sciences might encourage the arrogant impression that, with the latest theoretical trinket, the veil has once and for all been sundered, the evolution of the sciences, a history of abandonment, stands as an eloquent refutation.[111] Few serious scientists will regard present innovations as more than the planting of one foot upon the ground while the other swings forward, leaving in the sands so many footprints bespeaking the failure, indeed, the ineluctable failure, of consummation. Speculative metaphysics, equally prolific, equally insanguine, so crowds the highways of the mind that occasionally a Kant must appear to demand the epistemic credentials of its practitioners. Occasionally a positivism must appear to uproot the weeds ever threatening the well-ordered garden of the sciences. From theory, scientific or speculative, we can expect no closure, no summary, and thus, no perfection. The perfection enjoined is not an attribute of the view, but rather of the manner in which the view is entertained. As Husserl observes: "To be sure, we still have philosophical congresses. The philosophers meet but, unfortunately, not the philosophies. The philosophies lack the unity of a mental space in which they might exist for and act on one another."[112] The truth of phenomenology is never among the competing philosophical views. Phenomenology is not itself a position, but the reflective investigation of the very sense of position taking.[113] We must, as the commonplace insists, agree to disagree. Disagreement, the op/position of position, assumes a shared sense of the possibility, meaning, and strategies of disagreement, and thus harbors, at least implicitly, a common understanding of the nature of position taking itself.[114] The agreement, deeper than the conflicting positions, is exactly the mental space of which Husserl speaks. Challenged by an alternative agreement, a competing sense of the nature of position and op/position, the proper phenomenological comportment is to duck.[115] Imbued with a gentleness and freedom from hostility entirely congruent with the Buddhist spirit, phenomenology remains harmless, unimpeded, never entering the fray of positional combat. A view, a position, is a given style of relatedness to our world. Views are relative, and by no means to be confounded with Absolute Truth.[116] "Now, what is Absolute Truth? According to Buddhism, the Absolute Truth is that there is nothing absolute in the world, that everything is relative. . . ." (WBT, 39). No more vivid expression could be offered of the unshakable *transcendentalism* of Buddhist thought. The Buddha renounced the petty dogmatism poetically described in the *Sutta-Nipata*:

> Fixed in their pet beliefs,
> these divers wranglers bawl—
> "Hold this, and truth is yours";
> "Reject it, and you're lost."
>
> (TCB, 37)

His response rises beyond the reach of sectarianism:

> if dissent denotes
> a "fool" and stupid "dolt,"

then all are fools and dolts,
—since each has his own view.

Or, if each rival creed
proves lore and brains and wit,
no "dolts" exist,—since all
alike are on a par.

. . . There's one sole "Truth" (not two). . . .
(TCB, 37)

With the gladness of one who empties his hand of dust in order to receive an inestimably more valuable bestowal, phenomenology, like Buddhism, relinquishes its hold upon any purported truth which, because of opposition, proves itself to be a mere view.[117] Thus is born the *motion* of communalization recognized in the *Crisis*:

> In this communalization . . . there constantly occurs an alteration of validity through reciprocal correction. . . . If one attends to the distinction between things as "originally one's own" and as "empathized" from others, in respect to the how of the manners of appearance, and if one attends to the possibility of discrepancies between one's own and empathized views, then what one actually experiences *originaliter* as a perceptual thing is transformed, for each of us, into a mere "representation of," "appearance of," the one objectively existing thing. . . . "The" thing itself is actually that which no one actually experiences as really seen, since it is always in motion. . . . [118]

Like a slippery bar of soap, "*the* thing" perpetually eludes the grasp of "representation," "appearance."[119] And this slippage is accompanied by a concomitant in-turning, a progressive purification of the permissive space within which discrepancy occurs.

The Modes of Reflection

The untutored assumptions over which most of our quotidian affairs are transacted are precarious and fragile. Who, for example, is not secretly prepared to intone "excuse me" upon brushing unwittingly against a department store manikin? And who has not felt the searing embarrassment of hailing a "friend" half a block away only to be met by the uncomprehending stare of a perfect stranger? Upheavals such as these, in which the error of our ways (our modes of apprehending) are brought, with painful piquancy, to light, comprise, to be sure, a form of reflection, but a reflection wholly immersed within the natural attitude. Natural reflection appears as an undisciplined occurrence, a cacophonous lapse from the otherwise mellifluous dynamic of the daily round. As Natanson tells us, "the 'suddenness' with which self-awareness occurs . . . means that self consciousness is not being practiced or appropriated in some routine fashion but as a matter of happenstance."[120] For this reason, "The irruption of a reflective self-awareness in the individual going about his business may strike him as odd or strange and is, most commonly, brushed aside or shaken off."[121] Natural reflection strikes us as an unwanted and practically deleterious disengagement, as when, in driving through heavy traffic, we manage quite accidentally to shift into neutral. Our praxiological "gears" cease to mesh, and we want nothing more than to return to our prereflective engagements.[122]

Natural reflection is "accidental." But there remains a species of reflection which, though pre-phenomenological, is nonetheless deliberate, and, indeed, methodical. Establishing himself on the assumption that "the understanding is . . . alone capable of perceiving the truth,"[123] and that it performs the dual functions of "self-evident intuition and necessary deduction,"[124] Descartes admonishes us to "treat of things only in relation to our understanding's awareness of them."[125] The injunction becomes problematic, however, when coupled with the test for self-evidence proposed by the *Meditations*: failure of dubitability. What we cannot doubt is exactly the indubitable. Thus, if we "try" to doubt and "fail," we have struck granite, and can begin on the spot to erect our philosophical edifice. Yet our granite crumbles immediately into *aporia*. We might first puzzle over the unusual specimen of self-evidence which allows for such a test. Self-evidence is its own criterion. That which is evident "in itself" has no need to pass a further examination. But perhaps, if passing is not required, it is at least permitted: a sufficient, if not a necessary condition. Here our aporetic qualms wax epistemic. Self-evidence is the most flattering epistemic compliment we can pay. If the flattery attends failure of dubitability, we must know, *with lucid self-evidence*, that doubt has failed.[126] And thus, as a moment's thought will attest, is born an endless and vicious regress. If failure is merely sufficient, on the other hand, it is epistemically useless. For we will never know with consummate apodicticity that doubt has been tried and that it has failed. Perhaps, for example, we neglected to try hard enough. Perhaps, that is, there remains an unconsidered, but entirely conceivable, falsifying possibility. In any case, where the criterion is of a lower epistemic order than self-evidence, the criterion is clearly otiose.

Moreover, the very notion of "trying" to doubt is altogether vulnerable to question. If Husserl is right in his assessment that Descartes' "attempt to doubt universally is properly an attempt to negate universally,"[127] and if, as reason demands, universal negation is logically incoherent, what could the attempt come to? If attempt is tied to possibility, the answer must be: "nothing." Even allowing that we might attempt the impossible, especially before apprising ourselves of its impossibility,[128] we cannot pass unscathed before Peirce's challenge: "A proposition that could be doubted at will is certainly not believed."[129] Peirce amplifies:

> We cannot begin with complete doubt. We must begin with all the prejudices which we actually have when we enter upon the study of philosophy. These prejudices are not to be dispelled by a maxim, for they are things which it does not occur to us *can* be questioned. Hence this initial scepticism will be a mere self-deception, and not real doubt: and no one who follows the Cartesian method will ever be satisfied until he has formally recovered all those beliefs which in form he has given up. It is, therefore, as useless a preliminary as going to the North Pole would be in order to get to Constantinople by coming down regularly upon a meridian. A person may, it is true, in the course of his studies, find reason to doubt what he began by believing; but in that case he doubts because he has a positive reason for it, and not on account of the Cartesian maxim. Let us not pretend to doubt in philosophy what we do not doubt in our hearts.[130]

Peirce envisions a certain doxastic economy in which doubt is exchanged for belief. We doubt what we formerly believed because we come to believe its negate. Otherwise, doubt would be unmotivated, a mere pose, not an affair of the heart.

"Doubt," in common parlance, suffers ambiguity, meaning both *(positive doubt:)* a positive inclination toward disbelief, and *(negative doubt:)* a certain hesitation before the alternatives of belief and disbelief. It is the former, the positive variety, which informs the Peircean argument. Merleau-Ponty comments that "doubt as a destruction of certitudes is not doubt" (VI, 106), thereby reinforcing Peirce's negative assessment of the Cartesian project, though dismissing as spurious the Peircean notion of positive doubt. Positive doubt is not doubt, but *disbelief.* Reserving as genuine only the negative of the species, Merleau-Ponty clears the way for the phenomenological project of pure equipoise.

Peirce, of course, has his point. His argument efficiently dispels any lingering suspicion that Cartesian doubt is a "real" heartfelt movement of the psyche. Cartesian doubt is not psychological doubt. But then, perhaps, methodological doubt was never intended as more than a certain intellectual posturing, the practice of which illuminates the space of possibility, enabling the practitioner to discern, from the margins of *de facto* correctness, a purely possible falsity. Certainly this would appeal to Husserl, who aligns himself, at least in spirit, with a certain universal doubt:

> Cannot the disconsolateness of our philosophical position be traced back ultimately to the fact that the driving forces emanating from the *Meditations* of Descartes have lost their original vitality—lost it because the spirit that characterizes the radicalness of philosophical self-responsibility has been lost? Must not the demand for a philosophy aiming at the ultimate conceivable freedom from prejudice, shaping itself with actual autonomy according to ultimate evidences it has itself produced, and therefore absolutely self-responsible—must not this demand, instead of being excessive, be part of the fundamental sense of genuine philosophy?[131]

Yet even the radical demands of a Husserlian philosophy as a "strict science" do not compel the incoherent practice of universal negation. "Doubt," if it can have universal application at all, must portend, not denial, an infra-economic transaction, but rather a certain distancing, a certain "dropping out," from economic interaction. It may, that is, be possible to effect universal "suspension" (the *epochē*), but not universal negation.[132]

Or is "suspension" what we need here? Certainly it is not, if the word imports a cessation of doxastic activity. The Husserlian *epochē* is not the blockage, but the revelation, of world-belief, "the first authentic *discovery of the belief in the world*: the discovery of the world as a *transcendental dogma*."[133] Suspension, in the unwanted sense of cessation, would profoundly modify the economy, bringing about an aberrant disruption, not normal functioning, to the reflective spectator.

Moreover, what Levin contends with regard to our ineluctable believing-in-the-world may prove more generally valid:

> If one regards doubt, strictly speaking, as either a stage in or the outcome of a reflective, thematic posture . . . then one should say that this simple, lived belief in the existence of the world is prior to doubt, and in that unique sense, absolutely certain, that is, neither dubitable nor indubitable.[134]

Belief is a denizen of reflection. Prereflective naïveté simply takes the world "for granted" (*simpliciter*, as instanced by the general positing, or in some modalized manner of "grantedness"). We act. And we enjoy a certain prethematic trust that the world will support our endeavors.[135] "Grantedness" is a quality of naïveté and is thus impervious to both doubt and belief. "Grantedness" must be thematized, and thus phenomenally altered, to function, for reflection, as "belief." And only *as belief* does it play a role in the Peircean economy. Thus, Merleau-Ponty can say that "doubt is a clandestine positivism" (VI, 120). Doubt belongs inextricably to the "positivity" of reflection. As a "positive" phenomenon, it *excludes* and is *excluded by* belief. Yet both the dubitable and the indubitable have their roots in the rich dark "negativity," the "absolute certainty," of prereflective grantedness.

Though, on occasions which do not celebrate the nuance, Husserl may use the terms *epochē* and "reduction" interchangeably,[136] there is, as Zaner clarifies, a significant difference between them:

> This deliberate, explicitly adopted philosophical shift of attention . . . is what is to be understood as the '*epoche*'; the resultant 'orientation' or 'attitude'—that self-consciously maintained resolve to reflect radically on whatever presents itself—is the 'reduction'.[137]

The *epochē* opens the door, allowing us to enter; the reduction examines the furniture and wall hangings once we have stepped inside. The *epochē* is "*getting* there"; the reduction is "*being* there." The *epochē* is the "path"; the reduction is the "destination."[138] The *epochē* finds its home among Shen-hsiu's praxiological commitments; the reduction is more comfortably settled in the vicinity of Hui-neng's penetrating (anti-)ontological insight. The *epochē* is, in certain dimensions of comparability, the Husserlian counterpart of "tranquility" cultivation *(samatha bhāvanā)*; and the reduction, of the cultivation of insight *(vipassanā bhāvanā)*.

What segregates the "Cartesian reduction," the method of "hyperbolic" doubt, from the Husserlian is, as Sokolowski makes plain, the extrinsity of its methodological worth. In the Cartesian method of systematic doubt:

> The attempt to doubt is naturally performed in order to change the modality of our belief in a certain object or to reconfirm with new reasons, what we already believe. . . .
>
> The disconnection from a convinced life effected in the attempt to doubt is carried out in order to return to the same life with better conviction. . . .[139]

The phenomenological reduction is unmoved by the prospect of reimmersion in the currents of "natural" concern, a reentry marked only by the possession of a fund of "better," less vulnerable, beliefs. The reduction is radically "impractical," representing, as Fink says of the *epochē*, "not a 'royal path,' but the most extreme striving for a theoretical self-surmounting of man."[140] It is not simply that the reduction is its own presupposition, the very "space" of possibility which it occupies, the very "form" for its own "subject-matter."[141] It embraces not only its own formal, but also its own final, *aitia*. Like the Self-Thinking Thought of Aristotle's theology, the reduction, in its elucidation of transcendental subjectivity, brings to noetic light its own ground and its own end, a ground and an end which are not merely inseparable from the reduction, but profoundly at one with it.[142]

Reflections on Reflection

Yet, in Husserl's view, there would seem to yawn a fatefully unbridgeable abyss between reflection and its thematic subject, prereflective consciousness. Duméry voices an Husserlian position in his insistence that

> philosophy always comes after life. Philosophy is a recovery of life, but it cannot be identified with life. . . . There exist . . . two planes that must never be confounded: the *speculative plane* and the *concrete plane*. They are distinct yet interdependent. Reflection lives on concrete life. For its part, the concrete would never become "reason" and system without a technically reflected ordering.[143]

In the performance of the "Great Doubt" to which we will soon advert, *telos* and *teleology*, destination and path, embrace:[144] equipoise, mirrorlikeness, is accomplished for its own sake. The end of Buddhist phenomenology must not, however, be confounded with a finished conceptual edifice (the science, perhaps, of which Husserl dreamed). Nor is *beginning* to be identified with the *thought* of the beginning furnishing the theoretical estate.[145] Merleau-Ponty stoutly repudiates the claim, urged by philosophers of reflection, that "the universe of thought that is opened up by reflection contains everything necessary to account for the mutilated thought of the beginning, which is only the ladder one pulls up after oneself after having climbed it. . . ." (VI, 35). The methodological ascension to the uncommunicating heavens of phenomenality is imperiled by a pernicious amnesia. The rich and tolerant earth, the "wild" earth, matrix of "savage" being, bearing the impress of each faltering step, the earth of prereflective experience, which offers support to our methodological ladder is now tossed, like an orange peel robbed of its inner succulence, into the deep and uncomprehending waters of Lethe, forgotten in favor of its vapid successor: the *thought* of the earth. The ladder, rooted fast in the dark, rich humus of earthly antepredicative experience, will not be taken up.[146] The paradise of separated phenomenality, giving the lie to a reflection which would betray its source, now whirls in its virtigous self-pursuit[147] until, should this ever occur, the experiential wellspring (not its eidetic *Ersatz*) is rediscovered.

> With one stroke the philosophy of reflection metamorphoses the effective world into a transcendental field; in doing so it only puts me back at the origin of a spectacle that I could never have had unless, unbeknown to myself, I organized it. (VI, 44)

Naïveté is, however, misplaced. It is not to be found in a failure to recognize that "I organized it." Reflection, if it pretends disclosure of ingenuous life through idealization, falls itself, not into the regenerate innocence of "natural" experiencing, but into an untoward naïveté that, far from childlike, is fatefully ignorant, unapprised of the Sisyphusean fate which awaits it.

> The whole reflective analysis is not false, but still naïve, as long as it dissimulates from itself its own mainspring and as long as, in order to constitute the world, it is necessary to have a notion of the world as preconstituted—as long as the procedure is in principle delayed behind itself. (VI, 34)

The philosophy of reflection "thinks it can comprehend our natal bond with the world only by *undoing* it in order to *remake* it, only by constituting it, by fabricating it" (VI, 32). Yet the radiant lotus, exfoliating in the sun's good cheer, would not forget its rootedness in the mud.[148] This spells, of course, the impossibility of a "complete" reduction. But it also comports the possibility, and, we might add, the last and only hope, of a genuine reflection. If origin and its reflective suitor are loosed to prowl endlessly about one another, one will, in the end, be unable to tell them apart.[149]

Yet, though dualism seems our only recourse, the dualism of reflecting and "reflected" consorts no more intimately with Buddhist insights than with Sartre's own portrayal of consciousness as "all lightness, all translucence" (TE, 42). I am indebted to Phyllis Morris for drawing my attention to the Larousse definition of Sartre's operative term, translucence *(translucidité):* the translucid "permits the passage of light, yet without permitting objects to be seen clearly through its thickness: frosted glass is translucent."[150] "Translucence" is afflicted with the same ambiguity in French as it suffers in English, signifying either the utter transparency of crystal or the semiopacity of "frosted glass." There is much in Sartre, especially in the early writings, to suggest not only an insensitivity to the equivocation, but also, and tellingly, a commitment to the transparency (as opposed to the muddied translucence) of consciousness. And it is *this* side of Sartre which clashes with reflective duality. For if consciousness is genuinely and thoroughly transparent, then to look *at* consciousness is exactly to look *through* it. No more would be seen in reflection than is apparent in prereflective experience.[151] There would be no phenomenal basis for the discrimination. Thus, the theory of reflection would fall into the hands of a metaphysic entirely at variance with the strictures of phenomenological loyalty to experience precisely as it is given.

Reflection can be saved only by invoking the very different translucidity which imbues Hart's description of the Husserlian *Bewußt/sein*:

> But this absolute, diaphanous medium is an ongoing achievement with lights and shadows, delineations and obscurities; it can appear as a comprehensive, homogeneous atmosphere only when one abstracts from its essential contours of temporality and contrast. The medium is

> diaphanous only in the sense that its unity and continuity of continua are already achieved; but the contingency and facticity of this achievement insert at the heart of this luminosity something like blind spots and cracks that, however, de facto are incessantly healed.[152]

Everything shifts into question, however, in view of Merleau-Ponty's searching criticism:

> [W]e come to think that to reflect on perception is, *the perceived thing and the perception remaining what they were*, to disclose the true subject that inhabits and has always inhabited them. But in fact I should say that there was there a thing perceived and an openness upon this thing which the reflection has neutralized and transformed into perception-reflected-on and thing-perceived-within-a-perception-reflected-on. (VI, 38)

Reflection dramatically alters the phenomenal character of the thing perceived, transforming it into a thing-perceived-within-a-perception-reflected-on, and transforming "openness" into "perception-reflected-on," all the while assuming that the products of transformation were *there from the beginning* and come to light as they genuinely are only at the end. In effect, reflection creates both thing-perceived-within-a-perception-reflected-on and perception-reflected-on, while self-deceptively assuming their discovery.

In thus repulsing its detractions, we have not, to be sure, thereby vindicated reflection. Reflection—even Merleau-Ponty's self-correcting "hyper-reflection"—rests upon translucency. And the undecidability thesis will not permit the decisive predication of translucency. Haunted by Vaihinger, we must affirm, once again, in the mode of the *als ob*, that if it is exactly *as if* consciousness were translucent, it is also exactly *as if* consciousness were transparent. Thus, it is quite possible for the phenomenal to be configured exactly *as if* reflection were occurring. And it follows, inexorably and strikingly, that, *pace* Sartre, consciousness is by no means subject to "the absolute law of consciousness for which no distinction is possible between appearance and being" (TE, 63). Undecidability, as we recognize, drives an ineluctable wedge between the *appearance* and the *being* of consciousness, rupturing the putative self-contained immanence of consciousness.

But let us take stock. To assume, in conformity with Sartre's early proclivities, that consciousness is utterly transparent is to nullify the very possibility of reflection. And to assume, with Husserl, that consciousness is translucent, is to incur the censure of self-deceptive creation which Merleau-Ponty heaped upon reflection. The only navigable course between our Scylla and our Charybdis—indeed, the only consistently phenomenological course, is to surpass both Sartre and Husserl by adopting a radical "loyalty" to experience *exactly as it is lived (yathā bhūtaṃ)*. And the Middle Way is, of course, the Buddhist. Recall Tsung-mi's depiction of the mind as "a crystal ball with no colour of its own." Place the crystal against a dark surface. The "ignorant" conclude that "However pure it may have been before, it is now a dark-coloured ball, and this colour is seen as belonging from the first to the nature of the ball." This, of course, is exactly the charge which Merleau-Ponty levels against reflection. Yet, in faithfulness to *die Sache selbst*, it is no less ignorant to conclude, as did Sartre, that the ball is crystal clear. For, in light of our guiding insight, genuine transparency to color is phenomenally indistinguishable from colored translucency. Thus, to condemn reflection on the ground of the invisibility of prereflective consciousness is rank infidelity to the phenomenal. And to condemn reflection with the allegation of a self-deceptive transition from original transparency to resultant translucence is to assume, with equal disloyalty, the phenomenological legitimacy of affixing the one attribution before, and the other attribution after, reflection. We can speak of the *object* of perception ("thing perceived") only upon a conceptual terrain informed by the Cartesian divide. And we can speak of a "perception-reflected-on" only if we have decided, in advance, that perceptual consciousness is, or can be, translucent.

For the present, I shall be content if reflection can be retired with the solemnity and ceremony befitting one of philosophy's noblest and ablest of benefactors, and more satisfied still if a suitable station can be prepared for the venerable heir of reflection, to which Buddhism contributes the name mindfulness or awareness *(sati)*.

While Merleau-Ponty's cumbersome "thing-perceived-within-a-perception-reflected-on" appears adversely to presuppose the phenomenal decidability of transparency and translucence (a perception-reflected-on *must* be translucent to be reflectively seen), the neater and more typically Husserlian formula for the *noēma*, the object exactly *as presented*, does not. The consummate usefulness and value of our "emeritus" notion of reflection can only be explained by appeal to that which, manifest within the object-*as*-perceived, is not granted by the object perceived. What, then, is contributed by the *as?*

The Eidetic Reduction

Champions of the separation of reality from conceptual scheme, matter from form, *Inhalt* from *Auffassung*, will urge that what is clearly *not* contributed by the phenomenological "as" is enriched sensory presence.[153] To effect the reflective transition from object perceived to object-*as*-perceived is by no means to enjoy an expanded fund of sensation.[154] In this, however, we might well be governed by Edward Kasner who, as we are told,

> had a way of teaching large numbers to children. He would ask them to guess the length of the eastern coast line of the United States. After a "sensible" guess had been made—say 2,000 miles—he would proceed step by step to point out that this figure increased enormously if you measured the perimeter of each bay and inlet, then that of every projection and curve of each of these, then the distance separating every small particle of coastline matter, each molecule, atom, etc. Obviously the coastline is as long as you want to make it.[155]

While form delimits matter, as the coast delimits the continent, we have discovered, in the Zenonian proclivities of Buddhist thought, a similar suggestion of the instability of form. Matter does not *have* an invariant form, but every progressively more intimate vantage point we assume offers its own form. Form is horizonal, an ineluctable feature, not of the *viewed*, but of the *viewing*. And our horizons, like our coastline, expand, the presentational matter surging to the eye, the upsurge of an inexhaustible spring. It is not that we do, or even could, hold all the sensory spray in view as we throw ourselves headlong into the bottomless fountaining. But the very boundlessness of sensory enrichment argues conflation of the ossified divarication of "scheme" and "content." There is no given length which, rigidly and finally, measures our coastline. And there is no scheme, no system of concepts, no view, which seizes reality in its proflux.[156] Merleau-Ponty, hospitable to our present insistence, frames a congruent vision, noting, of the manifold profiles through which the *res* is disclosed, that

> the reality is their common inner framework *(membrure)*, their nucleus, and not something *behind them*: behind them, there are only other "views" still conceived according to the in itself-projection schema. The real is *between them*, this side of them. (VI, 226)[157]

Reality *(realitas)* is not accessible to view. It cannot be suspended from a conceptual platform, enframed by a theoretical scheme. It lies always between such in-formings. The common inner framework of views is recognizably the space of which Sartre speaks:

> [T]he continuous background suddenly when apprehended as figure bursts into a multiplicity of discontinuous elements. Thus the world . . . appears as an evanescent totality. . . . Space cannot be *a being*. . . . Space is not the world, but it is the instability of the world apprehended as totality, inasmuch as the world can always disintegrate into external multiplicity. Space is . . . the ideality of the ground inasmuch as it can always disintegrate into figures; it is . . . the permanent passage from continuous to discontinuous. (BN, 254)

It is, then, with some care that we repeat our denial. We must repudiate the indifference of the *as* to its content. But we must do so with a vital caution. The formalist is assuredly correct in urging that our fund of presence is not enriched through eidetic articulation. But we accept this for reasons uncongenial to formalist proclivities.[158] The fund, to begin with, is boundless, and cannot be delimited by any form. Hence, there is no question of "enrichment." Nor, second, is there any question of fattening our coffers. For the fund, as we have called it, will not submit to conceptual seizure. Though given, it cannot be taken.[159]

Nor, through reflective disclosure, is our perception rendered clearer, more distinct, more adequate, or more intense.[160] Reflection purports to disclose the perceptual object exactly as perceived.[161] The indistinctness of original perception would be violated were reflection to transubstantiate mud into beryl. Nor, again, does reflection give us a new object to inspect. The object-as-perceived is not a *second* object additional to the original object perceived. Once more, what is contributed by the *as*?

The object-*as*-perceived is *exactly* the object perceived. Yet, in virtue of a certain procedure of abstraction—a drawing *(trahere)* away from *(ab-)*, or separation—certain of its qualitative features are taken up, isolated, for independent examination.[162] What results is not unlike a certain body of text displayed on a computer monitor, a portion of which, or perhaps all of which, has been highlighted. The highlighting does not alter the text. Indeed, not a single character, not a single qualitative characteristic, has been inserted, deleted or moved.[163] Yet the text (as thus displayed) has been subtly transformed. And the transformation is one of abstractive emphasis. The object-as-perceived is the object as highlighted. To the extent that the object's features receive notice, they rise to the fore. Those unnoticed fall to the ground. Thus, the *as* contributes no less than a *Gestaltung*, a figuration which submerges the unnoticed in the external horizon of the noticed. Where once the object itself figured as figure, it has now become the ground of its qualitative isolates.

Qualitative features thus highlighted, thus abstractively drawn from the object for thematic consideration, have, through thematization, shed their insistent facticity, and, inasmuch as such qualities are examined in themselves, take on the formality of the ideal, "the [very] possibility of the fact."[164] We are on the verge of the "eidetic reduction."[165] But we must first see that what is *not* selected for abstractive thematization is *de*/selected, that what is not idealized is *de*/idealized. And we must see that de/idealization is itself a form of idealization.[166] It is not that abstractive thematization simply releases its hold over the nonthematic. The decision *for* one feature is a decision *against* others—others which *could* have been thematized instead. Thus, the de/selected, de/thematized, de/idealized qualities relegated to the ground are themselves seen as *possibilities* for thematization.[167] And thus, background qualities are themselves, in a curious negative sense, seen to be ideal. Neg-idealities and ideal positivities are both idealities. But this being so, the contribution of the *as* exceeds by far the mere provision of a handful of highlighted qualities. The *as* transforms the entire field, figure and ground alike. With the *as,* all becomes ideal. With the *as* we have entered upon the eidetic reduction. Writes Gurwitsch:

> By eidetic reduction, the real existent is divested of its actuality, of its existential character. . . . Every real existent can be regarded as an actualized possibility. Under the eidetic reduction, the fact of its actualization is considered as immaterial, and hence, is disregarded. What is encountered as a matter of fact, is "irrealized"; i.e., considered as to its imaginableness and not as to its actuality, it is transformed into a "pure possibility" among other possibilities. From the status of a real existent, it is transferred to that of an example or exemplar. . . . [168]

The real blessing of our hoary mythology of reflection is its anticipation, indeed, its Mosaic indication of the promised realm of "pure possibility."[169] Like Moses, reflection only leads, and, at the threshold, can only point.[170] We must, finally, enter in without our guide. What reflection portends must be accomplished without reflection. And, indeed, the profoundly transformative conversion to possibility brought about by the eidetic reduction owes nothing, for its accomplishment, though much for its prophesy, to reflection.

We have heard the Buddha's words, as recorded in The Foundations of Mindfulness Sutra *(Satipaṭṭhāna-sutta)*, instructing his disciples to dwell

> contemplating the body in the body *[kāye kāyānupassī]* . . . contemplating the sensations in the sensations *[vedanāsu vedanānupassī]* . . . , the mind in the mind *[citte cittānupassī]* . . . , mental objects in mental objects *[dhammesu dhammānupassī],* ardent, clearly comprehending and mindful, having overcome covetousness and grief concerning the world. (TI, 76; my interpolations)

For the present, what seems here of particular import are the curious iterations mediated by the preposition *in,* grammatically suggested, but not explicitly present in the Pali. The eidetic reduction enables to us to reclaim the body *as body*, the sensations *as sensations*, mind *as mind*, and mental objects *as mental objects*. The "as such" elucidates the subsumption of body and its sensations, mind and its objects, under their respective *eidē*, thus rendering the elements of experience merely illustrative. Mind *qua* mind becomes a "pure possibility." And "the fact of its actualization is considered as immaterial."[171] And Merleau-Ponty, in his early captivation with Husserlian phenomenology, registers the urgency of the "reduction" to possibility.

> [O]ur existence is too tightly held in the world to be able to know itself as such at the moment of involvement, and that it requires the field of ideality in order to become acquainted with and to prevail over its facticity. (PhP, xiv–xv)

Mind *in* mind *(citte cittānupassī)* does not, however, comport subsumption. Yet, though the intuition of mind *in* mind appreciates the suchness *(tathatā)* of mind without degrading its actuality to mere exemplary status, the form of mind is not thereby sacrificed. For the mind-form is to be found precisely *in* mind. Phenomenology neither requires nor can it justify the two-tiered Platonic ontology of timeless *eidē* and their mutable and contingently exemplified illustrations.[172] Phenomenology, as Merleau-Ponty observes, "puts essences back into existence" (PhP, vii). And Sartre, conflating formality and its material exemplification, is in solid accord:

> [T]he concrete "flesh and blood" existence must *be* the essence, and the essence must itself be produced as a total concretion; that is, it must have the full richness of the concrete without however allowing us to discover in it anything other than itself in its total purity. Or, if you prefer, the form must be to itself—and totally—its own matter. And conversely the matter must be produced as absolute form. (BN, 267–68)

Yet Merleau-Ponty would not, at least not without qualification, simply identify *eidos* and instance:

> As the nervure bears the leaf from within, from the depths of its flesh, the ideas are the texture of experience, its style, first mute, then uttered. Like every style, they are elaborated within the thickness of being and . . . could not be detached from it, to be spread out on display under the gaze. (VI, 119)

There is no question of detachment. Dialect is inseparable from phonic production. Artistic style is inseparable from the assemblage of forms and pigments covering the canvas.[173] Current is inseparable from the water of the stream. And, though the essential "style" of experience assuredly can be highlighted, it cannot be abstractively isolated, uprooted from the vital tissue of conscious life.[174]

Hyper-Reflection

It may be, in part, the undecidability of reflection which motivates Merleau-Ponty's report that

> we are catching sight of the necessity of another operation besides conversion to reflection, more fundamental than it, of a sort of *hyper-reflection (sur-réflexion)* that would also take itself and the changes it introduces into the spectacle into account. (VI, 38)

Such a hyper-reflection would

> plunge into the world instead of surveying it, it [would] descend toward it such as it is instead of working its way back up toward a prior possibility of thinking it—which would impose upon the world in advance the conditions for our control over it. (VI, 38–39)

Several years ago, at a Buddhist meditation retreat, I had occasion to converse with a Vietnamese Zen monk known for his assiduous work on behalf of world peace, the Venerable Thích Nhất Hạnh. I had been troubled at that time by what I then saw as a conflict of two loves, philosophy and meditation (how, after all, could I both think and not-think?), and submitted the issue for resolution. The answer I was given was hyper-reflective in a recognizable sense. We have spoken of the "openness" of thought. Thích Nhất Hạnh spoke of its penetration. Let the mind seep into things, I was advised, like water seeping into parched ground or like sunshine absorbed by a leaf. This, truly, is meditative thinking. And in meditative thinking, thought and meditation embrace.

We have already begun to suspect the doctrine of synthesis, the unwarranted persuasion that, prior to serving up its steaming dish of transcendence,[175] the mind dashes together *(syn-)* certain ingredients of immanence which, in reflection, could become thetic.[176] The dish is nothing without its ingredients. And vigilance has apprised us of the intrusion of theory into our stock of immanence. The unity disclosed through the conscious descent into the world and its objects "is not a *synthesis*; it is a metamorphosis by which the appearances are instantaneously stripped of a value they owed merely to the absence of a true perception" (VI, 8). Appearances, to be sure, are articulated from the matrix of primordial experience. Yet the unity of experienced objectivity is a unity given, not, for ingenuous perception, the product of constitutive *poiēsis*.[177] There is analysis with no need for prior synthesis. In reflection, we witness the process of loosening *(lysis)*, arrogating to ourselves the credit for an original tightening. Synthesis however, is always, and necessarily, presented *post facto*: an account, an afterthought.[178] A world brought about through synthesis would bespeak the "missing God" of Sartre's hypothetical theology:

> Everything happens as if the world, man, and man-in-the-world succeeded in realizing only a missing God. Everything happens therefore as if the in-itself and the for-itself were presented in a state of disintegration in relation to an ideal synthesis. Not that the integration has

> ever *taken place* but on the contrary precisely because it is always indicated and always impossible. (BN, 792)[179]

Consciousness, though incapable of constitutive "integration," nonetheless plunges headlong into the abyssal "integrity" of its object.[180] And in the hyperreflective descent, in its absorption and penetration, the disintegration of the object appears as the spray of an inexhaustible fount.

The Great Doubt

The Buddhist meditative tradition has its own *epochē*, more radical by far, because of its holistic transformation of experience, than the Husserlian, a movement of withholding, or *holding* (Greek: *echein*) *in* (or "upon": *epi-*), titled the Great Doubt. We are admonished to

> Doubt deeply in a state of single-mindedness, looking neither before nor after, right nor left, becoming wholly like a dead man and becoming unaware even of your own person being there. When this method is practiced more and more deeply, you will come to a state of being totally absent-minded and vacant. Even then, you must raise up the Great Doubt . . . and must doubt further, being all the time like a dead man. And after that, when you are aware no more of your being wholly like a dead man, are no more conscious of your procedure of "Great Doubting" and become, yourself, through and through a Great Doubt-mass, there will come all of a sudden a moment when you come out into a transcendence called the Great Enlightenment, as if you woke up from a great dream, or as if you, being completely dead, suddenly revived.[181]

The Buddhist *epochē* oversteps at a single bound both the Peircean stricture against universalization and the Husserlian modification which would transmute doubt into simple dis/covery. The Great Doubt is not a "clandestine positivism." Indeed, what is missing in both the Peircean and Husserlian doxastic modalizations is any sense of the inner dialectic of ambiguity which doubt imports. Peirce's conception of doubt is clearly "positivistic" inasmuch as it trades on the mutual exclusion of doubt and belief. The Husserlian *epochē* is positivistic, of course in a different sense, inasmuch as world-belief is brought to light *as such*, in its positivity, without modification. Yet, *pace* Peirce, doubt signifies more than inclination toward the negative; and *pace* Husserl, it signifies more than revelatory suspension. Doubt is, in its oldest sense, a wavering, a vacillation, a hesitation before the abyss of doxastic commitment. If doubt, in this archaic sense, is possible at all, it must concomitantly be possible to find ourselves poised on the brink, entirely capable of making the leap and entirely capable of refraining. What Kierkegaard says of dread might equally be said of the doxastic equipoise that withdraws from both the security of the cliffs and the danger of the abyss:

> Thus dread is the dizziness of freedom which occurs when the spirit would posit the synthesis, and freedom then gazes down into its own possibility, grasping at finiteness to sustain itself. In this dizziness freedom succumbs. . . . That very instant everything is changed, and when freedom rises again it sees that it is guilty. Between these two instants lies the leap. . . . [182]

To act is to "fall," to be "fallen" (thus: guilty), to plunge from the secure serenity of universality into the fray of particularity (thus: partiality). And to believe (or positively to disbelieve) is likewise to fall from the Great Doubt. The Great Doubt is the deeply transformative moment of sus/pension, thus, pensiveness (from the Latin *pensare:* "to weigh"; hence, "to measure") between affirmation and denial, the Middle Way, the way of doxastic equipoise, the achievement of poise (Old French: *pois*), establishing a counterweight (Latin: *pensum*) to the gravity of doxastic enticement. The Great Doubt is no friend of negation.[183] It rises, in Hui-neng's words, "above existence and non-existence" (PS/pw, 27). Thus, Peirce need have no fear that the economy of belief will be disrupted by the very irrationality of its concept. But neither is the Great Doubt allied with the epochetic affirmation that would simply allow the economy to pursue its own transactional course. The Great Doubt effects neither upheaval nor disclosure. It "freezes" the economy.

To be sure, narcosis is no prelude to enlightenment. But the Great Doubt, by which we become "like the dead," enlivens and intensifies awareness precisely by disengaging activity (somatic and intentional, or the two inextricably) from the very presuppositions that would support it. The seemingly innocent act of extending one's hand to pick up a cup of coffee is upheld by a thousand tacit assumptions, assumptions which come to light most perspicuously in our counterfactual musings. Suppose, for example, that we quite sincerely believe the arm that we now so casually and easily extend to be amputated or paralyzed. The belief would wither the attempt to lay hands on the steaming mug. Or again, suppose that some psychopathology led us to believe that the gods, offended by the deep pleasure which we take in our morning brew, had decreed all further cups of coffee to be illusory or tainted with a deadly poison. Certainly, we would comport ourselves toward the cup in a very different way, perhaps, in the one case, attempting to pass our hand through it instead of grasping it by the handle, or in the other, avoiding the deceitful brew with horror. I would not presume to unfurl a systematic treatment of the relationship between belief and action. Nor is that required. But I would commend the insight, more searching than at first appears, that action is neutralized by the belief that action is impossible. Were this belief to spread through every corner of the doxastic web, we would, indeed, become as one who is dead.

The point, as thus couched, is perhaps Peircean. Not only does universal negation point the way to theoretical perdition, but also, from the standpoint of praxis, a certain cryogenic suspension of animation is brought about. In a formula at once suggestive and insufficiently nuanced, doubt paralyzes action. For, as Bataille suggests, "inner experience is the opposite of action. Nothing more" (IE, 46). A certain deathlike cessation of performance grows in soil which, though logically poorer, is nonetheless rich in transformative potential, the soil of hesitation, doxastic equipoise. One need not cast supporting praxiological possibilities into *disbelief*. Contravening Husserl, one need only *cease to believe* in order to effect cryogenesis.

Yet we are admonished to "doubt further," and ever further. An action, or rather a *purposive* action, can be regarded as a means to an end. We jog *in order to* stay fit, read *in order to* be better informed, and, in our precaffeinated stupor, take up our morning coffee *in order to* prop open the heavy-shuttered windows of the soul. Hesitation before the very possibility of such mediate action effects paralysis. But we are admonished not only to absent ourselves from the mediate motility of our bodies, but also to "come to a state of being totally absent-minded and vacant." And here, again, we are instructed at the knees of mediation. Familiar though our coffee mug might be, we have not, and indeed, cannot enjoy its presence as given simultaneously through the infinite array of its possible presentational profiles. The object, in Husserlian parlance, is an identity sewn through a potentially endless and boundlessly rich fabric of "modes of givenness." We recur, again and again, to the "sameness" skewering manifold difference out of an investment of interest, thematic or pre-thematic. The object *interests* us. We therefore *value* it. And we therefore return to it. Its differentiated manners of presentation "matter" to us exactly because the object itself "makes a difference" to us.[184] For Husserl, seizure of the object under its sundry profiles is our way, our *only* way, of *appropriating* it, making it properly our own, "grasping" it.[185] Thus, difference becomes a means employed in the service of apprehension. And the concomitant utilization of the differentiated profile in this service, the enactment of (active) synthesis, becomes no less vulnerable to paralysis than its overt praxiological cousin. The mere hesitation before the possibility of active synthesis is sufficient to halt the active-synthetic process, thus, in the most intimate way, bringing about the absent-mindedness of the Great Doubt.

The lovely autochthonous flower of Taoism, exfoliating in deep insight, and flourishing in the rich soil of the Chinese philosophical tradition, pollinates freely with the Buddhism which, by a tradition perhaps more venerable than accurate, was transplanted to China by Bodhidharma. The history of cross-fertilization cannot concern us here, though the *Tao* is quite at home in Chinese Buddhist documents. *Wu wei* might, however, give us brief pause. Despite its literal configuration, the term no more suggests inaction than the exhortation to deathlikeness invites the enactment of suicide. *Wu wei*, far from a simple failure of motility, imports an enlivening atelic spontaneity of action. The interresonance of *wu wei* and the Great Doubt is sonorous and compelling. The equipoise of the Buddhist *epochē* short-circuits the disingenuousness of mediate activity, clearing the ground for the liberating upsurge of spontaneous immediacy.

In the project "to emerge through project from the realm of project" (IE, 46), the fundamental project is, and must be recognized to be, no-project. The atelicity of spontaneous action, though signifying a certain playfulness, no more comports a bacchanalian anti/nomianism, the setting of itself *against* established normative principles, than the simple suicide of overt behavior. *Wu wei* is brought to evidence no less in purposeful, deliberative action than in lawless revelry, and the deeper significance of the Way is not the abandonment of oneself to the vagaries of natural impulse, like driftwood borne by an unpredictable tide, but rather the recognition of spontaneity, however manifest—the celebration of spontaneity at the root of even the most rigid, autonomic, mechanical and purpose-bound forms of human action.

Eidetic metanoesis further illuminates the Great Doubt. The Buddhist *epochē* purges facticity, leaving no positive commitment, no praxiological suppositions, not even the "general positing" of the world, to grasp. We find ourselves utterly without doxastic support. In Hakuin's harrowing portrayal:

> What does it mean to release one's hold over the abyss? A man went astray and arrived at a spot which had never been trodden by the foot of man. Before him there yawned a bottomless chasm. His feet stood on the slippery moss of a rock and no secure foothold appeared around him. He could step neither forward or backward. Only death awaited him. The vine which he grasped with his left hand and the tendril which he held with his right hand could offer him little help. . . . Were he to release both hands at once, his dry bones would come to nought.
>
> . . . All thoughts vanish and in his bosom burns hot anxiety. . . . both body and mind break. This is the instant when the hands are released over the abyss. . . . This is termed seeing into one's own nature.[186]

Surely, no more "gripping" portrayal of the eidetic reduction has ever appeared. Accustomed, as we have been since Plato, to consign detachment from the factical to the dispassionate rationality of the philosophical mind, it may prove salutary to feel the "hot anxiety" of those who, in an existentially authentic sense, have released both hands over the abyss of pure possibility. All of our projects, all of our hopes, our very motility, are pinned to facticity. The releasement of all of our commitments is the precipitation of certain death, the death of egocentric telicity, the death of grasping life.

Yet, as Merleau-Ponty avers, "fundamental thought," thought open to reality, thought which renounces prehension, "is bottomless. It is, if you wish, an abyss."[187] The abyss of possibility is groundless—utterly. There is no question of violent impactment upon the stony facticity below. The leap finds one in endless "free fall." Indeed, the abyss of possibility *is* freedom. Heidegger writes:

> Reason *[Grund]* has its unreason *[Un-wesen]*, because it arises from infinite freedom; the latter cannot rid itself of what arises from it. Reasons, which have their origin in transcendence fall back on freedom, which, *as origin*, itself becomes a "reason." *Freedom is the reason for reasons*. . . . As *this* kind of reason *[Grund]*, however, freedom is the "abyss" of Dasein. . . . [188]

In releasement, detachment from the self-imposed bondage of the fist, we do, indeed, die to a life of servitude, a life mastered by the ends we serve. But we are "reborn" in midair. Again, Heidegger: "The meaning of Being can never be contrasted with entities, or with Being as the 'ground' which gives entities support; for a 'ground' becomes accessible only as meaning, even if it is itself the abyss of meaninglessness."[189] The boundless abyss of pure possibility, the vast "emptiness" *(śūnyatā)*[190] the realization of which brings final surcease of sorrow, final liberation *(mokṣa)* from the cares of *saṁsāra*, is not a "ground." It will not bear the ponderous weight of the factical world. It is neither the founding epistemic bedrock of foundationalist epistemology nor the deific *causa sui* of "onto-theo-logic." Ideality is not the platform of the factical, but its very possibility. Nothing, neither knowledge nor being, stands upon it.[191] But everything "floats" within it. Everything remains perpetually in free fall within it. And we have Merleau-Ponty's observation that

> The progress of the inquiry toward the *center* is not the movement from the conditioned unto the condition, from the founded unto the *Grund*: the so-called *Grund* is *Abgrund*. But the abyss one thus discovers is not such by *lack of ground*, it is upsurge of a *Hoheit* which supports from above . . . that is, of a negativity that *comes to the world*. (VI, 250)

The magisterial sublimity *(Hoheit)* which upholds from on high is not, as it might first appear, the grace of some pitying deity loathe to witness the lemming-like leap of suffering humanity beyond the verge of insufferable facticity only to be cruelly shattered by concussion upon some putative *fundamentum inconcussum*. Rather, the exalted majesty of which Merleau-Ponty speaks is precisely the bottomlessness of the abyss, precisely the Boundless *(apeiron)* which renders "fundamental concussion" unthinkable.

The Transformative Phenomenology of Liberation

The ingenuous spontaneity and atelicity of a Buddhist phenomenology would not "impose upon the world in advance the conditions for our control over it." Though "transcendental" in its articulation of the "Absolute Truth" of relativity, Buddhism renounces a certain Kantian transcendentalism which would dredge "Absolute Truth" from the bog of subjectivity. The conditions for experience, and for our praxiological manipulation of it, are not, *pace* Kant and *pace* Husserl, embedded in transcendental "subjectivity," for this would import the very subject-object dualism which Buddhism insistently rejects. Yet possibilitation *by subjectivity* is not the only available sense of the transcendental. Buddhist phenomenology remains transcendental in its lotuslike ability to remain rooted in the murky bed of prediscriminate ("antepredicative") experience while rising resplendently to the light, thus gaining lucid vantage upon the suffering world *(saṁsāra)*[192] itself.[193]

A Husserlian echo is returned by Schmitt's admission that "The world before the transcendental-phenomenological reduction and the world which I have transformed into 'mere phenomena' do not differ in content, but in the way in which I am related to each of them."[194] In the familiar Mahāyāna formula, *nirvāṇa* is not different from *saṁsāra*.[195] Yet were the formula naïvely to be read as strict identity, *nirvāṇa* could not entail releasement from suffering.[196] It may be well, then, in alignment with Wagner's observation, to regard *nirvāṇa* as "*saṁsāra* in quotes":[197] "I perform the *epochē* in order to distinguish between world and 'world', and with this I introduce the reduction. . . . The *terminus a quo* of the reduction is the 'world', its *terminus ad quem* is the achieving ground for this world."[198] The samsaric "text" remains, with its suffering, its dissatisfaction *(duḥkha)*. Yet the unconditional bracketing, the ideological equipoise that neutralizes (or better: balances) doxastic gravitation, makes all the liberatory difference.

Kohák's musings over the term *epochē* advance our own:

> Literally, the word means "switching off,' as when we switch off an electric lamp. The lamp is still there, but now as one of the objects in the room, not as that which illuminates everything else. This is what the phenomenologist does when he 'switches off the world' or, more precisely, the common-sense assumption that the world explains experience. The world, like the lamp, is still there, but no longer as that which makes experience 'visible' (here, intelligible).[199]

One cannot remain insensitive to the deep tremors of association with which *epochē*, in Kohák's serviceable metaphor, and *nirvāṇa* reverberate. *Nirvāṇa* is, in its root sense, the privation *(nir-)* of blowing *(-vāṇa)*, the winds of craving quelled, or, as often, if somewhat misleadingly, suggested, a blowing out.[200]

"Switching off" will do. More, perhaps, than a simple quotation of the world, *nirvāṇa* is depicted as its discontinuance. "The 'world' being a positive datum of experience, and mankind having on the whole no knowledge of anything beyond the world, Nirvāṇa had necessarily to be described to them in terms of the cessation of the world. . . ."[201] *Nirvāṇa* is, if you like, a reversal of polarity. Where once the mind was fetched with the world, like a giddy moth taken with its flame, now the world has gone out, no longer a fatal attraction. But the enlightened mind does not find itself abandoned to the dark. It rather finds "itself" as the very light of the world.[202]

Nirvāṇa, the "other shore" toward which the dharmic raft, wave-tossed but seaworthy, makes its relentless way, is the final ground of distinction, though itself beyond distinction. "There is, O monks, an unborn, not become, not made, uncompounded, and were it not, monks, for this unborn, not become, not made, uncompounded, no escape could be shown here for what is born, has become, is made, is compounded" (TCB, 113). Yet, though the ground of samsaric genesis is "unborn," though the ground of "form" *(rūpa)*[203] is unformed, *nirvāṇa*, though beyond the pale of description by means of conceptual formalities and beyond specification by means of conceptual polarities,[204] seems no antagonist to certain of the more evocative functions of language.[205] Compiling from the Buddhist canon a budget of attributions, Conze itemizes:

> Nirvana is permanent, stable, imperishable, immovable, ageless, deathless, unborn, and unbecome, . . . it is power, bliss and happiness, the secure refuge, the shelter, and the place of unassailable safety; . . . it is the real Truth and the supreme Reality; . . . it is the Good, the supreme goal and the one and only consummation of our life, the eternal, hidden and incomprehensible Peace.[206]

The Husserlian *epochē*, by contrast, though it illuminates a realm of timeless eidetic truth, is nonetheless an *event*: impermanent and perishable. It is not "supreme Reality," but a methodical and temporalized preparation for the elucidation of certain formal structures of reality.

Thus, despite their evident resonance, *epochē* and *nirvāṇa* are not to be conflated. The *epochē* is, for Husserl, the beginning of a life of rational self-responsibility; whereas, *nirvāṇa* is, for the Buddhist tradition, the end of the spiritual quest.[207] Husserl portrayed himself as a "perpetual beginner." And Merleau-Ponty, no less devoted to disclosure of the *archē,* steps decisively beyond Husserlian subjectivism:

> The core of philosophy is no longer an autonomous transcendental subjectivity, to be found everywhere and nowhere: it lies in the perpetual beginning of reflection, at the point where an individual life begins to reflect on itself. (PhP, 62)

Seizing the pertinent contrast, it might be said that the Buddha was not at all reticent in announcing his attainment of the end: "In me emancipated arose knowledge of my emancipation. I realized that rebirth has been destroyed, the holy life has been lived, the job has been done, there is nothing after this."[208] The resonance of Husserlian beginning and Buddhist end linger beyond the verbal polarity. The end of phenomenology *is* the elucidation of its beginning. Yet in admitting this, we must admit its consequence:

> [I]f this is so, there is no longer any philosophy of reflection, for there is no longer the originating and the derived; there is a thought traveling a circle where the condition and the conditioned, the reflection and the unreflected, are in a reciprocal, if not symmetrical, relationship, and where the end is in the beginning as much as the beginning is in the end. (VI, 35)

Still, a deeper and more immediate homophony commands our attention. It would serve no present purpose to luxuriate in the many exquisite descriptions of the enlightenment experience. Nor, except where necessity compelled, have the practical details of Buddhist meditation claimed our attention. The literature, both serious and popular, on both subjects is a flood tide. Instead, the present work contributes, from a Buddhist vantage point, to the incipient dialogue of Buddhism with the luminaries of Occidental phenomenology. Buddhism has much to say under the heading of "phenomenological methodology." Its voice is both a well-heeded challenge and a great reservoir of supplemental considerations.

The "Buddhist *epochē*" is the threshold opening upon a new life, a new life risen from the crematory ashes of the Great Death. Here *telos* and teleology embrace. Product is process. The end of that doxastic equilibrium by which one is rendered "deathlike" is precisely the equilibrium itself. And we have seen that the "death" of mediate activity is the quickening of spontaneity. Enlivenment is rooted in "paralysis."

The Great Doubt does not reveal, but rather, in evident contrast with the Husserlian *epochē*, disrupts, those mediate activities of mind which owe their enactment to a doxology of the factical. Assuredly, however, disruption is not practiced for its own sake, but as a pathway toward the joyous fullness of life of which Hakuin speaks:

> If a person is confronted with the Great Doubt, then in the four directions of heaven there is only wide, empty land, without birth and without death, like a plane of ice ten thousand miles in expanse, as if one sat in an emerald vase. Without there is bright coolness and white purity. As if devoid of all sense one forgets to rise when he is sitting, and forgets to sit down when he is standing. In his heart there remains

> no trace of passion or concept, only the word "nothingness," as if he stood in the wide dome of heaven. He has neither fear nor knowledge. If one progresses in this fashion without retrogression, he will suddenly experience something similar to the breaking of an ice cover or the collapse of a crystal tower. The joy is so great that it has not been seen or heard for forty years.[209]

Disruption pacifies our telic inclinations, putting an end to the mediate activity which serves a *telos* beyond itself. Activity, somatic or intentional, which does not display its intrinsic worth in the very possibility of its performance comes to a halt. Absent-mindedness, however, though importing a radical liberation from active-synthetic unification, does not signify a lapse into utter unconsciousness. It is, after all, "as if one sat in an emerald vase."

The Buddhist *epochē* and the Husserlian, congruent in several important dimensions, are perhaps nowhere more strikingly conformal than in the theory *(theoria)* of their very possibility. As Fink says of the Husserlian reduction:

> In truth . . . it does not at all present a possibility for our *human* existence. The unfamiliarity of the reduction is therefore not only an unfamiliarity with it as a fact, but is also an unfamiliarity with its possibility. . . . The reduction becomes knowable in its *transcendental* motivation only with the transcending of the world. This means that the reduction is its own presupposition insofar as it alone opens up that dimension of problems with reference to which it establishes the possibility of theoretical knowledge.[210]

The Great Doubt "hesitates" at the threshold of mediate activity, casting in question every "possibility for our human existence."[211] Unenlightened human existence comprises the entire spectrum of disingenuity, in all of its nuances and intensities, the entire spectrum of "suffering" activity incapable of finding peace and contentment within itself, ceaselessly deferring value and fulfillment to an end beyond itself. The very possibility of atelic spontaneity, the very possibility of action performed solely *for its own sake*, is, indeed, unfamiliar.

The Buddhist *epochē* is transformative, not in the Husserlian sense in which "the phenomenological reduction first exposes a subjectivity which *already* accepts the world,"[212] but in its existential-metanoetic transmutation of the very possibility-form of mediate, disingenuous activity. The unsatisfied telicity of mediate action presents the possibility *first*, leaving for calculative deliberation the subsequent actualization or refusal of actualization. Spontaneous action, like the Husserlian *epochē*, is its own possibility. From the standpoint of the mediate, the possibility of every spontaneous action is "unfamiliar," fathomlessly mysterious.[213]

Enlivened spontaneity is exhibited in thought no less than in deed. As *wu wei* does not signify a privation of action, "no-thought" does not signify empty-headedness. "What is no-thought? The Dharma of no-thought means: even though you see all things, you do not attach to them. . . ." (PS/y, 153).[214] Thus, "No-thought is not to think even when involved in thought. Non-abiding is the original nature of man" (PS/y, 138).[215] Buddhism, so often deprecated as thoughtless irrationalism, is, on the contrary, an unwavering champion of rigorous and original thought. Yet Buddhism reenvisages the function of thought.[216] If thought-engagement has the result of riveting us more firmly and more possessively to its object, if we intend, through thinking, to "grasp" the matter at hand, if we presume, more fundamentally, that truth turns a handle to the mind's hand, then Buddhism must eschew this deleterious species of "thinking." "Attachment," for the Buddhist tradition, is predicated upon the illusion of substantiality, the mirage of an abiding substratum subtending change.[217] With shadows chased away by the luminous realization of non-abiding, enlightened thought, no-thought,[218] seeks not to grasp, to tighten the fist around the chestnut of reality, but opens naturally, palm upward, toward the light.

> [D]o not activate thoughts. If there were no thinking, then no-thought would have no place to exist. "No" is the "no" of what? "Thought" means "thinking" of what? "No" is the separation from the dualism that produces the passions. "Thought" means thinking the original nature of True Reality. True Reality is the substance of thoughts; thoughts are the function of True Reality. (PS/y, 139)

Reality is like a melody. There is no underlying "drone." Or if there is, it, too, is subject to the law of impermanence, changeable, if unchanged.[219] To think "the original nature of True Reality" is to open oneself to impermanence,[220] to the "between" which beckons us ever onward toward the manifestation of "other views." To "activate thoughts" is to incur the inevitable frustration of grasping at that which, in principle, cannot be grasped. This is because "Intrinsically our transcendental nature is void and not a single dharma (thing) can be attained" (PS/pw, 26).[221] Reality, like a butterfly, alights upon the outstretched palm. To close the hand is, if not to kill the lovely creature outright, at least to suffocate it, to inhibit its spontaneous movements, and thus to rob it of the very charms which inspired our desire to possess it.[222] Reality can no more be ensnared in our con/ceptual nets than wind can be confined in a cardboard box. Yet the breeze ever wafts through the vale. And the sun ever shines upon the open palm. A thought open to reality is thus a thought imbued with transformative gratitude. Reality gives itself desportively. Yet the shattering comedy of this "gift" is its very disruption of the logic of giving.[223] For the gift is always given, but can never be taken.[224] To take, to prehend, to lay hands on reality,[225] is to return for the gift, not gratitude, but violence.[226] There is no economy in reality's self-giving. The gift is absolute. We cannot take it, refuse it, or contribute to it.[227]

Heidegger touches a deep chord in his identification of thinking *(Denken)* and thanking *(Danken)*. Gratitude is the only possible response of open thought.

Yet our cognitive language is hopelessly infected with the logic of the tightened fist. We con/ceive, and thus take *(capere)* by the hand, a fate reflected in the German *be/greifen*. Ap/prehend and com/prehend as we may, the mind still serves the unembellished violence of prehension.[228] We are not blessed with a repertoire of cognitive terms suggesting the "opening," the "giving," the "yielding" of no-mind.[229] But if we are to understand in any measure the function of enlightened thought,[230] we must find ways to substitute liberation for seizure. For, as Hui-neng assures us, "When all things are illumined by wisdom and there is neither grasping nor throwing away, then you can see into your own nature and gain the Buddha Way" (PS/y, 149). The delightful tale of monkey catching illustrates the liberatory power of "releasement."[231] As the ancient wisdom has it, the way to catch a monkey is to cut a hole in a coconut, secured to a tree, just the size of the monkey's outstretched hand. Leave a banana inside the coconut, and the monkey, in its refusal to release the banana, will do the rest.

That there is only one

is unbelievable tonight.

This harvest moon!

(RYŌTA, 1718–87),

Mindless Minding

REFLECTIONS ON INTENTIONALITY

The Mystery of Consciousness

Light, as our Prelude testifies, has a story to tell, an autobiography. It is born from the luminous, enabled by the transparent or foiled by the reflective, and is swallowed up in the crypt of the opaque. In "The Mirrorless Mirror," we have related only the adventure of light, the contest with reflection in which light is turned from its given course. But we are charged with the narration of the entire account. Reflection, it is claimed, elucidates the signal structures of consciousness. Consciousness, in the Husserlian acceptation, is a certain transparent medium giving uninhibited passage to intentional illumination. Intentionality is the vector of death, the directedness, exhibited by consciousness, "through" consciousness, toward lightless opacity. And, again in the Husserlian acceptation, this illumination that seeks its own extinction is emitted from the ego. The present chapter will bring this doleful parable to a close with a few final remarks on intentionality, intentional objectivity, and the ego.

"Conceit," conceptual consciousness, as Shakespeare well knew, "soaks up, "draws in"—is rather *of*—the "common blocks," the *objects*, of experience.

> Was this taken
> By any understanding pate but thine?

For thy conceit is soaking, will draw in
More than the common blocks.[1]

Con/sciousness is the event of being (or acting)[2] with *(con-)* knowing *(scire)*.[3] To *act* knowingly (with knowing) is to act conscientiously (with conscience). To *be* with knowing *(con/scire)* is more than merely being knowledgeable.[4] It is to be reflexively *with* one's very knowing itself, if not actually, at least virtually.[5] The Greek *gignoskein*, the Latin *cognoscere*, the French *connaître*, the English *recognize*—all resonate with the etymological suggestion that to know is *to be with*. Consciousness is virtual reflection.[6] Thus, as Trotignon remarks, "the universal category of all [conscious] teleology is the *wish to see*, and even the *wish to be seen*."[7] But the *act* of reflection is as much acting as seeing, as much *praxis* as *theoria*, and cannot, then, disdain the office of conscience. Consciousness thus entails a virtual self-commentary, the "second-order" normative assessment of its "first-order" activity. Consciousness is the subject of its own judiciary activity. And judgment (German: *Urteil)* is the primordial *(Ur-)* division *(-teil)* separating consciousness judged from the consciousness judging. Consciousness is, at least incipiently or virtually, a house divided, if not against, then within, itself; it is a desperate process that, as if out of fear or self-distrust, is always on the verge of catching itself red-handed.

The *Bewußtsein* of Husserl's German is not thus freighted. *Bewußt/sein* is not, of course, being *(Sein)* that, as an adventitious accretion, merely happens to be "known" *(bewußt)*, but rather, being *as known*: the very formula for the phenomenon. Phenomenology is exactly the elucidation of being *as it appears* (as *known*).[8] And perhaps it is the paucity of the Latinate form which prompted Sartre to regard consciousness as an "abstraction" (Cf. BN, 34). Though the phenomenon is the object of consciousness, in the fullness of its articulation, it is seamlessly integral with *Bewußtsein* itself. And given his evident assumption that the phenomenon is an appearance,[9] it is little wonder that Sartre regarded the phenomenon as abstract. *Bewußtsein* might seem to be concordant with consciousness inasmuch as the reflective thematization, *being as known*, may well offer itself to conscience, yield itself up to the canons of eidetic normativity. Yet it is wise to note the locus of attribution. *Bewußtsein* is *being* (as known), not the *knowing* of being (as reflectively accompanied). The German richly suggests a certain groundedness *in being* barely adumbrated in its pallid Latinate counterpart.[10]

The intentionality of consciousness is its vectorial character, its object-directedness, or "of-ness." Consciousness "stretches" *(in tendere)* in the direction of its object, "aims" for it.[11] In Sartre's extraordinarily intriguing trope:

> All at once consciousness is purified, it is clear as a strong wind. There is nothing in it but a movement of fleeing itself, a sliding beyond itself. If, impossible though it be, you could enter "into" a consciousness you would be seized by a whirlwind and thrown back outside, in the thick

> of the dust, near the tree, for consciousness has no "inside." It is just this being beyond itself, this absolute flight, this refusal to be a substance which makes it a consciousness.[12]

"Intentionality," Gurwitsch says, "means the objectivating function of consciousness."[13] Those who have suffered the daunting experience of teaching the basics of phenomenology to expectant young minds will know what the intentional act "looks like." It is, of course, an arrow. And its object is an *X* (or on days of particular artistic inspiration, a target with its bull's-eye). I find myself surrounded by objects (not, or not necessarily, *pace* Heidegger, by beings). There are, of course, books stacked haphazardly at the corner of my desk, a telephone, my grandmother's antique lamp, even a pair of hands resting expectantly at the keyboard to capture the next fleeting semiarticulate thought.[14] I am conscious *of* each of these objects in turn. But I am also conscious *of* a vague suspicion of hunger, a passing flush of embarrassment, the agitated state of my soul. Nor are the theory of relativity, the Fairy Godmother and inconceivable spherical tetrahedra exempt from object status. Even the mind and, of course, even our present shibboleth, intentionality, are endowed, through reflection, with a certain objectivity.[15]

It was Husserl's notable teacher, Franz Brentano, who first extirpated the term *intentionality* from its exclusive subservience within the narrow confinement of Scholastic quibble. Brentano's resuscitation of the vectorial nature of consciousness has propagated tremors and opened chasms throughout twentieth-century consciousness-theory. He writes:

> Every mental phenomenon is characterized by what the Scholastics of the Middle Ages called the intentional (or mental) inexistence of an object, and what we might call, though not wholly unambiguously, reference to a content, direction toward an object (which is not to be understood here as meaning a thing), or immanent objectivity. Every mental phenomenon includes something as object within itself, although they do not all do so in the same way. In presentation something is presented, in judgement something is affirmed or denied, in love loved, in hate hated, in desire desired and so on. . . . *This intentional inexistence is characteristic exclusively of mental phenomena.* No physical phenomenon exhibits anything like it. (Emphasis added)[16]

As an able philosophical psychologist, Brentano was understandably eager to delimit his own field of enquiry, and commissioned intentionality to perform just this task. In Brentano's service, intentionality becomes the mark of the mental. The experiment, however, was notoriously ill-fated. Intentional inexistence, signaled by the failure of existential generalization over a given term, proves a false friend. Brentano was wisely impressed by the fact that the object of presentation, love and desire *need not exist*. And we would detract nothing from the philosophical wonder that contemplation of such an astonishing fact must inevitably occasion. Surely, here is something rock-bottom, something essential. Yet here, also, is something merely necessary, and clearly insufficient. "Next year's harvest will be bounteous," we say. Yet few would pretend that "next year's harvest" refers to some solidly existing entity. And it assuredly does not follow that "next year's harvest" belongs, with tickles and touchings, pains and perceptions, to the concrete stratum of living immanence. The failure of existential generalization itself fails as a criterion of the mental. And *this* failure has spawned numerous attempts to refine or replace the criterion.[17]

It is not my intent here to enter the swarm of enigmas plowed up in the wake of Brentano's consequential revivification. But it would not be out of place to suggest a general failing of all such attempts to establish a criteriology demarcating the mental from the nonmental, subject from object.[18] Reserving "con/sciousness" for an awareness which presupposes the subject-object divide, the world stands decisively aloof from its conscious presentation. To say that *this* year's harvest is bounteous makes for a different world than would its negation.[19] To say that the harvest is manifest to consciousness makes not the least difference either to the harvest in particular or to the world in general. Thus, assuming that criterial entailments intended, in the spirit of Brentano, to capture the mental are "difference-making," intentionality cannot be netted by examining such ramifications. And thus, no difference-making criterion, Brentano's candidate or another's, can brand the mental.

Adorno speaks of "Husserl's will to replace the *intentio obliqua* with the *intentio recta*" (ND, 61). For Husserl, intentionality, no longer criterial, becomes constitutive of consciousness. The entire course of Husserl's philosophical development was shaped by his early yielding to Brentano's tutelage. Husserlian phenomenology in its entirety is an endlessly rich and intricate elaboration of the inherited notion of "intentionality." Yet the flowers of the Husserlian notion spring from the grave of the Brentanonian. Intentionality, for Husserl, was no longer an "exam" to which the phenomena of experience were to be subjected. It no longer determined their type. Brentano's problematic was accommodated methodologically. What appears within the phenomenological reduction is immanent (including the "transcendence-in-immanence" characteristic of the spatiotemporal object as perceived). And the task was now to elicit and to understand the intentionality of the immanent—to distill its meaning, not to secure for it a sinecure as proctor.

The "indifference" we have witnessed with regard to the objects of mentality has its historical precedents. Plato, with his "two worlds" ontology, and its consequent assumption of a chasm between the eternal Forms and the realm of sensible particularity, confronts a similar demand for substantial modification of the faculty of intellection *(noēsis)*. We do not invariantly intuit, with explicitness and clarity, any given Form. For the most part, our eyes are fixed upon the shadows. There are moments, however, when our powers of intellection are sufficiently engaged, when the mist of forgetfulness has lifted from our minds, and we do, indeed, come to re/cognize our Formal friends.[20] At other times, we are lost in the fog. Are the Forms thereby altered? Do they alternatively gain and then loose the property of being seen? To admit as much is to contravene the essential immutability of the Forms. It is *we* who change, not eidetic reality. In Augustine's subtle appropriation of Neoplatonism, the problem is particularly poignant. For the Forms have become Ideas in the Mind of God. To suggest that we might disturb their immutable serenity is more than a contravention of Platonic doctrine. It is now blasphemy! Who are *we* to arrogate to ourselves the power of altering the Divine in any way? Instead of transforming our conscious relationship with the Forms, providing it with a certain "Cambridge" accent, as did Plato, Augustine assumes the affective power of cognition in order to refute any direct apprehension of the Divine Ideas. Thus was born the early medieval doctrine of illuminationism. Not The Good only, but *every* Form is now illuminative. We cannot look directly upon them, but rather see in their light. Like Plato before him, Husserl fitted his "consciousness-of" with a certain Cambridge air. If I do not shorten as my papaya tree surpasses me in height, neither does the world tremble as I become conscious of it. The Cambridge eccentricities of intentionality are there, *in semine*, from the methodological beginning.

The *epochē* crucially assumes the possibility of systematic phenomenal deception, the possibility that "seeing" pink elephants could be exactly like *seeing* them in every phenomenal respect. Attending the zoo's exhibition of rare animals, I manage, in my enthusiasm, to frighten the curiously tinted pachyderm that so few have had occasion to *see*. Yet the indistinguishable twin that I "see" in my inebriated stupor is assuredly not frightened by my excited gesticulating. It isn't *there*. Restricting ourselves entirely to the phenomenal, as Husserl insists, no genuine relationship of adequation can be licensed between consciousness and an object purportedly endowed with the blessing of extraphenomenal reality. We can never be phenomenologically warranted in the arrogant assumption that our conscious powers have brought about a *real* change in the world. For any change admissible by phenomenological standards is *phenomenal*.

Despite the ontic and ontological overtones of *Bewußtsein*, the very activity of consciousness, its very upsurge, argues against any ontological pronouncement one might wish to put forward regarding the *Sein* thus *bewußt*. And it may be well to reserve the customary object, with its patent connotation of objective or aim, for the terminus of intentional activity. Like "running," however, the gerundive "being-conscious" is ambiguous. In Fisk's demarcation:

> If I say that the running took four minutes, I am referring to the complete action, to the performing of the running. If, however, I say that the running continues to be done or that the running is swift, I am referring to the progressive action.

> . . . progressive action is not extensive and hence not extensively divisible. The running you are doing just does not have a first half and a second half. This is not because it is an extended whole that somehow cannot be divided. Rather it is because it is not an extended whole at all.[21]

Borrowing the idiom, it is evident that the reflective *con-* of consciousness holds sway only over a "being-conscious" understood as completed action. *In progress*, consciousness offers no leverage to reflection.[22] "Swift" is attributable only to a running completed. For such an attribution engages a second-order ("normative") judgment of distance over time: extensive magnitudes both, and patently absent from progressive running.[23] Likewise, the reflective intuition of eidetic structure rests upon a completed conscious activity that offers itself as extensive display. And we would thus do well to heed Merleau-Ponty's admonition that "We must stop constructing . . . consciousness . . . according to a certain essence or idea of itself which compels us to define it in terms of some sort of absolute adequation. . . ." (PhP, 336). Only when the race is over, the running past, are we in a position to declare the running "slow" or "fast," "awkward" or "well trained." Indeed, whether the finish line is reached at all is not given until the running is over. And whether the *telos* of intentional activity (its "finish line") has been attained, whether the mind has genuinely seized upon its object *in its very existence*, can be adjudged, through reflection, only at the closure of the intentional act.[24] The signet of existential phenomenology is its rooting of perception in being. Yet, whatever else we might find to admire in Sartre and Merleau-Ponty, a Buddhist phenomenology must, as we have noted before, rise "above existence and non-existence" (PS/pw, 27).

The requirements of the "real" relation are familiar enough. What remains puzzling is the aberrant mode of relatedness in virtue of which consciousness enjoys the presentation of a possibly nonexistent object. If the positing of a certain *relation* between two items, *X* and *Y*, requires their conjoint existence (and what sense *could* it make to say that *X* is north of *Y*, for example, if there were no *Y* for *X* to be north of?), then intentionality is assuredly no "relation." For we can (and, for all the phenomena warrant, consistently may) stand in the presence of objects which fail to exist. Roquentin, the soured protagonist of Sartre's *Nausea*, confronts, in his own way, the utter unrelatedness, the absoluteness, of the present,[25] through the "second death" of his biographical subject, De Rollebon:

> M. de Rollebon had just died for the second time. . . .
>
> Nothing more was left now. No more than, on these traces of dry ink, is left the memory of their freshness. . . . suddenly, noiseless, M. de Rollebon had returned to his nothingness. . . .
>
> . . . Nothing existed but a bundle of yellow pages which I clasped

> in my hands. . . . Rollebon was no more. No more at all. If there were still a few bones left of him, they existed for themselves, independently. . . .[26]

The past has silently slipped from existence. Yet we are ruled by the relation's demand for the existence of its *relata*. Only one conclusion is allowed us: the present is unsupported by any "real" relations of causal-explanatory sufficiency that might otherwise lend it intelligibility.[27] Before this moment, Roquentin was nourished by the illusion that his present rested securely upon the past like a bust on a pedestal. The pedestal has disappeared. And the bust floats in midair like some absurd balloon. The analogy is patent. Were intentionality properly to be accounted a *relation* at all, it would be vacuous, a mere notion without illustration. Consciousness and its activity would, then, simply "float," mooringless, untethered to its putative, object.

Yet surely (the riposte might come), though it seems demonstrably illegitimate to foist upon progressive running such unwanted attributes as "slow" and "swift," we are not thereby reduced to muteness. Do we not at least perceive, while the race is in progress, that activity proceeds *in the direction* of the finish line, *toward* the objective? And do we not, analogously, apprehend, through reflection, the *intentionality* of consciousness? The answer, I urge, is "No." For, in the analogue, the sense of directedness is constituted by a relentless series of completed segments, *A* to *B*, *A* to *C*, *A* to *D*, . . . , each longer, each more remote from the starting line, than its predecessor. It is only through *successive segmentation*, and then *comparison* of the segments, that the vectorial nature of the running is given. Strictly speaking, the *progressive* action gives us nothing of the sort. The parallel is evident. Gurwitsch voices the Husserlian position:

> *Consciousness* is not to be mistaken for a mere unidimensional sphere composed of acts, as real psychical events, which co-exist with and succeed one another. Rather it ought to be considered as a *correlation, or correspondence, or parallelism between the plane of acts, psychical events, noeses, and a second plane which is that of sense (noemata)*. This correlation is such that to each act its noema corresponds, but the same noema may correspond to an indefinite number of acts. It is then not a one-to-one correspondence.
>
> The noetico-noematic correlation is what has to be meant by the term intentionality. In this light, the formula "consciousness *of* something" is to be understood: a conscious act is an act of awareness, presenting the subject who experiences it with a sense, an ideal atemporal unity, identical, i.e., identifiable.[28]

The conflation of intentionality with the abstract many-one structure of "correlation" cannot be attractive to one who takes the progressive activity of consciousness with the seriousness it deserves, but who, at the same time, insists upon leaving the tooth marks of intentionality in the living flesh of progressively occurring experience.[29] The progressively more extensive "segments" constituting the "direction" of intentionality are the profiles or *noēmata*, retained and remembered, disclosing the object. Intentionality is not displayed in the progressive activity of minding, but only *post facto*, in the second-order pattern of the profiles.[30] And the general resistance of progressive experience to the analytic structurations that are typical only of its ossified remains prompts Merleau-Ponty's methodological caution:

> [W]e . . . do not allow ourselves to introduce into our description concepts issued from reflection, whether psychological or transcendental: they are more often than not only correlatives or counterparts of the *objective* world. We must, at the beginning, eschew notions such as "acts of consciousness," "matter," "form," and even "image" and "perception." (VI, 157–58)

Intentionality is thus a feature only of the "act." And the act always arrives "too late" for conscious life.

Philonous, the protagonist of Berkeley's *Three Dialogues,* and standard-bearer for the "love" *(philos)* of "mind" *(noûs)*, queries, "is not *distance* a line turned endwise to the eye?"[31] If so, then, like distance, our "intentional threads" are strung "endwise to the eye,"[32] and cannot, *for this reason,* be seen in the act of seeing.[33] This may, of course, be the case for a "God who is everywhere," and for whom, therefore, "breadth is immediately equivalent to depth" (PhP, 255). Yet, while Merleau-Ponty would not deny the consequence that perception itself is overlooked in the act, he emphatically, and, I believe, wisely, rejects the identification of depth with "*breadth seen from the side*" (PhP, 255).

> What makes depth invisible for me is precisely what makes it visible for the spectator as breadth. . . . The depth which is declared invisible is, therefore, a depth already identified with breadth and, this being the case, the argument would lack even a semblance of consistency. (PhP, 255)

Consistently wary of importing reflective sophistication into prereflective naïveté Merleau-Ponty sets in abeyance the indemonstrable presumption that those structures accessible within the purview of the reflective spectator are already in play prior to the reflective act.[34] Depth, the distantiation which renders positional consciousness positional, is rather to be conceived as "the means the things have to remain distinct, to remain things, while not being what I look at at present" (VI, 219).[35]

The wisdom *(bodhi)* of Buddhism is a wisdom of equilibrium, equilibrium illustrated and confirmed in the centered, well-balanced posture of the lotus. The immediate disciples of the Buddha sensed, in the life of their teacher, a dimension of inexpressible depth that presented neither handle nor lever to description through the categorial word. Description frustrated led only to invigorated attempts at description, culminating in depictions of the Tathāgata typified by the following:

> The Lord as usual first sitting quietly became absorbed in Samadhi, radiating from the crown of his head rays of soft and tender brightness, like lotus petals surrounded by innumerable leaves. In the center of the lotus petals there was a vision of the Nirmanakaya Buddha sitting with feet crossed intuiting and radiating the intrinsic Dharani.[36]

The Buddha is consistently pictured as the serene source and center of a certain spiritual radiance. From the Buddha,

> there shown forth a glorious, blazing brightness, which radiated forth brilliantly into hundreds and thousands of colored rays reaching to the ten quarters of the universes, which were instantly turned into innumerable Buddha-lands. . . .[37]

Images such as these culminate in suggestions of perfect balance. And "Balance," as Levin tells us, "is a question of centering. When we are properly centered, our experience of Being is in equilibrium."[38]

Iconography has much to teach us. Though admitting the evident embellishment of such depictions, the pattern is recognizable. The teachings of the Buddha foster an attitude of perfect balance, a Middle Way, exemplified not only by the mediating withdrawal from extremes of sensuous indulgence and ascetic deprivation, but also in the Mādhyamika refusal of affirmation and negation, the determination to rise above existence and nonexistence. It is striking, in this connection, that, although Sartre postulated, on the part of prereflective consciousness, an irremediable ontological commitment, he was also able to see intentionality as a certain disequilibrium:

> [I]f consciousness is a slippery slope on which one can not take one's stand without immediately finding oneself tipped outside onto being-in-itself, this is because consciousness does not have by itself any sufficiency of being as an absolute subjectivity; from the start it refers to the thing. (BN, 786)

Consciousness, the third link of the twelvefold chain of *pratītya-samutpāda*, is perpetually destabilized, decentered, always in process of catching its balance, but condemned in the attempt to hopeless failure. The image, though slapstick, is nonetheless apropos. In being thus ecstatically "tipped," consciousness falls perpetually out of itself without hope of recovery. Indeed, the constancy of the slippage effectively deprives consciousness of an "itself" from which to fall. Consciousness, as Sartre would have it, is a "nonsubstantial absolute."[39]

Con/sciousness, in Sartre's chilling trope, "devours" its object much as "The spider which draws things into its web, coats them with its own drivel, and slowly swallows, reducing them to its own nature."[40] Consciousness is voracious for presence.[41] Prowling about its prey, consciousness intends to assuage its own dys-integrity, putting an end to its "ecstatic" disequilibrium, converting *ek/stacy* into *stasis*. Yet the for-itself is an irremediably abortive movement.[42] It is a primal lack of fit, an original imbalance. With less flourish,

> if [as Sartre believes] the transcendence of the object is based on the necessity of causing the appearance to be always transcended, the result is that on principle an object posits the series of its appearances as infinite. Thus the appearance, which is *finite*, indicates itself in its finitude, but at the same time in order to be grasped as an appearance-of-that-which-appears, it requires that it be surpassed toward infinity. (BN, 6)

The transcendent object is, in Sartre's alternative account, an actual infinity of appearances disclosed in its entirety through each serial advance of an inactual but potentially endless augmentation of lived presentational aspects.

> It is altogether *within* [the finite aspect], in that it manifests itself *in* that aspect; it shows itself as the structure of the appearance, which is at the same time the principle of the series. It is altogether outside, for the series itself will never appear nor can it appear. Thus the outside is opposed in a new way to the inside. . . . (BN, 6)

The series, though not itself appearing, serves nonetheless as the structure of the appearance.

Buddhism roundly concurs that "consciousness does not have by itself any sufficiency of being as an absolute subjectivity." But are we thereby warranted in supposing that "from the start it refers to the thing," that awareness is ineluctably intentional? There is, of course, a facile reply. Reserving "consciousness," as we have thus far, for object-directed awareness, the implicative passage is, of course, tautologous. But this is to found the intentionality thesis upon a definition, not, as is inevitably the phenomenological intent, to *see* its purported truth. How, then, is the mind to be "righted," "centered,"[43] "stabilized"? Is there not a balanced, pre-intentional awareness (in Loy's idiom, a consciousness-*as*, in contrast to consciousness-*of*)[44] that antedates the perpetual slippage of intentionality and robs it of its ultimacy? Should the object of intentional reference turn out to be "empty"—subject, that is, to a certain "deconstruction" into its manifold conditions—nothing will remain to obstruct an affirmative response.[45]

The Rupture of Immanence

Consider, then, any available perceptual object that might be at hand. A book, a lamp, a teacup would do. Philosophers, like children, seem quite adept at marveling over the most trivial, the most obvious aspects of our experience.[46] And phenomenologists are particularly subject to this tedious tendency. But it should not go unappreciated that the best place to hide something is precisely the most patent. And philosophers, in giving voice to the altogether taken-for-granted aspects of experience, seem to be peculiarly savvy to this trick.[47] Surely, upon reflection, one can think of few things more familiar than the plain fact that this chair, this bookcase, appear in different ways from different angles. From one point of view, a coin appears circular; from another, elliptical; and from yet another, rectangular. Yet, throughout our investigatory pursuits, as we examine the objects of our perception from this angle and that, it is, Husserl would insist, precisely the *object itself* that appears.[48] The object is an invariant strand woven through the variegated warp of "ways" in which it presents itself in perception: an "identity-in-manifold."[49]

How extensive is this warp, this manifold, through which the selfsameness constituting the Husserlian object is threaded? We have not yet seen the object as it appears through all of the strands of its appearing. Nor could we. This is yet another of those painfully obvious and unassailable facts of experience, available to reflection, of which phenomenologists make much. While we may, in fact, have only perceived the object through a finite array of appearances, we could nonetheless always entertain further manners of its presentation. The manifold is, then, *actually* finite, but *potentially* infinite. The perceptual object is thus a unitary ideality that presents itself throughout a potentially endless array of appearances. It is striking, however, that, despite the evident fact that it could always present itself alternatively, the perceptual object never does appear through more than a single appearance at a time. At any given time, we experience the compulsive, irruptive sensory givenness of the object only as it is given *from here*.

Ecstatic intentionality, the elemental conception of Occidental phenomenology, though it brightens whatever insight falls beneath its illumination, is itself wrapped in deep mystery. Sokolowski's comment is, then, directly to the point:

> It still remains a paradox that reality, something which is transcendent to consciousness, is accessible to consciousness in its very transcendence. What reality is in itself can be reached by consciousness even

> though it must remain, in principle, radically distinct from and transcendent to consciousness. This is the mystery of intentionality, the mystery of consciousness.[50]

And Findlay sniffs the same uncanny air of paradox:

> How can mind be thus "ecstatic," thus self-transcendent, we are inclined to ask, and it does not seem a sufficient answer at a sufficiently deep level of reflection to say that such ecstasy, such self-transcendence, is the very mark of the mental.[51]

The mystery, however, is quite literally artificial *(ars facio),* created by the art of distinction. Consciousness, on the Husserlian account, is immanent, indeed, immanence itself. Its object is transcendent. How is it that the wall of partition between them is broken down, the transcendent looming through the breach, without the immanent being remainderlessly absorbed into the transcendent, or the transcendent wholly assimilated to the immanent? How can the distinction hold without "perfect continence"? I answer: It cannot. But then, I am no champion of the distinction.

Heidegger, it seems, may own one piece of this fabricated puzzle. Recall the Heideggerean claim that "The matter of thinking is difference *as* difference."[52] Does not the thinking of the difference of transcendence from immanence—*qua* difference, of course—restore to us the cloven field of the distinction?[53] And are we not thus enabled to see the subject/object divide as Heidegger sees the severance of world and thing?

> For world and things do not subsist alongside one another. They penetrate each other. Hence the two traverse a mean *[Mitte]*. In it, they are at one. Thus at one, they are intimate [*innig*]. The mean of the two is inwardness *[Innigkeit]*. . . . The intimacy or inwardness of world and thing is not a fusion *[Verschmelzung]*. Intimacy obtains only where the intimate—world and thing—divides itself cleanly and remains separated *[rein sich scheidet und geschieden bleibt]*. In the midst *[Mitte]* of the two, in the between of world and thing, in the *inter*, division prevails: a *dif-ference [UnterSchied]*. The intimacy of world and thing is present in the boundary [*Schied*: border, limit, divide; case, sheath, vagina] of the between *[Zwischen];* it is present in the dif-ference. . . . [Dif-ference] exists only as this single difference. It is unique. Of itself, it holds apart the mean in and through which the world and things are at one with each other. The intimacy of the difference is the unifying element of the *diaphora*, the carrying out that carries through. The difference carries out world in its worlding, carries out things in their thinging. Thus carrying them out, it carries them toward one another.

> The dif-ference does not mediate after the fact by binding together world and things through a mean added on to them. Being the mean, it first determines world and things in their presence, i.e., in their being toward one another, whose unity it carries out.[54]

Does not the dif/ference in which immanence and transcendence find their intimate mean effect a similar interpenetration? And if so, if subjectivity and objectivity pass wraithlike through one another in virtue of the very distinction that prevents their fusion, what mystery remains?

The question, as Sokolowski frames it, is one of accessibility, the yielding *(ad cedere)* of the object to conscious givenness. To find the object drifting spectrally through consciousness, effortlessly penetrating its intimacy yet utterly devoid of the resistance that "touching" would impart, may well give account to "accessibility," though what "yields" in this ghostly unidirectional passage is consciousness, not object. Our experience would not, however, be falsified by the supposition that the object also yields to the specter of subjectivity, that consciousness penetrates its object. On the Heideggerean account, the ghost of immanence haunts the object as well.[55] The event of phenomenality is the crux, the intercrossing, the reciprocal passing through, of subjective immanence and objective transcendence.[56] But to say that the phenomenon emerges from, or is constituted by, the interpenetration of coeval principles of greater antiquity is precisely to lapse into a speculative metaphysic designed to account for the phenomenon. Phenomenology has no recourse but to the phenomenon. And we have repeatedly registered our complaint against the very immanence which would haunt the transcendent. And if transcendence is read *against* immanence, the curious prephenomenal diptych of principles falls, as a pair, under the axe of phenomenological scrutiny.

The Heideggerean "metaphysics of experience" is complemented by a second polarity of *aitia*: universality and particularity. Husserl, a Kantian in spirit, though by no means in letters and syllables, understands the phenomenon in terms congruent with Kantian hylomorphism. The phenomenon is the object *as it appears*, and thus represents a certain "material" particular considered under a given constitutive "form." For Heidegger, particularity and formality are hypostatized. In words which Fell extracts from Heidegger:

> Universal and particular are what they are—are distinct—only by playing into each other and out of each other. They are the same *and* different, unity and disunity. . . . Particular and universal must each defer and yield to the other while at the same time preserving their difference or independence.[57]

Again, a willingness to inaugurate the philosophical enterprise before the advent of phenomenality displays a commitment to metaphysics inimical to the theoretical asceticism of phenomenology. Moreover, we would well be guided by Merleau-Ponty's counsel that "we cannot apply the classical distinction of form and matter to perception" (PP, 12). The Heideggerean account, like the Husserlian, posits the immediate unity of *morphē* and *hylē*. Merleau-Ponty challenges their very discriminability. Every "stylistic" structuration of experience *is* material. Every hyletic datum *is* itself a "style." There is, then, no question of the interpenetration of two primordial *aitia*. For experience eludes the Aristotelian bipolarity.

The bottomless ambiguity of consciousness, its indifference to the epithets "transparent" and "translucent" here breaks forth in significant ramifications. On the early Sartrean transparentist view, the view that "All is clear and lucid in consciousness" (TE, 40), once the plane of distinction has been severed into subject and object, nothing will serve to bring the severed plane itself to presence. There is no seeing, no theoretical apprehension, of a purported synthetic unity of content and extent of which dif/ference is the mean. If subject and object comprise a synthetic "totality," it is, in Sartre's paradoxical phrase, a "detotalized totality." The totality itself can never be seen, since "in" consciousness there is nothing to see. To "see" consciousness in any sense is exactly to see *through* it. Nothing remains to be seen but the object. On the contrasting Husserlian view that reflection uncovers the phenomenal structure of living experience, the dialectical whole comprised of subject and object, their "correlation," is opened to transcendental reflection. Both views are equally warranted "seemings." Both are to be accorded the dignity of the "exactly as if." Yet it follows, for this very reason, that neither is to be granted adequation with experience. Experience, in the living of it, eschews both the realist "objectivism" that offers no phenomenal shelter to the subject and the transcendental idealism that installs the subject as an ineluctable polar referent of correlation.

Klaus Hartmann distinguishes the several distinct senses in which Husserl employs the related notion of transcendence. The term *transcendent* imports:

(1) "the opposite of being contained *realiter* [*reell*] in consciousness. . . ."
(2) "a kind of givenness, a mediated [*nicht selbstschauende*] cognition, in which we go beyond what is given in a true sense. . . ."
(3) "In this third sense the noema also is transcendent since it is not *realiter* [*reell*] contained in consciousness and since it is displayed in a manifold of shades."
(4) "And in yet another sense in the phenomenological reduction the object as a unity of noematic multiplicity . . . possesses transcendence."[58]

And, of course, "immanence," as the obverse of "transcendence," is endowed with an equal and corresponding ambiguity: (1) ingredience in the "real" *(reell)*; (2) cognitive immediacy; and appurtenance to the manifold of the profiles constituting (3) the *noēma*, and (4) the object. "Immanence" in the first, and primary, sense is an ontological notion, applying to that which conforms, in Sartre's early description, to "the absolute law of consciousness for which no distinction is possible between appearance and being" (TE, 63). Cognitive immanence, the second sense, rests upon the ontological together with the auxiliary assumption that an item of immanence is "self-showing" *(selbst schauende)* only if there is no gap, indeed, no *possible* gap, between its *being* and its *appearing.*[59] For the present, it is sufficient to register our suspicion of the dubiousness of this assumption. The final two senses, articulating the function of immanence in the enactment of synthesis, are likewise rooted in the ontological, and, like the cognitive, rest upon a questionable assumption that the real *(reell)*, the locus of the identity of being and appearing, is, and indeed, *can be*, parceled out in a manifold of immanent objectivities.

Again, the primordial sense of immanence, presupposed by all the rest, is the ontological. An objectivity, whether a tickle or a touch, a pain or a perceiving, is immanent (in any sense) only if its being and its appearing are not merely organically united, not merely inseparable, but strictly *identical.* Like dominoes, the remaining senses will topple with the fall of the first. And phenomenal undecidability does, in a decisive way, precipitate the ruin of ontological immanence.[60]

Consciousness is immanent only if it *is* the way it *appears* to be. But the lesson of phenomenal undecidability is that the purportedly immanent inevitably "appears to be" in two different, and indeed belligerently quarrelsome, ways. What, then, can we say of its being? We must be advised against the alluring, but treacherous, ontological leap. Ontology, if not phenomenology, would seem (now a dangerous word) to owe allegiance to consistency. Theological partisans of the ontological argument are given to claiming parity for the ontological commitments of impossibility and necessity. If the logical incoherence of a set of properties proscribes their conjoint instantiation, why should we not expect necessity of concept to entail the necessary instantiation of a Necessary Being?[61] I have no wish to settle, or even explore, the theological issue here. My present interest is in the antecedent. *Does* impossibility foreclose instantiation? Assuredly yes—*if* ontology submits itself to the canons of consistency.

Yet we find in Sartre a most intriguing ontology featuring a being (the *for-itself)* that seems the very instantiation of a flagrant contradiction: "[T]he being of *for-itself* is defined . . . as being what it is not and not being what it is" (BN, 28). Or more generally, the for-itself, itself a "being" of an odd sort,[62] is the universal nihilation of beings—the nihilation even of itself.[63] What it is, as a being, is its very *not-being* a being, indeed, its very *not-being* itself.[64] Given the logic of analysis, the contradiction is patent. But the contradiction is also *real.* Consciousness is itself a living contradiction. Has Sartre, then, succeeded in providing an ontology?

To lay it down by *a priori* fiat that reality glows with the cheerful harmony of a good-natured coherence, or conversely, that reality glowers with the gaunt sunkenness of an inner and twisted logical rebellion, is a convenient—if wholly antiphenomenological—approach to the problem.[65] Nor can we take mindless refuge in the mechanics of the truth table without incurring the censure of arbitrary foreclosure. Our sophomores are taught to intone, "A contradiction implies everything." Yet surely an innocent inconsistency does not bring down upon the universe of our rational deliberations the logical havoc that this trivial truth table result would inculcate—nor should it. And likewise, the vital "contradictions" of Sartre's ontology are much too well mannered to plunder the in-itself of its stolid logical complacency.[66] The truth table adjudicates, moreover, against any ontology which, like Hegel's, would preserve truth and meaningfulness from shattering, in instantiation, into numberless propositional shards. If Hegel has given birth to an ontology (and Hegel is assuredly among the most august and imposing of its avatars), then it cannot be the truth table that decides the issue.

If we would not approach the question by speculative fiat, let us then approach it as practitioners of phenomenology. What do we *see*?[67] If Sartre is right, the for-itself will prove "invisible." And this is because only a *being* (in-itself) can possess phenomenal determinacy.[68] The very lack of being, the very "not-being a being" that is the for-itself,[69] is wholly devoid of qualitative determination.[70] Phenomenology must pass over the for-itself in silence. There is *nothing* to see.[71] Or is it that what there is to "see" is an invisibility? It is sometimes said that, far from a privation of vision, death and dreamless sleep are the very vision of Nothingness.[72] Are we, in either case, to repudiate the *act* or the phenomenality of its *object*? Phenomenologically, it simply makes no difference. The issue is undecidable. Nothing phenomenal encourages a decision in favor of either "not seeing" or "seeing nothing." It is *exactly as if* there existed invisible being-privations. And equally, it is *exactly as if* there were none. It is, then, *exactly as if* an ontology of instantiated contradiction were possible.[73] And equally, it is *exactly as if* it were not. Is there, finally, an incoherent *being* subtending the "appearances" of monism and dualism? Our answer must be: it is *exactly as if* there were; and it is *exactly as if* there were not.

Immanence recoils at both the "Yes" and the "No." An incoherent being would hold no response to the question, *ti esti*? As Sartre perspicuously perceived, that which "is not what it is" certainly is not, nor does it, in any ordinary sense, possess, a "what." Nothingness—as much the privation of essence, an "anti-essence,"[74] as the absence of being—is the name for this utter failure of phenomenological describability.[75] A subtending incoherence could only be a nothing, an ontological vacuity.[76] Thus, at best, the law of our regenerate immanence would formulate the indistinguishability of appearance and emptiness—a formula strikingly reminiscent of the central doctrine of the vast *Prajñāpāramitā* literature, enshrined in the resounding formula of the *Heart Sutra:* "Form is emptiness; emptiness is form. Emptiness is not other than form; form is not other than emptiness."[77] But we no longer have an immanence that *is* as it *appears*. We have, in the Buddhist acceptation, a phenomenal *dharma* that *is-not* as it appears.[78]

The logical pedant, eager to demonstrate the contrast between "nothing" in its barbarous service as a noun and "nothing" in its prim adverbial deployment, chalks out the infamous syllogism:

> Nothing is better than Absolute Bliss.
> A peanut butter sandwich is better than nothing.
> Therefore: A peanut butter sandwich is better than Absolute Bliss.

The malady, of course, lies in the nominalization of "nothing." And, our logician queries, raising a learned eyebrow: Should we not expect more from our philosophers, even those who, like Sartre, hold mere logic in contempt, than the willingness to fall prey to the most obvious of fallacies? Does not Sartre move all too readily from the supposition that nothing separates me from the in-itself to the inference that this "nothing" is itself *nothingness?* Sartre, ever the more acute student of experience, finds fallacy in the very distinction that the logician connives. "Seeing nothing(ness)" and there being "nothing to see" designate a seamless phenomenological fact. The logician fissures the fact in a way wholly unsanctioned by phenomenological discipline.

The "No," then—the denial of a self-conflictual being subtending quarrelsome appearances—is a formality enacted in deference to the serviceable, if misplaced, acumen of our logician. The "No," however, affords nothing that could answer to the identity of appearance and being.[79] Incoherent being, the conjoint instantiation of incompossibilities, is all that could underlie undecidable and reciprocally belligerent appearances. If being of the only securable sort is precluded, immanence is lost.[80]

If Sartre posits the for-itself as a radically self-contradictory immanence, Merleau-Ponty resolutely abandons the very notion: "[T]here is no sphere of immanence, no realm in which my consciousness is fully at home and secure against all risk of error. . . . Consciousness is transcendence through and through, not transcendence undergone. . . ." (PhP, 376). And we are not spared the patent election of "nothing to see" over the "seeing of nothing." The conclusion of the matter belongs to Nāgārjuna (c. 150–250), the great Mādhyamika dialectician: "Nothing could be asserted to be *śūnya*, *aśūnya*, both *śūnya* and *aśūnya*, and neither *śūnya* nor *aśūnya*. They are asserted only for the purpose of provisional understanding" (MK 22:11; N, 134).[81] And the "knowledge" conveyed, knowledge of undecidability, both phenomenological and ontological, is the paradoxical province of phenomenology.

Experience is inhospitable to immanence. Nothing, not even an itch, *is* as it appears. Nor, as Nāgārjuna insists, are we even in a position to postulate "emptiness,"[82] since a decision between emptiness (the positive vacuity of instantial incompossibility) and sheer nonexistence is not welcomed by experience either. Buddhism involves a training of the will. And the knowledge conveyed by the "saying" of emptiness, though cognitive in its appreciation of undecidability, nonetheless exceeds the domain of *theoria*. To "know" emptiness is to know *how* to effect a certain detached cognitive equilibrium.[83] Hui-neng, recall, admonished his disciples: "[S]eparate yourselves from views" (PS/y, 136). It is not that we must first distinguish emptiness from the view of it, and then deactivate the view.[84] For again, the vision of emptiness cannot be distinguished—phenomenologically—from the having of no vision.[85] Rather, the knowing of emptiness is precisely the knowing of how to live without driving the wedge.[86]

Reduction and the Immanence of Intentionality

With immanence falls the phenomenological reduction as Husserl typically conceived it. Nothing, of course, could be more welcome to the Mādhyamika Buddhist than the "universal depriving of acceptance" to "all existential positions."[87] Yet Husserl would seem to deviate from his own preferred path at just this crucial juncture: "We must regard nothing as veridical except the pure immediacy and givenness in the field of the *ego cogito* which the *epochē* has opened up to us."[88] The dubious Husserlian bridge principle that would make of "self-showing" the guarantor of ontological immanence now stands as ironic witness to the bankruptcy of a quest for apodicticity instituted upon this trembling foundation. Dillon keenly observes that "The search for truth is an attempt to pierce the opacity of the world. . . . The quest for certainty . . . is an attempt to eliminate the opacity of the world altogether. . . ."[89] If cognitive transparency is the mark of the immanent, and if, moreover, the identification of the immanent with its being, coherent or otherwise, is the assumption of an existential position, Husserl has retreated from his otherwise scrupulous adherence to self-evidence.

But perhaps we are overeager. The suspension of existential position-taking removes from countenance the existence of the *object*, not, as it might be retorted, its *being* (identical with its appearing or not). The retort is either double-speak or, at best, unhelpful. Are we to discriminate "existence" from "being"? To save consistency, we must. Indeed, the import of the *epochē* is to bring to light the domain of immanence *as such*, and to find therein the "transcendence-within-immanence" presumably typical of the transcendent object: "Transcendency in every form is an immanent existential characteristic. . . ."[90] The *epochē* leaves the being of the object untouched. And it must, then, be acknowledged that the deeper dialectic of undecidability has uncovered in Husserl's thought a fateful diptych of presuppositions.[91] Husserl assumes, pre-phenomenologically, both that the being of the immanent is coherent, and that immanent being is discriminable from sheer privation of being.

The founding of *world-for-us* in immanent subjectivity,[92] the "ontological path" to the reduction, is, then, gravely imperiled by our thesis of undecidability. Husserl writes: "The world is for me absolutely nothing else but the world existing for and accepted by me in such a conscious cogito."[93] And again: "The *epochē* . . . leads us to recognize, in self-reflection, that the world that exists for us, that is, our world in its being and being-such, takes its ontic meaning entirely from our intentional life."[94] The world can only be suspended upon the "dharmic," for which appearing and not-being are identical.[95] There is no security here, nothing for the epistemological orientation to fix upon. The "world-phenomenon" *is not* as it appears.[96]

There is little comfort for a transcendence that, through reversion, would simply transmit the ills to which immanence is heir. And I take no delight in perpetuating the agony (either in its original or in its derived sense). But the fate of transcendence, and with it the Husserlian theory of constitutive synthesis, is at stake, and a remark or two would not be out of place. An object is transcendent, in Hartmann's fourth sense, the sense reserved for "intentional analysis," if it functions as "a unity of noematic multiplicity." And intentionality, if not a relation (which it cannot be), is at least the relationship between the constitutive manifold of immanence and the constituted unity of transcendence (or "transcendence-in-immanence").[97] Without the initial term (immanence), intentionality, a notion than which, in Husserlian phenomenology, there simply is no notion more fundamental, would be impossible. The rupture of immanence[98] ensures that every appearance, every *sensum,* every act is ambiguously presentable.[99] Immanence, as we have seen, is presentable in *both* the apophantic *and* the cataphantic mode: *both* as "transparency to color" (mirror-image) *and* as "colored translucency" (reflected object). Every ostensibly immanent objectivity is thus, in this curious way, transcendent, an identity-in-manifold.[100] We have lost the *terminus a quo*. Or, as we might rather say, intentionality can begin anywhere. There is no vicious inward regress of transcendence. The object, as well as the putatively immanent objectivity, always *can* be given *as profiled*, but *need not* be. Disclosed naïvely, the object terminates the regress. Presented *as profiled*, the object defers termination to its profile. Intentionality needs only a temporary branch on which to alight, not a permanent and absolutely solid ground on which to plant its feet. But what can we say of the branch? What we shall say is that intentionality can perch only upon a peculiar ignorance *(āvidyā)*, a blindness to the intrinsic ambiguity of experience, and thus that an enlightened mind, a mind liberated from *āvidyā*, will offer no refuge to intentionality.[101]

The World-Horizon

In perception, as we know, the mind reaches significantly farther than its sensory grasp. In Merleau-Ponty's paradoxical setting, "To see is as a matter of principle to see further than one sees."[102] We not only bask in the immediate sensory sunshine of the object's presence, but anticipate, apperceive, in an indistinct and not fully explicit way, what it would look like from various alternative vantage points. And in this prethematic anticipation, "we may *feel* how our thought presses on beyond the bounds of what it principally illuminates."[103] Apperception is not saturated by the presence of the object as given from alterior angles. It is, in fact, generally quite vague and of less experiential intensity than one finds in perception, "a stream of dispersed light enveloping the central ray and terminating in a dimly lit halo."[104] But its vital role in perception comes sharply into relief when it is realized that without apperception we could not re-cognize *in presence* the appearances that we originally anticipated *in absence*, and thus, on shifting from one appearance to another, could not appreciate the new appearance as an appearance of *the same* object as that appearing through the old.

Imagine, now, a large sailing vessel in its journey outward toward the open seas. The ship proceeds toward that demarcation which we call the horizon, and then beyond. Though it has passed beyond the purview of sensory givenness, the mind still follows it, anticipating what vistas greet the sailors from their present vantage point.[105] Yet, as Van Peursen notes,

> The really striking fact about the horizon is that it recedes. . . . There is a horizon everywhere man gazes. . . . it is not a question of an "over there" which we can approach. The horizon is not in the world, among trees and walls. . . . The world does not become fuller because something like a horizon exists. The horizon does not enrich the world. . . . The horizon is the translation of man into the world.[106]

The horizon is not a boundary that merely confines the sensory presence of the earth as manifested within our perspective. "The horizon sums up all possible perspectives."[107] It is the linear locus of unity whereby the impressionally present passes continually off into that region of absence that is the province of apperception. It is the infinite ensemble of possible passageways beyond the immediately given, the Way of all (perceptual) ways. At the same time, the horizon functions not merely to demarcate this side from that, but also to deliminate figure from ground. The great sphere of the earth appears upon the vast ground of the celestial firmament with its stars and heavenly bodies. We can, then, with Husserl, call the ensemble of possible alternative views of the selfsame object the "*internal* horizon,"[108] and the ensemble of possible grounds or backgrounds the "*external* horizon" of the planet. Apperception, as Husserl observes,

> reaches . . . in a fixed order of being the limitless beyond [Kersten: "the unlimited"]. What is actually perceived, and what is more or less clearly co-present and determinate (to some extent at least), is partly pervaded, partly girt about [Kersten: "penetrated and surrounded"] with a *dimly apprehended depth or fringe of indeterminate reality* [Kersten: "*actuality*"]. . . . an empty mist of dim indeterminacy gets studded over with

> intuitive possibilities or presumptions [Kersten: "an empty mist of obscure indeterminateness is populated with intuited possibilities or likelihoods"], and only the "form" of the world as "world" is foretokened [Kersten: "predelineated"]. Moreover, the zone of indeterminacy [Kersten: "indeterminate surroundings"] is infinite. The misty horizon that can never be completely outlined [Kersten: "the misty and never fully determinable horizon"] remains necessarily there.[109]

It should, of course, be clear that these horizonal functions are operative in our perception of any object. A common pencil manifests itself to our perceptual gaze, from a certain angle, in sensory presence.[110] But, through apperception, it invites us to fulfill our expectations regarding its "look" from various other perspective slants, thus exhibiting an internal horizon.[111] And the pencil seen against the background of wall or desk or writing paper, brings to light its external horizon as well.

Suppose, now, that the pencil rests upon a sheet of paper on my desk. As it occupies my focal attention, the paper that forms its background is quite lucidly "there" for me in its full sensory presence. The desk, while still present, exhibits a somewhat weakened intensity of conscious presence, and the objects surrounding my desk are yet more faded. At the focal center of the visual field, we find the greatest clarity and intensity, a conscious lucidity that is progressively attenuated as the periphery of the field is approached, until, at the extremity, there remains nothing but the dullest phosphorescence. Beyond this liminal asymptote, we find apperception functioning in the dimension initiated by the external horizon. Pencil, paper, desk, and a few objects are, in whatever degree, perceptually present to me. The house in which these items are located is not. Nor is the neighborhood in which the house is located, or the terrestrial sphere on which the neighborhood is inscribed. These progressively more encompassing contexts are apprehended, in absence, through apperception.

But can this nested Chinese-box series of contexts continue indefinitely? Must there be a *single* most widely embracing context, a Context of all contexts? Suppose there were not. We could not, of course, see the pencil were it not for the contrast between it and its ground. Nor could we see the writing paper on which it rests were it not, in turn, cast in relief upon its own ground. Context is a necessary condition for the appearance of text. We can perceive a given focal "text" *only if* its context is apperceived. And we thus know that the outermost member of the series must be a context. Husserl would argue that, were the series of ever-wider perceived and apperceived contexts indeed endless, we could never succeed even in perceiving so much as a humble pencil, since we could never arrive at a "final" member of the series, and thus every context would turn out to be a new text. Perception must, then, be anchored in a final, all-embracing external horizon—in Husserl's designation: the World-Horizon.[112]

While the need for "ultimacy" is patent, and the Husserlian intimations in this respect are cogent, we witness here a certain unwarranted slippage from "ultimacy" to "uniqueness." Merleau-Ponty has voiced in our hearing the *Gestalt*-inspired doctrine that "To be conscious = to have a figure on a ground. . . ." (VI, 191). And we have nodded assent. Surely, conscious intensity is "the work of the negative" inasmuch as discrimination is the setting of parts apart. To discriminate is to place the parts of a whole *a se*, to se/parate by an act of negation, to bring it about experientially that this part *is not* that part. Discrimination is thus an act of *parturition*, an act that "gives birth" to conscious intensity.

The distribution of intensity across the field of consciousness is a manifestation of the distributed "depth" of the activity of discrimination, and intensity is "highest" where discrimination is "deepest." In discrimination, the object *as a whole* is taken as the background for its parts, and if these parts are discriminated, they in turn serve as background for their parts. In such a case, there would be foreground objects upon a background of backgrounds. Nor need the iteration of backgrounds stop there. The original object may itself be apprehended as a figure upon some wider ground—as, say, an object within a room—and so on indefinitely. The "bite" of discrimination is thus a measure of our simultaneous apprehension of iterated backgrounds. The more backgrounds we keep distinctly in mind, the more intense our awareness of the "shallowest" foreground figure.

The typical differentiation of consciousness in continual descent from noonday brilliance to the highly attenuated gloaming of conscious intensity is a descent in the direction of that which has no intensity, that of which we are unconscious. And with respect to the *relatively* unconscious, or *relatively* little discriminated denizens of the field, Merleau-Ponty is assuredly correct:

> This unconscious is to be sought not at the bottom of ourselves, behind the back of our "consciousness," but in front of us, as articulations of our field. It is "unconscious" by the fact that it is not an *object*, but it is that through which objects are possible. . . . It is between them as the interval of the trees between the trees, or as their common level. (VI, 180)

Yet, though the "common level" may be spectral and faint in comparison with the trees, there could be no comparison at all if the common level made no showing within the field of consciousness. Every level *which has a level*, which is itself a figure upon some further level, is granted some degree of intensity.

Every discriminable level is parturient, "pregnant." A level is a *matrix* (a womb) which "gives birth to" discriminated parts. The logic of the field demands, however, in conflict with Husserl's intent to shelter the World-Horizon as the terminus of an entirely *finite* regress to ultimacy, that discrimination plunge asymptotically, in an infinite series of higher and higher attenuations of intensity (or lower and lower degrees of awareness), toward a limit that it is hopeless to attain. Suppose that a figure, *A*, rests upon a ground, *B*. If *B* is to have any degree of intensity—which it *must* in order to provide the necessary contrast with *A*—then *B* must, in turn, be situated upon a further ground, *C*. And this reasoning will perpetuate itself to infinity in an infinite series of figures upon grounds . . . : *A* upon *B*, *B* upon *C*, *C* upon *D* . . . We know, however, that the field is not infinite in extent. Thus, the field boundary must provide a limit within which this asymptotic drama is played out—a limit, however, which, of necessity, cannot reside *within* the field. This result is, in the etymologically primary sense, simply "paradoxical": beyond *(para)* belief *(doxa)*. In Loy's brisk commentary, "Husserl's attempt to analyze [the] horizon phenomenologically" amounts to "bringing that background into the foreground, a feat no less extraordinary than levitating by pulling on one's shoelaces."[113]

The contrast between any figure and its ground is one of *greater* to *lesser* intensity. The contrast between the field and what lies beyond it is existential: that of *some* intensity to *no* intensity. The field boundary is the boundary of a "silhouette," as it were. Our ability to silhouette the field relies upon our ability to contrast the totality of the *filled*, the experientially present, with the totality of the *empty*, the absent. If we silhouette only a portion of the filled, we fail to capture the field in its entirety. And were we able to silhouette any portion of the empty—in particular, that portion of the empty which contains the field boundary which has been expelled from the field—we would, contrary to hypothesis, permit within the empty a distinction between silhouetted (figure) and nonsilhouetted (ground), thus incoherently filling a portion of the empty. The simultaneous salvage of coherence and the phenomenal givenness of the field boundary requires an alternative to discriminating consciousness (the third link of the twelvefold chain of conditions). This, in the Buddhist tradition, is the awareness or mindfulness *(sati)* that arises, through the meditative cultivation of inner peace and insight, upon the revocation of the gestalt structuration of the field.

We know that discriminating consciousness evaporates without an ultimate horizonal ground. Yet we must not be tempted to infer from this desideratum that *the same* ground enframes every episode of consciousness. Intentionality is precisely the *écart* deliminating text and context, figure and ground. And intentionality, to entertain its figural end, must assuredly begin. As we have urged, however, the destabilized vectoriality of awareness can fly from any branch.

Or shall we put the matter another way? The enactment of intentionality is, for Husserl, the actualization of horizonal potentiality. If the horizon is, indeed, "an empty mist of obscure indeterminateness . . . populated with intuited possibilities or likelihoods," then to shift one's focus is to realize an alternative possibility for focal presencing, to actualize an alternative likelihood. Of course, were the realized focus itself simply one among the manifold focal possibilities, exactly the same fund of possibility would ground every intentional occurrence. There would be a single ground for every act, a single all-embracing horizon, a world-horizon:[114] the incomprehensibly vast reservoir of possibility of which the present act is but a flickering realization.[115] But we may well be given to wonder whether the present focus, the present focusing, is among the possibles.

It may be, as Hartshorne and others would commend, that the necessary is that which is common to all possibilities.[116] But the *factical*, whether contingent or necessary, is among the possibles only under the presumption that an alternative possible could have been realized in its stead. And to harbor the consequent is to unleash the evident regress. If possibility *A* could have been realized instead of *B*, the realizability of *A* is itself a third possibility, *C*, which, if among the possibles, demands the possibility, *D*, of its own realization, and thus without end. Or again, to claim that even though I presently entertain, in focal presence, the book on my desk, I can, here and now, lend attention to the lamp instead, strikes one as immediately suspect. To be sure, I *cannot* focally entertain *both* at one and the same time—unless, of course, both become moments of a more expansive theme, perhaps the corner of my desk at which both lamp and book are located. And then there is no question of maintaining the focus that I *now* enjoy. But the issue is one of disjunction, not conjunction. It would give us pause to be informed that, though now drinking our morning coffee, we *could* be drinking tea, instead. Formally couched, "what I am drinking now" picks out Colombian Supremo, not Darjeeling, and cannot be conflated with "whatever I might happen to be drinking now," which would select coffee or tea, depending on the morning's whim. Likewise, if I am gazing lovingly at my weathered and faithful copy of *Being and Nothingness*, it is *that* volume, and not another thing, that occupies my attention.[117] It is not simply *true* that the Sartrean classic obturates my gaze, but, in an intriguing sense, *necessarily* true. If, though I see *this* one, I *could* see that, if *this very object* that I presently regard could compete in the same lists with a mere possibility—and could *lose*—then this very object is itself, to our great surprise, and certainly contrary to our solid intuitions, a mere possibility.

To deny this Kripkean commonplace is to neglect the concrete individuality of the object before me. The general point, and certainly a thesis congruent with our own Buddhist proclivities, is ratified in Kripke's insightful ruminations:

> Now could *this table* have been made from a completely *different* block of wood, or even of water cleverly hardened into ice—water taken from the Thames River? We could conceivably discover that, contrary to what we now think, this table is indeed made of ice from the river. But let us suppose that it is not. Then, though we can imagine making a table . . . from ice, identical in appearance with this one, and though we could have put it in this very position in the room, it seems to me that this is *not* to imagine *this* table as made of . . . ice, but to imagine another table, *resembling* this one in all external details, made of . . . ice.[118]

This does not, of course, amount to the thesis, perhaps more at home in Hegel's philosophy, that everything is necessary. Necessity rather supervenes upon that which is independently and contingently true.

Remarkably, almost eight centuries before Kripke, Dōgen composed the

Genjokoan fascicle of the *Shōbōgenzō,* comprising a remark which, while considerably stronger than the Kripkean thesis, entails the supervenience of necessity upon contingent facticity:

> We should not take the view that what is latterly ashes was formerly firewood. What we should understand is that, according to the doctrine of Buddhism, firewood stays at the position of firewood. . . . There are former and later stages, but these stages are clearly cut.[119]

Firewood "exerts" the entire fund of its potentiality in being precisely what it is—as, of course, does ash. Firewood cannot become ash inasmuch as becoming assumes a certain reserve of potentiality underlying the purported transition. But equally, and to the present point, the "position" of firewood cannot be supplanted by any further possibility, since all the relevant possibilities of that position are actualized in its suchness.

Facticity is not, then, to be accounted among the possibles. It is, if you like, "impossible," or at least deeper than the possible. Or more tellingly, every likelihood inhabiting the horizon is the modalization of facticity, a way the factical could be. The actual world is not one among the possible worlds. Rather, possible worlds are alternative modes of the actual.[120] To invoke the Buddhist idiom, possibility is rooted in suchness *(tathatā).*[121] Rather than delivering us over to a new focus, the true actualization of horizonal potential is revolutionary in Magliola's sense: "[T]he authentic experience of *śūnyatā* runs a sort of Maoist 'continuing revolution' against focus!"[122]

A Buddhist "deconstruction," if we can, without misleading, bend the term to our own purposes, is not, of course, an exotic variation on the theme of ontological reduction. The object is empty, not solely because it owes its very existence to the manifold of its requisite conditions, nor even because this ontological debt is marked "paid," but also, and crucially, because the creditor (for Husserl, the stratum of immanence) is itself bankrupt of own-being. It remains, then, in a parallel way, to deconstruct the ego *(ātman)*, the purported agent of intentional activity and patient of sensory givenness that clings to the event of consciousness by the fragile filaments of mere grammar.

The Ego as Reflection

We have found reason to celebrate the notable sagacity of the parakeet. Bennett dampens the fête, however, by recounting Skinner's rather disappointing experiment with the pigeon:

> The birds were trained to peck at blue spots, and were adorned in such a way that blue spots on their own breasts could be seen by them only

> in mirrors; after a while, they learned to use the mirror images as evidence and to peck at the spots that were painted on themselves.[123]

Gallup, hoping to demonstrate self-awareness, performed a similar experiment with chimpanzees:

> Place a large mirror beside a chimpanzees cage, and within a few days the chimpanzee will start using her image in the mirror as a means of exploring parts of her body that she cannot see directly. A chimpanzee that has long shown an interest in strange marks on her arms, say, will use her mirror image to explore marks that she otherwise couldn't see on her forehead.[124]

While "The pigeon's use of mirrors . . . did not reflect any special attentiveness to their own bodies in particular," we notice that "the chimpanzee is not merely interested in paint marks that are on her, but is interested in them *because* they are on her."[125] Yet, according to Bennett, significantly more is required in order to demonstrate that our primate cousin is endowed with self-awareness, namely, "some reason to say that the chimpanzee attends to the mark on her brow because 'it is on *me*' and not merely because 'it is on *this*.'. . ."[126]

It is, of course, quite tempting to suppose, with Bennett, that the "'I' thought," indeed the "'I think' thought," marks the "me" off from the "this."[127] But this account assumes, without phenomenological warrant, that the "me" is not at the same time a "this."[128] In Sartre's view, a view which Buddhist (anti)egology thoroughly underwrites, "The *me* appears only with the reflective act" (TE, 60), "the psychic and psycho-physical me is a transcendent object" (TE, 36), and thus, an objectual "this."[129] For Sartre, both *reflecting* and *reflected* consciousness are impersonal, anonymous.[130] While there is, I believe, sound reason to dismiss the "two consciousness" model of reflection, and indeed reflection itself insofar as it requires the "two," anonymity remains as a fundamental phenomenal feature of our mental life. The chimpanzee may gaze into the mirror at the mark on her brow because "it is on *this*," and not because "it is on *me*."[131] But in this respect, we do not differ.[132]

Of the searching insights elucidated by Buddhist meditative practice, none plumbs deeper, none is more powerfully transformative, none effects greater upheaval of affect and perspect, than the realization of self-lessness *(anātman)*.[133] "All *dhammas* are without self."[134] And in adumbration, if not in the minutiae of its detail, the Sartrean egology, though perhaps Cartesian in its inspiration, proves a worthy companion. Yet companions, however dear, seldom accompany us in all of our chosen byways. And we must therefore mark the junctures at which Sartre departs our company.

Though Sartre is assuredly correct in regarding the Husserlian ego as "a sort of X-pole which would be the support of psychic phenomena," to say only this much would be to misrepresent through deficiency. For the indifferent unity of the "X-pole" cannot convey the sense of spontaneous *source* implicit in the Husserlian acceptation. For Sartre, consciousness itself assumes certain functions assigned to the Husserlian ego, and is, like the latter, a "wellspring," an "upsurge" *(jaillissement)*, a fulmination which "unifies," not as an objective synthesis, but as a virtual locus of origination. Sartre divides the functions of unification and originary spontaneity, assigning the one to the ego and the other to consciousness itself.[135] "Thus," as Sartre admits, "the consciousness which says *I Think* is precisely not the consciousness which thinks" (TE, 45).[136] For Husserl, on the contrary, the "I Think" is given thought and given voice precisely by the *I,* the *ego*, who thinks.[137]

There is, for Descartes, no truth more solidly and inalienably "possessed" than "the *cogito*,"[138] our elliptical expression for the familiar Cartesian thesis, formulated in the *Discourse* as "I am thinking, therefore I exist"[139] and in the *Meditations* as "this proposition: I am, I exist, is necessarily true, each time that I pronounce it or that I mentally conceive it."[140] The divergence of the two articulations is of some import, the one seeming to allow continuance of my existence beyond the momentary occurrence of thinking, and the other inhibiting this suggestion.[141] Sartre, our present delegate for the Cartesian tradition, commits himself, in the *Transcendence*, to a version of the latter formulation, forsaking the former, in positing the identity of being and appearing. Consciousness, as conceived in the *Transcendence*, simply *is* the appearing of its object. And, of course, "consciousness" embraces all the modalizations *(modi cogitandi)* covered by the richly expansive Cartesian *cogito* and its equally comprehensive vernacular counterpart, *je pense*. Among the forms of cognition *(perceptio)*, Sartre would assuredly admit "sensation, imagination and pure intellection," and among the volative functions of mind, the "desiring, holding in aversion, affirming, denying, doubting"[142] of Descartes's catalog. Sartre would not, however, admit the disjunction of will and intellect. "[W]e must return to Spinoza's doctrine and identify will and consciousness."[143] The *being* of consciousness, in any of its modalities, cannot exceed the momentariness of objectual appearing, the revelation of object or project, since Sartre, in his devotion to pellucid subjectivity, is still under the spell of immanence.

Cogito and *sum*—occurrences, but not propositions, identical, but not equivalent—cannot serve as premise and conclusion of an argument.[144] "Ergo" is not earnest of implication.[145] Indeed, were "the *cogito*" to function as an inference, it would issue enthymematic demands that could only be fulfilled by assurances from without the circuit of apodicticity.[146] The major of the syllogism could only be the extensional, "Whatever thinks, exists," or the intensional, "To think is to exist." In the drama of the *Meditations*, all has fallen in devastation to the axe of doubt—all, that is, with the exception of the *cogito*. And to complement the purported enthymeme with a problematic major is thereby to problematize the *sum*, a result that neither Descartes nor Sartre would countenance. The extensional thesis, "Whatever thinks, exists," cannot rise to the requisite measure of apodicticity, requiring survey for its verification, a procedure porous to doubt. Or if the extensional variant is an *implicandum* of the intensional, we must remind ourselves that even the cherished securities of logic, mathematics and geometry, "clear and distinct" one and all, have been subverted by the Evil Genius. "To think is to exist," no matter how hospitable to the light of reason, articulates a mere conceptual connection that the malevolent deity of Descartes's hypothesis, eager to confuse, to lead cognitively astray, may have implanted for his own mischievous amusement. The *cogito* surpasses, however, even the typical desiderata of Descartes's epistemology. As Dillon assures us:

> If clarity and distinctness were indeed sufficient to assure the certainty of our ideas . . . then there would be no reason to begin with the cogito rather than with any other clear and distinct idea. The indubitability of the cogito must accordingly rest upon some other foundation.[147]

The searching radicalism of the hyperbolic doubt pushes beyond the mere diaphaneity of the thought. For, as Descartes cogently perceived, it is not yet apparent that thought is internal to the thinking of it.[148] And only the slightest breach between *cogitatum* and *cogito* is needed for the devil's cognitive mischief. We must have, not transparency, but *self-transparency*.[149] And we must therefore be absolutely assured that "thinking" and "thought" are *one* and pellucid.[150]

There is another reason compelling rejection of the inferential reading of "ergo." Let us once again follow the argument: I think. Whatever thinks, exists. Therefore, I exist. The logic of quantification[151] has taught us to parse the extensional major: "For any *x*, if *x* thinks, then *x* exists." Thus, "I" becomes a "substitution instance" of the variable. But the major premise, packed or unpacked, is affirmed in the *third person*. "I think" is, of course, given voice in the *first person*. And the substitution of "I" for *x* is possible only if the Cartesian subject can be found among its third-person objects.[152] Neither Descartes nor Sartre would license the replacement, since *subject* is not, and cannot be, *object*.[153] Nor is it of any avail to repair to the intensional formulation. For "I think" could have no purchase upon "To think is to exist" unless the latter were extensionally parsed.[154]

The oneness of thinking and thought within the self-transparency of nonobjectifiable subjectivity is itself disclosed, and is itself the disclosure, in Sartrean prethematic self-lucidity.[155] "What can properly be called subjectivity is consciousness (of) consciousness" (BN, 23), the parenthetical "of" marking the hazard of objectification. Of course,

> if my consciousness were not consciousness of being consciousness of the table, it would then be consciousness of that table without consciousness of being so. In other words, it would be a consciousness ignorant of itself, an unconscious—which is absurd. (BN, 11)

But while Sartre might here appear to endorse the rationalist "bell" (when we really know, we *know* that we know—a bell rings, something chimes), he is not unaware of the regress, by no means benign, thus propagated.

> Either we stop at any one term of the series—the known, the knower known, the knower known by the knower, *etc.* In this case the totality of the phenomenon falls into the unknown; that is, we always bump up against a non-self-conscious reflection and a final term. Or else we affirm the necessity of an infinite regress (*idea ideae ideae*, etc.), which is absurd. (BN, 12)

The dilemma is dispatched by appeal to the "prereflective *cogito*," the prethematic "consciousness (of) consciousness" which provides a final term without condemning us to the absurdity of an unconscious consciousness.[156]

It can only be the prereflective *cogito*—not, as we shall see, the Sartrean ego—that answers the Cartesian demand for a flexuous arcing of subjectivity upon itself.[157] The self-enclosed curvilinearity typified by Ouroboros devouring its own tail, subject and object united in seamless self-consumption, images forth the primordial sense of self exemplified in the spontaneous and originary upsurge of prereflective consciousness. This self, however, is as yet "no one."[158] The prereflective *cogito* remains staunchly impervious to thematization. And indeed, prereflective consciousness, though entirely transparent to itself, remains radically impersonal, anonymous, neither mine nor thine, an undeclined disclosure of the world.[159]

While, in reflection, "we are in the presence of a synthesis of two consciousnesses, one of which is consciousness *of* the other" (TE, 44), both the reflecting and the reflected are prepersonal and prereflective.[160] "All reflecting consciousness is, indeed, in itself unreflected" (TE, 45). Yet, through reflection, there emerges the response to our evident sense of first-person "declension." The ego is, as it were, the mirrored reflection of the *reflecting* consciousness within the *reflected*: "[T]he *I* proffers itself to an intuition of a special kind which apprehends it, always inadequately, behind the reflected consciousness" (TE, 53). The reflected consciousness, however, has by no means relinquished its prereflective engagement with the world and its objects. As a mirror of the world, the reflected brings to conscious prominence ("reflects") a given object and its horizonal ground. And it is thus that the ego, as a second-order reflection, is given to the reflecting consciousness only as an horizonal structure:[161]

> The ego never appears, in fact, except when one is not looking at it. The reflective gaze must be fixed on the *Erlebnis*, insofar as it emanates from the state. Then, behind the state, at the horizon, the ego appears. It is, therefore, never seen except "out of the corner of the eye." As soon as I turn my gaze toward it and try to reach it without passing through

> the *Erlebnis* and the state, it vanishes. This is because in trying to apprehend the ego for itself and as a direct object of my consciousness, I fall back onto the unreflected level, and the ego disappears along with the reflective act. (TE, 88–89)

Thus, while Sartre persistently refers to the ego as an object, it cannot, in principle, perform the same thematic role as the less remarkable objects of our acquaintance. The ego does not obturate. It is not thrown (from the Latin, *jacere*) in our way *(ob-)*, but perpetually retires, withdraws, a renunciation rather than an annunciation, a revocation, not an invocation. And inasmuch as the extroverted world heralds itself in casting its ob/jects before our gaze, the ego is seen as "an object which appears only to reflection, and which is thereby radically cut off from the World. The ego does not live on the same level" (TE, 83).

The ego is the most general structure of the psychic, the "outside" of consciousness. The psychic is, however, a "contradictory compound" (TE, 84). For "an absolute interiority never has an outside" (TE, 84). If the for-itself is, as Sartre so vigorously inculcates, a "hole in being," the psychic is neither the absolute vacuity of conscious nothingness nor the plenary fullness of stolid being, but precisely the "boundary" between them, a lamination without thickness, but in its dimensional privation, without thinness as well.[162] The ego, "a constantly gulling mirage" (TE, 87),[163] is a mere patinal shimmer. "The *outside* of the for-itself is to *be*, as negation of the in-itself, in the same way as the in-itself."[164] Thus, the ego "frolics on the surface of the for-itself and is a kind of insubstantial phantom of [the] in-itself."[165] Again, the psychic generally, and the ego as its exemplary instance, is a certain "reflection."[166]

The duality suggested by Sartre's portrayal of reflection as "a synthesis of two consciousnesses" (TE, 44) becomes immediately problematic in view of his assertion that "reflection and reflected are only one" (TE, 84). Sartre has not lapsed here into perverse, or even careless, inconsistency. For we are immediately apprised of the significantly differing respect informing the oneness of the "two": "[T]he interiority of the one fuses with that of the other" (TE, 84). Duality is apparent only, as it were, "from the outside." The event of reflection "transpires as if interiority closed upon itself and proffered us only its outside; as if one had to 'circle about' it in order to understand it. . . . It is inward *for itself, not for consciousness*" (TE, 84).[167] Yet, paradoxically, consciousness is an "absolute interiority," and thus "never has an outside" (TE, 84). Reflection, incapable of objectifying its own interiority, can only disclose the indistinctness, the very failure of qualitative difference, which, as Sartre observes, "is interiority seen from the outside; or, if one prefers, indistinctness is the degraded projection of interiority" (TE, 85).[168] And indistinctness "may be interpreted as a primitive undifferentiation of all qualities, now as a pure form of being, anterior to all qualification" (TE, 85). Or, in a phrase redolent with suggestions for the splendid Hua-yen vision of phenomenal reality as the jewel-studded Net of Indra, indistinctness may, in its positive presentation, be reclaimed as "interpenetrative multiplicity" (TE, 85).[169] Sartre temporalizes this Bergsonian notion, relativizing it to the past, and speculating that, "with respect to the future" indistinctness may be read as "bare power" (TE, 86). While the *future* may be the fount of potentiality (thus, "potency"), the *present* its actualization, and the *past* its repository of actualities, it is crucial to see that the Buddhist denial of substantiality *(nihsvabhāvatā)* entails the untenability of a supposed underground reservoir of potentiality surging into actuality in a succession of nows. Potentiality *thoroughly exhausts itself* in each moment. And in this sense, each temporal presence is *its own* future-in-act. Thus, the negativity, intuited by Shen-hui, characterizing the inner indifference of the mind-mirror is not a "bare power" eluding the present as the carrot perpetually escapes the donkey, but is rather the potentiality exhaustively actualizing itself in the mirror's positive interpenetration.[170]

But to say as much does not yet insinuate the telling ambiguity of the for-itself. And accordingly, Sartre appends to the image of simple reflection a nuance that both potentiates its fruitfulness and withers its potency:

> I shall compare this 'in-itself', that comes to tinge the for-itself and constitute an exterior for it, to those reflections one can see on a window-pane when viewing it from an angle and which suddenly mask its transparency—only to vanish as soon as one changes position in relation to the pane.[171]

Consciousness, itself informed with a certain perspectivity, a certain transcendence, grants to us its ambiguity. We are offered alternative views: consciousness *as mirror*, scene of the illusory "dance" that is the ego, and consciousness *as utter transparency*, disclosure of the world. Charming and compelling as the more subtle analogue might seem, it could exert the requisite phenomenological leverage only if there were an experientially discernible difference between "mirror" and "glass." And this, as we have so often intoned, there flatly is not. Description of the psychic as a contradictory compound leaves nothing to forgive. For experience itself, in the very pattern of its flow, is paradoxical. But phenomenology cannot exculpate a theory that roots itself in a distinction that, in principle, cannot be parsed in terms of alternative modalities of presentation.

The Ego as Gestalt

There is, on the part of Buddhist egology, no effort to repugn or suppress the evident *appearance* of the ego, the latter, to be sure, a *phenomenon bene fundata*.[172] But neither have we come to expect repudiation of the appearance of the possessable object. What we have discovered from the doctrine of "dependent co-origination" *(pratītya-samutpāda)* is not the nonexistence of the object, but its merely *conditional* (or, as we might say, "horizon-grounded") existence, not the privation of quality, but the bankruptcy of monadicity. The object has no "own-being" *(svabhāvatā)*.[173] Nor has it any "own-appearing." And the possessive ego is like unto its possessions, an emergence or upsurge, a gestalt, without intrinsic determination and enjoying only a borrowed existence.[174] Clearly in consonance, Sartre rejects the Husserlian doctrine that "What is logically first are unilateral relations by which each quality belongs (directly or indirectly) to this X like a predicate to a subject" (TE, 73). The ego is not a logical subject, and thus, not a subject of monadic predication.[175] The ego cannot, then, function as a unitary "pole" tethering the extroverted "acts" of consciousness. Indeed,

> an indissoluble synthetic totality which could support itself would have no need of a supporting X, provided of course that it were really and concretely unanalyzable. If we take a melody, for example, it is useless to presuppose an X which would serve as a support for the different notes. The unity here comes from the absolute indissolubility of the elements which cannot be conceived as separated, save by abstraction. The subject of the predicate here will be the concrete totality, and the predicate will be a quality abstractly separated from the totality, a quality which has its full meaning only if one connects it again to the totality. (TE, 73–74)

Three marbles tossed randomly to the floor, in relative proximity to one another, will, if not forming a line, quite readily be seen as the corners of a triangle. The triangle "emerges." We *know* that in reality only the three agates are "there" to be seen. Yet undeniably, we do perceive the triangle.[176] We *see* more than is there to be seen. Indeed, we see it *first*: the whole *before* the parts. Appearance thus quarrels with being. Or rather, the very *being* of the triangle is "on loan." Like the moon, it *appears* the "lender" while *being* the "borrower." Congruently,

> the ego is an object apprehended, but also an object *constituted*, by reflective consciousness. . . . *really*, consciousnesses are first; through these are constituted states; and then, through the latter, the ego is constituted. But, as the order is reversed by a consciousness which imprisons itself in the world in order to flee from itself, consciousnesses are given as emanating from states, and states as produced by the ego. It follows that consciousness projects its own spontaneity into the ego-object in order to confer on the ego the creative power which is absolutely necessary to it. . . . Whence the profound irrationality of the notion of an ego. (TE, 80–81)

The ego is afflicted with a curiously retroflexive species of transcendence. Not content with simple divergence of *being* from *appearing*, the ego, itself an "emergent" phenomenon, is hostile to the very conditions that sustain its life, repudiating in its appearing the ontological indebtedness that, in fact, maintains its ungrateful existence.[177]

Remove, now, one of the marbles. The figure which rises to the eye is now a line. The triangle, wholly dependent, and dependent *as such*, in its essence as well as its existence, upon the three marbles, has now vanished, not modified, but supplanted, by the line. And the ego, "nothing outside of the concrete totality of states and actions it supports" (TE, 74), enjoys the same "sensitivity" to the matrix of conditions which gives birth to it.

> For these very reasons we shall not permit ourselves to see the ego as a sort of X-pole which would be the support of psychic phenomena. Such an X would, by definition, be indifferent to the psychic qualities it would support. But the ego . . . is never indifferent to its states; it is "compromised" by them. (TE, 74)

The Husserlian ego, "whose mission," Sartre misguidedly asserts, "is only to unify" (TE, 74), is endowed with the indifference of the mirror. But the mirror, in Sartre's view, is misplaced. The gestalt play of co-origination does, of course, invoke the anonymous reflectivity of mind. But for Sartre, it is consciousness, not a purported opacity imbedded within it, standing behind it, or projecting through it which is "mirrorlike."[178] And it is not the "mind-mirror," but a peripheral "reflection" twinkling upon it, which accounts for the personal declension, the "I-ness," of consciousness.

Like the picture that emerges from the myriad and variously shaded dots of the newsprint, the ego is a pattern arising from the states, actions, and optionally, qualities, that inform the psychic exterior of consciousness.[179] Transcendent in the Sartrean infinitary sense, the ego is "the infinite totality of states and actions which is never reducible to *an* action or to *a* state" (TE, 74), or again, to *a* quality. Sartre says of the state of hatred, itself constituted through a concrete flux of momentary *Erlebnisse*, experiences of repugnance,

> It is given precisely as not being limited to this experience. My hatred was given *in* and *by* each movement of disgust, of repugnance, and of anger, but at the same time it is not any of them. My hatred escapes from each of them by affirming its permanence. (TE, 62–63)

Action, similarly transcendent and including the acts of consciousness which largely absorbed Husserl's investigatory attention, "is not only the noematic unity of a stream of consciousnesses: it is also a concrete realization" (TE, 69). And the quality (or better: "disposition"),[180] conceived as "a unity of objective passivities" (TE, 71), "is given as a potentiality, a virtuality, which, under the influence of diverse factors, can pass into actuality. Its actuality is precisely the state (or the action)" (TE, 70). The ego is, in Sartre's incompletely illuminating idiom, the open-ended "totality" of states, actions and qualities. It is as if, in ascending vertically in a helicopter, the individual stones, the distinct blades of grass, all the detail which companions our accustomed range, were to pour together, lost in indistinction. The blades of grass, once seen severally, now meld into a continuous sea of green. And as we ascend, even the verdant fields, once articulate, now dissolve into an overall terrain. It is not, of course, the terrain that is indistinct. For we see it, in precisely the pertinent way, the only way, and the clearest way, it can appear, from our elevated vantage. It is rather the fields which, in loosing themselves in the terrain, become indistinct. The fields, in turn, were also revealed in an appropriately distinct way simultaneously with the dissolution of earth-bound detail.

The ego, is a phenomenon of "altitude," a *pensée de survol*, as Merleau-Ponty would say, the terrain that lies open to the reflective gaze. But the Sartrean analysis belies tacit commitment to the "realist distinction," the relocation of the real beyond the merely apparent. "*[R]eally*," in Sartre's emphatic pronouncement, "consciousnesses are first." The twigs and pebbles of immediate experience are *real*. The egological landscape is merely *apparent*. In *Being and Nothingness*, Sartre claims to have "ruled out a *realistic* conception of the relations of the phenomenon with consciousness" (BN, 26). But this early lapse into realism bodes ill. The realist wedge is driven deeper by Sartre's distinction between pure and impure reflection.

> We see here two reflections: the one, impure and conniving, which effects then and there a passage to the infinite, and which through the *Erlebnis* abruptly constitutes hatred as its transcendent object; the other, pure, merely descriptive, which disarms the unreflected consciousness by granting its instantaneousness. These two reflections apprehend the same, certain data, but the one affirms *more* than it knows, directing itself through the reflected consciousness upon an object situated outside consciousness. (TE, 64–65)

The brunt of the distinction is, however, substantially modified by Sartre's parenthetical admission that pure reflection "is not necessarily phenomenological reflection" (TE, 64). Though he may falter at the precipice, no one has recognized more perspicaciously than Sartre the unyielding aspiration of phenomenology to liberate itself from the polarity of idealism and realism. Thus, the lapse into realism is especially grievous.

"Neither a borrower nor a lender be": prosaic counsel at best—from any quarter, that is, but the phenomenological. The Sartrean ego is unmistakably a "borrower," owing its very existence to the flux momentary lived experience, and the river of living *Erlebnisse* is no less certainly a "lender." The purported reversal of illumination, the lunar refraction which informs the apparent ego's dispute with its very being, is, however, itself a posit of speculation loosed from its moorings in the phenomenal. We are thus firmly aligned with the Buddhist view voiced by Trinh thi Minh-hà:

> When i say "I see myself seeing myself," I/i am not alluding to the illusory relation of subject to subject (or object) but to the play of mirrors that defers to infinity the real subject and subverts the notion of an original "I." . . . No primary core of irradiation can be caught hold of, no hierarchical first, second, or *third* exists except as mere illusion. All is empty when one is plural.[181]

Sartre assumes a "primary core of irradiation." But if, as our study persistently inculcates, original and reflection are phenomenally indiscernible, we have no right to this assumption. Again, in Trinh's words:

> From mirage to mirage, the subject/object takes flight and loses its existence. Trying to grasp it amounts to stopping a mirror from mirroring. It is encountering the void. Not a transitory void, but one (the one) that has always been there despite our eternal effort to banish it from conscious sight.[182]

If it is true that "the consciousness which says *I Think* is precisely not the consciousness which thinks," it is equally true that *no* consciousness, reflecting or reflected, is endowed with this agential and originary power. There is no "source."

We find wisdom in the tutelage of infants. And wisdom accrues no less to the primordial impression, undistorted by subsequent accretions of sense, unravaged, indeed, by even the informing of "truth."[183] It is a phenomenological insight of far greater moment than mere accuracy of representation that mirror *qua* mirror is hopelessly indistinguishable from glass *qua* glass, that reflectivity and transparency enjoy, at best, a merely speculative or theoretical difference, but coalesce in undefiled experience. And this being so, the Sartrean egology is precisely what Sartre claims it to be: "an existentialist *theory* of consciousness." Only now the epithet turns bitter. For "theory," in this sense, is exactly the betrayal of the phenomenal.

Leading me along

my shadow goes back home

from looking at the moon

(SODŌ, 1641–1716)

The Diary of a Moon-Gazer

I.

A storm wind blows
out from among the grasses
the full moon grows

Suddenly it was there—uninvited—at first only dimly distinguished from the frenzied gossamer that all but obscured it. It emerged *ex nihilo* from the logic and mystery of Universal Process—a plenum presence converting adumbral dalliance with Being into round and centered plenitude of contact. "It left me breathless. . . . It had lost the harmless look of an abstract category: it was the very paste of things, this root was kneaded into existence. . . ." (*Nausea,* J.-P. Sartre). Its luminous sphericity was at once profoundly engaging and profoundly placid—curvilinearity folded into itself with nirvanic serenity, like a slumbering kitten.

II.

The moon on the pine—
I keep hanging—taking it off—
and gazing each time.

With the inception of perspective it no longer overspilled the rim of consciousness. Arrested by comparison and critical examination it surrendered the dynamic of its Suchness. *Hanging* and *Taking-off* became hypostatized polarities, and the tension generated by this artificiality shattered the smooth stone of Unity into jagged perplexities.

III.

In all this cool
is the moon also sleeping
there in the pool?

A chill wind blew up out of the "future" (a mere phantasmal postexistence) laden with miasma, and companioning with grim specters brandishing cruel and foreboding scimitars. The invasion of the wraiths-of-fancied-futurity occurred in a world between the eyes—yet each pool in isolation swallowed up the moon without disturbing her sleep.

IV.

Whatever we wear
we become beautiful
moon viewing!

Invoking the benign Origin—the transcendental present—bathing in its luminescence we are suddenly denuded, our chrysalid and crustacean essences dropping like a robe, our pristine being buoying up, individual-yet-formless like a mirror. Peering into each other's universe, we see one another naked of all but identity. These glimpses are the sparks flying upward—toward the benign Origin.

V.

That there is only one
is unbelievable tonight.
This harvest moon!

Its singularity is miraculous! Still, there is something disturbing, agitating, fracturing tranquility into ten thousand "possibilities." That liberation is quiescence seems incredible—perhaps *is* incredible. Who can navigate all these refractions?

VI.

Leading me along
my shadow goes back home
from looking at the moon.

Lacerating the narrow footpath, my all too definite silhouette informs me of the positions of the moon—behind me! Someone cut a whole in my mind and the moon fell out. Yet emptiness is a friend.

Epilogue

Nothing exists only by invitation. It is Expectation that requests the presence of Absence. Luna, huddled in chaste and sensuous circularity, still smiles. As for me, an old mystic of Yellow Plum Mountain kicking at the stumps, I sometimes laugh. I think I know the game she likes to play. Each time I turn my back upon her, her absence will grow so luminous that I can never distinguish her presence from her absence. In more quiet moments the prophecy engraved in the marrow of my bones makes me serene and buoyant. Someday the slumbering kitten will awaken and turn to lightning!

Notes

An Incident at Wang-mei Shan

The haiku by Chora is from Harold G. Henderson, *An Introduction to Haiku: An Anthology of Poems and Poets from Bashō to Shiki* (Garden City, N.Y.: Doubleday, 1958), p. 122.

1. In the Wade-Giles transliteration:

   Shen shih p'u t'i shu,
   Hsin ju ming ching t'ai.
   Shih shih ch'in fu shih,
   Mo shih jo ch'en ai.

2. In an address delivered in Los Angeles on 12 June 1985, the Venerable Thích Mạn-Giác, president of the Congregation of Vietnamese Buddhists in the United States, remarked: "In the books it's always related that the sixth patriarch, Hui Neng, was Chinese, but I know he was Vietnamese. . . . Before he became the sixth patriarch, when he first came to the fifth patriarch to ask for the teachings, do you remember what the fifth patriarch said? He said, 'You barbarian from the south, what do you know?' The sixth patriarch replied, 'Buddha nature is in everyone, so what's the difference if I live in the south?'" Thích Mạn-Giác, "The Branch That Gleams in the Dark: An Introduction to Vietnamese Buddhism" (Los Angeles: The First American-Vietnamese Buddhist Monastery, 1985), pp. 10–11. The word "Nam" appearing in "Việt-Nam" meaning *south,* the compound, "Việt-Nam," bears the dual signification of "southland of the Việts" and "transcendence *[vượt]* toward the south."

3. Transliterating once again:

   P'u t'i pen wu shu,
   Hsin ching i fei t'ai.

Pen lai wu i wu,
He ch'u jo ch'en ai.

Prelude in the Key of Emptiness

1. As Quasha correctly senses, taking a position "implies a certain fixity, requiring defense and perhaps aggressiveness in advancing the position. . . ." George Quasha, "A Virtual Account" (BSM, 212). Of the divergences that separate one such view from another, Jean-Luc Nancy writes: "Each of these breaks is a break of philosophy, and not within philosophy. Therefore they are incommensurable with and incommunicable to one another. They represent a disarticulation of the common space and of the common discourse of 'philosophy'. . . ." Jean-Luc Nancy, "Introduction" (WCAS, 2). Indeed, "Many lines of rupture traverse *us* . . . philosophy separated from itself, outside of itself, crossing its own limits—which means, perhaps, discovering that it never did have proper limits, that it never was, in a sense, a 'property'." Nancy, "Introduction" (WCAS, 2).

2. From the outset, we should affirm with Hayward that "Buddhism is the study of mind—its essence, nature, and functioning. . . . ," and thus an investigation of the mind *as mirror*. Jeremy W. Hayward, foreword to Herbert V. Guenther, *From Reductionism to Creativity: rDzogs-chen and the New Sciences of Mind* (Boston: Shambhala, 1989), p. ix.

3. Placing the accent on the "thing," it is interesting, in this light, to ponder Merleau-Ponty's proposal that "the thing is much less a pole which attracts than one which repels" (PhP, 324). As argued in "Hui-neng and the Transcendental Standpoint," "The operator, 'originally' *(pện lái)*, determines the *way* in which the statement 'Not one thing exists' is true. 'Originally' is a mode of truth, but not, obviously, for the Ch'an tradition, a mode of *propositional* truth. 'Originally' is more faithfully understood as a mode of conscious revelation, a way of being conscious, an attitude or stance of mind. Whatever stance 'originally' may refer to, it must be such that, for consciousness engaged in that mode of conscious life, 'not one thing exists.'" Steven W. Laycock, "Hui-neng and the Transcendental Standpoint," *Journal of Chinese Philosophy* 12 (1985).

4. This reading clearly conflicts with Suzuki's contention that "Zen knows no contradictions; it is the logician who encounters them, forgetting that they are of his own making." D. T. Suzuki, "Existentialism, Pragmatism and Zen," in *Zen Buddhism*, ed. William Barrett (Garden City, N.Y.: Doubleday, 1956), p. 269.

5. Still, phenomena are regulated by that deep insight according to which "Each experience we have is in conflict with others, every thought contradicts others." Bob Boldman, "Zen, Art, and Paradox" (BSM, 33).

6. Is time, for example, Plato's "moving image of eternity," Augustine's subjective extension, or Sartre's "shimmer of nothingness on the surface of a strictly atemporal being" (BN, 294)? Each such prelogical notion establishes a distinct sense in which attribute and complement prove incompossible *at a given time.*

7. As the Prajñā Gāthā suggests, *Prajñā*, etymological kin to "pro/gnosis," denotes a certain precognitive, preintentional intuition:

Prajna, unknowing, knoweth all;
Prajna, unseeing, seeing all.

(HH, 47)

Suzuki finds in prajñā both the condition and the disruption of reason: "[T]he functioning of Prajñā is discrete, and interrupting to the progress of logical reasoning, but all the time it underlies it, and without Prajñā we cannot have any reasoning whatever. Prajñā is at once above and in the process of reasoning. This is a contradiction, formally considered, but in truth this contradiction itself is made possible because of Prajñā" (NM, 55).

8. Clarice Lispector bears convincing witness to a "seeing" which, while not devoid of significance, is, at the same time, not constitutive of significance: "I saw it. I know I did because I didn't give it its meaning. I know that I did because I don't understand it. I know I did because what I saw isn't good for anything" (GH, 9).

9. In his remark that "Phenomenology let itself be defined as the paradoxical search for a theory-free theory" (AE, 125), Adorno conflates two significantly distinct senses of theory: the genuinely phenomenological sense that imports a certain modality of vision, and the remotely derivative sense purged of any quasi-visual presence and preserving only the abstract form of an explanation or account.

10. Merleau-Ponty drives the wedge even deeper between presence and essence: "In the very measure that I see, I do not know *what* I see. . . ." (VI, 247).

11. In Nāgārjuna's words: "What is never cast off, seized, interrupted, constant, extinguished, and produced. . . . this is called *nirvāṇa*" (MK 25:3; N, 154). Concomitantly, Merleau-Ponty is emphatic that he does not wish to "*exclude the possibility that we find in our experience a movement toward what could not in any event be present to us in the original and whose irremediable absence would thus count among our originating experiences*" (VI, 159), a claim that accords well with the "irremediable absence" of *nirvāṇa*.

12. There is an ancient Hawaiian parable of unexcelled loveliness and depth that expresses as powerfully and directly as any text of Hui-neng's the latter's doctrine of original enlightenment: "Each child born has at birth, a Bowl of Perfect Light. If he tends his Light it will grow in strength and he can do all things—swim with the shark, fly with the birds, know and understand all things. If, however, he becomes envious or jealous he drops a stone into his Bowl of Light and some of the Light goes out. Light and the stone cannot hold the same space. If he continues to put stones in the Bowl of Light, the Light will go out and he will become a stone. A stone does not grow, nor does it move. If at any time he tires of being a stone, all he needs to do is turn the bowl upside down and the stones will fall away and the Light will grow once more." Pali Jae Lee & Koko Willis, *Tales from the Night Rainbow: Mo'olelo na Pō Mākole: The Story of a Woman, a People, and an Island* (Honolulu: Night Rainbow, 1990), pp. 18–19. Indeed, the Hawaiians relate, "Our people had been taught by holy men who had come to our shore centuries earlier that there was an Enlightened One. They spoke of him as if the sun shone from his back. . . ." Lee and Willis, *Night Rainbow*, p. 44.

13. For Merleau-Ponty, "The visual field is that strange zone in which contradictory notions jostle each other because the objects . . . are not, in that field, assigned to the realm of being, in which a comparison would be possible, but each is taken in its private context as if it did not belong to the same universe as the other" (PhP, 6).

14. "Everything is, then, truth within consciousness" (PhP, 378).

15. The real prize, of course, was the intuitive wisdom already manifest in Hui-neng's *gāthā*. The honorific name conferred upon Hui-neng by the emperor was a tribute to his resplendence. He was known as "Great Mirror" *(Ta-chien)*.

16. Merleau-Ponty's assertion that "There could not possibly be error where there is not yet truth. . . ." (PhP, 344) does not merely set the two notions in a framework of binary exclusion, but, as a consequence of the deep ambiguity of experience, formulates his recognition that every "position" is simultaneously infected with error and graced with truth. The intellectual humility expressed in the claim, "[E]very position I take is partially erroneous," though leading perhaps to paradox, or at least puzzlement, when applied to itself, is a welcome palliative for the vaulting excesses of philosophical arrogance.

17. Nāgārjuna imparts: "Without relying on everyday common practices (i.e., relative truths), the absolute truth cannot be expressed. Without approaching the absolute truth, *nirvāṇa* cannot be attained" (MK, 24:10; N, 146). In Murti's rendering, "Paramārtha is the end or goal that we seek to attain, and samvṛti is the means; it is the ladder or the jumping board which enables us to reach that objective. . . . samvṛti is the means . . . and Paramārtha is the end. . . ." (CPB, 253). But the "end" is no more than the "beginning" revisioned: "Happenings" can be regarded in a "gathered" *(samvṛti)* and "ungathered" *(paramārtha)* way" (CPB, 119).

18. The Buddhist distinction of two orders of truth does not gainsay Merleau-Ponty's declaration that "There would be no experience of truth, and nothing would quench our 'mental volubility' if we thought *vi formae*, and if formal relations where not first presented to us crystallized in some particular thing" (PhP, 385). The lotus of universality is rooted in the mud of particularity.

19. In any case, as Merleau-Ponty suggests, "The world and reason are not problematical. We may say . . . that they are mysterious, but their mystery defines them. . . ." (PhP, xx).

20. It may be that "Any rationalism admits of at least one absurdity, that of having to be formulated as a thesis" (PhP, 295). But Buddhist insight is prethetic.

21. For Merleau-Ponty, "rationality is neither a total nor an immediate guarantee. It is somehow open, which is to say that it is menaced" (PP, 23).

22. "A truth seen against a background of absurdity, and an absurdity which the teleology of consciousness presumes to be able to convert into truth, such is the primary phenomenon" (PhP, 296).

23. In Adorno's useful characterization, "The name of dialectics says no more, to begin with, than that objects do not go into their concepts without leaving a remainder, that they come to contradict the traditional norm of adequacy" (ND, 5).

24. Richard Rorty, *Philosophy and the Mirror of Nature* (Princeton: Princeton University Press, 1980), p. 12. Rorty, of course, is not alone in his construal of the mirror metaphor. He is joined, for example, by Annette Baier, who explicitly opposes "a Kantian cum Schopenhauerian version of mind as a magic mirror that both reflects the way the world around it is (with some possible 'distortion' provided by its own intrinsic features), and also causes an occasional fire or two in the world by its own presence there, its own efficacious representations." Annette Baier, *Postures of the Mind: Essays on Mind and Morals* (Minneapolis: University of Minnesota Press, 1985), p. 3.

25. Rorty, *Philosophy and the Mirror of Nature*, p. 376.

26. Merton, in describing Hui-neng's view, expresses a complementary and equally vital point in his assertion that "the 'purity' of sunyata is not purity and void considered as an object of contemplation, but a non-seeing, a non-contemplation, in which precisely

it is realized that the 'mirror' or the original mind (of prajñā and emptiness) is actually a non-mirror, and 'no-mind'. . . ." Thomas Merton, *Mysticism and Zen Masters* (New York: Farrar, Straus and Giroux, 1967), p. 32.

27. Baudrillard claims that "Alternation . . . is the end of the end of representation. . . ." (SS, 131). This is illustrated in his account of Andy Warhol's work: "[T]he multiple replicas of Marilyn's face are there to show at the same time the death of the original and the end of representation" (SS, 136). Indeed, "Here not only the syntagmatic dimension is abolished, but the paradigmatic as well. Since there no longer is any formal flection or even internal reflection, but contiguity of the same—flection and reflection zero" (SS, 144).

28. We should here remind ourselves that "philosophy . . . does not begin by being *possible*. . . ." (PhP, xx).

29. Uchiyama Kosho Roshi, *Dogen Zen As Religion* (DZ, 191). Amplifying: "As soon as we become conscious that we have hit the mark, we have already viewed it from our personal point of view as a yardstick. Letting go and throwing down our personal point of view as a yardstick is actualized only beyond our consciousness, in just aiming at zazen with our bones and muscles" (DZ, 194).

30. Perhaps Rorty would wish to transpose into a philosophical register Lyotard's fantasy of a "revolt of things represented [that would be] a world without mirrors, without theatre and without painting [La révolte des choses représentées, sera-ce un monde sans miroir, sans théâtre et sans peinture]." Jean-François Lyotard, "Contributions des tableaux de Jacques Monore," in Gérald Gassiot-Talabot et al., *Figurations 1960–1973* (Paris: Klincksieck, 1973), p. 155.

31. What, for Borch-Jacobsen, is a warranted deliverance of investigation, for Rorty would be a stumbling block: "[W]e cannot (but) represent the unrepresentable, we cannot (but) present the unpresentable." Mikkel Borch-Jacobsen, "The Freudian Subject, from Politics to Ethics" (WCAS, 76).

32. Rodolphe Gasché, *The Tain of the Mirror: Derrida and the Philosophy of Reflection* (Cambridge: Harvard University Press, 1986), p. 238.

33. Trinh thi Minh-hà, *Woman, Native, Other: Writing, Postcoloniality and Feminism* (Bloomington: Indiana University Press, 1989), p. 22. I am indebted to Professor Huma Ibrahim for calling my attention to this extraordinary text.

34. If, as Merleau-Ponty suggests, "each colour, in its inmost depths, is nothing but the inner structure of the thing overtly revealed" (PhP, 229), if "colour in living perception is a way into the thing" (PhP, 305), then an object's possession of color is inconsistent with its being a mirror-reflection.

35. Since, for Merleau-Ponty, "there is no longer any way of distinguishing a level of *a priori* truths and one of factual ones" (PhP, 221), indeed, since "*a priori* truths amount to nothing other than the making explicit of a fact" (PhP, 221), one should hope, on his view, to seize the purity of the ideal mirror *through* the impurity of the empirical.

36. In this connection, consider the "stain" that discolors the mirror of Blofeld's intriguing deployment: "Until we have learnt to control our minds, every single thing perceived affects our consciousness or subconsciousness exactly as a mirror would be affected if all the objects mirrored in it left their individual stains upon its surface! Whether that surface were stained by things 'good' or 'bad' would be immaterial, for their total conglomeration would inevitably produce that dense, muddy colour we get

from mixing all the paints in the paintbox in a single mess." Blofeld, "Translator's Introduction" (HH, 23).

37. Hsüeh-fêng I-ts'un (822–908 C.E.) reports: "A monk argued, 'From the infinite past, it has been nameless. Why do you call it an ancient mirror?' The Master said, 'Now it has a flaw'" (OT, 282).

38. Anaxagoras speculates that "In everything there is a portion of everything except Mind; and there are some things in which there is Mind as well." Fr. 11, *Simplicius, Phys.* 164, 23, as translated in G. S. Kirk, J. E. Raven and M. Schofield, *The Presocratic Philosophers: A Critical History with a Selection of Texts* (Cambridge: Cambridge University Press, 1985), p. 366. Is it not concomitantly the case that in every mirror, no matter how flawed, there is a "portion" *(moira)* of the unflawed, that it falls to every mirror, as its "portion," its "destiny," to be unflawed?

39. For Merleau-Ponty, "This new conception of reflection which is the phenomenological conception of it, amounts . . . to giving a new definition of the *a priori*. . . ." (PhP, 220).

40. It is intriguing to set beside Tsung-mi's words those of the Buddha himself: "This consciousness is luminous but it is defiled by adventitious defilements. The uninstructed average person does not understand this as it really is. Therefore I say that for him there is no mental development.

"This consciousness is luminous, and it is freed from adventitious defilements. The instructed Aryan disciple understands this as it really is. Therefore I say that for him there is mental development." *A/guttara NikOya* [Gradual sayings], trans. I. B. Horner, i.8.10, in Edward Conze, ed., *Buddhist Texts Through the Ages* (New York: Harper and Row, 1954), p. 33. In consonance, Bassui tells us that "The essence of your mind is not born, so it will never die. It is not an existence, which is perishable. It is not an emptiness, which is a mere void. It has neither color nor form. It enjoys no pleasures and suffers no pains" (ZFZB, 78).

41. Merleau-Ponty thus remarks that "the formula of radical reflection is not: 'I know nothing'—a formula which it is all to easy to catch in flat contradiction with itself—but: 'What do I know?'" (PhP, 399).

42. We have Bataille's word that: "*circular, absolute knowledge is definitive non-knowledge.* Even supposing that I were to attain it, I know that I would know nothing more than I know now" (IE, 108).

43. Merleau-Ponty foils the possibility that the mirror-image might in any sense represent its occasioning mirror. "There is no *metaphor* between the visible and the invisible. . . ." (VI, 221). This does not, however, preclude the employment of "mirror" as metaphor.

44. It must, of course, be admitted that whereas light travels *through* a crystal ball, it is remitted, turned back, by the mirror. Metaphors are notoriously limited in their application, and it is best to specify from the outset that the course of illumination is a metaphysical issue. As I shall claim, *both* the perfect mirror *and* the perfect crystal ball are *invisible*, and thus, in this trivial sense, indistinguishable. The usefulness of either metaphor extends no farther than its curious (in)visibility.

45. In Merleau-Ponty's intriguing account: "[W]hen I look closely at snow, I break its apparent 'whiteness' up into a world of reflections and transparencies. . . ." (PhP, 211).

46. Even the remarkable stone of Daumal's description is, by our stringent standards, afflicted with a fateful opacity: "This stone is so perfectly transparent and its index

of refraction so close to that of air in spite of the crystal's great density that the inexperienced eye barely perceives it. But to any person who seeks it with sincerity and out of true need it reveals itself by a brilliant sparkle like that of a dew drop." René Daumal, *Mount Analogue: A Novel of Symbolically Authentic Non-Euclidean Adventures in Mountain Climbing*, trans. Roger Shattuck (Baltimore: Penguin Books, 1974), p. 92.

47. In a very different context, Merleau-Ponty notes that "the course of time is no longer the stream itself: it is the landscape as it rolls by for the moving observer" (PhP, 412). We should note that the continuity of the landscape is not disrupted by the *dis/* continuity of distinct photographic or painterly "views." There are no landscape-regions corresponding to the regions bounded by our faithful representations. Thus, the representation is "of" the landscape in its entirety, not "of" a putative landscape-region.

48. The same, of course, can be said for the photograph: "Counterfeit and reproduction imply always an anguish, a disquieting foreignness: the uneasiness before the photograph, considered like a witch's trick. . . ." (SS, 153 n. 1).

49. Gongora, quoted in Octavio Paz, *Conjunctions and Disjunctions*, trans. Helen R. Lane (New York: Viking, 1969), p. 4.

50. "[T]hought is assigned to its place only if it takes up its place itself" (PhP, 130).

51. Martin Heidegger, *Being and Time*, trans. John Macquarrie and Edward Robinson (New York: Harper and Row, 1962), p. 51.

52. "*The real*," for Sartre, "*is realization*" (BN, 249).

53. While the "light" of enlightenment indeed "brings to an end the bounded, dark kingdom of privileged knowledge," Buddhism might well demur from regarding it as a form of "majestic violence." Michael Foucault, *The Birth of the Clinic: An Archaeology of Medical Perception*, trans. A. M. Sheridan Smith, (New York: Pantheon, 1973), p. 39.

54. Tetsuaki Kotoh voices the existential import of this resorption: "Our existence is thrown into total darkness. No matter how much our insights may illuminate it, darkness not only obscures the path we have come along and where we are heading for, but also casts shadows over our everyday life. If we are thrown into this world and are to be taken away from it without knowing why, this means that we exist as merely ephemeral and lack an ultimate goal. . . . This absolute lack of ground constitutes the abysmal darkness of human existence. At the bottom of our existence is total nothingness which repels any kind of reasoning from the human perspective." Tetsuaki Kotoh, "Language and Silence: Self-Inquiry in Heidegger and Zen," in Graham Parkes, ed., *Heidegger and Asian Thought* (Honolulu: University of Hawaii Press, 1987), p. 201.

55. "Light," Ricoeur reminds us, is "the space of appearance, but light is also a space of intelligibility. Light, as openness, is a medium of appearance and expressibility." Paul Ricoeur, *Fallible Man*, trans. Charles Kelbley (Chicago: Henry Regnery, n.d.), p. 62.

56. Margaret Gibson's piece, "The Glass Globe," gives eloquent voice to the silent transparency of things: "But at times, I see light and the silence of light turn wide the horizon of each leaf and sill, each facet of screen, each spoon, each cup—and I see the space that spins within things, the table now serried particles, a dance of tendencies toward light I can feel beneath my fingers" (BSM, 86).

57. Adorno may be correct in supposing that "to think in general categories is to enter into collusion with the compulsion of totality" (LD, 232), yet, without wishing to "collude," and remaining receptive to additional suggestions, I must confess here an exhaustion of imagination. It might be supposed that *shadow* comprises the locus for a fundamental and irreducible mode of luminal relatedness. But shadow is rather the very

absence of light, not a presence with which light is destined to contend. And one might appropriately regard shadow as the "inside" of the mirror, the result of the mirror's repulsion of light. Heidegger's insight is here of particular poignancy: "Everyday opinion sees in the shadow only the lack of light, if not light's complete denial. In truth, however, the shadow is a manifest, though impenetrable, testimony to the concealed emitting of light." Martin Heidegger, *The Question Concerning Technology and Other Essays*, trans. W. Lovitt (New York: Harper and Row, 1977), p. 154.

58. Analogously, one can speak of the "secret blackness of milk," a phrase that Sartre attributes to Audiberti (BN, 766), and Merleau-Ponty to Valéry: "[T]he secret blackness of milk, of which Valéry spoke, is accessible only through its whiteness. . . ." (VI, 150).

59. Rovatti observes, "The blinding is the ultimate experience of an exercise in which the subject proceeds against the grain. We might say that the subject negates itself as self. That is, it negates itself as ability to see itself fully and, therefore, to control itself. But at the same time and following this same path, it searches for itself." Pier Aldo Rovatti, "The Black Light" (RM, 132).

60. The "Admonition on Sitting in Meditation" resonates:

> Pure is the water and transparent, where fish move slowly, slowly in it.
> Boundless is the sky where flying birds disappear, disappear into the unseen.
>
> (OT, 55)

61. Thus, in the words of Niu-t'ou Fa-yung (594–657 C.E.), "When there is an image occupying a mirror-mind, where can you find mind?" (OT, 21).

62. The ambiguity of lightlessness is caught in Merleau-Ponty's words: "[T]his blackness is less the sensible quality of blackness than a sombre power which radiates from the object, even when it is overlaid with reflected light. . . ." (PhP, 305). The radiance of lightlessness is recapitulated, though from precisely the inverse vantage point, in the words of Nelson Foster's verse, "Pieces from the Night":

> The whole blackness turns toward me
> as to its sole point
> or end. . . .
>
> (BSM, 77)

63. Suzuki hints an intriguing "opacity" associated with the Buddhist conception of *śūnyatā:* "Emptiness is not a vacancy—it holds in it infinite rays of light and swallows all the multiplicities there are in this world." D. T. Suzuki, *Mysticism: Christian and Buddhist* (New York: Harper, 1957), p. 30. And recent astronomical discoveries that, paradoxically, black holes may be among the brightest bodies in our universe converge with the Taoist expression, "Great white is as if it is black." Chang Chung-yuan, *Tao: A New Way of Thinking* (New York: Harper and Row, 1975), p. 106.

64. While one might imagine, at the heart of the black hole, a singularity of infinite, if introverted, illumination, Bachelard finds in the most dazzling emblem of luminosity that "it is only its covering of dust which shines. . . . The sun is dark: its rays are dark [«c'est seulement son vêtement de poussière qui brille. . . . Le soleil est obscur; ses rayons

sont obscurs»]." Gaston Bachelard, *La terre et les rêveries du repos* (Paris: Corti, 1948), p. 28 (Bachelard is here quoting *L'Homme et la poupée*, a French translation of D. H. Lawrence). Or, in Derrida's summation, "[T]he heart of light is black." Jacques Derrida, "Cogito and the History of Madness," in *Writing and Difference*, trans. Alan Bass, (Chicago: University of Chicago Press, 1978), p. 61.

65. Bataille notes: "Here darkness is not the absence of light (or of sound) but absorption into the outside. In simple night, our attention is given entirely to the world of objects by way of words, which still persist" (IE, 17). And again: "[N]ight surpasses this limited 'possible' and yet IT is nothing, there is nothing in IT which can be felt, not even finally darkness" (IE, 124–25).

66. In Nāgārjuna's lucid "deconstruction": "We provisionally assert that impurity cannot exist without being mutually dependent on purity and that, in turn, purity exists only as related to impurity. Therefore, purity per se is not possible.

"We provisionally assert that purity cannot exist without being mutually dependent on impurity and that, in turn, impurity exists only as related to purity. Therefore, impurity per se does not exist." (MK 23:10–11; N, 139)

67. Our "paradox of phenomenological optics" may bear some distant resemblance to the captivating, if also quite limited, "Olbers's paradox" that Poundstone discusses: "Assume that the universe is infinite and that the stars . . . extend out in all directions forever. In that case, a straight line extended in any direction from the earth . . . must hit a star *eventually*. . . . if *every* straight line extended from the earth hits a star, the entire sky should consist of the overlapping disks of stars—each as blindingly bright as the solar disk—fusing into an all-enclosing celestial sphere. It should be as if the sun were a hollow sphere, with us in the middle. There should be no such thing as a shadow, including the shadow we call night." William Poundstone, *Labyrinths of Reason: Paradox, Puzzles, and the Frailty of Knowledge* (New York: Anchor, 1988), p. 153.

68. This inverts Daumal's insistence that "*The door to the invisible must be visible*." Daumal, *Mount Analogue*, p. 42.

69. For Descartes, "thought is light, the light of representation, the light of the world, the light in which things and their geometric shapes shine—Greek light." Michel Henry, "The Critique of the Subject" (WCAS, 166). However, as Rovatti makes plain, a certain Cartesian literalism finds itself shaken by the metaphor: "Descartes encounters metaphor as a disturbance of natural light." Pier Aldo Rovatti, "The Black Light" (RM, 129). But is this uneasiness not occasioned by a fixated literalizing of the metaphor of "natural light"?

70. Merleau-Ponty affirms that "For an absolute evidence, free from any presupposition, to be possible, and for my thought to be able to pierce through to itself, catch itself in action, and arrive at a pure 'assent of the self to the self', it would . . . have to cease to be an event and become an act through and through . . . its formal reality would have to be included in its objective reality. . . ." (PhP, 395).

71. Dōgen sees that "For Dharma even metaphors *(hiyu)* are ultimate realities *(hisso)*." Dōgen, *Shōbōgenzō*, "Muchu-setsumu," in Hee-Jin Kim, *Dogen Kigen: Mystical Realist* (Tucson: University of Arizona Press, 1987), p. 82.

72. David Loy, *Nonduality: A Study in Comparative Philosophy* (New Haven: Yale University Press, 1988), p. 75.

73. Alternatively, writes Merleau-Ponty: "Plato still allowed the empiricist the power of pointing a finger at things, but the truth is that even this silent gesture is

impossible if *what* is pointed out is not already torn from instantaneous existence and monadic existence and treated as representative of its previous appearances in me, and of its simultaneous appearances in others, in other words, subsumed under some category and promoted to the status of a concept" (PhP, 120–21).

74. "The work of the mind exists only in act [L'oeuvre de l'esprit n'existe qu'en acte]." Paul Valéry, *Introduction à la poétique* (Paris: Gallimard, 1938), p. 40.

75. Helmut Kuhn, "The Phenomenological Concept of 'Horizon'," in Marvin Farber, ed., *Philosophical Essays in Memory of Edmund Husserl* (New York: Greenwood, 1968), p. 115.

76. But as a systematic redirection of light, does not reflection function as an analogue of Lispector's magnifying glass? "[I]f I look into the darkness with a magnifying glass, will I see more than darkness? The glass won't disperse the darkness, it will only reveal it all the more. And if I look at brightness with a magnifying glass, I shall see, with a shock, only greater brightness" (GH, 13–14).

77. It is, of course, ironic, in view of his evident *Lichtmetaphysik*, that "Husserl continually warns us against these metaphors." Jacques Derrida, *Speech and Phenomena and Other Essays on Husserl's Theory of Signs*, trans. David B. Allison (Evanston, Ill.: Northwestern University Press, 1973), p. 84 n. 9.

78. "As soon as it admits the existence of the point, *the mind is an eye*. . . ." (IE, 118). Consider "the sorrow of the eye exceeded by light." Emmanuel Lévinas, "Philosophy and Awakening" (WCAS, 215).

79. In Carr's apt illustration, "[G]iven two convincing visual experiences of, say, a dancing bear, one of which is a seeing and the other an illusion (and supposing perspective, background and the like to be the same), the two would be described in just the same way. . . ." David Carr, "Intentionality," in Edo Pivcevic, ed., *Phenomenology and Philosophical Understanding* (London: Cambridge University Press, 1975), p. 32.

80. Prufer sees that "difference" presupposes an "indifferent matrix"—the latter, we must add, remarkably consonant with the Buddhist conception of emptiness: "The differentiated (those which are different, the differents) are different from each other and from the undifferentiated or indifferent matrix out of which they are differentiated and which they cover over and hide. The matrix, however, is by anticipation the matrix of the differents, but as matrix it itself is different from them by its indifference. The differents, as differentiated, are still indifferent by recapitulation, by remaining being different out of the matrix from which they were not different and in which they were not different from each other." Thomas Prufer, "Welt, Ich und Zeit in der Sprache," *Philosophische Rundschau* 20 (1973): 226.

81. Ex/sistence, that is, is precisely the failure of objectivism of which Merleau-Ponty speaks: "If the synthesis could be genuine and my experience formed a closed system, if the thing and the world could be defined once and for all, if the spatio-temporal horizons could, even theoretically, be made explicit and the world conceived from no point of view, then nothing would exist" (PhP, 331–32).

82. It is not, of course, our business "to extinguish that other light, a black and hardly natural 'light' to which Descartes paid his debt." Derrida, "Cogito," p. 61.

83. For Merleau-Ponty, "Living thought . . . does not consist in subsuming under some category. The category imposes on the terms brought together a meaning external to them" (PhP, 128).

84. Intelligence, for Aristotle, is typified as "a sort of positive state like light; for in a sense light makes potential colours into actual colours." *De anima* iii.5.430a16-17, in Richard McKeon, ed., *The Basic Works of Aristotle* (New York: Random House, 1941), p. 592.

85. This is not, of course, to gainsay the patent observation of the ensuing passage, but rather to contextualize the solar illumination of which it speaks as "ordinary," or "impure," and thus not referring to the pure and extraordinary brilliance of the Platonic Good: "The sun seems safer to many of us. It is the golden deity of the day, of sharp awareness, disciplined work, focused goals, and distinctions between elements. The shadows of daytime are in sharp relief against the sunlit ground. There is 'yes' and 'no,' black and white, sinner and saint, and absolute facts." Rita Knipe, *The Water of Life: A Jungian Journey through Hawaiian Myth* (Honolulu: University of Hawaii Press, 1989), p. 81.

86. Like light, "the mind is that milieu where there is *action at a distance* (memory)" (VI, 242).

87. The void, as Adorno might say, thereby becomes infinite, the infinite being "the paradoxical shape in which absolute and, in its sovereignty, open thought took control of what is not exhausted in thought, and which blocks up its absoluteness" (AE, 31).

88. Derrida insightfully speculates that "Light perhaps has no opposite, certainly not night [La lumière n'a peut-être pas de contraire, surtout pas la nuit]." Jacques Derrida, *L'Écriture et la différance* (Paris: Éditions du Seuil, 1967), p. 137.

89. Menzan discloses that "When you make mental struggle, the light becomes illusory mind and brightness becomes darkness. If you do not make mental struggle, the darkness itself becomes the Self illumination of the light. This is similar to the light of a jewel illuminating the jewel itself." Menzan Zuiho Osho, *Jijuyu-zanmai* [Samādhi of the self] (DZ, 55).

90. And emptiness, for Lispector, is "a medium of transport" (GH, 106).

91. In Menzan's splendid trope, "[W]hen sunlight streams into a room through a window and you hit a straw mat, you will see dust rising up in clouds. After the dust settles, there is nothing but empty space. In this analogy, thoughts are the rising dust and original mind is the empty space." Menzan Zuiho Osho, *Jijuyu-zanmai* [Samādhi of the self] (DZ, 65).

92. John Blofeld, "Translator's Introduction" (HH, 48).

93. Thus, in Merleau-Ponty's articulation, "[A]lthough I do not manage to encompass my death in thought, I nevertheless live in an atmosphere of death in general, and there is a kind of essence of death always on the horizon of my thinking" (PhP, 364). Indeed, "A present without a future, or an eternal present, is precisely the definition of death. . . ." (PhP, 333).

94. For Sartre, "Play, like Kierkegaard's irony, releases subjectivity. What is play indeed if not an activity of which man is the first origin, for which man himself sets the rules, and which has no consequences except according to the rules posited?" (BN, 741).

95. Like the Bodhisattvas, Murti suggests, "The Buddhas are but the realised ideal of the devotee, his higher self. It is as it were the actual becomes the ideal, which it really is, by constantly having it before the mind's eye and venerating it. True worship is self-worship; the lower is completely transmuted into the higher which it is in fact; the lower surrenders itself, and the higher attracts and raises the lower" (CPB, 226).

96. Merleau-Ponty gives voice to an entirely admissible conception of the dialectic: "[D]ialectical thought is that which admits reciprocal actions or interactions—which admits therefore that the total relation between a term *A* and a term *B* cannot be expressed in one sole proposition, that that relation covers over several others which cannot be superimposed, which are even opposed, which define so many points of view logically incompossible and yet really united within it—even more that each of these relations leads to its opposite or to its own reversal, and does so by its own movement. Thus Being, through the very exigency of each of the perspectives, and from the exclusive point of view that defines it, becomes a system with several entries. Hence it cannot be contemplated from without and in simultaneity, but must be effectively traversed. In this transition, the stages passed through are not simply passed, like the segment of the road I have traveled; they have called for or required the present stages and precisely what is new and disconcerting in them. The past stages continue therefore to be in the present stages—which also means that they are retroactively modified by them. Hence there is a question here not of a thought that follows a pre-established route but of a thought that itself traces its own course, that finds that the way is practicable. This thought wholly subjugated to its content, from which it receives its incitement, could not express itself as a reflection or copy of an exterior process; it is the engendering of a relation starting from the other." (VI, 89–90)

97. Thus, Merleau-Ponty can say, "Night is not an object before me; it enwraps me and infiltrates through all my senses, stifling my recollections and almost destroying my personal identity" (PhP, 283).

98. Metaphysics, Nietzsche affirms, is "an attempt to take by force the most fertile fields." Nietzsche, *Human, All-Too-Human*, part 2, translated by Paul V. Cohn and edited by Oscar Levy (1909–11; rpt., New York: Russell & Russell, 1964), p. 239.

99. We find phenomenology "assisting at the birth of this knowledge. . . ." (PP, 25). Or rather, in the words of Nan-ch'üan P'u-yüan (748–834 C.E.), "Tao is not a matter either of knowing or of not-knowing. Knowing is a delusion; not knowing is indifference" (OT, 165).

100. Lévinas sensitizes us to the indexical and prehensile construals of "truth": "To truth itself . . . there belongs a primary technical success, that of the index which points at something and of the hand which grasps it." Emmanuel Lévinas, "Beyond Intentionality" (PFT, 103). And "The idea of truth as a *grasp* on things must necessarily have a non-metaphorical sense somewhere." Lévinas (PFT, 103).

101. "The perceptual 'something' is always in the middle of something else, it always forms part of a 'field'" (PhP, 4).

102. Sartre, on the contrary, sponsors an "emptiness" which, in principle, refuses self-emptying: "[E]ach *for-itself* is a lack of a certain coincidence with itself. . . . it is haunted by the presence of that with which it should coincide in order to be *itself*. . . . the being which the For-itself lacks, the being which would make the For-itself a Self by assimilation with it—this being is still the For-itself" (BN, 153).

103. Sartre is not unaware of the fragility of reflection: "For consciousness is a reflection *(reflet)*, but *qua* reflection it is exactly the one reflecting *(réfléchissant)*, and if we attempt to grasp it as reflecting, it vanishes and we fall back on the reflection" (BN, 122).

104. Derrida deplores "the un-thought-out axiomatics of Husserlian phenomenology, its 'principle of principles', that is to say, its intuitionism, the absolute privilege of

the living present, the lack of attention paid to the problem of its own phenomenological enunciation, to transcendental discourse itself . . . to the necessity of recourse, in eidetic or transcendental description, to a language that could not itself be submitted to the *epochē*—without itself being simply in the world—thus to a language which remained naïve, even though it was by virtue of this very language that all the phenomenological bracketings and parentheses were made possible." Jacques Derrida, "The Time of a Thesis: Punctuations" (PFT, 39).

105. Sartre proposes that "There is only intuitive knowledge." As the raft is abandoned, in the familiar Buddhist trope, when the "other shore" *(nirvāṇa)* is attained, so "When intuition is reached, methods utilized to attain it are effaced before it. . . ." (BN, 240).

106. Nothingness, for Sartre's Heidegger, "is given as that by which the world receives its outlines as the world" (BN, 51).

107. Clearly, as Merleau-Ponty notes, "in so far as I can deny each thing, it is always by asserting that there is something in general. . . ." (PhP, 360).

108. Adorno submits that "To negate a negation does not bring about its reversal; it proves, rather, that the negation was not negative enough" (ND, 160).

109. We must, then, credit Merleau-Ponty's remark, "[B]eneath affirmation and negation, beneath judgment . . . , it is our experience, prior to every opinion, of inhabiting the world by our body, of inhabiting the truth by our whole selves, without there being need to choose nor even to distinguish between the assurance of seeing and the assurance of seeing the true, because in principle they are one and the same thing. . . ." (VI, 28).

110. "Mediacy," advances Adorno, "is not a positive assertion about being but rather a directive to cognition not to comfort itself with such positivity" (AE, 24).

111. Gödel's results were first published under the title, "Über formal unentscheidbare Sätze der Principia Mathematica und verwandter System I."

112. The illustration is inspired by Raymond Smullyan's musings and amusings on the Gödel theorem as presented in a seminar on the topic that I attended some years ago at Indiana University. And I was pleased to discover a text condensing his presentation in *5000 B.C. and Other Philosophical Fantasies* (New York: St. Martin's Press, 1983). In Smullyan's example, Abe cannot print "NPR*NPR*" (read: "The Repeat of 'NPR*' is not printable"): "[T]he repeat of NPR* is the very sentence NPR*NPR*! So this sentence is true if and only if it is not printable. If the sentence is false, then it *is* printable (since the sentence says that it isn't) . . . so the sentence NPR*NPR* must be true, but the machine says it cannot print it" (p. 45).

113. Another illustrative paradox is provided by Daumal: "'Don't be afraid,' said the crocodile. 'I promise to spare your life if you can contrive to explain to me what is truth. I hear all those passing by talking about it endlessly, and I have no idea what they mean. So tell me what is truth, and I'll not eat you.'

"'The truth,' replied the passerby, 'is that you are going to gobble me up.'" (Daumal, *Mount Analogue*, p. 11)

114. This is one way of demonstrating the curious property articulated in Baudrillard's observation that "As for the Moebius strip, if it is split in two, it results in an additional spiral without there being any possibility of resolving its surfaces" (SS, 34).

115. In this sense, the Möbius strip finds much in common with the arabesque. "The synthesis—in itself impossible—of absolute contradictions within a manifestation . . . is an essential sign of the arabesque [Die—an sich unmögliche—Synthese der absoluten

Gegensätze innerhalb einer Erscheinung . . . ist ein wesentliches Merkmal der Arabeske]." K. K. Polheim, *Die Arabeske, Ansichten und Ideen aus Friedrich Schlegels Poetik* (Paderborn: Schöningh, 1966), p. 113.

116. Edward Conze, trans., *Selected Sayings from the Perfection of Wisdom* (Boulder: Prajñā Press, 1978), pp. 101–2.

117. Conze, *Selected Sayings*, p. 20.

118. J. W. N. Sullivan, *The Limitations of Science* (New York: Mentor, 1949), p. 140.

119. E. N. da C. Andrade, *An Approach to Modern Physics* (New York: Doubleday Anchor, 1957), p. 255.

120. Werner Heisenberg, *The Physicist's Conception of Nature* (New York: Harcourt, Brace, 1958), p. 24.

121. The "middle," medium of communication, commensuration, is, as Murti has it, "beyond concepts or speech; it is the transcendental, being a review of all things" (CPB, 1970 ed., 129).

122. Vision, in Merleau-Ponty's acceptation, "is a mirror or concentration of the universe or . . . the *idios kosmos* opens by virtue of vision upon a *koinos kosmos*. . . ." "Eye and Mind" (PP, 166).

123. Though philosophy, for Bataille, "is never supplication," still "without supplication, there is no conceivable reply; no answer ever preceded the question: and what does the question without anguish, without torment mean?" (IE, 36).

124. Adorno sees the dialectic as "the attempt to untie the knot of paradoxicality by the oldest means of enlightenment: the ruse" (ND, 141). While liberation from selfhood may be brought about through "skillful means" *(upāya)*, the Buddhist dialectic neither begins nor ends in deception.

125. Assuredly, as Sartre maintains, "Neither affirmation nor negation can confer the character of possibility on a representation" (BN, 151).

126. Consonantly, Merleau-Ponty asserts, "I can remain within the sphere of absolute self-evidence only if I refuse to make any affirmation, or to take anything for granted, if, as Husserl has it, I stand in wonder before the world, and ceasing to be in league with it, I bring to light the flow of motivations which bear me along in it, making my life wholly aware of itself, and explicit. When I try to pass from this interrogative state to an affirmation, and *a fortiori* when I try to express myself, I crystalize an indefinite collection of motives within an act of consciousness, I revert to the implicit, that is, to the equivocal and to the world's free play" (PhP, 295).

127. "Negation," for Sartre, "is an abrupt break in continuity which can not in any case *result* from prior affirmations; it is an original and irreducible event" (BN, 43).

128. As Adorno teaches, "Dialectic reaches the insight that the closed process also includes the non-included. It thus reaches a boundary to knowledge itself" (AE, 39).

129. In an affiliated sense, Gargani maintains that "'True' is a primitive term that indicates the acknowledgment of the encounter of a thought with the necessity of this thought." Aldo G. Gargani, "Friction of Thought" (RM, 79). We need only append that the Buddhist vision of the arising of vision is "silent," unmediated.

130. One must, of course, confront Dews's extroverted Kantian query, "[H]ow must one imagine the world to be if pure affirmation is to be possible?" (LD, 133). But the world thus disclosed will, in the Buddhist idiom, be recognized as the cycle of suffering denominated *saṁsāra*.

131. Merleau-Ponty complains of Sartre's view that it "begins by opposing being and nothingness absolutely, and it ends by showing that the nothingness is in a way within being, which is the unique universe. When are we to believe it? At the beginning or at the end?" (VI, 66).

132. Nothingness, then, pursues the cessation of a certain "questioning," for, in Merleau-Ponty's view, "The sensible quality is the peculiar product of an attitude of curiosity or observation . . . it is the reply to a certain kind of questioning on the part of my gaze. . . ." (PhP, 226).

133. It is, rather, as Merleau-Ponty would say, "the difference between the identicals" (VI, 263).

134. In this connection, Hui-neng regards as a "confused notion" the assumption that "the greatest achievement is to sit quietly with an emptied mind, where not a thought is to be conceived" (NM, 26–27). He counsels: "When you sit quietly with an emptied mind, this is falling into a blank emptiness" (NM, 26).

135. The interrogative character of the Sartrean for-itself is its openness: "The being by which the 'Why' comes into being has the right to posit its own 'Why' since it is itself an interrogation, a 'Why'" (BN, 788). Since, however, the for-itself is ineluctably a "looking-for," a "questioning-about," its nothingness, failing in "purity," is determinately modalized.

136. If, as Adorno claims, "ontology is understood as readiness to sanction a heteronomous order that need not be consciously justified" (ND, 61), Sartre's ontological project is open to serious question.

137. In Gargani's taunting portrayal, "This is the subject that with its colored crayons tints the world that surrounds it. . . ." Aldo G. Gargani, "Friction of Thought" (RM, 80). He continues: ". . . a purer, more gaseous, and more rarefied Ego that tinges the world with its lights. The philosophers of this type run about at dawn in the streets of the city in order to color things red and yellow and then declare at midday that the world is red and yellow because of their constitutive acts of meaning. In reality none of them actually went into the city or the countryside at dawn; they stayed in bed like everyone else. Nevertheless, someone did go, but who? Not them, but their delegates, the speculative agents, the 'transcendental Ego', the 'constitutive subjects of possible experience'—the new modern figures, in other words, of the guardian angel" (RM, 81).

138. Edmund Husserl, *Phenomenological Psychology*, trans. John Scanlon (The Hague: Martinus Nijhoff, 1977), sect. 9a, p. 54. Adorno finds, rather, a mediative function for the *eidē:* "The ideas live in the cavities between what things claim to be and what they are" (ND, 150).

139. Being quite explicit that intuitive "seeing" is subject to progressive clarification, Husserl would quite cheerfully accept Merleau-Ponty's assessment that "Husserl himself never obtained one sole *Wesenschau* that he did not subsequently take up again and rework, not to disown it, but in order to make it say what at first it had not quite said" (VI, 116). In Merleau-Ponty's more pictorial ideolect, the Husserlian *eidos* has become a "hinge": "Husserl's eidetic variation, and its in-variant, designates only these *hinges* of Being, these structures accessible through quality as well as through quantity—" (VI, 236).

140. Husserl is not insensitive to the (perhaps paradoxical) self-referentiality of *Wesenschau:* "Only in eidetic intuition can the essence of eidetic intuition become clarified." Edmund Husserl, *Formal and Transcendental Logic*, trans. Dorion Cairns (The Hague: Martinus Nijhoff, 1969), p. 249.

141. Husserl, *Phenomenological Psychology*, sect. 9a, p. 54.

142. "[I]nstead of the figure's appearing on an undifferentiated ground," Sartre informs us, "it is wholly penetrated by the ground; it holds the ground within it as its own undifferentiated density" (BN, 260). Again: "[T]he continuous background suddenly when apprehended as figure bursts into a multiplicity of discontinuous elements" (BN, 254).

143. Lyotard instructs us that "it is metaphysical to struggle against oblivion. . . ." Jean-François Lyotard, "Presentations" (PFT, 132).

144. Husserlian phenomenology is, if you like, the science of beginning. For Adorno, however, "The problem of the first itself is retrospective. Thinking which like Plato's has its absolute in memory, can really no longer be expected" (AE, 32).

145. On the contrary, "It is essential to [philosophy] that it be autocritical—and it is also essential to it to forget this as soon as it becomes what we call *a philosophy*" (VI, 92). Indeed, "The core of philosophy . . . lies in the perpetual beginning of reflection, at the point where an individual life begins to reflect on itself" (PhP, 62).

146. The complete proverb runs: "Playing with ink will get your hands black; standing near a lamp will make you bright" *(Gần mực thì đen; gần den thì sáng).*

147. Lispector's ruminations suggest that a faithful reception of the "given" is not itself "given" within the same experience: "Did something happen, and did I, because I didn't know how to experience it, end up experiencing something else instead?" (GH, 3).

148. Understanding by "reproduction" the production of indiscernible likeness, we find salient insight in Baudrillard's comment that "The very definition of the real becomes: *that of which it is possible to give an equivalent reproduction. . . .* the real is not only what can be reproduced, but *that which is always already reproduced"* (SS, 146). In fact, "it is reality itself that disappears utterly in the game of reality. . . ." (SS, 148). Thus: "Reproduction is diabolical in its very essence; it makes something fundamental vacillate" (SS, 153 n. 1). A similar point is given voice in Trinh thi Minh-hà's statement, "A shattered mirror still functions as a mirror; it may destroy the dual relation of I to I but leaves the infiniteness of life's reflections intact. Here reality is not reconstituted, it is put into pieces so as to allow another world to rebuild (keep on unbuilding and rebuilding) itself with its debris. Mirrors multiplied and differently disposed are bound to yield fallacious, fairy-like visions, thus constituting a theater of illusions within which countless combinations of reflecting reflections operate." Trinh, *Woman, Native, Other*, p. 23.

149. Gary Snyder suggests the estate of a Buddhist phenomenology in his remark that "Meditation is not just a rest or retreat from the turmoil of the stream or the impurity of the world. It is a way of *being* the stream, so that one can be at home in both the white water and the eddies. Meditation may take one out of the world, but it also puts one totally into it" (BSM, 1).

150. This "space" has little to do with the "Cartesian 'spirituality'" which follows upon the "*identity* of space with the mind" (VI, 37).

151. We find, in Sartre, an intriguing analogue: "Space is not the world, but it is the instability of the world apprehended as totality, inasmuch as the world can always disintegrate into external multiplicity. Space is neither the ground nor the figure but the ideality of the ground inasmuch as it can always disintegrate into figures; it is neither the continuous nor the discontinuous, but the permanent passage from continuous to discontinuous. . . . Space is the ideality of the synthesis" (BN, 254–55).

152. Bhikkhu Ñaṇamoli, *The Life of the Buddha* (Kandy: Buddhist Publication Society, 1972), p. ii.

153. This articulation is indissociably "poetic." "The poem," writes Robert Kelly, "is not an artifact, not a picture of reality; it is a weapon or at least a tool in the ceaseless and necessary battle for simple vigilance, *pour éveiller*, wake up—the basic meaning of the verbal root *budh-*, of which the past participle is Buddha, the One Who Woke Up." "Going With the Poem" (BSM, 163). Husserl's comment resounds: "On close inspection, sleep has meaning only in relation to waking and carries in itself the potentiality for awakening" [Schlaf hat, näher besehen, nur Sinn in Bezug auf Wachen und trägt eine Potentialität des Erwachens in sich]." Edmund Husserl, *Phänomenologische Psychologie*, ed. Walter Biemel, Husserliana IX (The Hague: Martinus Nijhoff, 1968), p. 209.

154. Sangharakshita, *A Survey of Buddhism: Its Doctrines and Methods through the Ages* (London: Tharpa Publications, 1987), pp. 4–5.

155. Ibid., p. 26.

156. Indeed, "the spirit of Gautama is existential rather than intellectual." Howard L. Parsons, *The Value of Buddhism for the Modern World,* Wheel Publication no. 232–33 (Kandy: Buddhist Publishing Society, 1976), p. 12.

157. Indeed, space, in Merleau-Ponty's interesting phrase, "is the evidence of the 'where'." "Eye and Mind" (PP, 173).

158. Merleau-Ponty cautions that "philosophy itself must not take itself for granted, in so far as it may have managed to say something true; that it is an ever-renewed experiment in making its own beginning; that it consists wholly in the description of this beginning, and finally, that radical reflection amounts to a consciousness of its own dependence on an unreflective life which is its initial situation, unchanging, given once and for all" (PhP, xiv).

159. The spirit *(pneuma)* of Western philosophy would seem, by certain accounts, to be that of "argumentative cantankerousness," "aggressive belligerence." Or as Burtt amplifies, "Occidental philosophy typically makes what progress it does through the medium of hostile argumentation." E. A. Burtt, "What can Western Philosophy Learn from India?" *Philosophy East and West* 5 (1955): 206. And certainly, "the pugnacious atmosphere of philosophic discussion" does, as Burtt says, make for "spicy debates and hilarious argumentation; when two redoubtable pugilists engage in such intellectual sparring the rest of us crowd the side-lines in the philosophical journals and watch the fray with excited absorption" (p. 207). In Lin Yu-tang's graphic expression, "European intellectuals seem to have been born with knives in their brains" (quoted in BTI, 214).

160. This does not, however, contravene the fact that genuine "Understanding requires a kind of resolute renunciation of itself." Parsons, *The Value of Buddhism*, p. 17.

161. Consider here the words of Blanchot: "[The image] is light, and [nothingness] is immensely heavy. [The image] shines and [nothingness] is the diffuse thickness where nothing reveals itself. [The image] is the crack, the mark of this black sun, the tear which, under the appearance of the dazzling burst, gives us the negative of the inexhaustible negative depth. That is why the image seems so profound and so empty, so menacing and so attractive, rich in ever more senses than we lend it, and also poor, void and silent, because in it advances this dark impotence, deprived of master, which is that of death as recommencement [Elle est légère, et il est immensément lourd. Elle brille, et il est l'épaisseur diffuse où rien ne se montre. Elle est l'interstice, la tache de ce soleil noir,

déchirure qui nous donne, sous l'apparence de l'éclat éblouissant, le négatif de l'inépuisable profondeur négative. De là que l'image semble si profonde et si vide, si menaçante et si attirante, riche de toujours plus de sens que nous ne lui en prêtons et, aussi, pauvre, nulle et silencieuse, car, en elle, s'avance cette sombre impuissance privée de maître, qui est celle de la mort comme recommencement]." Maurice Blanchot, *L'Amitié* (Paris: Gallimard, 1971), p. 51.

162. As Trinh thi Minh-hà makes plain, this would involve not merely suturing, but thoroughly healing the deep laceration that separates appearance and reality: "In this encounter of I with I, the power of identification is often such that reality and appearance merge while the tool itself becomes invisible. Hence the superstitious fear of broken mirrors and the recurring theme (and variations) in Western literature of the poet who smoothly *enters* the mirror for a journey in the dark or the man who, fighting desperately against death, shatters mirror after mirror, only to come again and again, after each attempt at eliminating his reflection, face to face with himself." Trinh, *Woman, Native, Other*, p. 22.

163. Cf., for example, "Hui-Neng and the Transcendental Standpoint," *Journal of Chinese Philosophy* 12 (1985); "Harmony as Transcendence: A Phenomenological View," *Journal of Chinese Philosophy* 16 (1988); "Sartre and a Chinese Buddhist Theory of No-Self: The Mirroring of Mind," *Buddhist-Christian Studies* 9 (1989); "Consciousness Without Identity: Buddhist Reflections on Sartrean Bad Faith." *Buddhist-Christian Studies,* 1994.

164. We shall rely heavily upon what Adorno dismissively, though amusingly, calls "The corny exoticism of such decorative world views as the astonishingly consumable Zen Buddhist one. . . ." (ND, 68).

165. Or rather, as Mehta suggests, "Comparative philosophy, if we still retain the name, would then be a name for the task, infinitely open, of setting free, bringing into view and articulating in contemporary ways of speaking, in new ways of speaking, the matter of thinking which, in what has actually to be realized in thought, still remains unsaid and so unthought in the traditions of the East. Otherwise, comparative philosophy will amount to no more than an unthinking attempt at perpetuating Western 'philosophy' by translating Eastern thinking into the language of Western metaphysics, taken as the universally valid paradigm." J. L. Mehta, "Heidegger and Vedanta: Reflections on a Questionable Theme," in Parkes, *Heidegger and Asian Thought*, p. 29.

166. Bataille concurs that "one reaches the states of ecstasy or of rapture only by *dramatizing* existence in general" (IE, 10).

167. Jacob Loewenberg, *Hegel's* Phenomenology: *Dialogues on the Life of Mind* (La Salle, Ill.: Open Court, 1965), p. 17. Loewenberg's helpful reading thus illuminates the murky "dialectic" strategy of the *Phenomenology*: "The simulation of identity between the impersonator and the impersonated continues until the very histrionic effort leads to the exhibition of the empirical persuasion's inward discrepancy" (p. 18). Thus "The *Phenomenology* is a sort of comedy of errors" (p. 20). Also, regarding such "experiments," we would do well to recall that "Poetry, like Zen, is an experimental science." Dale Pendell, "Some Reveries on Poetry as a Spiritual Discipline" (BSM, 201).

168. Mumon reports that "Old Zuigan sells out and buys himself. He is opening a puppet show. He uses one mask to call 'Master' and another that answers the master. . . . If anyone clings to any of his masks, he is mistaken" (ZFZB, 99–100).

169. We cannot, then, accept Danto's disappointing assessment that "The fantastic architectures of Oriental thought . . . are open to our study and certainly our admiration, but they are not for us to inhabit." Arthur C. Danto, *Mysticism and Morality: Oriental Thought and Moral Philosophy* (New York: Columbia University Press, 1988), p. xiii.

170. Johann Gottlieb Fichte, *Die Wissenschaftslehre—Zweiter Vortrag im Jahre 1804* (Hamburg: Felix Meiner Verlag, 1975), p. 4, as translated by Walter E. Wright in his essay, "Fichte and Philosophical Method," *Philosophical Forum* 19 (1988): 69.

171. In fairness, however, we should remind ourselves that:

> Like a good Zen student Mephistopheles says "Myself am hell."
>
> . . . .
>
> for his screams, read "delight,"
> and for the tortures he undergoes,
> read "he does not shut out
> any part of himself."

John Tarrant, "Spell to Be Recited for Banishing Loneliness" (BSM, 310)

172. Fichte, *Wissenschaftslehre*, p. 13.

173. Ibid., p. 5. Thus, as Wright amplifies, "Fichte holds philosophical truth to be communicable only indirectly and not through declarative sentences. For him, philosophical truth is something which must be recreated within the individual thinker by that individual's own act, and this is best done in the living presence of philosophical discourse." Wright, "Fichte and Philosophical Method," p. 66. Thus, "Philosophical truth cannot be formulated discursively, either in a single sentence or in an entire treatise" (p. 69).

174. "There are," as Merleau-Ponty proposes, "no principal and subordinate problems: all problems are concentric" (PhP, 410).

175. "The body," suggests Merleau-Ponty, "is our general medium for having a world" (ibid., 146). Indeed, "Each 'sense' is a 'world'. . . ." (VI, 217).

176. The "amusement" of thought is nicely captured in Gargani's description: "[T]hought is not a determined sequence between a premise and a conclusion but a scenario looking onto the open backdrop of life and time in the same way in which we say that a room looks onto the garden or that a room faces the garden." Aldo G. Gargani, "Friction of Thought" (RM, 84).

177. Guenther elucidates: "[I]f we let U denote the 'thematic set', that is, the set of those things . . . to which we are naïvely accustomed, and if we denote the empty set by ø, then closer (epistemological) investigation reveals that U = ø." Guenther, "'Meditation' Trends in Early Tibet" in Whalen Lai and Lewis R. Lancaster, *Early Ch'an in China and Tibet*, Berkeley Buddhist Studies Series 5 (Berkeley, Calif.: Asian Humanities Press, 1983), p. 356.

The Mirrorless Mirror: Reflections on Buddhist Dialectic

The haiku by Hokushi is from Harold G. Henderson, *An Introduction to Haiku: An Anthology of Poems and Poets from Bashō to Shiki* (Garden City, N.Y.: Doubleday, 1958), p. 66.

1. We know, at least, that the abstract and "absolute" space of Euclidean geometry is not that of experience. In Merleau-Ponty's words: "The Euclidean space is the model for perspectival being, it is a space without transcendence, positive, a network of straight lines, parallel among themselves or perpendicular according to the three dimensions, which sustains all the possible situations. . . ." (VI, 210).

2. Of such intraperspectival representations claiming extraperspectival validity, Nietzsche heralds: "[T]ruths are illusions about which one has forgotten that this is what they are; metaphors that are worn out and without sensuous power; coins that have their obverse effaced and now matter only as metal, no longer as coins." Nietzsche, "On Truth and Lie in the Extra-Moral Sense," in *The Portable Nietzsche*, edited and translated by Walter Kaufmann (New York: Penguin, 1980), pp. 46–47.

3. Is there a fate worse than falsehood? In Merleau-Ponty's lucid pronouncement: "The intellectualist analysis, here as everywhere, is less false than abstract" (PhP, 124).

4. To the frequent claim that necessity is truth in all "possible worlds," Merleau-Ponty voices the Husserlian, and more generally phenomenological, rejoinder that "'The "other possible worlds' are ideal variants of this one" (VI, 228). Thus, "it is the possible worlds and the possible beings that are variants and are like doubles of the actual world and the actual Being" (VI, 112).

5. Brown suggests that the "anomaly" is inseparable from a certain understanding of logic: "If the weakness of present-day science is that it centres round existence, the weakness of present-day logic is that it centres round truth" (LF, 101).

6. Daumal's ruminations regarding Mount Analogue open intriguing questions regarding what prodigy might lie wrapped within the curvature of logical space: "But may there not exist unknown substances—unknown for this very reason in fact—capable of creating around them a much stronger *curvature of space*? . . . Because of it, *everything takes place as if Mount Analogue did not exist*." René Daumal, *Mount Analogue*: *A Novel of Symbolically Authentic Non-Euclidean Adventures in Mountain Climbing*, trans. Roger Shattuck (Baltimore: Penguin, 1974), pp. 64–65.

7. The meaning of the two gāthās may have much in common with the "meaning" of Merleau-Ponty's bouquet: "The flowers are self-evidently a love bouquet, and yet it is impossible to say what in them signifies love. . . . There is no way of understanding them other than by looking at them, but to the beholder they say what they mean" (PhP, 321). Since meaning resides in the gestalt and evaporates upon analysis, we court a grave risk: "[I]t is not only a risk of non-sense, therefore, but much worse: the assurance that the things have *another sense* than that which we are in a position to recognize in them" (VI, 94).

8. It is, of course, significantly true that "The region surrounding the visual field is not easy to describe, but what is certain is that it is neither black nor grey" (PhP, 6). The "field" of the field, being non-sensory, is of a radically different order from the field itself. Perhaps a sensory field can only be apprehended upon the ground of a certain ideality. And perhaps, then, the field is itself ideal, though its content is hyletic. Be that as it may, a divine "field" of fields cannot, it seems, be understood on analogy with a sensory field.

9. Edmund Husserl, *Ideas*: *General Introduction to Pure Phenomenology*, trans. W. R. Boyce Gibson (New York: Humanities, 1969), p. 123.

10. See, for example, my "Actual and Potential Omniscience," *International Journal of Philosophy of Religion* 26 (1989) and the second chapter of my *Foundations for a Phenomenological Theology* (Lewiston, N.Y.: Edwin Mellen Press, 1988).

11. In Merleau-Ponty's challenging, almost koanlike, proclamation: "The experience of absurdity and that of absolute self-evidence are mutually implicatory, and even indistinguishable" (PhP, 295–96).

12. The "richness" of reality may function as a certain resistance, a certain recalcitrance both to analytic penetration and to physical manipulation. "The real," says Lacan, "is the collision, it's the fact that things don't work out straight away, as the hand which reaches towards external objects would like." Jacques Lacan, *The Four Fundamental Concepts of Psycho-Analysis* (London: Hogarth Press, 1977), p. 167.

13. Analytic elucidation would, it seems, reach so far as to chase the "little shadow" which is the very being of the analyst: "There is nothing hidden behind these faces and gestures, no domain to which I have no access, merely a little shadow which owes its very existence to the light" (PhP, xii).

14. What Merleau-Ponty calls "physical explanation" is, of course, set out upon a plane. Yet "Phenomenology is . . . the recognition that the theoretically *complete*, full world of the physical explanation is not so, and that therefore it is necessary to consider as ultimate, inexplicable, and *hence as a world by itself* the whole of our experience of sensible being and of men" (VI, 256).

15. Lispector, acutely aware of the deeply enigmatic character of experience, observes that "the explanation of an enigma is the mere repetition of the enigma. What are You? and the answer is: You are. What do you exist? and the answer is: what you exist. I had the ability to question but not the ability to hear the answer" (GH, 127).

16. Husserl, in Adorno's reading, attempts "to counter Wittgenstein by uttering the unutterable" (ND, 9). Let us bear in mind, as Agamben counsels, that "*There is, thus, even a 'grammar' of the ineffable; or rather, the ineffable is simply the dimension of meaning of the* gramma, *of the letter as the ultimate negative foundation of human discourse*" (PN, 30).

17. It is not that the "wilderness" of experience is devoid of form. For Merleau-Ponty, it is rather indistinguishable from its form. "Matter is 'pregnant' with its form. . . ." (PP, 12).

18. "The fact is," as Suzuki proposes, "that there is nothing explicable or inexplicable in Reality itself, which is the state of all things that are" (EZB III, 22).

19. Planar analysis "deteriorates into the technique of conceptless specialists amid the concept, as it is now spreading academically in the so-called 'analytical philosophy,' which robots can learn and copy" (ND, 30). And it is not surprising, as Rorty reports, that "The notion of 'logical analysis' turned upon itself and committed slow suicide." Richard Rorty, *Consequences of Pragmatism* (Minneapolis: University of Minnesota Press, 1982), p. 227.

20. Reality, in Merleau-Ponty's concordant view, is not the stuff of "flat" propositional asseveration: "[T]he existing world exists in the interrogative mode. Philosophy is the perceptual faith questioning itself about itself" (VI, 103).

21. Mumon images the consonant inexplicability of Zen: "Even such words are like raising waves in a windless sea or performing an operation upon a healthy body. If one clings to what others have said and tries to understand Zen by explanation, he is like a dunce who thinks he can beat the moon with a pole or scratch an itching foot from the outside of a shoe. It will be impossible after all" (ZFZB, 88).

22. Derrida clearly sees that "the analysis produces always more and something other than an analysis. It transforms; it translates a transformation already in progress.

Translation is transformative." Jacques Derrida, "'Eating Well,' or the Calculation of the Subject: An Interview with Jacques Derrida" (WCAS, 109).

23. The curiosity of this Kantian bequest is reflected in Merleau-Ponty's comment that "the cube itself, with six equal faces, is only for an unsituated gaze, for an *operation* or inspection of the mind seating itself at the center of the cube, for a field of *Being*. . . ." (VI, 202). Even the Sartrean counterpart displays a certain oddity: "[I]t is actually impossible to say of the in-itself that it is *itself*. It simply *is*" (BN, 156).

24. H. G. Alexander, ed., *The Leibniz-Clarke Correspondence, Together With Extracts from Newton's* Principia *and* Optiks (Manchester: Manchester University Press, 1956), p. 26.

25. *The Leibniz-Clarke Correspondence*, p. 26.

26. In Derrida's arresting statement: "Predication is the first violence. Since the verb *to be* and the predicative act are implied in every other verb, and in every common noun, nonviolent language, in the last analysis, would be a language of pure invocation, pure adoration, proffering only proper nouns in order to call to the other from afar." Jacques Derrida, "Violence and Metaphysics: An Essay on the Thought of Emmanuel Lévinas," in *Writing and Difference*, trans. Alan Bass (Chicago: University of Chicago Press, 1978), p. 147.

27. *The Leibniz-Clarke Correspondence*, p. 26.

28. Robinson explicates that Nāgārjuna's repudiation of the principle of identity "is not a denial of the concept of identity, but simply a denial that identity to the exclusion of difference, or vice versa, can be attributed to anything existential." R. H. Robinson, *Madhyamika Studies in Fifth-Century China* (London: Thesis, 1959) (quoted in BTI, 76).

29. "[W]e are," in Merleau-Ponty's allusion to Sartre's famous phrase, "*condemned to meaning*. . . ." (PhP, xix).

30. We are not, then, remote in spirit from Gadamer's dedication to the "fundamental unclosability of the horizon of meaning." Hans-Georg Gadamer, *Truth and Method* (London: Sheed & Wood, 1975), p. 361.

31. We would do well to heed Adorno's counterclaim that, rather, "Arbitrariness, the complement of compulsion, already lurks in the assumption that such a recourse is the sufficient condition of truth. . . ." (AE, 23).

32. The logical "symbols" manipulated by analytic logic remind us of the "metaphysical coins" of which Anatole France graphically speaks: "[T]he metaphysicians, when they make up a new language, are like knife-grinders who grind coins and medals against their stone instead of knives and scissors. They rub out the relief, the inscriptions, the portraits, and when one can no longer see on the coins Victoria, or Wilhelm, or the French Republic, they explain: these coins now have nothing specifically English or German or French about them, for we have taken them out of time and space; they now are no longer worth, say, five francs, but rather have an inestimable value, and the area in which they are a medium of exchange has been infinitely extended [les métaphysiciens, quand ils se font un langage, ressemblent à des rémouleurs qui passeraient, au lieu de couteaux et de ciseaux, des médailles et des monnaies à la meule, pour en effacer l'exergue, le millésime et l'effigie. Quand ils ont tant fait qu'on ne voit plus sur leurs pièces de cent sous ni Victoria, ni Guillaume, ni la République, ils disent: 'Ces pièces n'ont rien d'anglais, ni d'allemand, ni de français; nous les avons tirées hors du temps et de l'espace; elles ne valent plus cinq francs: elle sont d'un prix inestimable, et leur cours

est étendu infiniment']." From Anatole France's "Garden of Epicurus" cited at the beginning of Jacques Derrida's "La Mythologie Blanche," in *Marges de la Philosophie* (Paris: Les Éditions de Minuit, 1972), p. 250. To this, we must append Philip Whalen's verse:

> a symbol doesn't MEAN
> anything
> it IS
> something . . . relationship of that kind doesn't exist except in the old philosophy whose vocabulary you insist on using. . . .

"All About Art & Life." Quoted with the author's permission from *On Bear's Head,* copyright © 1960, 1965, by Philip Whelan. Reprinted in BSM, 333.

33. "As a 'law of thought'," writes Adorno, the "content [of the law of noncontradiction] is prohibition: Do not think diffusely. Do not let yourself be diverted by unarticulated nature, but rather hold tight to what you mean like a possession. By virtue of logic, the subject saves itself from falling into the amorphous, the inconstant, and the ambiguous. For it stamps itself on experience, it is the identity of the survivor as form" (AE, 80).

34. Merleau-Ponty perceives that "The dialectic become *thesis* (statement) is no longer dialectical," and regards this aporetic dialectic as "embalmed" (VI, 175).

35. And, of course, here, above all, Merleau-Ponty's rejection of a Platonism of meaning is apposite: "The meaning is not on the phrase like the butter on the bread, like a second layer of "psychic reality" spread over the sound: it is the totality of what is said, the integral of all the differentiations of the verbal chain. . . ." (VI, 155).

36. In Dews's summary of the Derridian stance: "[A]ny specification of meaning can only function as a self-defeating attempt to stabilize and restrain what he terms the 'dissemination' of the text. Meaning is not retrieved from apparent unmeaning, but rather consists in the repression of unmeaning" (LD, 13).

37. Consider: (Fr. 58) "[P]hysicians, who cut and burn, demand payment of a fee, though undeserving, since they produce the same *(pains as the disease)*"; (Fr. 59) "For the fuller's screw, the way, straight and crooked, is one and the same"; (Fr. 60) "The way up and down is one and the same"; (Fr. 61) "Sea water is the purest and most polluted: for fish, it is drinkable and life-giving; for men, not drinkable and destructive." Kathleen Freeman, *Ancilla to the Pre-Socratic Philosophers*: *A Complete Translation of the Fragments in Diels*' Fragmente der Vorsokratiker (Cambridge: Harvard University Press, 1983), pp. 28–29.

38. Ibid., p. 31.

39. Ibid., p. 28.

40. Ibid., p. 29.

41. The example is Findlay's: "My brother as I think of him is in fact not properly an actual object and can be identical with no actual object except in an entirely special sense of identity, which has of course the special peculiarity of evading Leibniz's Law, so that only *some* of the things predicable of the real object can be predicated of the intentional object that is 'identified' with it." J. N. Findlay, *Ascent to the Absolute*: *Metaphysical Papers and Lectures* (New York: Humanities, 1970), p. 242.

42. Blyth supplements: "We live supposedly in a world of opposites, of white against black, of here versus there. But beneath this level of opposition lies a sea of tranquillity in which all things are complementary rather than contradictory." R. H. Blyth, *Games Zen Masters Play* (New York: New American Library, 1976), p. 14.

43. It is this circular relationship that prompts Conze to assert that "*absolute* identity . . . does not exclude an absolute difference" (BTI, 264).

44. The "nay" is glimpsed in Hui-hai's provocation: "The moon is reflected in that deep pond; catch it if you like." John Blofeld, "Translator's Introduction" (HH, 89).

45. Thus: "The miracle of consciousness consists in its bringing to light, through attention, phenomena which re-establish the unity of the object in a new dimension at the very moment when they destroy it" (PhP, 30).

46. "Yea" and "nay" are, that is, internal negates. Contrastingly, external negation "appears as a purely external bond established between two beings as by a witness" (BN, 243).

47. The Buddhist sense of voidness is poignantly expressed in Anne Waldman's "Makeup on Empty Space":

> There is a better way to say empty space
> Turn yourself inside out and you might disappear

48. "Space is the intimate experience of the nature of one's mind." A. H. Almaas, *The Void: A Psychodynamic Investigation of the Relationship between Mind and Space* (Berkeley, Calif.: Diamond Books, n.d.), p. 22. Thus, in the conversation which Hui-hai recounts, there is no place to dwell:

> Q: Whereon should the mind settle and dwell?
> A: It should settle upon non-dwelling and there dwell.
> Q: What is this non-dwelling?
> A: It means not allowing the mind to dwell upon anything whatsoever."
> (HH, 45)

49. Principle 10, part 2, in René Descartes, *The Principles of Philosophy*, trans. Elizabeth S. Haldane and G. R. T. Ross (Cambridge: Cambridge University Press, 1972), p. 259.

50. Merleau-Ponty reminds us, however, that "*every concept is first a horizonal generality, a generality of style*—" (VI, 237).

51. The positive and the negative confront one another as, in Sartre's theory of self-deception, do belief and questioning reflection. Reflection renders the belief questionable, but cannot exist without feeding upon it. Belief is perpetually consumed while remaining constantly whole: "[B]elief, owing to the very fact that it can exist only as *troubled*, exists from the start as escaping itself, as shattering the unity of all the concepts in which one can wish to inclose it" (BN, 122).

52. This does not in the least abrogate the fact that "my experience breaks forth into things. . . ." (PhP, 303).

53. Plurality, as Hui-hai suggests, is a consequence of this insouciance: "[A]lthough only the one sun appears in the sky above, its reflections are caught by water held by

many different receptacles, so that each of those receptacles 'contains a sun' and every 'sun' is both complete in itself and yet identical with the sun in the sky" (HH, 65).

54. Ta-chu Hui-hai remarks that "It is like a brightly shining mirror reflecting images on it. When the mirror does this, does the brightness suffer in any way? No, it does not. Why? Because the Use of the bright mirror is free from affections, and therefore its reflection is never obscured. Whether images are reflected or not, there are no changes in its brightness. Why? Because that which is free from affections knows no change in all conditions" (NM, 50).

55. "Yet," for Adorno, "the appearance of identity is inherent in thought itself, in its pure form. To think is to identify" (ND, 5). Again: "We can see through the identity principle, but we cannot think without identifying. Any definition is identification" (ND, 149).

56. "Within identity there is yet difference" (OT, 230).

57. Merleau-Ponty thus remarks, "The need to proceed by way of essences does not mean that philosophy takes them as its object, but, on the contrary, that our existence is too tightly held in the world to be able to know itself as such at the moment of its involvement, and that it requires the field of ideality in order to become acquainted with and to prevail over its facticity. . . . Husserl's essences are destined to bring back all the living relationships of experience, as the fisherman's net draws up from the depths of the ocean quivering fish and seaweed" (PhP, xv).

58. For Nietzsche, "The concept of substance is a consequence of the notion of the subject: not the reverse! If we relinquish the soul, 'the subject,' the precondition for 'substance' in general disappears." Friedrich Nietzsche, *The Will to Power*, trans. Walter Kaufmann and R. J. Hollingdale (New York: Vintage, 1968), p. 485.

59. "Activity" is used here advisedly and without contrast. For we are not, as Merleau-Ponty insists, "in some incomprehensible way an activity joined to a passivity . . . but wholly active and wholly passive. . . ." (PhP, 428). Indeed: "[I]t is . . . certain that every attempt to fit a passivity upon an activity ends up either in extending the passivity to the whole—which amounts to detaching us from Being, since, for lack of a contact of myself with myself, I am in every operation of knowledge delivered over to an organization of my thoughts whose premises are masked from me, to a mental constitution which is given to me as a fact—or ends up by restoring the activity to the whole. This is in particular the flaw in the philosophies of reflection that do not follow themselves through; after having defined the requirements for thought, they add that these do not impose any law upon the things and evoke an order of the things themselves which, in contradistinction to the order of our thoughts, could receive only exterior rules" (VI, 43). Sartre's counsel is immediately apposite: "Being . . . is neither passivity nor activity" (BN, 27).

60. But, in Frauwallner's words, like "the breaking of a pot and the felling of a tree" which, though not realities, are nonetheless "facts," the mirror cannot be described as a "real separate datum." [Ebenso gibt est das Zerbrechen eines Topfes und das Umhauen eines Baumes. Es sind nur keine wirklichen gesonderten Gegebenheiten.] Erich Frauwallner, *Die Philosophie des Buddhismus* (Berlin: Akademie-Verlag, 1956), p. 139.

61. Merleau-Ponty typifies this latter act as an event of "generation": "the awesome birth of vociferation" (VI, 144).

62. The *dia-* of Merleau-Ponty's "good dialectic" is no mere idealization: "[T]he good dialectic is that which is conscious of the fact that every *thesis* is an idealization, that

Being is not made up of idealizations or of things said, as the old logic believed, but of bound wholes where signification never is except in tendency, where the inertia of the content never permits the defining of one term as positive, another term as negative, and still less a third term as absolute suppression of the negative by itself" (VI, 94).

63. Though no Zenonian, Sartre at least supposes that "A world without motion would be conceivable. To be sure, we cannot imagine the possibility of a world without change, except by virtue of a purely formal possibility, but change is not motion. Change is alteration of the quality of the *this*; it is produced . . . in a block by the upsurge or disintegration of a form" (BN, 286). The ostensible chasm between motion and rest is altogether annulled in the Merleau-Pontyan conception of the lived body: "It is not *in rest* either like some of them. It is beneath objective rest and movement—" (VI, 225).

64. Cf. J. E. Raven, *Pythagoreans and Eleatics* (Cambridge: Cambridge University Press, 1948), and G. E. L. Owen's contribution in David J. Furley and R. E. Allen, eds., *Studies in Presocratic Philosophy 2* (London: Routledge and Kegan Paul; New York: Humanities, 1970–75), pp. 143–65.

65. Merleau-Ponty agrees that "The possibilities by essence can indeed envelop and dominate *the facts*," yet we must remember that "they themselves derive from another, and more fundamental, possibility: that which works over my experience, opens it to the world and to Being, and which, to be sure, does not find them before itself as *facts* but animates and organizes *their facticity*" (VI, 110).

66. In Sartre's insightful rejoinder "The arrow, they tell us, when it passes by the position AB 'is' there, exactly as if it were an arrow at rest, with the tip of its head on A and the tip of its tail on B. This appears evident if we admit that motion is superimposed on being and that consequently nothing comes to decide whether being is in motion or at rest. In a word, if motion is an accident of being, motion and rest are indistinguishable. . . . it does not seem to us that *to pass* a place is the equivalent of *remaining there—i.e., of being there*. . . . the moving object only *passes* AB (*i.e.*, it never *is* there) . . . how could the arrow *not* be at AB since at AB it *is*? . . . in order to avoid the Eleatic paradox we must renounce the generally admitted postulate according to which being in motion preserves its being-in-itself. . . . In motion being changes into *nothing*. . . ." (BN, 287–89). Again: "When the *this is at rest*, space *is*; when it is in motion space *is engendered* or *becomes*. The trajectory *never is*, since it is *nothing*: it vanishes immediately into purely external relations between different places; that is, in simple exteriority of indifference or spatiality" (BN, 290).

67. While I find the interpretation useful, it would be remiss to suggest that it enjoys universal acceptance. For a vigorously opposing view, see D. J. Furley, *Two Studies in the Greek Atomists* (Princeton: Princeton University Press, 1967), pp. 71–75. No doubt, in Brumbaugh's moderate summation, the four-part scheme "makes history more orderly than it was." Robert S. Brumbaugh, *The Philosophers of Greece* (Albany: SUNY Press, 1981), p. 224.

68. Cf. Aristotle, *Prior Analytics* I, 24a–b; *Topics* I, 100a–b. Yet, as Kofman acutely observes regarding the principle that "The true is that which can be demonstrated," "This is an arbitrary definition of the word 'true'; *this definition cannot be demonstrated*." Sarah Kofman, "Descartes Entrapped" (WCAS, 189).

69. A demonstration, as Brown clarifies, "occurs inside the calculus, a proof outside. The boundary between them is thus a shared boundary, and is what is approached,

in one or the other direction, according to whether we are demonstrating a consequence or proving a theorem" (LF, 94).

70. While Aristotle would not abandon the pursuit of conceptual verity, he would assuredly salute the second of Benoit's injunctions: "Search not for the truth; only cease to cherish opinions." Benoit, "Salvation or Satori." Robert Sohl and Audrey Carr, eds., *The Gospel According to Zen: Beyond the Death of God* (New York: Mentor, 1970), p. 49.

71. Cf. Plato, *Sophist* 224e–226a; *Republic* 499a; *Phaedrus* 261c.

72. Cf. Plato, *Phaedo* 100b, 101d; *Republic* 511e, 532a–b, 533c–d.

73. In the verse of Sêng-ts'an (c. A.D. 600), the third patriarch of the Ch'an tradition:

> At the least thought of "Is" and "Is not,"
> There is chaos and the mind is lost . . .
> In its essence the Great Way is all-embracing.

(TCB, 228). The *Chao-lun* says: "[U]nless one has the special penetration of Holy Intelligence, how can one fit one's spirit to the interstice between the existent and the non-existent?" (BTI, 219).

74. In Nāgārjuna's summation, "Any thesis must lead to a counter-thesis. Neither one nor the other is to the point." (BTI, 209).

75. Alan W. Watts, *Psychotherapy East and West* (New York: Ballantine, 1969), p. 160.

76. "All the positivist bric-à-brac of 'concepts', 'judgments', 'relations', is eliminated," says Merleau-Ponty, and, in a Zen-like image, "the mind [is] quiet as water in the fissure of Being—" (VI, 235).

77. For Mādhyamika, "The dialectic reaches its fruition through three 'moments,' the antinomical conflict of opposed views of the real advanced by speculative systems. . . . ; their criticism, which exposes their hollowness (śūnyatā); and intuition of the Real in which the duality of 'is' and 'is not' is totally resolved (prajñā). It is the Absolute beyond Reason." (CPB, 226–27).

78. Regarding temporal unitization, Merleau-Ponty perceives that "The definition of time which is implicit in the comparisons undertaken by common sense, and which might be formulated as 'a succession of instances of *now*' has not even the disadvantage of treating past and future as presents: it is inconsistent, since it destroys the very notion of 'now', and that of succession" (PhP, 412). Indeed, as Royce claims, "Every *now* within which something happens is . . . *also* a succession." Josiah Royce, *The World and the Individual*, 2d ser.: *Nature, Man, and the Moral Order* (Gloucester, Mass.: Peter Smith, 1976), p. 139.

79. Of such logically determined "possibilities," Sartre insightfully suggests: "[I]f we define possible as non-contradictory, it can have being only as the thought of a being prior to the real world or prior to the pure consciousness of the world such as it is" (BN, 149).

80. "Is this," questions Merleau-Ponty "the highest point of reason, to realize that the soil beneath our feet is shifting, to pompously name 'interrogation' what is only a persistent state of stupor, to call 'research' or 'quest' what is only trudging in a circle, to call 'Being' that which never fully *is?*" "Eye and Mind (PP, 190).

81. Nāgārjuna demonstrates the deeply aporetic character of this distinction: "There is no darkness in light or in its abode. What does light illumine when, indeed, it destroys darkness?

"How could darkness be destroyed by a presently shining light? For, indeed, the presently shining light has not as yet extended over to darkness.

"If darkness is destroyed by light which is not extended, then light, in such a state, will destroy the whole world of darkness.

"If light illuminates both itself and other entities, then undoubtedly, darkness will also darken itself and other entities as well" (MK, 7:9–12; N, 65–66).

82. Suzuki adds: "Again it is like the sun illuminating the world. Does the light suffer any change? No, it does not. How, when it does not illuminate the world? There are no changes in it, either. Why? Because the light is free from affections, and therefore whether it illumines objects or not, the unaffected sunlight is ever above change" (NM, 50).

83. Lyotard has his own way of expressing this point: "[E]very statement advances into pathos in order to separate the this and the not-this, advances therefore armed with a cutter, a double-edged blade, and cuts [tout énoncé s'avance dans le pathos pour y départager le ceci et le non-ceci, donc s'avance armé d'un *cutter*, d'un biface, et tranche]." Jean-François Lyotard, *Économie libidinale* (Paris: Éditions de Minuit, 1974), p. 289.

84. The *aporia* attendant upon this severance is indicated in Merleau-Ponty's recognition that "The world is still the vague theatre of all experiences" (PhP, 343). *Both* sides of the breach are claimed by experience.

85. The universe is, of course, one *(unus)* turn (from *vertere*, to turn). Thus, in Brown's presentation: "A given (or captivated) universe is what is seen as the result of making one turn, and thus *is the appearance* of any first distinction, and only a minor aspect of all being, apparent and non-apparent. Its particularity is the price we pay for its visibility" (LF, 106n). Since the "verse (*versus*, from *verto*, the act of turning, to return, as opposed to *prorsus*, to proceed directly, as in prose)" (PN, 79) is inseparable from the uni/verse, there is, as the dual legacy of *versus* suggests, something profoundly "poetic" about the manifest single revolution *(saṁsāra)* constitutive of our realm of *res*: *realitas*.

86. For Merleau-Ponty, "[W]e dissolve the perceived *world* into a *universe* which is nothing but this very world cut off from its constitutive origins, and made manifest because they are forgotten" (PhP, 41). It may not be entirely incorrect to assimilate τὸ ὅλον and τὸ πᾶν, of Sartre's significant distinction to Brown's "all" and "world": "[T]he Greeks were accustomed to distinguish cosmic reality, which they called τὸ πᾶν, from the totality constituted by this and by the infinite void which surrounded it—a totality which they called Τὸ ὅλον" (BN, 791). Thus, "the ὅλον we are considering is like a decapitated notion in perpetual disintegration. . . . There is here a passage which is not completed, a short circuit" (BN, 793).

87. This was neither the muteness of incapacity before the known but inarticulable nor the failure of speech within the failure of knowledge. Rather, as Agamben suggests, "*Silence comprehends the Abyss as incomprehensible*" (PN, 63).

88. We must also include the "vertical" polarity: "I polarize a world which I do not create" (PhP, 359).

89. "The real language," Murti teaches, "is silence" (CPB, 232).

90. "Take the case of a bright mirror. When it is reflecting something, does its brightness waver? No, it does not. And when it is not reflecting something, does its brightness waver, then? No." Blofeld, "Translator's Introduction" (HH, 61).

91. Adorno's assessment is harsher still: "For the present, reason is pathic; nothing but to cure ourselves of it would be rational" (ND, 172).

92. Lyotard appositely maintains that "A sentence presents a universe" (PFT, 129). Indeed, "The universe which a sentence presents is not presented to something or to someone—as to a subject. A 'subject', whether addressor or addressee, referent or sense, is situated in a universe presented by a sentence. Even when the subject is declared outside the sentential universe *qua* addressor or addressee of the presentation . . . this subject is situated within the universe presented by the sentence which declares it to be outside. The metaphysical illusion consists in confusing presentation with situation" (PFT, 130).

93. Juo (1296–1380 C.E.) offers a proposal for enlightened realization: "unhitch the universe." Lucien Stryk and Takashi Ikemoto, trans., *Zen: Poems, Prayers, Sermons, Anecdotes, Interviews* (Garden City, N.Y.: Doubleday, 1963), p. 7.

94. For Merleau-Ponty, "Reality is not a crucial appearance underlying the rest, it is the framework of relations with which all appearances tally" (PhP, 300). This is not remote from Sartre's insistence that "There is . . . no substantial form here, no principle of unity to stand *behind* the modes of appearance of the phenomenon; everything is given at one stroke without any primacy" (BN, 272).

95. Emptiness, as Inada makes plain, is not universal negation, but rather, universal affirmation, absolute inclusion, not exclusion: "Thus the middle path is the 'vision of the real in its true form.' Nothing is excluded, nothing is negated, nothing is abstracted. Everything is ... in the sense of inclusive or immanent transcendence. The middle path might then be termed the ontological inclusiveness, excellence, purity or supremeness of being" (N, 22).

96. In Lyotard's relevant discussion: "All discourse of knowledge rests on a *decision*, namely that the two statements *the soup is served* and *it is true that the soup is served* do not belong to the same class and should be distinguished. But this decision is not itself demonstrable. In other words, what is called the 'paradox' of the Liar is not refutable; and at the same time, the decision constitutive of the discourse of knowledge, constitutive of the constituting order, appears as a fact of power and as the power of a fact [Tout le discours de savoir s'appuie sur une *décision*, à savoir que les deux énoncés *la soupe est servie* et *il est vrai que la soupe est servie* n'appartiennent pas à la même classe et doivent être distingués. Mais cette décision n'est pas elle-même démontrable. Autrement dit, ce qu'on apelle le «paradoxe» du Menteur n'est pas réfutable; et du même coup, la décision constitutive du discours de savoir, constitutive de l'ordre constituant, apparaït comme le fait d'un pouvoir et un pouvoir de fait]." Jean-François Lyotard, *Rudiments païens* (Paris: Union Générale d'Éditions, 1977), pp. 229–30.

97. Ekai (Mumon), "The Gateless Gate" (ZFZB, 124).

98. "We know that there are errors only because we possess truth. . . ." (PhP, 295).

99. Inada, writing of Y. Ueda's interpretation of Nāgārjuna, affirms that "The unique logical principle in brief is that of any two concepts, e.g., fire and wood, there are inherent conditions in each such that their ultimate relationship into a whole or unity entails a mutual denial of each other" (N, 80).

100. Mumon, "The Gateless Gate" (ZFZB, 124). In Conze's trenchant pronouncement, "The Mahayana dialectic will stop at nothing in its efforts to deprive us of all and everything and to prevent us from hugging and cherishing even the tiniest reward for all our renunciations and sacrifices. In fact the teachings become quite logical and unavoidable when regarded as the ontological counterpart to a completely selfless and disinterested attitude" (BTI, 232).

101. This event would be "a negation-reference (zero of . . .) or separation *(écart)*" (VI, 257).

102. In the lovely words of the *Pao-ching San-mei* [*Samādhi as Reflection from the Precious Mirror*]: "As snow is contained in a silver bowl, and as a white heron hides in the bright moonlight, when you classify them they are different from each other, but when you unify them they are the same in the Source" (OT, 47).

103. "The idea of 'being'" is the Archimedean point of Western thought." Yoshinori Takeuchi, "Buddhism and Existentialism: The Dialogue between Oriental and Occidental Thought," in Walter Leibrecht, ed., *Religion and Culture*: *Essays in Honor of Paul Tillich* (Freeport, N.Y.: Books for Libraries Press, 1972), p. 292.

104. However, as Murti notes, "The spiritual man is a one-level personality. In him there is no division of the inner and the outer, the surface motives and the deeper unconscious drives. He is not torn asunder by conflict and confusion; he is fully integrated and unified" (CPB, 259).

105. In Merleau-Ponty's query, "What is willing, if it is not being conscious of an object as valid. . . ." (PhP, 377).

106. "Either what I call depth is nothing, or else it is my participation in a Being without restriction, a participation primarily in the being of space beyond every [particular] point of view. Things encroach upon one another *because each is outside of the others*." "Eye and Mind" (PP, 173).

107. We should bear in mind, however, that "Even the sharpest sword cannot cut itself; the finger-tips cannot be touched by the same finger-tips. Citta [mind] does not know itself" (CPB, 317–18). Wittgenstein, who in many ways resonates with certain fundamental Buddhist assumptions, also asserts that "nothing *in the visual field* allows you to infer that it is seen by an eye." Ludwig Wittgenstein, *Tractatus Logico-Philosophicus* (London: Routledge and Kegan Paul, 1961), no. 5.633, p. 57.

108. B. J. Whorf, *Language, Thought, and Reality* (Cambridge: MIT Press, 1956), pp. 240, 213. A more recent statement of this position was voiced by John Searle in conversation with Bryan Magee: "The world doesn't come to us already sliced up into objects and experiences: what counts as an object is already a function of our system of representation, and how we perceive the world in our experience is influenced by that system of representation. The mistake is to suppose that the application of language to the world consists of attaching labels to objects that are, so to speak, self-identifying. On my view, the world divides the way we divide it, and our main way of dividing things up is in the language." Bryan Magee, ed., *Men of Ideas* (New York: Viking, 1978), p. 184.

109. "It is," as Merleau-Ponty articulates, "a diacritical, oppositional, relative system whose pivot is the *Etwas*, the thing, the world, and not the idea—" (VI, 206). Or as Robert Kelly testifies: "Deep in the planet of our incarnation the uncountably many relays switch on and off. Language, that gauge, gives our best local mapping of those (strictly) endless modifications motivated by everything else. Our syntax is our habit. . . ." "Going With the Poem" (BSM, 162).

110. Chögyam Trungpa tells us that "Things are symbols of themselves." Cited in Allen Ginsberg, "Meditation and Poetics" (BSM, 97). And for Cassirer, as Merleau-Ponty reminds us, "thought was the 'shuttlecock' of language." "An Unpublished Text" (PP, 8).

111. "In the beginning," proclaims Bourdieu, "is the *illusio*, adherence to the game. . . ." Pierre Bourdieu, "The Philosophical Institution" (PFT, 1). And: "The most funda-

mental reasons for acting are rooted in the *illusio*, that is in the relation, itself not recognized as such, between a field of play and a habitus, as that sense of the game which confers on the game and on its stakes their determining or, better, their *motivating* power" (PFT, 3).

112. Joseph Margolis, "Deconstruction; or, The Mystery of the Mystery of the Text," in Hugh J. Silverman and Don Ihde, eds., *Hermeneutics & Deconstruction* (Albany: SUNY Press, 1985), p. 144.

113. This is not at all to dismiss Merleau-Ponty's contention that "the real is coherent and probable because it is real, and not real because it is coherent; the imaginary is incoherent or improbable because it is imaginary, and not imaginary because it is incoherent" (VI, 40).

114. Margolis, "Deconstruction," p. 114.

115. Martin Heidegger, *Identity and Difference* (New York: Harper and Row, 1969), p. 47.

116. Ibid., p. 64.

117. Or as Tao-hsin expresses it: "Like the mirror on which your features are reflected, they are perfectly perceived there in all clearness; the reflections are all there in the emptiness, yet the mirror itself retains not one of the objects which are reflected there. The human face has not come to enter into the body of the mirror, nor has the mirror gone out to enter into the human face" (EZB III, 29).

118. Jacques Derrida, *Margins of Philosophy* (Chicago: University of Chicago Press, 1982), p. 67. Kierkegaard's musings on the Unknown may instantiate this speculation: "What then is the Unknown? It is the boundary to which reason repeatedly comes, and insofar, substituting a static form of conception for the dynamic, it is the different, the absolutely different. But because it is absolutely different, it has no distinguishing mark. When determined as absolutely different, it seems on the verge of disclosure, but this is not so, for reason cannot even conceive an absolute unlikeness. Reason cannot negate itself absolutely, but uses itself for this purpose, and thus only conceives a difference within itself as it can conceive by means of itself. It absolutely cannot go out of itself, and hence conceives only such a superiority over itself as it can conceive by means of itself." Søren Kierkegaard, *Philosophical Fragments*, trans. D. F. Swenson and H. V. Hong (Princeton: Princeton University Press, 1971), p. 55.

119. Jacques Derrida, *Of Grammatology* (Baltimore: Johns Hopkins University Press, 1976), p. 23.

120. As Sartre fruitfully appends, "This original relation between the all and the 'this' is at the source of the relation between figure and ground. . . ." (BN, 252).

121. In the words of Fa-i T'sao-an, "The awakening of Prajñā was the first grand deviation, and ever since we live in the midst of deviations. There is no way to escape them except living them as they follow one another" (NM, 150).

122. Perhaps this movement is akin to the "sliding" which, Sartre observes, "realizes a material unity in depth without penetrating farther than the surface . . . the sliding appears as identical with a continuous creation" (BN, 745–46).

123. "What we differentiate," Adorno maintains, "will appear divergent, dissonant, negative for just as long as the structure of our consciousness obliges it to strive for unity; as long as its demand for totality will be its measure for whatever is not identical with it" (ND, 5–6).

124. Rodolphe Gasché, "God, For Example," in André Schuwer, ed., *Phenomenology and the Numinous* (Pittsburgh: Simon Silverman Phenomenology Center, 1988), p. 51.

125. Ibid., p. 52.

126. Transposing this structure into a political key, Baudrillard affirms that "like two ends of a curved mirror, the 'vicious' curvature of political space henceforth magnetised, circularised, reversibilised from right to left, a torsion that is like the evil demon of communication, the whole system, the infinity of capital folded back over its own surface: transfinite?" (SS, 35).

127. Introduction to Robert Denoon Cumming, ed., *The Philosophy of Jean-Paul Sartre* (New York: Vantage, 1965), p. 9.

128. "There is always," Lyotard tells us, "a prereflective, an unreflective, a prepredicative upon which reflection and science are based, and which these latter always conjure away when explaining themselves." Jean-François Lyotard, *Phenomenology*, trans. Brian Beakley (Albany: SUNY Press, 1991), p. 33.

129. "Reflection moves all things away to a distance. . . ." (PhP, 399).

130. There are, of course, other possible responses, that of anxiety, for example. Baudrillard speaks of "the uneasiness before the mirror-image. There is already sorcery at work in the mirror" (SS, 153 n. 1).

131. Merleau-Ponty exemplifies this "humility" in his observation that "the donkey that goes straight to the fodder knows as much about the properties of the straight line as we do. . . ." (VI, 153).

132. Mediated self-awareness, depicted as the vision of oneself as one stands before the mirror, models Sartre's "circuit of selfness" *(circuit de ipséité),* which, as he says, is "the relation of the for-itself with the possible which it is. . . . The possible is *the something* which the for-itself lacks *in order to* be itself" (BN, 155).

133. In Trinh's sobering proclamation, "To see one's double is to see oneself dead." Trinh thi Minh-hà, *Woman, Native, Other: Writing, Postcoloniality and Feminism* (Bloomington: Indiana University Press, 1989), p. 22.

134. Should we add Lispector's G. H.?: "I am the priestess of a secret that I no longer know" (GH, 8).

135. D. E. Harding, "On Having No Head," in Douglas R. Hofstadter and Daniel C. Dennet, eds., *The Mind's I: Fantasies and Reflections on Self and Soul* (New York: Basic Books, 1981), pp. 28–29. In Merleau-Ponty's congruent explication: "A Cartesian does not see *himself* in the mirror; he sees a dummy, an 'outside,' which, he has every reason to believe, other people see in the very same way but which, no more for himself than for others, is not a body in the flesh." "Eye and Mind" (PP, 170).

136. Bataille proposes an unmistakably Buddhist resolution of the tension: "[W]e only become aware of them [inner states] to the extent that we let go of our discursive mania to know!" (IE, 140).

137. "We must not wonder whether we really perceive a world, we must instead say: the world is what we perceive" (PhP, xvi).

138. Yet, of a cognition which purports to be genuine and secure, Nietzsche propounds: "[A]bsolute and unconditional knowledge is wishing to know without knowledge." Daniel Breazeale, ed., *Philosophy and Truth: Selections from Nietzsche's Notebooks of the Early 1870s* (Atlantic Highlands, N.J.: Humanities, 1979), p. 40.

139. This is because phenomenology itself, "as a disclosure of the world, rests on itself, or rather provides its own foundation" (PhP, xx–xxi).

140. Bataille describes the "great derision" as "a multitude of little contradicting 'everythings', intelligence surpassing itself, culminating in multivocal, discordant, indiscrete idiocy" (IE, 25).

141. Yet, in Bataille's compelling vision, "Life will dissolve itself in death, rivers in the sea, and the known in the unknown. Knowledge is access to the unknown. Nonsense is the outcome of every possible sense" (IE, 101).

142. Something of the paradox embodied in this question is expressed in Severino's view: "Appearing is not the infinite appearing of Being, the epiphany in which the completed totality is disclosed and in which, therefore, no further revelation can occur. As finite Appearing, eternal truth is contradiction. ... The eternal appearing of the background is the manifesting of a contradiction, which could be resolved only in an occurrence. . . . the truth of Being, which eternally appears, includes finitude, namely, the essential contradiction of its own Appearing." Emanuele Severino, "The Earth and the Essence of Man" (RM, 182, 185).

143. Fa-yen Wên-i (885–958 C.E.) transmits the following repartee:

> Monk: "How can the ancient mirror reveal itself before it is uncovered?"
> Master: "Why should you reveal it again?"
>
> (OT, 224)

144. Reginald E. Allen, "Participation and Predication in Plato's Middle Dialogues," in Gregory Vlastos, ed., *Plato: A Collection of Critical Essays*, vol. 1: *Metaphysics and Epistemology* (New York: Doubleday, 1971), p. 174.

145. Phenomenological bedrock is struck in Blofeld's lucid remark that "even a mirror suggests a plurality of the reflector, the act of reflecting and the thing reflected, whereas these three do not in truth differ from one another; so that, beyond a certain point, even the mirror is a mere analogy—another raft to be discarded." John Blofeld, "Translator's Introduction" (HH, 33).

146. Allen, "Participation and Predication in Plato's Middle Dialogues," p. 174.

147. Sartre confirms that "The existent does not *possess* its essence as a present quality. It is even the negation of essence; the green *never is* green. But the essence comes from the ground of the future to the existent, as a meaning which is never given and which forever haunts it" (BN, 267). In Merleau-Ponty's concordant claim: "I am open to the world, I have no doubt that I am in communication with it, but I do not possess it; it is inexhaustible" (PhP, xvii).

148. "Considered as an instrument of self-knowledge, one in which I have total faith, it also bears a magical character that has always transcended its functional nature." Trinh, *Woman, Native, Other*, p. 22.

149. Nietzsche advises us to "regard as false that which has not made you laugh at least once." Friedrich Nietzsche, "Old and New Tables," in *Thus Spake Zarathustra* (IE, 80). Compare Common's translation: "And false be every truth which hath not had laughter along with it!" Friedrich Nietzsche, "Old and New Tables," in *Thus Spake Zarathustra: A Book for All and None*, trans. Thomas Common (Edinburgh: Darien Press, 1909), p. 257.

150. Harding, "On Having No Head," p. 24.

151. A congruent point is nicely expressed by Trinh thi Minh-hà: "Yet how difficult it is to keep our mirrors clean. We all tend to cloud and soil them as soon as the older

smudges are wiped off, for we love to *use them as instruments* to behold ourselves, maintaining thereby a narcissistic relation of me to me, still me and always me. Rare are the moments when we accept leaving our mirrors empty, even though we may laugh watching our neighbors pining away for their own images. The very error that deceives our eyes inflames them; searching after that which does not exist. This object we love so, let us just turn away and it will immediately disappear." Trinh, *Woman, Native, Other*, p. 22.

152. And Merleau-Ponty confirms that "There really is inspiration and expiration of Being. . . ." "Eye and Mind" (PP, 167). Spirit, in Bergson's poignant description, is "that faculty of seeing which is immanent in the faculty of acting and which springs up, *some*how, by the *twisting [torsion]* of *the will on itself*, when action is turned into knowledge, like heat, so to say, into light." Henri Bergson, *Creative Evolution*, trans. A. Mitchell (New York: Modern Library, 1944), p. 273.

153. This immediacy might be accommodated in virtue of Sartre's intriguing notion of "distinction through nothing": "[I]f the two curves were hidden so that one could see only the length A B where they are tangential to each other, it would be impossible to distinguish them. Actually what separates them is *nothing*; there is neither continuity nor discontinuity but pure identity . . . what separates the two curves at the very spot of their tangency is *nothing*, not even a distance; it is a pure negativity as the counterpart of a constituting synthesis" (BN, 247–48).

154. Norwood Russell Hanson, *Patterns of Discovery: An Inquiry into the Conceptual Foundations of Science* (Cambridge: Cambridge University Press, 1958), p. 17.

155. Continuing and culminating this line of inquiry, Baudrillard asks: "But what if God himself can be simulated, that is to say, reduced to the signs which attest his existence? Then the whole system becomes weightless, it is no longer anything but a gigantic simulacrum—not unreal, but a simulacrum, never again exchanging for what is real, but exchanging in itself, in an uninterrupted circuit without reference or circumference" (SS, 10–11).

156. Quoted in Trinh, *Woman, Native, Other*, p. 3.

157. As Merleau-Ponty expresses it, "[T]he knowing of nothingness is a nothingness of knowing. . . ." (VI, 85). In the eighth-century repartee of Chih of Yün-chü:

> Chih: "There is seeing, but nothing is seen."
> Monk: "If there is nothing seen, how can we say there is any seeing at all?"
> Chih: "In fact there is no trace of seeing."
> Monk: "In such a seeing, whose seeing is it?"
> Chih: "There is no seer, either."

D. T. Suzuki, *Zen Buddhism* (New York: Doubleday Anchor, 1956), p. 207.

158. Nicholas of Cusa, *The Vision of God* (New York: Frederick Ungar, 1960), p. 4.

159. It cannot consistently be maintained both that "phenomenology is also a philosophy which put essences back into existence" (PhP, vii) and that "existent" and reflection are phenomenologically indistinguishable.

160. In this connection, we are cautioned that "no attribute that may be brought under the supreme genus of quality can subsist in Him." Maimonides, *The Guide to the Perplexed*, trans. Schlomo Pines (Chicago: The University of Chicago Press, 1963), p. 116.

161. Thus, "it is permitted that this kind should be predicated of God . . . after you have . . . come to know that the acts in question need not be carried out by means of

differing notions subsisting within the essence of the agent, but that all His different acts . . . are all of them carried out by means of His essence, and not . . . by means of a superadded notion." Maimonides, *Guide to the Perplexed*, p. 119.

162. The "awareness of the essencelessness of things" is, as Misra propounds to us, "another way of expressing *nirvana* itself." Interview with R. S. Misra, in Dom Aelred Graham, *The End of Religion* (New York: Harcourt Brace Jovanovich, 1971), pp. 174–75. Thus, "*sunyata* is the realization of the essencelessness of things. . . ." Ibid.

163. If, as Sartre remarks, "the essence comes from the ground of the future to the existent" (BN, 267), we cannot expect the mirror to have a "future." The mirror (mirroring) is an entirely *present* occurrence.

164. Allen, "Participation and Predication in Plato's Middle Dialogues," p. 174.

165. Harding, "On Having No Head," p. 25.

166. Magliola voices the same point in a splendidly intriguing way: "There are things like reflecting pools, and images, an infinite reference from one to the other, but no longer a source, a spring. There is no longer a simple origin. For what is reflected is split *in itself* and not only as an addition to itself of its image. The reflection, the image, the double, splits what it doubles." Robert Magliola, *Derrida on the Mend* (West Lafayette, Ind.: Purdue University Press, 1986), p. 9.

167. Nietzsche sees that the abandonment of the in-itself entails the concomitant abandonment of intellectual self-critique: "The intellect cannot criticise itself simply because it cannot be compared with other species of intellect and because its capacity to know would be revealed only in the presence of 'true reality'. . . . This presupposes that distinct from every perspective kind of outlook or sensual spiritual appropriation, something exists, an 'in itself'." Nietzsche, *The Will to Power*, p. 263.

168. It would not be amiss to remind ourselves, in Adorno's words, that "There is no origin save in ephemeral life" (ND, 156).

169. "*In a certain sense, 'thought' means nothing*. . . . This thought has no weight." Jacques Derrida, *Edmund Husserl's Origin of Geometry: An Introduction*, trans. John P. Leavey (New York: Nicolas Hays, 1977), p. 93.

170. Lyotard is attuned to Buddhist insight in his claim that subject and object are "fragments deriving from a primary deflagration of which language alone was the starting spark [des fragments en provenance d'une déflagration première dont le langage justement a été l'étincelle initiale]." Jean-François Lyotard, *Discours, Figure* (Paris: Klinksieck, 1971), p. 109.

171. The anecdote was conveyed to me in conversation with Robert Aitken, roshi of the Koko An Zendo, Honolulu. Yamada Roshi, a splendid exponent of the Rinzai tradition, was Aitken's teacher. Dale Pendell amplifies the momentum of this event in his verse:

> The first thing to do is to kick spirituality in the rear—hard enough
> to send it through the window.

"Some Reveries on Poetry as a Spiritual Discipline" (BSM, 202).

172. And of course, if "The dis-illusion is the loss of one evidence only because it is the acquisition of *another evidence*" (VI, 40), the transcendental project can at best be limited and partial.

173. "Objectively"—objectivity concerning itself with the structures of the "map"—"dialectics means to break the compulsion to achieve identity, and to break it by means

of the energy stored up in that compulsion and congealed in its objectifications" (ND, 157).

174. This is glimpsed in the well-known exchange:

> Bodhidharma says: "If you bring me that mind, I will pacify it for you."
> The successor says: "When I search my mind I cannot hold it."
> Bodhidharma says: "Then your mind is pacified already."
> (ZFZB, 122)

175. In Bataille's ecstatic antidote: "A space constellated with laughter opened its dark abyss before me. . . . I laughed divinely . . . I laughed as perhaps one had never laughed; the extreme depth of each thing opened itself up—laid bare, as if I were dead" (IE, 34). Again, "laughter was revelation, opened up the depth of things" (IE, 66).

176. Perhaps, as Deleuze suggests, finding ourselves inverted from the impact: "To be walking with one's feet in the air is not something with which one dialectician can reproach another, it is the fundamental character of the dialectic itself." Gilles Deleuze, *Nietzsche and Philosophy* (London: Athlone, 1983), p. 158.

177. The Sartrean in-itself "is an immanence which can not realize itself, an affirmation which can not affirm itself, an activity which can not act, because it is glued to itself" (BN, 27). Indeed, "It is itself so completely that the perpetual reflection which constitutes the self is dissolved in an identity" (BN, 28).

178. Thus, in Murti's Kantian-Mādhyamikan proposal: "[P]henomena are the veiled form or false appearance of the Absolute. . . ." (CPB, 232). Murti would, contrary to the spirit of our present musings, make of emptiness a Kantian noumenon: "The absolute is known as the reality of the appearances, what they stand for" (CPB, 232).

179. As Henry maintains, "[T]o be means to appear, and appearing appears in and through unfolding, as the exteriorization of exteriority, the Openness of the Open, which is the light of the world and the world itself." Michel Henry, "The Critique of the Subject" (WCAS, 162).

180. In Lispector's immoderate declaration, "[N]othing exists unless I give it a form. And . . . what if the reality is precisely that nothing has existed?!" (GH, 6).

181. Nietzsche voices the comic irony of the Kantian project: "What Kant wished to prove, in a way that would offend 'all the world,' was that 'all the world' was right—this was that soul's secret joke. He wrote against the scholars and in favor of the prejudices of the people, but he wrote for scholars, and not for the people [Kant wollte auf eine 'alle Welt' vor den Kopf stoßende Art beweisen, daß 'alle Welt' Recht habe:—das war der heimliche Witz dieser Seele. Er schrieb gegen die Gelehrten zu Gunsten des Volks-Vorurteils, aber für Gelehrte und nicht für das Volk]." Friedrich Nietzsche, *Gesammelte Werke* (Munich: Musarion Verlag, 1924), 12:182–83.

182. Thus Merleau-Ponty's report, "[W]hen I approach them, the things dissociate, my look loses its differentiation, and the vision ceases for lack of seer and of articulated things" (VI, 100). Sartre's "unchangeable this" is "revealed across a flickering and an infinite parceling out of phantom in-itselfs. This is not how that glass or that table is revealed to me. They do not endure; they *are*. Time flows over them" (BN, 281). Yet, in the Buddhist view, neither the flickering "phantom in-itselfs" nor, indeed, the "this" enjoy the least substantiality or ipseity.

183. We shall see the wisdom of Merleau-Ponty's view that "The thing is that manner of being for which the complete definition of one of its attributes demands that of the subject in its entirety; an entity, consequently, the significance of which is indistinguishable from its total appearance" (PhP, 323).

184. As has Merleau-Ponty: "I cannot even for an instant imagine an object in itself" (PP, 16).

185. For Merleau-Ponty, "There can be no question of describing perception itself as one of the facts thrown up in the world, since we can never fill up, in the picture of the world, that gap which we ourselves are, and by which it comes into existence for someone, since perception is the 'flaw' in this 'great diamond'" (PhP, 207).

186. Buddhism, Paz suggests, "is a dialectic of conjunction: Buddhism tends to assimilate and absorb what is contrary rather than destroying it utterly." Octavio Paz, "Eve and Prajnaparamita," in *Conjunctions and Disjunctions*, trans. Helen R. Lane (New York: Viking, 1974), p. 61. Suggesting a more general application, Merleau-Ponty remarks, "What I call the essence of the triangle is nothing but this presumption of a completed synthesis. . . ." (PhP, 388).

187. "Outwardly," as Yün-mên Wên-yen (d. 949 C.E.) discloses, "not even the slightest explanation can be used to reveal your inner awareness" (OT, 286).

188. For Merleau-Ponty, "doubt, or the fear of being mistaken, testifies as soon as it arises to our power of unmasking error, and that it could never finally tear us away from truth. We are in the realm of truth and it is 'the experience of truth' which is self-evident. To seek the essence of perception is to declare that perception is, not presumed true, but defined as access to truth" (PhP, xvi).

189. Heidegger re/minds us of the inner significance of memory: "Re-collection or re-inwardization [*Er-innerung*] converts that nature of ours that merely wills to impose, together with its objects, into the innermost invisible region of the heart's space. Here everything is inward [*inwendig*]: not only does it remain turned toward this proper inner [*eigentlichen Innen*] of consciousness, but inside this inner, one thing turns, free of all bounds, into the other. The interiority of the inner-world-space [*Das Inwendige des Weltinnenraumes*] unbars the open for us." Martin Heidegger, *Poetry, Language, Thought* (New York: Harper, 1971), p. 130.

190. Writes Foucault: "[T]he will to truth, as it has imposed itself on us for a long time, is such that the truth which it wills cannot help but mask it." Michel Foucault, "The Order of Discourse," in Robert Young, ed., *Untying the Text: A Post-Structuralist Reader* (Boston: Routledge and Kegan Paul, 1981), p. 56.

191. In Kakuan's report, "[E]veryone I look upon becomes enlightened" (ZFZB, 154). Such smugness is therefore wholly out of place.

192. Voicing the Buddhist abrogation of bivalence, Inada is firm that "reason cannot and should not be used as an apogogic device, i.e., the rejection of a view does not automatically mean the acceptance of another" (N, 9).

193. Cf. Michael Dummett, *Truth and Other Enigmas* (Cambridge: Harvard University Press, 1978), pp. xix–xxxvi.

194. Ibid., p. xxviii. It should be clear that "antirealism" does not coincide with idealism. In consonance with Buddhism, Bergson maintains that the nexus of ontological dependence cannot be understood as a unidirectional vector. Thus, Bergson queries whether the task of metaphysics is not "to remount the incline that physics descends, to

bring back matter to its origins, and build up progressively a *cosmology*, which would be, so to speak, a reversed *psychology*." Bergson, *Creative Evolution*, p. 227f.

195. Dummett, *Truth and Other Enigmas*, p. xxix.

196. "The real," in Merleau-Ponty's comment, "lends itself to unending exploration; it is inexhaustible" (PhP, 324).

The Pathless Path: Reflections on Buddhist Meditative Practice

The haiku by Ryusui is from Harold G. Henderson, *An Introduction to Haiku: An Anthology of Poems and Poets from Bashō to Shiki* (Garden City, N.Y.: Doubleday, 1958), p. 88.

1. In Hua Yol Jung's resonant deposition, this sonorous repletion enjoys a certain emancipation from its origin: "Color does not separate itself from the object, whereas sound separates itself from its source (e.g., voice or the sound of a musical instrument). In other words, color is a dependent attribute of an object, whereas sound is not. While the color we see is the property of a thing itself and we confront color in space, the tone we hear is not the property of anything and we encounter it out of or from space. Color is locatable and localizable in one single position with the object, whereas sound, once separated from its source, has no definite topological property or determination although its source is locatable. Sound travels in no one direction; it travels in all directions. Musical tones have no locatable places: they are neither 'here' nor 'there' but everywhere (i.e., placeless or ubiquitous)." Hwa Yol Jung, "Heidegger's Way with Sinitic Thinking," in Graham Parkes, ed., *Heidegger and Asian Thought* (Honolulu: University of Hawaii Press, 1987), p. 242 n. 22.

2. And with "vigilance" is born philosophy. As Solomon observes, "Philosophy is not a particular body of knowledge; it is the vigilance which does not let us forget the source of all knowledge." Robert C. Solomon, "General Introduction: What is Phenomenology?" in Robert C. Solomon, ed., *Phenomenology and Existentialism* (New York: Harper & Row, 1972), p. 4.

3. J. N. Findlay, *The Discipline of the Cave* (New York: Humanities, 1966), p. 85.

4. Bataille puzzles: "Where is this insipid cloud of thoughts headed—this cloud which I imagine to be similar to the sudden blood in a wounded throat?" (IE, 55).

5. "The upsurge of time," writes Merleau-Ponty, "would be incomprehensible as the *creation* of a supplement of time that would push the whole preceding series back into the past. That passivity is not conceivable" (VI, 184). For Sartre, "The for-itself directs the explosion of its temporality against the whole length of the revealed in-itself as though against the length of an immense and monotonous wall of which it can not see the end" (BN, 280). The intimacy that enfolds consciousness and temporality is glimpsed in Buddhaghosa's words: "By time the Sage described the mind, and by mind described the time." Buddhaghosa, *Atthasālinī*, quoted in Bhikkhu Ñaṇajivako, "Karma—The Ripening Fruit," in *Kamma and its Fruit,* Wheel Publications no. 221–24 (Kandy: Buddhist Publication Society, 1975), pp. 35–36.

6. As Albrecht insightfully propounds: "*Quiet as* 'Grundbefindlichkeit,' *in contrast to anxiety, is not a structural moment in the disclosure of Dasein. Quiet has no*

disclosing function. There is no why and wherefore of quiet. *Quiet is not situational understanding*. The ontological structural moment of quiet cannot therefore constitute the disclosure of Dasein, but what may be glimpsed through its phenomenal state is something other, something essentially different—namely, *the structural moment of an openness of Dasein*. Anxiety is a self-situating in disclosure. *Quiet is a self-situation in openness*. The state of being open of being being-in-itself is the condition for the possibility of receptivity. Set within the horizon of beings within the world, Dasein is disclosed in the anxiety of being-in-the-world as such. But displayed against the horizon of beings in the word, being-in-itself as quiet *is* neither a disclosure of being-in-the-world nor a disclosure of being-in-itself. It is *openness pure and simple and indeed openness as the possibility of receptivity* [*Die Ruhe als »Grundbefindlichkeit« ist im Gegensatz zur Angst kein Strukturmoment der Erschlossenheit des Daseins. Ruhe hat keine erschließend Function*. Est gibt kein Wovor der Ruhe und es gibt kein Worum der Ruhe. *Die Ruhe ist kein befindliches Verstehen*. Das ontologische Strukturmoment der Ruhe kann also nicht die Erschlossenheit das Daseins konstituieren, sondern das, was sich aus ihrem Phänomenbestand herausschauen läßt, ist etwas anders, wesensverschiedenes: nämlich *das Strukturmoment einer Offenheit des Daseins*. Angst ist ein Sich-befinden im Erschließen; Ruhe ist ein Sich-befinden im Offensein. Das Offensein des In-sich-Seins ist die Bedingung der Möglichkeit der *Empfänglichkeit*. Herausgestellt aus dem Horizont des innerweltlich Seienden *ist* das In-sich-Sein als Sein der Ruhe nicht Erschlossenheit des In-der-Welt-Seins und auch nicht Erschlossenheit des In-sich-Seins, sondern *Offenheit schlechthin und zwar Offenheit als Möglichkeit der Empfängnis*]." Carl Albrecht, *Das mystische Erkennen. Gnoseologie und philosophische Relevanz der mystischen Relation* (Bremen: C. Schüneman, 1958), p. 360, following Hans Waldenfels, *Absolute Nothingness: Foundations for a Buddhist-Christian Dialogue*, trans. J. W. Heisig (New York: Paulist Press, 1980), pp. 128–29.

7. John Cage discovers that "silence is not acoustic." "Where'm Now" (BSM, 44).

8. Merleau-Ponty says substantially the same with respect to language: "It is the error of semantic philosophies to close up language as if it only spoke of itself: it lives only from silence; everything which we cast towards others has germinated in this great, silent landscape which never leaves us" (VI, 126).

9. Hui-hai also sees that "The nature of hearing being eternal, we continue to hear whether sounds are present or not" (HH, 49).

10. Bataille cautions, however, that "*the word silence is still a sound*, to speak is in itself to imagine knowing; and to no longer know, it would be necessary to no longer speak" (IE, 13). Indeed, "Silence is a word which is not a word and breath an object which is not an object. . . ." (IE, 16).

11. Zen reminds us that "Silence never varies. . . ." (OT, 12).

12. Dews presents us with an ostensibly conflicting view: "There is no domain of 'phenomenological silence', of intuitive self-presence prior to the representational, and therefore divisive, function of language" (LD, 19). But this view collides with our own only if phenomenology is understood as the attempt to "represent" or literally describe, rather than "evoke," experience.

13. Yung-chia Hsüan-chio (665–713) affirms that "Illusory thoughts come forth in disorder; yet when we trace them back to their source, they are nothing but silence" (OT, 31).

14. "If," as Blake famously hypothesizes, "the doors of perception were cleansed, every thing would appear to man as it is, infinite." William Blake, *The Marriage of Heaven and Hell*, with an introduction and commentary by Sir Geoffrey Keynes (London and New York: Oxford University Press, 1975), p. 197.

15. "Diese philosophie endet im Schweigen, da der Erleuchtete nichts mehr über Sein und Nichtsein auszusagen hat." Heinrich Dumoulin, *Östliche Meditation und christliche Mystik* (Freiburg and Munich: Alber, 1966), p. 106. Robert Kelly says the same with respect to the poet: "The poet is someone with nothing to say." "Going With the Poem" (BSM, 164). Indeed, "Silence is the life of poetry" (BSM, 165).

16. The elements of the Noble Eightfold Path, those concerned with the development of wisdom *(prajñā)*—Right Understanding (Pali: *sammā diṭṭhi*) and Right Thought (Pali: *sammā saṃkappa*)—those concerned with the development of ethical conduct *(śila)*—Right Speech (Pali: *sammā vācā*), Right Action (Pali: *sammā kammanta*) and Right Livelihood (Pali: *sammā ājīva*)—and those concerned with the development of mental discipline (Pali: *samādhi*)—Right Effort (Pali: *sammā vāyāma*), Right Mindfulness (Pali: *sammā sati*) and Right Concentration (Pali: *sammā samādhi*)—are not ordered sequentially as "steps," as if one first perfected the understanding, only then proceeding to perfect thought, and so on. The eight elements can be viewed both normatively and as diagnostic categories to be employed in analyzing the personality as a whole. The Path is itself "eightfold," then, inasmuch as every "step" represents the advancement of the entire person.

17. Merleau-Ponty speaks of "a communication with the world more ancient than thought. . . ." (PhP, 254).

18. There is, however, a silence far deeper than the mere absence of sound. For Zen seeks "freedom from the alternatives of words or silence" (OT, 90).

19. Bataille remarks that "In the projection of the point, the inner movements have the role of the magnifying glass concentrating light into a very small incendiary site. It is only in such a concentration—beyond itself—that existence has the leisure of perceiving, in the form of an inner flash of light, 'that which it is' ..." (IE, 118).

20. "Le Bouddhisme est une branche du *yoga* ... ." Louis de la Vallée-Poussin, *Nirvâṇa* (Paris: Gabriel Beauchesne, 1925), p. 11. A similar, but more appropriate, trope would feature Buddhism as the "flower" of certain strains of the Hindu tradition, drawing its nourishment therefrom, and being thus ever mindful of its great debt, but nonetheless growing *from* the rich soil in which it exfoliates. The same metaphor offers a way of understanding the almost autochthonous character of Chinese, Japanese and Tibetan Buddhism. The living organism transforms the cultural materials provided by its nourishing ground.

21. "Der ganze Buddhismus ist durch und durch nichts als Yoga." Hermann Beckh, *Buddha und seine Lehre* (Stuttgart: Verlag Freies Geistesleben, 1958), p. 138.

22. Edward J. Thomas, *The History of Buddhist Thought* (New York: Barnes and Noble, 1951), p. 17.

23. Deisetz Taitaro Suzuki, *An Introduction to Zen Buddhism* (Kyoto: Eastern Buddhist Society, 1934), p. 5.

24. Ibid., p. 101.

25. Ibid., p. 16.

26. An intriguing parallel to Zen koan-practice is the practice of Blake's visionary poet who, "as technician of the possible, is willing to frustrate and perplex the mind in

order to stand outside its drivenness and attachment, its mechanism. At the same time he creates a context in which the mind can come upon itself, extend its capacity to know itself as source, face its responsibility as author of experience, embrace a certain tropism toward essential delight in being while denying nothing that seems true—and all this within a field of sometimes terrifying intimacy." George Quasha, "A Virtual Account" (BSM, 212–13). In this connection, we should also recall Brown's important declamation that "To arrive at the simplest truth . . . requires *years of contemplation*. Not activity. Not reasoning. Not calculating. Not busy behavior of any kind. Not reading. Not talking. Not making an effort. Not thinking. Simply *bearing in mind* what it is one needs to know" (LF, 110).

27. Let us bear in mind that "Rapture is not a window looking out on the outside, on the beyond, but a mirror" (IE, 54).

28. Intuition, in a related, perhaps more ordinary, but nonetheless significant, sense can be viewed as "instinct that has become disinterested, self-conscious, capable of reflecting upon its object and of enlarging it indefinitely." Henri Bergson, *Creative Evolution*, trans. A. Mitchell (New York: Modern Library, 1944), p. 194.

29. Jay McDaniel, "Mahayana Enlightenment in Process Perspective," in Kenneth K. Inada and Nolan P. Jacobson, eds., *Buddhism and American Thinkers* (Albany: SUNY Press, 1984), p. 58. Heidegger, as is now commonly recognized, maintained a profound, if largely tacit, interest in Taoism, as evidenced in his musing that "Perhaps there lies concealed in the word 'Way,' *tao*, the mystery of all mysteries of thoughtful saying, as long as we let this name return to its unspokenness and are able to accomplish this letting. . . . All is Way." Martin Heidegger, *On the Way to Language*, trans. Peter D. Hertz (New York: Harper and Row, 1971), p. 92.

30. Again, as Heidegger remarks: "Yet *Tao* could be the way that gives all ways, the very source of our power to think what reason, mind, meaning, *logos* properly mean to say—properly by their proper nature. Perhaps the mystery of mysteries of thoughtful Saying conceals itself in the word 'way,' *Tao*, if only we will let these names return to what they leave unspoken, if only we are capable of this, to allow them to do so." Heidegger, *On the Way to Language*, p. 92.

31. Paul Ricoeur, "Philosophy of Will and Action," in Erwin W. Strauss and Richard M. Griffith, eds., *Phenomenology of Will and Action* (Pittsburgh: Duquesne University Press, 1967), p. 16.

32. In Levin's concomitant claim, "[W]hen I 'think,' I *reduce* the field of my being. . . ." David Michael Levin, *The Body's Recollection of Being* (Boston: Routledge, 1985), p. 143.

33. In Bataille's companion view, "It is through an 'intimate cessation of all intellectual operations' that the mind is laid bare. If not, *discourse* maintains it in its little complacency" (IE, 13).

34. Levin proclaims that "when 'thinking' frames the question of 'essence,' it tends to *stand opposite* the body, secretly detaching itself from 'the body' in a move that only perpetuates the conflict already inherent in dualism. 'Thinking,' spellbound by the authority it wields during the rule of metaphysics, is itself part of the problem. We must let go, finally, of our metaphysical conception of 'thinking.' We must simply *give* our thought *to* the body. We must take our thinking 'down' into the body. We must learn to think *through* the body. . . . we should *listen in silence* to our bodily felt experience. Thinking needs to learn by feeling, by just *being with* our bodily being. . . . Are we, as

thinkers, ready to quiet the conceptualizing mind in order to *listen* to the body's own speech, its own *logos*?" Levin, *The Body's Recollection of Being*, pp. 60–61.

35. Fa-yen Wên-i recalls the following dialogue:

> Monk: "What is the ground of Absolute Truth?"
> Master: "If there should be a ground, it would not be Absolute Truth."
> (OT, 244)

36. As a result, in Buddhaghosa's words, "Then his consciousness no longer enters into or settles down on or resolves upon any field of formations at all, or clings, cleaves, or clutches on to it, but retreats, retracts and recoils as water does from a lotus leaf. . . ." Bhadantācariya Buddhaghosa, *The Path of Purification (Visuddhimagga)*, xxii 4, trans. Bhikkhu Ñaṇamoli (Berkeley: Shambhala, 1976), p. 785.

37. In Guenther's words, "Out of its realm the radiant light of the magnificent appearance of the ground, representing a pattern of communication in the highest perfection, comes as a self-arising appearance where the light shed by the lamp of self-arisen analytical awareness marks the beginning, that of the lamp of distant vision marks the gates through which the ground appears, that of the lamp of pure value reveals the beauty of the ground that has appeared, and that of the lamp of glittering colors illumines the distinct features of the ground that has appeared." Herbert V. Guenther, "Indian Buddhist Thought in Tibetan Perspective," in *Tibetan Buddhism in Western Perspective* (Berkeley, Calif.: Dharma Publishing, 1977), pp. 125–26.

38. Friedrich Heiler, *Die buddhistische Versenkung: Eine religionsgeschichtliche Untersuchung* (Munich: Verlag von Ernst Reinhardt, 1918), p. 347, following Heinrich Dumoulin, *Zen Buddhism: A History*, vol. 1, *India and China*, trans. James W. Heisig and Paul Knitter (New York: Macmillan, 1988), p. 24.

39. Étienne Lamotte, *Histoire du bouddhisme indien* (Louvain: Institut orientaliste, Bibliothèque de l'Université, 1967), p. 48.

40. Merleau-Ponty sagely comments that "there is not something *rather than nothing*, the nothing could not *take the place* of something or of being: nothingness inexists. . . ." (VI, 64).

41. Nietzsche spares no words: "[T]he *causa sui* is the best contradiction that has been conceived so far; it is a sort of rape and perversion of logic." Friedrich Nietzsche, *Beyond Good and Evil*, trans. Walter Kaufmann (New York: Vintage, 1966), p. 21. Elsewhere, I have referred to the ontological impropriety of the *en-soi-pour-soi* as the "shadow of God." Cf. Steven W. Laycock, "Nothingness and Emptiness: Exorcizing the Shadow of God in Sartre," *Man and World* 24 (1991).

42. *Saṃyutta Nikāya*, xv, 1, following Sangharakshita, *A Survey of Buddhism: Its Doctrines and Methods through the Ages* (London: Tharpa Publications, 1987), p. 153.

43. Nowhere in Śākyamuni's exposition of the First Noble Truth is it said that "life" is suffering. The Buddha rather offers a catalogue of illustrations: "Now this, monks, is the noble truth of pain: birth is painful, old age is painful, sickness is painful, death is painful, sorrow, lamentation, dejection, and despair are painful. Contact with unpleasant things is painful, not getting what one wishes is painful. In short the five groups of grasping are painful" (TCB, 30). The exposition is thus "existential" and demonstrative (Pali: *ehi-passika*), inviting attention to the suffering that imbues human life, but not

formulating this suffering as a crisp packet of general "information" to be set beside so many others in the cupboard of the intellect.

44. Kant's excessively cognitive account of "the *faculty of desire*" as "the faculty such a being has of causing, through its ideas, the reality of the objects of these ideas" offers little room for the involvement of desire in grasping and attachment, and is thus inappropriate as a stand-in for the Buddhist conception of *taṇhā*. Immanuel Kant, *Critique of Practical Reason*, trans. Lewis White Beck (New York: Liberal Arts Press, 1956), p. 9 n. 7.

45. In Levin's helpful exposition: "Compassion, or solicitude, essentially involves an awareness of universality and wholeness: we are not alone; and we are not whole, without caring for others. Thus, to the extent that we are deeply *moved* by a deep compassion and can *feel* this compassion in the form of a strongly *grounded* motivation to move through the world for the sake of others, we are in fact also unfolding our more fundamental capacity to move in the motility-field of Being, moved not by the subjective springs of our own volition, but rather by grace of the 'energy' of Being as such.

"To move with compassion is to move *in response to* the calling—the sufferings and needs—of other sentient beings. But when deep compassion is the motivation, to move and to *be* moved are one and the same." (Levin, *The Body's Recollection of Being*, pp. 97–98.)

46. "Metta Sutta" (WBT, 97).

47. Bataille speaks perspicuously of "the disguised suffering which the astonishment at not being everything, at even having concise limits, gives us" (IE, xxxii).

48. Mahāvagga, *Vinaya* (WBT, 29).

49. "Mahāvedalla Sutta," *Majjhima Nikāya* [Collection of middle-length discourses] 43 (TI, 60).

50. Master Han Shan enjoins: "*Search out the point where your thoughts arise and disappear. See where a thought arises and where it vanishes*" (OT, 113).

51. Bhadantācariya Buddhaghosa, *The Path of Purification (Visuddhimagga)*, Bhikkhu Ñaṇamoli, trans. (Colombo: Semage, 1956), p. 151.

52. Ibid., p. 151.

53. In Merleau-Ponty's congruent affirmation, "[I]t is precisely within its particularity as yellow and through it that the yellow becomes a universe or an *element*. . . ." (VI, 218).

54. Buddhaghosa, *Path of Purification* (1956), pp. 149–50.

55. Ibid.

56. Buddhaghosa, *Path of Purification* (1976), p. 151.

57. An illustration of such a misguidedly "positive" conception of being is furnished by the Sartrean in-itself which "is full positivity. It knows no otherness. . . ." (BN, 29).

58. Sartre is emphatic that "*Non-being exists only on the surface of being*" (BN, 49).

59. Merleau-Ponty speaks relevantly of "a 'lake of non-being,' a certain nothingness sunken into a local and temporal *openness*. . . ." (VI, 201).

60. In Tu-shun's words, "when a Bodhisattva observes form, he sees Voidness, and when he observes Voidness, he sees form. . . ." Tu-shun, "On the Meditation of Dharmadhatu," in Garma C. C. Chang, *The Buddhist Teaching of Totality* (University Park: Pennsylvania State University Press, 1977), p. 211.

61. "The philosophy of reflection" that establishes itself upon this very distinction "is not wrong," as Merleau-Ponty says, "in considering the false as a mutilated or partial truth: its error is rather to act as if the partial were only a *de facto* absence of the totality, which does not need to be accounted for" (VI, 42).

62. The gentleness of this transformation is felt in Dōgen's statement that "Nondefilement is not trying to force yourself to stop doing things such as discriminating, seeking for something, or escaping from something. Nondefilement is not purposely trying to fabricate a state of nondiscrimination. Nondefilement can never be discriminated, adopted or rejected." Dōgen, *Shōbōgenzō Yuibutsu-yobutsu* [Only the Buddha together with the Buddha], quoted in Uchiyama Kosho Roshi, *Dogen Zen as Religion* (DZ, 169).

63. Nietzsche's Zarathustra probes: "Have you ever said Yes to a single joy? O my friends, then you have said Yes too to all woe. All things are entangled, ensnared, enamored; if ever you wanted one thing twice, if ever you said, 'You please me, happiness! Abide, moment!' then you wanted *all* back. All anew, all eternally, all entangled, ensnared, enamored." Friedrich Nietzsche, *Thus Spake Zarathustra*, in Walter Kaufmann, ed. and trans., *The Portable Nietzsche* (New York: Viking, 1954), p. 19.

64. Hua Yol Jung speaks of "the world of human existence as a realm of well-being, a realm in which human motility understands itself as, and is, a clearing for the truth of Being in the depth of its beauty and goodness." "Heidegger's Way with Sinitic Thinking," in Parkes, *Heidegger and Asian Thought*, p. 262. This "realm of well-being" is *nirvāṇa*.

65. The ensuing interchange is recorded by Tung-shan Liang-chieh (807–69 C.E.):

> "I came after wandering from mountain to mountain."
> "Have you reached the top?" asked the Master.
> "Yes, I have reached it," answered the monk.
> "Is there anyone there?" said the Master.
> "No, no one is there," replied the monk.
> "If so, it means that you have not yet reached the top," said the Master.
> "If I have not yet reached the top, how can I know there is no one there?" argued the monk.
> "Then why don't you stay there?" said the Master.
>
> (OT, 62–63)

66. In Lévinas's rhetorical query, "Isn't the liveliness of life excessiveness, a rupture of the containing by the uncontainable, a form that ceases to be its proper content already offering itself in the guise of experience . . . ?" Emmanuel Lévinas, "Philosophy and Awakening" (WCAS, 215).

67. "Poised in silence," says Kakuan, "I observe the forms of integration and disintegration" (ZFZB, 152).

68. In the tradition of Buddhist thought, "It is not said . . . that a man shall know the true 'I' but that he need not take for the 'I' *(ātmā*, Pali *attā)* what is not 'I'. . . . The Deliverance ensues not because a man is conscious of or knows the true 'I' but because a man knows everything which is falsely regarded as the 'I' as the 'not-I' *(anātmā*, Pali *anattā)* and thus the Desire is dissolved." Erich Frauwallner, *History of Indian Philosophy*, trans. V. M. Bedekar (Delhi: Motilal Banarsidass, 1973), 1:153.

69. Suzuki comments that "When 'I' is an illusion, all that goes on in the name of this agent must be an illusion too, including moral sins, various kinds of feelings and desires, and hell and the land of bliss. With the removal of this illusion, the world with all its multiplicities will disappear, and if there is anything left which can act, this one will act with utmost freedom, with fearlessness, like the Dharma-king himself, indeed as the One" (NM, 115–16).

70. "What desire wishes to be," writes Sartre, "is a filled emptiness but one which shapes its repletion as a mould shapes the bronze which has been poured inside it" (BN, 154).

71. Yet, in Conze's wise counsel, "What sensible person would enjoy having a boil just because it gives a little pleasure to bathe it occasionally?" (BTI, 35). Suffering incurred for the placation of suffering, or the amplification of pleasure, is not openness, but a more subtle way of battening the hatch.

72. Sartre confirms that "it is not exact to say that a Thirst tends toward its own annihilation as thirst; there is no consciousness which aims at its own suppression as such" (BN, 153–54).

73. Rather, in Heidegger's extensive and subtle probe, "But what is pain? Pain tears or rends *[reißt]*. It is the tear or rift *[Riß]*. But it does not tear apart into dispersive fragments. Pain indeed tears asunder, it separates *[scheidet]*, yet in such a way that it at the same time draws everything together to itself. Its rending, as a separating that gathers, is at the same time that drawing *[Ziehen]*, which, like the pre-drawing *[Vorriß]* and sketch *[Aufriß]*, draws and joins together what is held apart in separation. Pain is the joining *[Fügende]* in the tearing/rending that divides and gathers *[schneidend-sammelnden Reißen]*. Pain is the joining or articulation of the rift. The joining is the threshold. It delivers the between *[Zwischen]*, the mean *[Mitte]* of the two that are separated in it. Pain articulates the rift of the difference. Pain is dif-ference *[Unter-schied]* itself." Martin Heidegger, *Poetry, Language, Thought*, trans. A. Hofstadter (New York: Harper and Row, 1971), p. 204. For Bataille, "A pain means little and is not clearly different from a sensation of pleasure, before nausea—the intimate cold wherein *I succumb*. A pain is perhaps only a sensation incompatible with the tranquil unity of the *self:* some action, external or internal, challenges the fragile ordering of a composite existence, decomposes me, and it is the horror of this threatening action which makes me grow pale. Not that a pain is necessarily a threat of death: it unveils the existence of possible actions beyond which the *self* could not survive; it *evokes* death, without introducing a real threat" (IE, 72). And in Parsons's lyrical, if sobering, delineation, "Suffering arises out of a sense of the difference between what is and what might be. It is the tragic sense. It is the realization that creative possibilities have not or will not be fulfilled: that man can never fully 'find' or complete himself; that time is greater than one moment, and eternity vaster than time; that death conquers individual life, but that collective life transcends individual death; that no matter how rich or full a single life may be, it cannot begin to encompass the richness and fullness of the multiform cosmic life around it, and is destined to be singular and lonely in the midst of that great abundance." Howard L. Parsons, *The Value of Buddhism for the Modern World,* Wheel Publication no. 232–33, (Kandy: Buddhist Publishing Society, 1976), pp. 2–3.

74. Conze explains that "Whenever the yogin meets with the presentation of an object, he sizes it up and notices its short duration, as well as the vital fact that, by the time he comes round to reviewing it, it has happened already, has vanished and is no longer

there. He thus becomes convinced that it no longer concerns him and is not worth holding on to" (BTI, 70).

75. Annette Baier, *Postures of the Mind: Essays on Mind and Morals* (Minneapolis: University of Minnesota Press, 1985), p. xiii.

76. The deep paradox of selfhood is illuminated in Dews's remark that "The relation of reflection is intended to provide an account of what it is to be a self, yet in the very activity of reflection the self is already presupposed. . . ." (LD, 21).

77. And, of course, "Illuminating and acknowledging life and death is the ultimate concern for Buddhism." Tetsuaki Kotoh, "Language and Silence: Self-Inquiry in Heidegger and Zen," in Parkes, *Heidegger and Asian Thought*, p. 202.

78. For Bataille, "Movements inscribed within an order *arrest* time, which they freeze in a system of measures and equivalences. 'Catastrophe' is the most profound of revolutions—it is time 'unhinged'. . . ." (IE, 74). Concordantly, Sartre: "If Time is considered by itself, it immediately dissolves into an absolute multiplicity of instants which considered separately lose all temporal nature and are reduced purely and simply to the total atemporality of the *this*" (BN, 293). A sense of authentic temporality is glimpsed in Merleau-Ponty's remark that "there is at the core of time a gaze . . . an *Augenblick*. . . ." (PhP, 422). "Time," he says, "is 'the affecting of self by self'; what exerts the effect is time as a thrust and a passing towards a future: what is affected is time as an unfolded series of presents: the affecting agent and affected recipient are one, because the thrust of time is nothing but the transition from one present to another" (PhP, 425–26).

79. Perversity is fringed with hypocrisy in Merleau-Ponty's apposite observation: "What does not pass in time is the passing of time itself. . . . The feeling for eternity is a hypocritical one, for eternity feeds on time. The fountain retains its identity only because of the continuous pressure of water" (PhP, 423).

80. Yet time, as Bataille recognizes, "only signifies the flight of objects which seemed real" (IE, 74).

81. "Time," as Merleau-Ponty observes, "presupposes a view of time. It is, therefore, not like a river, not a flowing substance" (PhP, 411).

82. Bergson's presentation of William James's position is an elegant portrayal of our own: "reality . . . flows without our being able to say whether it is in a single direction, or even whether it is always and throughout the same river flowing." Henri Bergson, "The Perception of Change" in *The Creative Mind* (New York: Philosophical Library, 1946), p. 250.

83. The infinity here is, of course, "the infinity of *Offenheit* and not *Unendlichkeit*. . . ." (VI, 169).

84. Of stones and geological plications, Sartre insightfully remarks that they "do not destroy *directly*; they merely modify the distribution of masses of beings. There is no *less* after the storm than before. There is *something else*. Even this expression is improper, for to posit otherness there must be a witness who can retain the past in some manner and compare it to the present in the form of *no longer*" (BN, 39); "Fragility has been impressed upon the very being of this vase, and its destruction would be an irreversible absolute event which I could only verify. There is a transphenomenality of non-being as of being" (BN, 40).

85. Heidegger adds that "The pain which must first be experienced and borne out to the end is the insight and the knowledge that lack of need [*Notlosigkeit*] is the highest and

most hidden need which first necessitates [*nötigt*] in virtue of the most distant distance. Lack of need consists in believing that one has reality and what is real in one's grip and knows what truth is, without needing to know in what truth presences [*worin die Wahrheit west*]." Martin Heidegger, "Overcoming Metaphysics," in *The End of Philosophy* (New York: Harper and Row, 1973), p. 102.

86. "Mahāvedalla Sutta," *Majjhima Nikāya* 43 (TI, 60).

87. Gary Snyder reminds us that "to be truly serious you have to play" (BSM, 5).

88. Suzuki elucidates the functioning of *prajñā* in his simile: "It is like appreciating a fine piece of brocade. On the surface there is an almost bewildering confusion of beauty, and the connoisseur fails to trace the intricacies of the threads. But as soon as it is turned over all the intricate beauty and skill is revealed. Prajñā consists in this turning-over. The eye has hitherto followed the surface of the cloth, which is indeed the only side ordinarily allowed us to survey. Now the cloth is abruptly turned over; the course of the eyesight is suddenly interrupted; no continuous gazing is possible. Yet by this interruption, or rather disruption, the whole scheme of life is suddenly grasped; there is the 'seeing into one's self-nature'" (NM, 56).

89. Robert Sokolowski, *Husserlian Meditations: How Words Present Things* (Evanston, Ill.: Northwestern University Press, 1974), p. 106.

90. Kakuan declares: "When the first thought springs from enlightenment, all subsequent thoughts are true. Through delusion, one makes everything untrue" (ZFZB, 144).

91. It is, then, good advice, offered by Master Han Shan, that we should "Never treat the distracted thought as a concrete thing. When it arises, notice it right away but never try to suppress it. Let it go and watch it as one watches a calabash floating on the surface of a stream" (OT, 113).

92. Sokolowski, *Husserlian Meditations*, p. 106.

93. In Nietzsche's arresting formulation: "'Thinking,' as epistemologists conceive it, simply does not occur; it is a quite arbitrary fiction, arrived at by selecting one element from the process and eliminating all the rest, an artificial arrangement for the purposes of intelligibility." Sect. 477 in Friedrich Nietzsche, *The Will to Power*, trans. Walter Kaufmann and R. J. Hollingdale (New York: Random House, 1968), p. 264.

94. Sokolowski, *Husserlian Meditations*, pp. 73–74.

95. Buddhaghosa, *Path of Purification* (1956), p. 148. Sustained thought may have some common resonance with the later Heideggerian notion that "To answer the question 'What is called thinking?' is itself always to keep asking, so as to remain underway." Martin Heidegger, *What is Called Thinking*? trans. Fred D. Wieck and J. Glenn Gray (New York: Harper and Row, 1968), p. 169.

96. In Nishida's elucidation: "At the base of thought there is always concealed a certain mystical element; even a geometric axiom is a thing of this kind. . . . explanation means nothing more than being able to reduce to an even more basic intuition." Kitaro Nishida, *A Study of Good*, trans. V. H. Viglielmo (Tokyo: Japanese Government Printing Office, 1960), p. 35.

97. As Heidegger says, "[T]o think is to confine yourself to a single thought that one day stands still like a star in the world's sky." Heidegger, *Poetry, Language, Thought*, p. 4. For Levin, "Thinking . . . *is* the thoughtful gesture." Levin, *The Body's Recollection of Being*, p. 123.

98. Buddhaghosa, *Path of Purification* (1976), p. 148. "What is questionable can sometimes be worthy of thought, and what is unthinkable can sometimes be glimpsed as

that which thinking is about." J. L. Mehta, "Heidegger and Vedanta: Reflections on a Questionable Theme," in Parkes, *Heidegger and Asian Thought*, p. 15.

99. Yet, for Bataille, "Being is 'ungraspable'. It is only 'grasped' in error; the error is not just easy—in this case, it is the condition of thought" (IE, 82).

100. As Chang elucidates, "All thought is systematic, but at the base of any system there must be a unifying intuition. Intuition is beyond all thought, yet it is the ground from which all thought takes form" (OT, ix).

101. "There where there was nothing (and not even a 'there'—as the 'there is no there there' of Gertrude Stein). . . ." (WCAS, 7). This puts one in mind of Merleau-Ponty's "spiral": "My 'central' nothingness is like the point of the stroboscopic spiral, which is *who knows where*, which is 'nobody'" (VI, 264).

102. Baier, *Postures of the Mind*, pp. 23–24.

103. Merleau-Ponty thus speaks of "a question consonant with the porous being which it questions and from which it obtains not an *answer*, but a confirmation of its astonishment" (VI, 102).

104. Agamben reminds us that "Indication is the category within which language refers to its own taking place" (PN, 25). In Zen experience, as Margaret Gibson confirms:

> . . . I enter the complete
> absence of any indicative event,

Margaret Gibson, "Making Salad," in *Out in the Open* (Baton Rouge: Louisiana State University Press, 1989). Reprinted in BSM, 88.

105. Eugen Fink, "The Phenomenological Philosophy of Edmund Husserl and Contemporary Criticism," in R. O. Elveton, ed., *The Phenomenology of Husserl: Selected Critical Readings* (Chicago: Quadrangle Books, 1970), p. 105.

106. "But what is my treasure?" / "It is he who has just asked the question. It contains everything and lacks nothing. There is no need to seek it outside yourself." *Ching-tê Record of the Transmission of the Lamp*, compiled by Tao-yüan in 1004, edited by Yang-i (968–1024 C.E.), chüan 6 (OT, xi).

107. Hsiang-yen Chih-hsien relates the following conversation:

> A monk asked, "What is a word before it is said?"
> The Master replied, "I answered you the moment before you asked the question."
> The monk went on, "What is this moment?"
> The Master replied, "It is the same as the moment you asked the question."
> (OT, 222)

108. "[T]heories," as Sangharakshita tells us, "are rooted in desires." Sangharakshita, *A Survey of Buddhism*, p. 37. And in the remarkable declaration of Kiangsi Tao-i (709–88 C.E.), "Those who seek for the Truth should realize that there is nothing to seek. There is no Buddha but Mind; there is no Mind but Buddha" (OT, 149).

109. Perhaps the philosopher is thus the very type of Daumal's "Hollow-Men": "The Hollow-Men live in solid rock and move about in it in the form of mobile caves or recesses. In ice they appear as bubbles in the shape of men. But they never venture out into the air, for the wind would blow them away.

"They have houses in the rock whose walls are made of emptiness, and tents in the ice whose fabric is of bubbles. During the day they stay in the stone, and at night they wander through the ice and dance during the full moon. But they never see the sun, or else they would burst.

"They eat only the void, such as the form of corpses; they get drunk on empty words and all the meaningless expressions we utter.

"Some people say they have always existed and will exist forever. Others say they are the dead. And others say that as a sword has its scabbard or a foot its imprint, every living man has in the mountain his Hollow-Man, and in death they are reunited" (René Daumal, *Mount Analogue*, p. 83).

110. Albert Camus, "The Myth of Sisyphus," in Walter Kaufmann, ed., *Existentialism: From Dostoevsky to Sartre* (New York: New American Library, 1975), p. 378.

111. It is heartening to find in Descartes a confession of intellectual humility with respect to the very activity that Buddhist practice enjoins: "Admittedly, I am aware of a certain weakness in me, in that I am unable to keep my attention fixed on one and the same item of knowledge at all times. . . ." René Descartes, *Meditations on First Philosophy*, IV, trans. John Cottingham (Cambridge: Cambridge University Press, 1986), p. 43.

112. T. S. Eliot, "East Coker," in *The Complete Poems and Plays: 1909–1950* (New York: Harcourt, Brace & World, 1971), p. 126.

113. Eliot, "East Coker," p. 127.

114. The spaciousness of mind is illuminated in Conze's portrayal: "Not subject to conditions or restrictions it is free from obstructions and obstacles, and cannot be impeded or impede. In it everything is absent that might offend, resist, fetter, entrance, estrange or lead astray. It is everywhere, and everywhere it is the same. In it nothing is wanting, nothing owned. In perfect calm it remains by itself outside time, change and action. Nothing can be predicated of it, and nothing adheres to it as its attribute" (BTI, 165).

115. Place is lucidly explicated in Conze's exposition of certain concepts operative in the work of Vasubandhu and in the philosophical lineage of Theravada: "The Abhidharmakosa defines local space as a hole or cavity in which there are no material objects, but which, like the mouth or the aperture of a gate, is near them and can be perceived. The Theravadins concur by describing it as the gaps, interstices, vacua, holes, apertures, etc., which occur between visible, etc., objects, as for instance doors, windows, mouth or nose cavities. In them there is nothing to be seen or felt, but they delimitate forms, set bounds to them, environ them and make them manifest, and are the basis of such notions as 'below', 'above', 'across', etc. Local space is just lack of matter, and is finite, visible and conditioned" (BTI, 164).

116. For Vasubandhu, "Space is that which does not impede." Louis de la Vallée Poussin, *L'Abhidharmakosabhasyam de Vasubandhu* (BTI, 164).

117. Apropos, Merleau-Ponty refers to the "Mythology of a self-consciousness to which the word 'consciousness' would refer—There are only *differences* between significations" (VI, 171).

118. Buddhaghosa, *Path of Purification* (1976), p. 360.

119. The emptiness of the Sthaviras, no less than the nothingness of Sartrean ontology, "is like a termite hole—termites bore a hole into a piece of wood (absence of self in persons), but all around they leave thin outer walls standing (dharmic events)" (BTI, 198). In the Mahāyāna, emptiness is like unbounded space.

120. Agamben usefully explicates this term: "The verb *to solve*, from which the term 'absolute' derives, can be broken down into *se-luo*. . . . The verb *to solve* thus indicates the operation of dissolving *(luo)* that leads (or leads back) something to its own **se*, to *suus* as to *solus*, dissolving it—*absolving it*—of every tie or alterity. . . .

"To think the Absolute signifies, thus, to think that which, through a process of 'absolution,' has been led back to its ownmost property, to itself, to its own *solitude*, as to its own *custom*. For this reason, the Absolute always implies a voyage, an abandonment of the originary place, an alienation and a being-out-side. If the Absolute is the supreme idea of philosophy, then philosophy is truly, in the words of Novalis, nostalgia *(Heimweh)*; that is, the 'desire to be at home everywhere.' . . ." (PN, 92).

121. Buddhaghosa, *Path of Purification* (1976), p. 363.

122. Perhaps I should say "*only* dreamed of." There is, in Sartre, an implicit sense of being prior to ontological parturition which I have called the Sartrean *apeiron*. Cf. Laycock, "Exorcizing the Shadow of God."

123. In Brown's progression, "to experience the world clearly, we must abandon existence to truth, truth to indication, indication to form, and form to void. . . ." (LF, 101).

124. It is, as Badiou tells us, the "void that sutures every situation into being." Alain Badiou, "On a Finally Objectless Subject" (WCAS, 26).

125. Suzuki ponders: "I cannot tell just where the unconscious is. Is it in me? Or is it in the flower? Perhaps when I ask, 'Where?' it is nowhere. If so, let me be in it and say nothing." D. T. Suzuki, "East and West," in Robert Sohl and Audrey Carr, eds., *The Gospel According to Zen: Beyond the Death of God* (New York: Mentor, 1970), p. 86.

126. For Vasubandhu, "[P]erceptions are a sickness, an ulcer, a barb! Their mere absence in a state of unconsciousness is nothing but stupefaction. But this station of neither perception nor non-perception, that is calm, that is excellent!" Louis de la Vallée Poussin, *L'Abhidharmakosabhasyam de Vasubandhu* (BTI, 66).

127. Dews thus speaks of "the paradox that to grasp the unconscious is, at the same time, to fail to grasp it" (LD, 84).

128. Henry deepens this consideration: "*Cogito* means everything, except *I think*. *Cogito* designates that which appears to itself immediately in everything that appears, or rather in pure appearing (what Descartes calls thought). *Subjectivity* is the pathetic immediation of appearing as auto-appearing, such that, without this pathetic grasp of appearing in its original appearing to itself, no appearing—notably the aesthetic appearing of the world—would ever appear." Michel Henry, "The Critique of the Subject" (WCAS, 116).

129. "The for-itself *is* the nihilation of the in-itself, not 'something' which nihilates: an act, an event, perhaps, but not an agent. . . . Though the for-itself *is*, it is, not as *different* from, but as the very *differing* from, the in-itself. Or rather, while *differing-from-the-in-itself* is itself different from the in-itself, *it is* not this difference." Laycock, "Exorcizing the Shadow of God," p. 398.

130. In Chao-chou Ts'ung-shen's paradoxical formulation, "Buddhahood is passion [*kleśa*], and passion is Buddhahood" (OT, 166) Again, in conversation with a monk, Chao-chou says:

> "Buddha causes passion in all of us."
> "How do we get rid of it?"

"Why should we get rid of it?" asked Chao-chou.

(OT, 166)

131. "If one can fuse his mind into one whole, continuous piece, he cannot help but attain Enlightenment" (OT, 164).

132. "Mahāvedalla Sutta," in *Majjhima Nikāya* 43 (TI, 73).

133. In the report of Hsüeh-fêng I-ts'un, Hui-neng is featured as declaring that "It is neither the wind nor the banner that moves. It is your mind that moves" (OT, 264). Alternatively: "Not the wind, not the flag; mind is moving" (ZFZB, 114).

134. Sangharakshita, *A Survey of Buddhism*, p. 200.

135. Ibid.

136. Eliot, *Complete Poems and Plays*, p. 119.

137. In the well-known parable of *The Questions of King Milinda*, the chariot is neither to be identified with any single part, nor with the assemblage of its parts, nor—intriguingly—with an "extra" part or supervenient "wholeness" exceeding the sum of its parts.

138. Dōgen consonantly enjoins: "Let go of all relations. . . . " Dōgen, *Shōbōgenzō Zazengi*, quoted in Menzan Zuiho Osho, *Jijuyu-zanmai* [Samādhi of the self] (DZ, 104).

139. Adorno opines that "The construction of transcendental subjectivity was a magnificently paradoxical and fallible effort to master the object in its opposite pole. . . ." (ND, 185).

140. Corless cautions against a facile, but insidious, assumption correlative with this hierarchy: "If I think that liberation is a state of radical enstasis, I will probably come up with an elaborate map of more and more inward states, hierarchically arranged, until I reach the One or the One Point which is behind, or in, everything. What I may not notice is that if the goal is on the same continuum as the path, I may reach the end of the path but I cannot extract myself from the path-goal model. I sit at the end of the path, either doing nothing for ever and ever, or I eventually decide to return along the same path. The Buddha did not want to find the end of the path but the way out of all paths altogether." Roger J. Corless, *The Vision of Buddhism: The Space Under the Tree* (New York: Paragon House, 1989), p. 118.

141. Yet, in the words of Kiangsi Tao-i, "The mind does not exist by itself; its existence is manifested through forms" (OT, 149).

142. Yung-chia Hsüan-chio sees that "The source of motion and that of motionlessness are the same" (OT, 31).

143. Robert Sohl and Audrey Carr, eds., *The Gospel According to Zen: Beyond the Death of God* (New York: Mentor, 1970), p. 27.

144. Plotinus, *The Enneads*, trans. Stephen MacKenna (London: Faber and Faber, 1969), V, viii, 4, p. 425.

145. The Hawaiians believe, "We are all one, each a part of the eternal whole. There is no line that divides one from another or those in body from those in spirit. When men say they believe only this or that they put blinders on themselves." Pali Jae Lee and Koko Willis, *Tales from the Night Rainbow: Mo'olelo na Pō Mākole: The Story of a Woman, a People, and an Island* (Honolulu: Night Rainbow, 1990), p. 75. A concrete implication of this is expressed in the Hawaiian view, "[T]here is no dividing line between two people. You cannot hit your brother without hitting yourself, your father and your mother."

Lee & Willis, *Night Rainbow*, p. 20. Thus, "Anything said to hurt another would hurt you also." Lee & Willis, *Night Rainbow*, p. 59.

146. "All spirituality is the attainment of this universal interest and the elimination of private standpoints and values" (CPB, 259).

147. Indeed, as Bresson declares, "The phenomenological description is at the limit unrealizable and interior experience thus ineffable. To that extent it ceases to be the object of any communication and of any science, and it is sufficient to admit the existence of this experience, without occupying oneself with it any further [La description phénoménologique est à la limite irréalisable et l'expérience intime en tant que telle ineffable. Par là même elle cesse d'être l'objet d'une quelconque communication et d'une quelconque science, et il suffirait d'admettre l'existence de cette expérience, sans plus s'en occuper]." François Bresson, "Perception et indices perceptifs," in Bruner, Bresson, Morf, and Piaget, *Logique et perception*, in *Études d'épistémologie génétique*, vol. 6 (Paris: Presses Universitaires de France, 1958), p. 156.

148. Bataille reminds us that "suffering is, according to Buddha, what is individual. . . ." (IE, 22). And, of course, it is the individual, *this* as distinct from *that*, which inhabits the Lokadhātu.

149. In Merleau-Ponty's apposite reminder, "[T]here is no *Schein* without an *Erscheinung*. . . . (VI, 41).

150. Simplicius, *Phys*. 140, 28, in G. S. Kirk, J. E. Raven, and M. Schofield, eds., *The Presocratic Philosophers: A Critical History with a Selection of Texts* (Cambridge: Cambridge University Press, 1983), p. 266.

151. Lispector contributes concretely to the elucidation of infinite divisibility: "Between two musical notes there exists another note, between two facts there exists another fact, between two grains of sand, no matter how close together they are, there exists an interval of space, there exists a sensing between sensing—in the interstices of primordial matter there is the mysterious, fiery line that is the world's breathing, and the world's continual breathing is what we hear and call silence" (GH, 90).

152. Fragments 2 and 1, Simplicius, in *Phys*. 139, 9 and 140, 34, in Kirk et al., *Presocratic Philosophers*, p. 267.

153. Ibid.

154. Accordingly:

> Cloth is existent in its threads,
> The threads again in something else.
> How can these threads, unreal themselves,
> Produce reality in something else?

Candrakīrti, *Prasannapadā*, as quoted in Robert Magliola, *Derrida on the Mend* (West Lafayette, Ind.: Purdue University Press, 1986), p. 111. In Sprung's more prosaic translation: "Cloth is supposed to be realized from a cause and this cause from another cause; but how can what is not realized in its own right be the cause of something else?" Candrakīrti, *Lucid Exposition of the Middle Way: The Essential Chapters from the* Prasannapadā *of Candrakīrti*, trans. Mervyn Sprung (Boulder, Colo.: Prajñā Press, 1969), p. 73.

155. And the "one" thus resplendent takes on, in Ingarden's fine phrase, the character of "Opalescent Multiplicity." Roman Ingarden, *The Literary Work of Art*, trans. George G. Grabowicz (Evanston, Ill.: Northwestern University Press, 1973), p. 142.

156. Fragments 2 and 1, Simplicius, in *Phys*. 139, 9 and 140, 34, in Kirk et al., *Presocratic Philosophers*, p. 267.

157. James Thompson, "Tasks and Super-Tasks," in Wesley C. Salmon, ed., *Zeno's Paradoxes* (Indianapolis: Bobbs-Merrill, 1970), p. 95.

158. Sangharakshita, *A Survey of Buddhism*, p. 123.

159. The "spatio-analytic" and "dynamic-synthetical" approaches to emptiness are crisply delineated in ibid., p. 120.

160. Streng is surely correct in affirming that "most Western philosophies . . . think of the 'uncombined' as equivalent to 'simple' and . . . begin with the simple absolute as a fundamental category for interpreting the nature of reality. Nāgārjuna extended this *anātmā*-teaching to show how 'the uncombined' is logically and linguistically dependent on the 'combined' *(saṁskṛta)*" (E, 37).

161. Vasubandhu's approach "put[s] to a philosophy questions that it has not put to itself." Merleau-Ponty questions whether this is possible, and responds,"To answer no is to make of philosophy separate works, is to deny *philosophy*. To answer yes is to reduce history to philosophy.

My point of view: a philosophy, like a work of art, is an object that can arouse more thoughts than those that are "contained" in it. . . . (VI, 199)

162. Alan Watts's more graphic presentation is useful here and compelling: "For when we examine anything we see first of all the pattern, the shape, and then we ask the question, 'What is the shape composed of?' So we get out our microscope to look very carefully at what we thought was the substance of, say, a finger. We find that the so-called substance of the finger is a minute and beautiful design of cells. We see a structure, but then when we see these little patterns called individual cells, we ask again, 'What are they made of?' and that needs a sharper microscope, a more minute analysis. Turning up the level of magnification again, we find that the cells are molecules but we keep asking, 'What is the stuff of the molecule?' What we are in fact discovering through all of this is that what we are calling 'stuff' is simply patterns seen out of focus. It's fuzzy, and simply fuzziness is stuff. Whenever we get fuzziness into focus, it becomes patterns. So there isn't any stuff, there is only pattern. This world is dancing energy." Alan W. Watts, "Western Mythology: Its Dissolution and Transformation," in Joseph Campbell, ed., *Myths, Dreams and Religion* (New York: Dutton, 1970), pp. 13–14.

163. The "aggregates" (*skandhas*, the root of our word "skein," suggesting a certain reciprocal externality of elements) are catalogued in the Buddha's declaration that "All material phenomena, whether past, present or future, one's own or external, gross or subtle, lofty or low, far or near, all belong to the aggregate of material form. All sensations . . . belong to the aggregate of sensation. All perceptions . . . belong to the aggregate of perception. All mental formations . . . belong to the aggregate of mental formations. All consciousness . . . belongs to the aggregate of consciousness." "Mahāpunnama Sutta," *Majjhima Nikāya*, 109 (TI, 99).

164. "What is a *Gestalt*? A whole that does *not* reduce itself to the sum of the parts—a negative, exterior definition. . . ." (VI, 204).

165. The latter point deserves belaboring in an effort to rectify a not uncommon misconstrual of the Husserlian theory of constitution. In his essay, "The Ontology of Edmund Husserl," Bergmann exposes what he takes to be the insuperable ontological flaws of Husserl's "system." In my response, "Bergmannian Meditations," *Noûs* 21 (1987), I undertake to demonstrate that Bergmann's critique, while perhaps compelling

in its application to a position not unlike Husserl's in certain respects, is nonetheless inapplicable to Husserl. Bergmann assumes throughout that the Husserlian phenomenological categories bear ontological weight. And this assumption infects and distorts Bergmann's interpretation in its entirety. Grossmann, in consonance with Bergmann, reads Husserl as claiming that "No single perceptual act ever presents you with the whole perceptual object." Reinhardt Grossman, *Ontological Reduction* (Bloomington: Indiana University Press, 1973), p. 150. This is flatly erroneous. Husserl repeatedly insists that, in perception, the object is given "in person." We are presented with the object *itself*, and *as a whole*, but the object entire as given from a particular standpoint, or through a particular profile. Grossmann claims that "The structural source of Husserl's . . . view . . . consists in [his] belief that a perceptual object is nothing but the class of all its parts, including the relational ones" (p. 152). Nowhere does Husserl subscribe to this claim. Indeed, for Husserl, the object itself is the very principle whereby the elements of such a "class" are collected. Appearances are "classed" (i.e., comprise a manifold) precisely in virtue of their being appearances *of* a given perceptual object. See my review of Grossmann's work in *Husserl Studies* 4 (1987).

166. "Asserting being is false addition; denying being is false reduction; asserting both being and non-being is false contradiction; and the last, denying both being and non-being, is a joke" (OT, 130).

167. "Quality," for Sartre, "is nothing other than the being of the *this* when it is considered apart from all external relation with the world or with other *thises*" (BN, 257). The Buddhist vision of universal conditioning renders the Sartrean quality a floating abstraction.

168. For Sartre, "The first causality is the apprehension of the 'appeared' before it appears as being already there in its own nothingness so as to prepare its apparition. Causality is simply the first apprehension of the temporality of the 'appeared' as an ekstatic mode of being. . . . the relation of causality disintegrates into a pure relation of exteriority between the 'thises' prior to the 'appeared' and the 'appeared' itself" (BN, 284).

169. The Sanskrit *samutpāda* is richer in connotation than the rather odd rendering of "co-origination" might insinuate. *Ut* (up) combined with *pāda* (related to the Latin *ped*, and meaning "foot" or "step") would suggest a "standing-up" or "arising." But *ut* is also a constituent of compounds existing in many Indian languages which suggest "awakening." Thus, while *sam-* (indicating, like the Greek *syn-*, a certain multiplicity considered under the aspect of unity) *-utpāda* may indicate a universal "arising-together," it also suggests, as does the English "arising," a universal "waking-up."

170. In a very interesting, and apposite, Hawaiian account, we hear that "The ancient ones believed that all time is now and that we are each creators of our life's conditions. We create ourselves and everything that becomes a part of our lives. Any situation in which we might find ourselves is brought about by learning the many pathways of life. When we wish to change our circumstances, all we have to do is release our present condition. It will be gone. On the other hand, if we find it useful to continue, we can hang on to the problem and not let it go." Lee and Willis, *Night Rainbow*, p. 19.

171. It is rather akin to "this circle which I do not form, which forms me, this coiling over of the visible upon the visible. . . ." (VI, 140). Guenther tells us that "the Buddhist conception of causality, which is reticular and hierarchically fluctuating, not singly

catenarian and particulate. If any succession was recognized, it remained subordinate to the basic idea of interdependence." Herbert V. Guenther, *From Reductionism to Creativity: rDzogs-chen and the New Sciences of Mind* (Boston: Shambhala, 1989), 276–77 n. 6.

172. Cf. Sangharakshita, *A Survey of Buddhism*, p. 120.

173. And of course, as Hyakujo asserts, "The enlightened man is one with the law of causation" (ZFZB, 91).

174. Fa-tsang, "On the Golden Lion," in Chang, *Buddhist Teaching of Totality*, p. 229. In Fa-tsang's further explication, "[T]his is a demonstration of Totality in the dharmadhatu. In each and every mirror within this room you will find the reflections of all the other mirrors with the Buddha's image in them. . . . The principle of interpenetration and (mutual) containment is clearly shown by this demonstration. Right here we see an example of one in all and all in one—the mystery of realm embracing realm ad infinitum is thus revealed." Fa-tsang, "On the Golden Lion," p. 24.

175. Thus, "If the total number of conditions is unlimited, and most of them are unknown, it is impossible to say which condition of necessity brings about which event. In consequence it is impossible in any given case to prove by observation that one event necessarily follows from just these and only these conditions. Inevitably causality is therefore a mere surmise, and there is plenty of room for caprice and for the unusual. . . ." (BTI, 146).

176. Nāgārjuna concomitantly cautions that "At nowhere and at no time can entities ever exist by originating out of themselves, from others, from both (self-other), or from the lack of causes." (MK 1:1; N, 39).

177. Aron Gurwitsch, *The Field of Consciousness* (Pittsburgh: Duquesne University Press, 1964), p. 4.

178. Ibid., p. 340.

179. Ibid., p. 283.

180. *Pratītya-samutpāda* is "the form for expressing the phenomenal 'becoming' as the lack of any self-sufficient, independent reality" (E, 63).

181. "The effect itself, indeed, is nothing but the presence of the totality of its causes. If the seed and the necessary quanta of air, soil, heat and moisture are present in it, all other elements not interfering, the sprout is already there. The effect is nothing over and above the presence of the totality of its causes." F. Th. Stcherbatsky, *Buddhist Logic* (New York: Dover, 1962), 1:131.

182. Alternatively: "Never are any existing things found to originate" (MK, 1:1; E, 183). Sprung amplifies: "There are no things on the middle way; they disappear into the way itself." Mervyn Sprung, ed., *The Question of Being* (University Park: Pennsylvania State University Press, 1978), p. 136.

183. This possibility is implicit in Yehuda Amichai's remark that the "body remains forever an amateur." Cited in John Tarrant, "Zen, Poetry, and the Great Dream Buddha" (BSM, 304).

184. Bataille says of his own practice: "I fix a point before me and I represent this point to myself as the geometric place of all possible existence and of all unity, of all separation and of all anguish, of all unsatisfied desire and of all death.

"I adhere to this point and a deep love of what is in this point burns me to the point that I refuse to be alive for anything other than what is there—for that point which, being together life and death of a loved being, has the flash of a cataract.

"And at the same time it is necessary to strip what is there of its external representations until there is nothing more than pure interiority, a pure inner fall into a void: this point endlessly absorbing this fall into what is Nothingness within it, that is to say 'past' and, in this same movement, endlessly prostituting its fleeting but flashing appearance to love" (IE, 121–22).

185. Though we have not, for example, engaged the function of the breath, we must nonetheless pause to savor James's extraordinary observation that what we familiarly call the stream of consciousness is a process that, "when scrutinized, reveals itself to consist chiefly of the stream of [one's] breathing." William James, in *Classic American Philosophers* (New York: Appleton-Century-Crofts, 1951), p. 160. Crediting James, we cannot fail to note the indissociability of consciousness and poetry entailed by the conjunction of Kelly's further specification that "the poem shapes itself in syllables, which are breath-patterns, deep metabolic rhythms it borrows from the body of the writer, the ground swell." Robert Kelly, "Going With the Poem" (BSM, 164).

186. "In holding fast, or grasping, the whole universe vanishes. In letting go, or releasing, the individual world appears, in which everyone asserts his true existence." Katsuki Sekida, *Two Zen Classics*: *Mumonkan and Hekiganroku* (New York: John Weatherhill, 1977), p. 329.

187. Dōgen proclaims: "If you step on the path of practice assuming it to be the stairway to realization, not a single speck of dust will support your feet." Eihei Dōgen Zenji, *Gakudo-yojinshu* [Points to watch in practicing the Way] (DZ, 10).

188. Heidegger's description is poignantly applicable to the typical Buddhist expression of veneration: "Two hands fold into one, a gesture meant to carry man into the great oneness." Martin Heidegger, *What Is Called Thinking*? trans. Fred D. Wieck and J. Glenn Gray (New York: Harper and Row, 1968), p. 17.

189. For Merleau-Ponty, the body represents "a thinking older than myself of which those organs are merely the trace" (PhP, 351–52).

190. Paz sees that "Whatever the word and the particular meaning of *body* and *non-body* within each civilization, the relationship between these two signs is not, and cannot be, anything but unstable." Octavio Paz, "Eve and Prajnaparamita," in *Conjunctions and Disjunctions*, trans. Helen R. Lane (New York: Viking, 1974), p. 45.

191. As Merleau-Ponty affirms, "[M]y body is a movement towards the world, and the world my body's point of support" (PhP, 350). In Suzuki's lovely presentation, "Hands are no hands, have no existence, until they pick up flowers and offer them to the Buddha; so with legs, they are no legs, non-entities, unless their Use is set to work, and they walk over the bridge, ford the stream and climb the mountain" (NM, 42).

> I exercise occult and subtle power,
> carrying water, shouldering firewood.

Layman P'ang (Koji), in Katsuki Sekida, *Two Zen Classics*, p. 263. "Isan kicked over the pitcher. So wonderful is his Zen that every movement of his foot and hand is shining with the truth." Shibayama Zenkei, *Zen Comments on the Mumonkan* (New York: New American Library, 1974), p. 291.

192. In words attributed to the Buddha, "If one's body is straight, one's mind is easily straightened too. If one sits keeping one's body upright, one's mind does not become

dull." Dōgen, *Shōbōgenzō Zanmai-o-zanmai*, quoted in Menzan Zuiho Osho, *Jijuyu-zanmai* [Samādhi of the self] (DZ, 93).

193. M. C. Dillon, *Merleau-Ponty's Ontology* (Bloomington: Indiana University Press, 1988), p. 158.

194. The body, then, would seem have the attributes of "slime" in Sartre's depiction: "Slime is the agony of water. . . . In the slimy substance which dissolves into itself there is a visible resistance, like the refusal of an individual who does not want to be annihilated in the whole of being, and at the same time a softness pushed to its ultimate limit. For the *soft* is only an annihilation which is stopped halfway . . . it is a fluidity which holds me and which compromises me; I can not *slide* on this slime, all its suction cups hold me back. . . . The sliding however is not simply denied . . . it is *degraded*. Slime is the revenge of the In-itself. . . . water is the symbol of consciousness—its movement, its fluidity, its deceptive appearance of being solid, its perpetual flight—everything in it recalls the For-itself. . . . A consciousness which became slimy would be transformed by the thick stickiness of its ideas" (BN, 774–78).

195. This "gap" is disclosed in Merleau-Ponty's admission, "I do not entirely succeed in touching myself touching, in seeing myself seeing, the experience I have of myself perceiving does not go beyond a sort of *imminence*, it terminates in the invisible, simply this invisible is *its* invisible, i.e., the reverse of its specular perception, the concrete vision I have of my body in the mirror" (VI, 249).

196. It is also made linguistic: "With metaphor, the body enters the heart of every discourse. . . ." Franco Rella, "Fabula" (RM, 152).

197. For Merleau-Ponty, the body "is not a self through transparence, like thought, which only thinks its object by assimilating it, by constituting it, by transforming it into thought. It is a self through confusion, narcissism, through inherence of the one who sees in that which he sees, and through inherence of sensing in the sensed—a self, therefore, that is caught up in things, that has a front and a back, a past and a future. . . ." "Eye and Mind" (PP, 163).

198. Merleau-Ponty notes that "every reflection is after the model of the reflection of the hand touching by the hand touched . . . hence reflection is not an identification with oneself . . . but non-difference with self = silent or blind identification" (VI, 204).

199. In Merleau-Ponty's intriguing observation, "When through the water's thickness I see that tiling at the bottom of a pool, I do not see it *despite* the water and the reflections there; I see it through them and because of them. If there were no distortions, no ripples of sunlight, if it were without this flesh that I saw the geometry of the tiles, then I would cease to see it *as* it is and where it is—which is to say, beyond any identical, specific place. I cannot say that the water itself—the aqueous power, the syrupy and shimmering element—is *in* space; all this is not somewhere else either, but it is not in the pool. It inhabits it, it materializes itself there, yet it is not contained there; and if I raise my eyes toward the screen of cypresses where the web of reflections is playing, I cannot gainsay the fact that the water visits it, too, or at least sends into it, upon it, its active and living essence." "Eye and Mind" (PP, 182).

200. Adorno remarks that "Philosophical thinking crystallizes in the particular, in that which is defined in space and time. The concept of entity pure and simple is the mere shadow of the false concept of Being" (ND, 138).

201. D. T. Suzuki, *Zen Buddhism* (Garden City, N.Y.: Doubleday, 1956), p. 261.

202. This is implicit in the exquisite verse of Takuan (1573–1645):

> Though night after night
> The moon is stream-reflected,
> Try to find where it has touched,
> Point even to a shadow.

Lucien Stryk and Takashi Ikemoto, trans., *Zen: Poems, Prayers, Sermons, Anecdotes, Interviews* (Garden City, N.Y.: Doubleday, 1963), p. 13.

203. Findlay, *Discipline of the Cave*, p. 79.

204. Concomitantly, in the words of Fa-yen Wên-i: "Not knowing most closely approaches the Truth" (OT, 239).

205. Fa-yen Wên-i records the subsequent exchange:

> Question: "What is the first principle?"
> Master: "If I should tell you, it would become the second principle."
> (OT, 246)

206. Adorno lucidly contends that "The first must become ever more abstract to the philosophy of origin. The more abstract it becomes, the less it comes to explain and the less fitting it is as a foundation" (AE, 14). Again: "Whenever a doctrine of some absolute 'first' is taught there will be talk of something inferior to it, of something absolutely heterogeneous to it, as its logical correlate. *Prima philosophia* and dualism go together" (ND, 138).

207. Conze advances that "Emptiness is not a theory, but a ladder which reaches out into the infinite, and which should be climbed, not discussed. It is not taught to make a theory, but to get rid of theories altogether" (BTI, 243).

208. In Magliola's presentation, "a Nothing can only operate in dialectic with a non-Nothing . . . so that any theory of nothingness 'buys into' a theory of presence." Magliola, *Derrida on the Mend*, p. 25.

209. Edward Conze, *Buddhism: Its Essence and Development* (New York: Philosophical Library, 1952), p. 130.

210. This notwithstanding, "*There are mountains hidden in sky. There are mountains hidden in mountains. There are mountains hidden in hiddenness. This is complete understanding.*" Dōgen, "Mountains and Rivers," in Kazuaki Tanahashi, ed. and trans., *Moon in a Dewdrop: Writings of Zen Master Dogen* (San Francisco: North Point Press, 1985), p. 107.

211. "Being," for Sartre, "is equally beyond negation as beyond affirmation" (BN, 27).

212. This reversibility, for Merleau-Ponty, "is not an actual *identity* of the touching and the touched. It is their identity by principle (always abortive)—" (VI, 272). He muses: "Reversibility: the finger of the glove that is turned inside out—There is no need of a spectator who would be *on each side*" (VI, 263). Again: "[T]he end of the finger of the glove is nothingness—but a nothingness one can turn over, and where then one sees *things*—The only 'place' where the negative would really be is the fold, the application of the inside and the outside to one another, the turning point—" (VI, 263–64).

213. Paul Klee reports, "In a forest, I have felt many times over that it was not I who

looked at the forest. Some days I felt that the trees were looking at me, were speaking to me. . . . I was there, listening. . . ." Klee, in G. Charbonnier, *Le monologue du peintre* (Paris, 1959), following "Eye and Mind" (PP, 167). Lispector corroborates: "The world looks at itself in me. Everything looks at everything. . . ." (GH, 58). Indeed, "It seems as though man everywhere and always encounters only himself." Martin Heidegger, *The Question Concerning Technology and Other Essays*, trans. W. Lovitt (New York: Harper and Row, 1977), p. 27.

214. In Merleau-Ponty's exposition: "[T]he mirror arises upon the open circuit [that goes] from seeing body to visible body. Every technique is a 'technique of the body.' A technique outlines and amplifies the metaphysical structure of our flesh. The mirror appears because I am seeing-visible [*voyant-visible*], because there is a reflexivity of the sensible; the mirror translates and reproduces that reflexivity." "Eye and Mind" (PP, 168).

215. Erwin Schrödinger, *What is Life? and Mind and Matter* (London: Cambridge University Press, 1969), p. 146.

216. Suzuki, *Zen Buddhism*, pp. 261–62.

217. Conze points out that "Etymologically 'mindfulness' *(smr-ti)* [Pali: *sati*] is derived from the root for 'to remember', and it may be defined as an act of remembering that prevents ideas from 'floating away', and which fights forgetfulness, carelessness and distraction" (BTI, 52). Mindfulness is the attribute of a mind fully "collected" or "recollected."

218. Zen, as Margaret Gibson assures us, "offers . . . not revelation but awakening." "The Glass Globe" (BSM, 86).

219. For Merleau-Ponty, also, "Every incarnate subject is like an open notebook in which we do not yet know what will be written. Or it is like a new language; we do not know what works it will accomplish but only that, once it has appeared, it cannot fail to say little or much, to have a history and a meaning." "An Unpublished Text" (PP, 6).

220. As Adorno says, in admonishing Heidegger: "Dialectics—in which pure particularization and pure generality pass into each other, both equally indistinct—is shrouded in silence and exploited in the doctrine of Being" (ND, 76).

221. Accordingly, for Merleau-Ponty, "To get used to a hat, a car or a stick is to be transplanted into them, or conversely, to incorporate them into the bulk of our own body" (PhP, 143).

222. "The Hawaiian people have always believed in many lives; in a continuing river of life. A life that flowed in and out of the earth plane, learning something new each time, always moving forward." Lee and Willis, *Night Rainbow*, p. 60. "We were taught also in things we had always known, but had not been taught. These were called '*ohana* knowledge'. These were things we had brought with us from other lifetimes. We studied ourselves and why we had returned at this special time and place. Each person's lesson was different at this time. Each of us was her own teacher. We had to go into ourselves for every answer." Lee and Willis, *Night Rainbow*, p. 46. Dōgen (1200–1253) insists, "It is fallacious to think that you simply move from birth to death. Birth . . . is a temporary point between the preceding and the succeeding; hence it can be called birthlessness. The same holds for death and deathlessness. In life there is nothing more than life, in death nothing more than death: we are being born and are dying at every moment." "On Life and Death," in Lucien Stryk and Takashi Ikemoto, trans., *Zen: Poems, Prayers, Sermons, Anecdotes, Interviews* (Garden City, N.Y.: Doubleday, 1963), p. 39.

223. For Lispector, verity is, indeed, so lacking in ornament that "Truth doesn't make sense!" (GH, 11).

224. For Derrida, "[N]onpresence and nonevidence are admitted into the blink of the instant. There is a duration to the blink, and it closes the eye." Jacques Derrida, *Speech and Phenomena and Other Essays on Husserl's Theory of Signs*, trans. David B. Allison (Evanston, Ill.: Northwestern University Press, 1973), p. 65.

225. Of this blind spot, Merleau-Ponty observes: "*What* it does not see it does not see for reasons of principle, it is because it is consciousness that it does not see. *What* it does not see is what in it prepares the vision of the rest (as the retina is blind at the point where the fibers that will permit the vision spread out into it). *What* it does not see is what makes it see, is its tie to Being, is its corporeity, are the existentials by which the world becomes visible, is the flesh wherein the *ob*ject is born" (VI, 248). Bataille concomitantly observes, "There is in understanding a blind spot: which is reminiscent of the structure of the eye. In understanding, as in the eye, one can only reveal it with difficulty. But whereas the blind spot of the eye is inconsequential, the nature of understanding demands that the blind spot within it be more meaningful than understanding itself. To the extent that understanding is auxiliary to action, the spot within it is as negligible as it is within the eye. But to the extent that one views in understanding man himself, by that I mean an exploration of what is possible in being, the spot absorbs one's attention: it is no longer the spot which loses itself in knowledge, but knowledge which loses itself in it. In this way existence closes the circle, but it couldn't do this without including the night from which it proceeds only in order to enter it again" (IE, 110–11). Mehta advances that "'magic' is only the name of a category employed to indicate what a blind spot prevents one from seeing. . . ." J. L. Mehta, "Heidegger and Vedanta: Reflections on a Questionable Theme," in Parkes, *Heidegger and Asian Thought*, p. 28.

226. Merleau-Ponty speaks appropriately of "my body, as the system of all my holds on the world. . . ." (PP, 18).

227. In the proclamation of Niu-t'ou Fa-yung, "The teaching of the truth is not the Truth" (OT, 20).

228. Sprung thus declares that "the middle way is not a means to some final truth; it is not a path leading to knowledge. Whatever it is, it is the end of socratizing, of theory, and of knowing. It is the practice of wisdom, not a means to it. . . ." Sprung, *Question of Being*, p. 136.

229. *Satipatthana-sutta* [The foundations of mindfulness] (WBT, 111).

230. Ibid. (WBT, 112).

231. Or as Merleau-Ponty also notes, "My body is wherever there is something to be done" (PhP, 250).

232. In Yampolsky's interesting alternative: "Bodhi originally has no tree" (PS/y, 132).

233. Dōgen proclaims: "Since there is no mind in me, when I hear the sound of raindrops from the eave, the raindrop is myself." Quoted in Tetsuaki Kotoh, "Language and Silence: Self-Inquiry in Heidegger and Zen," in Parkes, *Heidegger and Asian Thought*, p. 206.

234. Jorge Luis Borges, "Borges and I," in *A Personal Anthology*, ed. Anthony Kerrigan (New York: Grove Press, 1967), pp. 200–201.

235. Kirk et al., *Presocratic Philosophers*, p. 364.

The Gateless Gate: Reflections on the Methodology of Reflection

The haiku by Chiyo is from Harold G. Henderson, *An Introduction to Haiku: An Anthology of Poems and Poets from Bashō to Shiki* (Garden City, N.Y.: Doubleday, 1958), p. 84.

1. Martin Heidegger, *Being and Time*, trans. John Macquarrie and Edward Robinson (New York: Harper & Row, 1962), p. 51. Guenther, in consonance, remarks that "That which 'lights up' and 'appears' as what we call a phenomenon (a Latinization of Greek *phaínomenon*) is the whole and not an appearance *of* something." Herbert V. Guenther, *From Reductionism to Creativity: rDzogs-chen and the New Sciences of Mind* (Boston: Shambhala, 1989), p. 273 n. 14.

2. Heidegger, *Being and Time*, pp. 56, 58.

3. There is deep phenomenological wisdom in Saraha's counsel: "Understand appearance [the phenomenon] to be the teacher." Cited in Michael Heller, "Notes" (BSM, 133).

4. Phenomenology does not, in the currently standard sense, proceed by argumentation. It is, however, "argumentative" in the richly provocative sense expressed in Agamben's etymological explicitation: "The term *argumentum* derives from the very theme *argu*, found in *argentum* and signifying 'splendor, clarity.' *To argue* signified originally, 'to make shine, to clarify, to open a passage for light.' In this sense, the argument is the illuminating event of language, its taking place" (PN, 67).

5. The "word" of phenomenology has much in common with the "first utterance" which, Fallico tells us, "asserts nothing and demonstrates nothing, but which nonetheless initiates everything by making possible for us to speak at all." Arturo B. Fallico, *Art and Existentialism* (Englewood Cliffs, N.J.: Prentice-Hall, 1962), p. 64. Indeed, "first utterance is not something which translates the unsaid, or what cannot be said, into speech: it is *its* very word or speech." Fallico, *Art and Existentialism*, p. 103.

6. Herbert Spiegelberg, *The Phenomenological Movement: A Historical Introduction*, 3d ed. (The Hague: Martinus Nijhoff, 1982), p. 693.

7. The liberation of the word from deep and sacred silence is expressed in the Hawaiian phrase, "*Āmama, Ua Noa, Lele Wale* [The Kapu is finished, the words fly free]." Pali Jae Lee and Koko Willis, *Tales from the Night Rainbow: Mo'olelo na Pō Mākole: The Story of a Woman, a People, and an Island* (Honolulu: Night Rainbow, 1990), p. v.

8. Edmund Husserl, *Ideas: General Introduction to Pure Phenomenology*, trans. W. R. Boyce Gibson (London: George Allen and Unwin, 1931), p. 209.

9. Perhaps an even greater affinity is exhibited in the "proto-speech" of Mumon's pronouncement:

> Before the first step is taken the goal is reached.
> Before the tongue is moved the speech is finished.
>
> (ZFZB, 127)

10. Heidegger, *Being and Time*, p. 56. This, of course, is the very formula of "logocentrism." But if Husserl, whom Derrida regards as the culminating expositor of

logocentrism, has veritably lapsed into a *metaphysics* at all, his is not a metaphysics of presence, but, in the spirit of Sokolowski's fine study, a metaphysics of presence and absence. Cf. Robert Sokolowski, *Presence and Absence: A Philosophical Investigation of Language and Being* (Bloomington: Indiana University Press, 1978).

11. Jacques Derrida, "Limited Inc abc . . . " *Glyph* 2 (1977):183.

12. Ibid., p. 186.

13. Jacques Derrida, *Edmund Husserl's Origin of Geometry: An Introduction*, trans. John P. Leavey Jr. (Lincoln: University of Nebraska Press, 1962), p. 77. Husserl may, as Merleau-Ponty believes, have implicitly recognized this in claiming, in a letter to Lévy-Bruhl (11 March 1935) that "the philosopher could not possibly have access to the universal by reflection alone. . . ." Maurice Merleau-Ponty, "The Philosopher and Sociology," in John O'Neill, ed., *Phenomenology, Language, and Sociology: Selected Essays of Maurice Merleau-Ponty* (London: Heinemann, 1974), p. 104.

14. As Dews puts it, "[I]n any attempt to capture a world prior to—or independent of—language, language is always presupposed. . . ." (LD, 112).

15. Jacques Lacan, "Of Structure as an Inmixing of an Otherness Prerequisite to any Subject Whatever," in *The Languages of Criticism and the Sciences of Man: The Structuralist Controversy*, ed. Richard Macksey and Eugenio Donato (Baltimore: Johns Hopkins Press, 1970), p. 188. Agamben's position is, perhaps, equivalent: "*[T]he limit of language always falls within language; it is always already contained within as a negative*" (PN, 17).

16. Gadamer, forsaking a rigid dichotomization of language and reality, maintains that "Being that can be understood is language." Hans Georg Gadamer, *Truth and Method* (New York: Seabury Press, 1975).

17. If, as Adorno postulates, the argument is a certain "meditative contraction" (ND, 29), perhaps this demonstrativeness is a further, more tightly involuted, contraction of the argument.

18. Thomas helpfully observes that "Buddhist thinkers had without realizing it stumbled upon the fact that the terms of ordinary language do not express the real facts of existence. Words are static, but not the objects to which they refer. The contradictions were attributed not to the defects of verbal expression, but to the nature of experience." Edward Joseph Thomas, *The History of Buddhist Thought* (New York: Barnes and Noble, 1951), p. 218.

19. For Suzuki, "Spiritual experience is like sense-experience. It is direct, and tells us directly all that it has experienced without resorting to symbolism or ratiocination" (EZB III, 100).

20. Jacques Lacan, *Écrits: A Selection*, trans. Alan Sheridan (London: Tavistock, 1977), p. 86.

21. In this respect, Adorno rings somewhat truer to the spirit of Buddhism than does the founder of phenomenology: "Phenomenology forbade the prescription of laws by a subject that was already obliged to obey them: in that sense, the subject experiences something objective in the laws. Yet because Husserl, like the idealists, put all mediations on the noetic side, on the subject's, he could not conceive the objective moment in the concept as anything but an immediacy sui generis, and he was forced to commit an act of epistemological violence and copy the mediations from sense perception" (ND, 167–68).

22. Gurwitsch's summary comment, "Objectivity is identifiableness," notwith-

standing. Aron Gurwitsch, "On the Intentionality of Consciousness," in Marvin Farber, ed., *Philosophical Essays in Memory of Edmund Husserl* (Cambridge: Harvard University Press, 1940), and reprinted in Joseph J. Kockelmans, *Phenomenology: The Philosophy of Edmund Husserl and Its Interpretation* (Garden City, N.Y.: Doubleday, 1967), p. 136. Butchvarov's "indefinite identifiability" more aptly captures the sense of a perceptually possible "sharing." Panayot Butchvarov, *Being Qua Being: A Theory of Identity, Existence and Predication* (Bloomington: Indiana University Press, 1979), pp. 40, 120.

23. Menzan is luminously cognizant of this: "An entire library of sutras is merely a collection of recipes of the true taste of reality. . . . all the scholars spent their time arguing with each other about which recipe was better without ever tasting reality." Menzan Zuiho Osho, *Jijuyu-zanmai* [Samādhi of the self] (DZ, 60).

24. Aron Gurwitsch, *The Field of Consciousness* (Pittsburgh: Duquesne University Press, 1964), p. 167.

25. Dōgen's famous report plumbs the mind-sense to its depths:

> When the Great Master Yakusan Kodo was sitting, a certain monk asked him, "What do you think of when you sit?"
> The master replied, "I think of not-thinking."
> The monk asked, "How do you think of not-thinking?"
> The master said, "Beyond-thinking."

Dōgen, *Shōbōgenzō Zazenshin*, in Menzan Zuiho Osho, *Jijuyu-zanmai* [Samādhi of the self] (DZ, 94–95).

26. Agamben is emphatic that "*Thought is the suspension of the voice in language*" (PN, 107).

27. Or as Heidegger affirms, "[L]anguage is the language of Being, as clouds are the clouds of the sky." Martin Heidegger, "Letter on Humanism," trans. Frank A. Capuzzi, in David Farrell Krell, ed., *Martin Heidegger: Basic Writings* (New York: Harper and Row, 1977), p. 242.

28. This is not, of course, the mock-homicide proposed by Lin-chi (d. 867 C.E.): "When you meet a Buddha, kill the Buddha; when you meet a Patriarch, kill the Patriarch" (OT, 96).

29. Lévinas offers the consideration that "The necessity of a Reduction in Husserl's philosophy bears witness to a closure at the heart of the opening onto the given, to a drowsiness in spontaneous truth." Emmanuel Lévinas, "Philosophy and Awakening" (WCAS, 214).

30. A certain "brutality" is evidenced in the severance of thought from speaking. In Merleau-Ponty's words: "[A]s soon as we distinguish thought from speaking absolutely we are already in the order of reflection. . . ." (VI, 130).

31. Thus Lacan can say that "In its symbolizing function, speech is moving towards nothing less than a transformation of the subject to whom it is addressed by means of the link that it establishes with the one who emits it. . . ." Lacan, *Écrits: A Selection*, p. 83.

32. In Lacan's concordant view, "[T]he real does not wait, and in particular not for the subject, since it expects nothing from speech. But it is there, identical with its existence, a noise in which one can hear anything, and ready to burst in and submerge what the 'reality principle' constructs there in the name of the external world [Car le réel n'attend pas, et nommément pas le sujet, puisqu'il n'attend rien de la parole. Mais il est

là, identique à son existence, bruit où l'on peut tout entendre, et prêt à submerger de ses éclats ce que le «principe de réalité» y construit sous le nom de monde extérieur]." Lacan, *Écrits* (Paris: Éditions du Seuil, 1966), p. 388.

33. Indeed, in the wisdom of Yang-shan Hui-chi (814–90 C.E.), "there is no single truth that can be considered adequate" (OT, 215).

34. Alternatively, language must exhibit the "spaciousness" implicit in Quasha's remark that "Poetry's most challenging ontological claim is to be the space that preserves the very possibility of authentic language." George Quasha, "A Virtual Account" (BSM, 213).

35. The eikonic undecidability of original and copy, presentation and representation, reality and appearance, entails that the real "becomes an allegory of death, but it is reinforced by its very destruction; it becomes the real for the real, fetish of the lost object—no longer object of representation, but ecstasy of denegation and of its own ritual extermination: the hyperreal" (SS, 142). And conversely, "The unreal is no longer that of dream or of fantasy, of a beyond or a within, it is that of a *hallucinatory resemblance of the real with itself*" (SS, 142).

36. Somewhat mystically, Badiou writes that "One must come to conceive of truth as making a hole in knowledge." Alain Badiou, "On a Finally Objectless Subject" (WCAS, 25).

37. Though affirmed in a somewhat different vein, we find concurrence in Merleau-Ponty's statement that "The wonderful thing about language is that it promotes its own oblivion. . . ." (PhP, 401).

38. Brown observes that "The process of justification can be thus seen to feed upon itself, and this may comprise the strongest reason against believing that the codification of a proof procedure lends evidential support to the proofs in it. All it does is provide them with coherence. A theorem is no more proved by logic and computation than a sonnet is written by grammar and rhetoric, or than a sonata is composed by harmony and counterpoint, or a picture painted by balance and perspective. Logic and computation, grammar and rhetoric, harmony and counterpoint, balance and perspective, can be seen in the work *after* it is created, but these forms are, in the final analysis, parasitic on, they have no existence apart from, the creativity of the work itself" (LF, 102).

39. Blanchot speaks of the grisly freight borne by this barque: "[T]he word, in its perpetual vanishing, carries death, emptiness, absence. . . . [la parole, dans son perpétuel évanouissement, porte la mort, le vide, l'absence. . . .]." Maurice Blanchot, *Le Pas au-delà* (Paris: Gallimard, 1973), p. 46.

40. The paradox is expressed in the account rendered by Fa-yen Wên-i:

> A monk asked, "As for the finger, I will not ask you about it. But what is the moon?"
>
> The Master said, "Where is the finger that you do not ask about?" So the monk asked, "As for the moon, I will not ask you about it. But what is the finger?"
>
> The Master said, "The moon!"
>
> The monk challenged him, "I asked about the finger; why should you answer me, 'The moon'?"
>
> The Master replied, "Because you asked about the finger."
>
> (OT, 242)

41. "One may well affirm that everything is sayable," claims Lyotard. "[T]his is true, but what is not true is that the signification of discourse gathers up all the sense of the sayable. One can say that the tree is green, but one will not have placed the color into the sentence [On peut bien affirmer que tout est dicible, c'est vrai, mais ce qui ne l'est pas, c'est que la signification du discours recueille tout le sense du dicible. One peut dire que l'arbre est vert, mais on n'aura pas mis la couleur dans la phrase]." Jean-François Lyotard, *Discours, Figure* (Paris: Klincksieck, 1971), pp. 51–52.

42. We cannot disregard Robert Kelly's complementary insight that "Speech is the deep sound of language." "Going With the Poem" (BSM, 164).

43. "Word and form," declares Lispector, "will be the plank on top of which I shall float over billows of silence" (GH, 12).

44. Tradition attributes to Śākyamuni the statement that "The true Dharma-body of Buddha is like the empty sky, and it manifests itself according to sentient beings like the moon [reflected] on the water." In Dōgen's intriguing commentary: "'Like' in 'like the moon [reflected] on the water' should mean the water-moon *(sui-getsu)*. It should be the water-thusness, the moon-thusness, thusness-on, on-thusness. We are not construing 'like' as resemblance: 'like' is 'thusness'." Dōgen, "Tsuki," *Shōbōgenzō*, quoted in Hee-Jin Kim, *Dogen Kigen: Mystical Realist* (Tucson: University of Arizona Press, 1987), p. 191.

45. There is much to learn from Nott's observation that "the poet was the primitive physicist." Kathleen Nott, *The Emperor's Clothes* (London: Heinemann, 1953), p. 248. In Emerson's concordant words: "The poets made all the words, and therefore, language is the archives of history, and, if we must say it, a sort of tomb of the muses. For, though the origin of most of our words is forgotten, each word was at first a stroke of genius, and obtained currency, because for the moment it symbolized the world to the first speaker and to the hearer. The etymologist finds the deadest word to have been once a brilliant picture. Language is fossil poetry. As the limestone of the continent consists of infinite masses of the shells of animalcules, so language is made up of images, of tropes, which now, in their secondary use, have long ceased to remind us of their poetic origin. But the poet names the thing because he sees it, or comes one step nearer to it than any other." Ralph Waldo Emerson, "The Poet," *Essays: Second Series* (New York: Lovell, Coryell, n. d.), p. 21.

46. Derrida addresses this regrettable assessment in his statement that "Metaphor . . . is determined by philosophy as a provisional loss of meaning, an economy of the proper without irreparable damage, a certainly inevitable detour, but also a history with its sight set on, and within the horizon of circular reappropriation of literal, proper meaning. This is why the philosophical evaluation of metaphor always has been ambiguous: metaphor is dangerous and foreign as concerns *intuition* (vision or contact), *concept* (the grasping of proper presence of the signified), and *consciousness* (proximity of self-presence); but it is in complicity with what it endangers, is necessary to it in the extent to which the detour is a re-turn guided by the function of resemblance *(mimesis* or *homoiosis)*, under the law of the same." Jacques Derrida, *Margins of Philosophy*, trans. A. Bass (Chicago: University of Chicago Press, 1982), p. 270.

47. The ancient Hawaiians enjoyed a vivid and powerful sense of the concreteness of language: "Words once spoken became actual entities and caused changes in the world. The mana of words affected the physical, as well as the metaphysical world. . . .

A word is spoken with breath, which is spirit that moves what is uttered in a manner that can never be altered." Rita Knipe, *The Water of Life: A Jungian Journey through Hawaiian Myth* (Honolulu: University of Hawaii Press, 1989), p. 7.

48. Sartre locates this realm of "logical" ideality in the future: "[T]he abstract is always there but *to-come*; I apprehend it in the future with my future" (BN, 261).

49. Stanley Cavell, *Must We Mean What We Say? A Book of Essays* (New York: Charles Scribner's Sons, 1969), pp. 78–79.

50. Richard Rorty, *Essays on Heidegger and Others: Philosophical Papers*, vol. 2 (New York: Cambridge University Press, 1991), p. 12.

51. Ibid., p. 13.

52. Poetry, in Bataille's phrase, is "the simple holocaust of words" (IE, 137): a conflagration devoutly to be wished!

53. Analogously: "[T]he sun rises and shines all over the world but it does not light the Void; when the sun sets, darkness comes to the world but the Void is not darkened" (OT, 87).

54. It is interesting, in this connection, to hear Magiola's ruling that "*Śūnyatā* is not voidness but devoidness. . . ." Robert Magliola, *Derrida on the Mend* (West Lafayette, Ind.: Purdue University Press, 1986), p. 116.

55. It is no *thing*, no (particular) *one*, or rather, *merely* "one" in the sense of Merleau-Ponty's declaration: "[I]f I wanted to render precisely the perceptual experience, I ought to say that *one* perceives in me, and not that I perceive" (PhP, 215); "Perception is always in the mode of the impersonal 'One'" (PhP, 240).

56. Consonantly, Suzuki attests that "No designation whatever is possible. Therefore I say that *Wu-nien* [no-mind] is beyond the range of wordy discourse. The reason we talk about it at all is because questions are raised concerning it. If no questions are raised about it, there would be no discourse. It is like a bright mirror. If no objects appear before it, nothing is to be seen in it. When you say that you see something in it, it is because something stands against it" (NM, 30).

57. Hui-hai comments that "Mind has no colour . . . it is not long or short; it does not vanish or appear; it is free from purity and impurity alike; and its duration is eternal. It is utter stillness. Such, then, is the form and shape of our original mind, which is also our original body. . . ." (HH, 46).

58. In the notable proclamation of Huang Po Hsi-yün (d. 849 C.E.), "This Mind has no beginning, was never born, and will never pass away . . . it has no shape, no form; it does not belong to [the category of] being and non-being . . . it transcends all measurements, nameability, marks of identification, and forms of antithesis. . . . It is like vacuity of space, it has no boundaries. . . ." (NM, 129).

59. This resonates with Kelly's striking poetic articulation: "To define the world: *Nothing remembering something*." "Objections to the Unsatisfactoriness of Cyclic Existence" (BSM, 168).

60. O. K. Bouwsma, "Descartes' Evil Genius," *Philosophical Review* 58 (1949): 142.

61. David Hume, *Dialogues Concerning Natural Religion*, ed. Norman Kemp Smith (Indianapolis: Bobbs-Merrill, 1980), p. 149.

62. Hume, *Dialogues*, p. 147.

63. This, in part, is why Nāgārjuna charges that "A wrongly conceived *śūnyatā* can ruin a slow-witted person. It is like a badly seized snake or a wrongly executed incantation" (MK 24:11; N, 146). *Śūnyatā* conceived at all is wrongly conceived.

64. Takayama thus discloses that "Zen, which disowns all that has form, rejects any and all kinds of vision. According to it, a mountain is not high, nor is a pillar vertical. Emptiness in Zen is that in which being and non-being originate. It is realized, if you continue to insist on the term, when the dualism of being and non-being is done away with. The emptiness is not there as something to be seen or not seen, it is what you have become. And its realization is instantaneous, meaning timeless, without beginning or end. It is perhaps to be conceded that one can experience emptiness at a given moment, but the experience itself transcends time." Takayama, in Lucien Stryk and Takashi Ikemoto, trans., *Zen: Poems, Prayers, Sermons, Anecdotes, Interviews* (Garden City, N.Y,: Doubleday, 1963), p. 140.

65. Trinh thi Minh-hà, *Woman, Native, Other: Writing, Postcoloniality and Feminism* (Bloomington: Indiana University Press, 1989), p. 23.

66. The Pali texts relate the Buddha's attestation: "*Mindfully discerning the 'nothing-whatever-anywhere', supported by the conviction 'it is not' [there is nothing?], you will cross the flood.*" *Saṃyutta Nikāya* (BTI, 77).

67. Maurice Natanson, *Edmund Husserl: Philosopher of Infinite Tasks* (Evanston, Ill.: Northwestern University Press, 1973), p. 15.

68. Fink elucidates: "What is of decisive importance is the awakening of an immeasurable astonishment over the mysteriousness of this state of affairs [i.e., the reality of the world]. To accept it as a self-evident fact is to remain blind to the greatest mystery of all, the mystery of the being of the world itself. . . ." Eugen Fink, "The Phenomenological Philosophy of Edmund Husserl and Contemporary Criticism," in R. O. Elveton, ed., *The Phenomenology of Husserl: Selected Critical Readings* (Chicago: Quadrangle Books, 1970), pp. 109–10.

69. "Sanity," while, perhaps, consistent with "the 'madness' of the *epoché*" (RM, 133) of which Gargani speaks, is not necessarily infected by it.

70. Despite its length, it seems appropriate to have before us one of the earliest, clearest, and certainly one of the most elucidative of Husserlian texts concerning the "natural positing": "*We put out of action the general thesis* [Kersten: "general positing"] *which belongs to the essence of the natural standpoint*, we place in brackets whatever it includes respecting the nature of Being: *this entire natural world therefore* which is continually "there for us," "present to our hand" [Kersten: "on hand"], and will ever remain there, is a "fact-world" [Kersten: "actuality"] of which we continue to be conscious, even though it pleases us to put it in brackets.

"If I do this, as I am fully free to do, I do *not* then *deny* [Kersten: "I am *not negating*"] this "world," as though I were a sophist, *I do not doubt that it is there* as though I were a sceptic; but I use the "phenomenological" [*epochē*], which *completely bars me from using any judgement that concerns spatio-temporal existence. . . .*

"Thus *all sciences which relate to this natural world*, though they stand never so firm to me, though they fill me with wondering admiration, though I am far from any thought of objecting to them in the least degree, I *disconnect* [Kersten: "exclude"] *them all, I make absolutely no use of their standards* [Kersten: "the things posited in them"], *I do not appropriate a single one of the propositions that enter into their systems, even though their evidential value is perfect, I take none of* them, *no one of them serves me for a foundation—so* long, that is, as it is understood, in the way these sciences themselves understand it, as a truth *concerning the realities* [Kersten: "actualities"] of this world. *I may accept it only after I have placed it in the bracket* [Kersten: "parentheses"]. That means: only in the modified consciousness of the judgement as it appears in disconnexion [Kersten: "the consciousness of judgement-excluding"], and *not as it figures within the science as its proposition, a proposition which claims to be valid and whose validity I recognize and make use of.*" Husserl, *Ideas*, trans. Gibson, pp. 99–100; Edmund Husserl, *Ideas Pertaining to a Pure Phenomenology and to a Phenomenological Philosophy: First Book: General Introduction to a Pure Phenomenology*, trans. F. Kersten (The Hague: Martinus Nijhoff, 1982), pp. 61–62.

71. And assuredly, "philosophical questioning habitually knows more than its audience." Jacques Rancière, "After What" (WCAS, 246).

72. As Wagner avers, "Naïveté has no suspicions concerning what takes place within the unfathomable; it speaks without suspicion of the world, of man, and of his consciousness; it lives without suspicion in the world. . . . This naïveté would come to an end if it should be asked: what does it mean to say that *there is* (a world, that we are within it, that we have our familiar capabilities)?" Hans Wagner, "Critical Observations Concerning Husserl's Posthumous Writings" in Elveton, *Phenomenology of Husserl*, pp. 217–18.

73. David Michael Levin, "Husserl's Notion of Self-Evidence," in Edo Pivcevic, ed., *Phenomenology and Philosophical Understanding* (London: Cambridge University Press, 1975), p. 59n.

74. In Hui-hai's contrasting transmission:

> Q: What does right perception mean?
> A: It means perceiving that there is nothing to perceive.
>
> (HH, 51)

75. For Merleau-Ponty, "[T]he 'object' of philosophy will never come to fill in the philosophical question, since this obturation would take from it the depth and the distance that are essential to it" (VI, 101). And "Philosophy does not raise questions and does not provide answers that would little by little fill in the blanks" (VI, 105).

76. Aron Gurwitsch, "On the Intentionality of Consciousness," p. 128. Gurwitsch's "Husserl" is clearly preferable, on this crucial point of interpretation to that of Føllesdal who claims that "noemata are not perceived through the senses." Cf. Dagfin Føllesdal, "Husserl's Notion of Noema," *Journal of Philosophy* 66 (1969).

77. Merleau-Ponty queries: "But are there any absolute commitments? Is it not the essence of commitment to leave unimpaired the autonomy of the person who commits himself, in the sense that it is never complete, and does it not therefore follow that we have no longer any means of describing certain feelings as authentic?" (PhP, 382).

78. In Adorno's words: "[C]onsciousness is at the same time the universal medium and cannot jump across its shadow even in its own *données immédiates*. They are not the truth" (ND, 40).

79. Merleau-Ponty adopts the quasi-Berkeleyan position that "if I attempt to imagine some place in the world which has never been seen, the very fact that I imagine it makes me present at that place" (PP, 16). Not only is the imaginary a modality of the real, the real is at once the terminus of the imagination.

80. In Lao-Tzu's poetic articulation:

> Endless the series of things without name
> On the way back to where there is nothing.

They are called shapeless shapes.
Forms without form
Are called vague semblances.
Go towards them, and you see no front;
Go after them, and you see no rear.

Arthur Waley, *The Way and its Power: A Study of the* Tao Tê Ching *and its Place in Chinese Thought* (London: George Allen & Unwin, 1934), chap. 14, p. 159.

81. J. N. Findlay, *The Discipline of the Cave* (New York: Humanities, 1966), p. 90.

82. Jeffrey Gordon, "Dream-World or Life-World? A Phenomenological Solution to an Ancient Puzzle," *Husserl Studies* 2 (1985): 190.

83. Gordon, "Dream-World or Life-World?" p. 188.

84. Jean-Paul Sartre, *The War Diaries of Jean-Paul Sartre: November 1939/March 1940*, trans. Quintin Hoare (New York: Pantheon, 1984), pp. 37–38.

85. Discernment, to credit Nietzsche's speculation, may be possible even if dream cannot be discriminated *from reality*: "I suddenly woke up in the midst of this dream, but only to the consciousness that I am dreaming and that I must go on dreaming lest I perish." Friedrich Nietzsche, *The Gay Science: With a Prelude in Rhymes and an Appendix of Songs*, trans. Walter Kaufmann (New York: Vintage, 1974), sec. 54, p. 116.

86. Bataille's heart-wrenching query, "Am I awake? I doubt it and I could weep" (IE, 34), demonstrates, by contrast, the aptness of the epithet "Blessed One" in its application to the Buddha.

87. In Bataille's similar, but assuredly more arresting, trope: "The mind of man has become his own slave and through the work of autodigestion which the operation assumes, has consumed, subjugated, destroyed *itself*" (IE, 133).

88. "At bottom," affirms Merleau-Ponty, "Pyrrhonism shares the illusions of the naïve man. It is the naïveté that rends itself asunder in the night. Between Being in itself and the 'interior life' it does not even catch sight of the *problem of the world*" (VI, 6).

89. Zen solves the problem directly: "Open your hands. Just let everything go, and see" (DZ, 35).

90. Baudrillard posits that "there is no longer apparition, but instead subpoena of the object, severe interrogation of its scattered fragments—neither metaphor nor metonymy: successive immanence under the policing structure of the look" (SS, 143).

91. In the notable impartation of Mumon [No-Gate]:

The great path has no gates,
Thousands of roads enter it.
When one passes through this gateless gate
He walks freely between heaven and earth.

(ZFZB, 88)

92. Adorno warns that "What they subsume under ἐποχή will avenge itself by enforcing its power behind the back of philosophy" (ND, 51).

93. Existence loosed, like lightning, from the brackets may have much in common with what Adorno calls "the violence of unleashed quantification" (ND, 43).

94. The reflective strategies of phenomenology involve an inner transformation of the reflecting consciousness. And in this light, it is intriguing to consider Corless's

assertion that "The Buddha Dharma is *trans*formation manifesting as *in*formation." Roger J. Corless, *The Vision of Buddhism: The Space Under the Tree* (New York: Paragon House, 1989), p. 124.

95. Saxe Commins and Robert N. Linscott, ed., *Man and the Universe, the Philosophers of Science* (New York: Washington Square Press, 1969), p. 457.

96. In Krell's explication, "'the true,' 'truth' in the traditional metaphysical sense, is a *fixation* of an apparition; it clings to a perspective that is essential to life but in a way that is ultimately destructive to life." David Farrell Krell, "Analysis," in Martin Heidegger, *Nietzsche*, vol. 1: *The Will to Power as Art*, trans. David Ferrell Krell (New York: Harper & Row, 1979), p. 237.

97. Though not, in my estimation, a form of pragmatism, since the doctrine of *upāya* is not a theory of truth, but, if you will, of "perlocutionary force," Buddhism regards theoretical construction as "skillful means," and in this is joined by Foucault, who avers: "Theory is merely a 'tool-kit' in the service of a particular struggle, and may be discarded as soon as it loses its utility." Michel Foucault, *Language, Counter-Memory, Practice: Selected Essays and Interviews*, ed. Donald F. Bouchard (Ithaca, N.Y.: Cornell University Press, 1977), p. 208.

98. Thus, Irigary tells us, "the Buddha's gazing upon the flower is not a distracted or predatory gaze, it is not the lapse of the speculative into the flesh, it is the at once material and spiritual contemplation that provides an already sublimated energy to thought. . . . Buddha contemplates the flower without picking it. He gazes upon this other than him without removing it at its roots. Moreover, what he gazes upon is not just anything—it is a flower, which perhaps offers us the best object for meditation on the adequation of form to matter." Luce Irigary, "Love Between Us" (WCAS, 171). We find also that "In holding fast, or grasping, the whole universe vanishes. In letting go, or releasing, the individual world appears, in which everyone asserts his true existence." Katsuki Sekida, *Two Zen Classics: Mumonkan and Hekiganroku* (New York: John Weatherhill, 1977), p. 329.

99. If bracketing is analogous to quotation, the lapse of *epochē* is, in Quine's phrase, "disquotation": "The truth predicate serves the function of . . . disquotation." W. V. Quine, *Philosophy of Logic* (Englewood Cliffs, N.J.: Prentice-Hall, 1970), p. 97.

100. John Blofeld, "Translator's Introduction" (HH, 49–50).

101. Schrag is concerned that "The use of the metaphor of foundations invites a disturbing self-arrogation on the part of philosophy." Calvin O. Schrag, *Radical Reflection and the Origin of the Human Sciences* (West Lafayette, Ind.: Purdue University Press, 1980), p. 17.

102. Edmund Husserl, *Cartesian Meditations: An Introduction to Phenomenology*, trans. Dorion Cairns (The Hague: Martinus Nijhoff, 1960), p. 6.

103. Buddhist ideological liberation is not alien to the "freedom" of Adorno's comment: "The freedom of philosophy is nothing but the capacity to lend a voice to its unfreedom" (ND, 18).

104. George Quasha attests that "when a mind-event self-liberates, it realizes an intrinsic state of possibility in which the energy that performed the mind-event becomes free in and of itself." "A Virtual Account" (BSM, 212n).

105. Husserl, *Cartesian Meditations*, p. 2.

106. Ibid.

107. Ibid.

108. Bataille speaks of the "paradox in the authority of experience" that is "based on challenge, [and] is the challenging of authority; positive challenge, man's authority defined as the challenging of himself" (IE, 7n).

109. Merleau-Ponty elucidates the impossibility of "adequation" as an entailment of the repudiation of immanence: "*Because there is Einströmen*, reflection is not adequation, coincidence: it would not pass *into* the *Strom* if it placed us back at the source of the *Strom*—" (VI, 173).

110. Parsons notes that "We continuously seek closure in our meanings and identities, yet we cannot tolerate the constrictions they lay upon us. . . ." Howard L. Parsons, *The Value of Buddhism for the Modern World,* Wheel Publication no. 232–33 (Kandy: Buddhist Publishing Society, 1976), p. 3.

111. Baudrillard expresses a certain Kuhnian sentiment—a proclivity, indeed, even less congenial to the "normal" assumption of internal validity, and certainly a view out of step with progressive positivism—in his rather sinister assertion that "science never sacrifices itself: it is always murderous" (SS, 14).

112. Husserl, *Cartesian Meditations*, p. 5. "Philosophy," as Lévinas counters, "is philosophers in an intersubjective 'intrigue' that nobody resolves, while nobody is allowed a lapse of attention or a lack of rigor." Emmanuel Lévinas, "Philosophy and Awakening" (WCAS, 215).

113. Reflection, for Merleau-Ponty, is curiously insidious: "Once one is settled in it, reflection is an inexpugnable philosophical position, every obstacle, every resistance to its exercise being from the first treated not as an adversity of the things but as a simple state of non-thought, a gap in the continuous fabric of the acts of thought, which is inexplicable, but about which there is nothing to say since it is literally '*nothing*'" (VI, 44).

114. In the narrative of Hsüeh-fêng I-ts'un: "The Master said, 'You don't entirely agree with Yang-shan? If someone asked you, what would you say?' Hui-leng answered, 'I would just say he is mistaken.' The Master went on, 'Then you are not mistaken?' Hui-leng said, 'My answer would not be any different from a mistake'" (OT, 278).

115. "Ch'an takes no sides" (OT, 11).

116. "Relativism," as Magliola observes, "is the absence of truth conditions." Magliola, *Derrida on the Mend*, p. 81.

117. Truth, for Nietzsche, is "the kind of error without which a certain species of life could not live." Indeed, knowledge is "a measuring of earlier and later errors by one another." Friedrich Nietzsche, *The Will to Power*, trans. Walter Kaufmann and R. J. Hollingdale (New York: Vintage, 1968), pp. 272, 281.

118. Edmund Husserl, *The Crisis of European Sciences and Transcendental Phenomenology: An Introduction to Phenomenological Philosophy*, trans. David Carr (Evanston, Ill.: Northwestern University Press, 1970), pp. 163–64.

119. Indeed, as Merleau-Ponty observes, the appearances themselves are ineluctably elusive: "[T]hose appearances which are not yet firmly fixed intercommunicate, run into each other, and all radiate from a central *Würfelhaftigkeit* which is the mystical link between them" (PhP, 324).

120. Natanson, *Philosopher of Infinite Tasks*, p. 21.

121. Ibid.

122. As Zaner insightfully observes, "Any 'problem' (or: disturbance, crisis, dilemma, in life) stands out from a background of what is unproblematic; in fact it is only

by reference to the latter that anything can stand out as 'problematic', 'unfamiliar', 'unexpected', and the like. Moreover not only does the unexpected, unfamiliar or unusual call attention to itself, but what has hitherto been accepted as familiar, expected and usual is brought into question. . . . To the extent the person takes his situation—ultimately, his life—seriously, the problematic situation is critical for him; and to the extent that he seriously *seeks to know* 'what and how things actually are', he is himself called on to be critical: to question, seek, find out, assess, justify. That is, he must cease taking for granted what has been up to now accepted as unquestionable." Richard M. Zaner, "On the Sense of Method in Phenomenology," in Pivcevic, *Phenomenology and Philosophical Understanding*, p. 134.

123. René Descartes, Rule XII in *Rules for the Direction of the Mind*, in *The Philosophical Works of Descartes*, edited and translated by Elizabeth S. Haldane and G. R. T. Ross (New York: Dover, 1955), p. 35. "To understand," in an apposite sense, "is to delay immediate response and belief. . . ." Parsons, *The Value of Buddhism*, p. 11.

124. Descartes, Rule XII in *Rules*, p. 45. Standing in significant opposition to Descartes's assumption, Levin asserts: "To deduce is not to elucidate." David Michael Levin, *Reason and Evidence in Husserl's Phenomenology* (Evanston, Ill.: Northwestern University Press, 1970), p. 11.

125. Descartes, Rule XII in *Rules*, pp. 40-41.

126. Merleau-Ponty calls into question the appropriateness of this "complement": "'I doubt': there is no way of silencing all doubt concerning this proposition other than by actually doubting, involving oneself in the experience of doubting, and thus bringing this doubt into existence as the certainty of doubting. . . . if I try to verify the reality of my doubt, I shall again be launched into an infinite regress, for I shall need to call into question my thought about doubting, then the thought about that thought, and so on" (PhP, 383).

127. Husserl, *Ideas*, trans. Kersten, 59.

128. Bataille speaks, in this connection, of "the voyage to the end of the possible. . . ." (IE, 23). He proclaims: "There all possibilities are exhausted; the 'possible' slips away and the impossible prevails. To face the impossible—exorbitant, indubitable—when nothing is possible any longer is in my eyes to have an experience of the divine. . . ." (IE, 33).

129. Charles Sanders Peirce, "Critical Common-Sensism," in Justus Buchler, ed., *Philosophical Writings of Peirce* (New York: Dover, 1955), p. 299.

130. Peirce, "Some Consequences of Four Incapacities," in Buchler, *Philosophical Writings of Peirce*, pp. 228–29.

131. Husserl, *Cartesian Meditations*, pp. 5–6.

132. As the Venerable Bhikkhu Ñaṇajivako points out, the *epochē*, the act of abstaining from "views" (Greek: *doxa*; Sanskrit: *dṛṣṭi*; Pali: *diṭṭhi*) was a method brought from India by Pyrrho of Elis at the time of Alexander the Great. Cf. "Karma—The Ripening Fruit," in *Kamma and its Fruit,* Wheel Publication no. 221–24 (Kandy: Buddhist Publication Society, 1975), pp. 35–36.

133. Fink, "Phenomenological Philosophy of Husserl," p. 221.

134. Levin, *Reason and Evidence*, p. 3.

135. As Natanson discloses, "Underlying the moments of self-consciousness there is a continuous believing in the world, a nonself-conscious 'faith' in the reality which encompasses the believer." Natanson, *Philosopher of Infinite Tasks*, p. 22.

136. A harmless example is provided by Husserl's certification that "the 'transcendental' epochē is meant, of course, as a habitual attitude which we resolve to take up once and for all. Thus it is by no means a temporary act which remains incidental and isolated in its various repetitions." Husserl, *Crisis*, p. 150. Had the context demanded greater precision, Husserl might have replaced *"epochē"* with "reduction."

137. Zaner, "Method in Phenomenology," p. 137.

138. As illustrated by Nansen's words, Zen "deconstructs" this distinction: "The path does not belong to the perception world, neither does it belong to the nonperception world. Cognition is a delusion and noncognition is senseless. If you want to reach the true path beyond doubt, place yourself in the same freedom as sky. You name it neither good nor not-good" (ZFZB, 105).

139. Robert Sokolowski, *Husserlian Meditations: How Words Present Things* (Evanston, Ill.: Northwestern University Press, 1974), pp. 173–74.

140. Fink, "Phenomenological Philosophy of Husserl," p. 126.

141. If, as Merleau-Ponty suggests, "The world is that reality of which the necessary and the possible are merely provinces" (PhP, 398), and if the actual is, at the same time, possible (if not necessary), then reduction must, of course, be "incomplete," since *world* includes both the empirically actual and the transcendentally required.

142. Merleau-Ponty postulates that "a sufficient reduction leads beyond the alleged transcendental 'immanence', it leads to the absolute spirit understood as *Weltlichkeit*, to *Geist* as the *Ineinander* of the spontaneities. . . ." (VI, 172).

143. Henry Duméry, *The Problem of God in Philosophy of Religion*, trans. Charles Courtney (Evanston, Ill.: Northwestern University Press, 1964), pp. 5–6.

144. Merleau-Ponty confesses, "I am not a finalist, because the interiority of the body (= the conformity of the internal leaf with the external leaf, their folding back on one another) is not something *made, fabricated*, by the assemblage of the two leaves; they have never been apart—" (VI, 265).

145. Merleau-Ponty supplements: "The end of a philosophy is the account of its beginning" (VI, 177).

146. For Bataille: "Experience would only be an enticement, if it weren't revolt: in the first place against the attachment of the mind to action (to project, to discourse—against the verbal servitude of reasonable being, of the servant); in the second place against the reassurances, the submissiveness which experience itself introduces" (IE, 115).

147. Merleau-Ponty labels this "the reflective cramp" (VI, 57).

148. Is the lotus, perhaps, genetic kin to "the 'flower' of philosophy—the heliotrope or sunflower" (RM, 127) of which Rovatti speaks?

149. Merleau-Ponty remarks that "precisely inasmuch as they are a return or a reconquest, these operations of reconstitution or of re-establishment which come second cannot by principle be the mirror image of its internal constitution and its establishment, as the route from the Etoile to the Notre-Dame is the inverse of the route from the Notre-Dame to the Etoile: the reflection recuperates everything except itself as an effort of recuperation, it clarifies everything except its own role" (VI, 33).

150. Cf. Phyllis Sutton Morris, "Sartre on the Self-Deceiver's Translucent Consciousness," *Journal of the British Society for Phenomenology* 23 (1992): 105. In the original: "Translucidité: qui laisse passer la lumière, sans permettre toutefois de voir clairment, les objets à travers son épaisseur: les verres dépolis sont translucides." *Larousse*

Classique, 1957, following Morris, p. 116 n. 8. A later version offers a somewhat more abstract, less nuanced, definition: "Said of a substance which allows light to pass, but through which one does not neatly distinguish objects [Se dit d'une substance qui laisse passer la lumière, mais au travers de laquelle on ne distingue pas nettement les objets]." *Larousse de la langue française* (Paris: Librairie Larousse, 1979), p. 1923.

151. With this concurs Merleau-Ponty's observation that "If it is not unaware of itself—which would be contrary to its definition—the reflection cannot feign to unravel the same thread that the mind would first have woven, to be the mind returning to itself within me, when by definition it is I who reflect" (VI, 33–34).

152. James G. Hart, "A Précis of an Husserlian Philosophical Theology," in Steven W. Laycock and James G. Hart, eds., *Essays in Phenomenological Theology* (Albany: SUNY Press, 1986), p. 98.

153. In Adorno's disparaging appraisal, "[T]he thought of passing into subject-matter was more chilling to Husserl than to any neo-Kantian of the University of Marburg who might find the infinitesimal method helpful in such a passage" (ND, 78).

154. This is, in part, because "the sensible itself is *invisible. . . .*" (VI, 237). "The sensible," furthermore, "is precisely that medium in which there can be *being* without it having to be posited. . . ." (VI, 214).

155. P. Hughes and G. Brecht, *Vicious Circles and Infinity* (New York: Penguin, 1979), pp. 64–65.

156. Indeed, "concepts are simply indications of the relative capacity and resistance of a particular space. . . ." Tarthang Tulku, *Time, Space and Knowledge: A New Vision of Reality* (Emeryville, Calif.: Dharma Publishing, 1977), p. 14.

157. With this accords Adorno's striking assertion that "Truth is, rather, a field of force" (AE, 72).

158. We align ourselves with the "positivist" proclivities of Merleau-Ponty's construal: "The eidetic method is the method of a phenomenological positivism which bases the possible on the real" (PhP, xvii). The possible, that is, stands as one of the manifold "ways" the real could be.

159. In Gary Snyder's crystalline summation:

> A flower
> for nothing;
> an offer;
> no taker;
>
> "For Nothing" (BSM, 264)

160. Merleau-Ponty emphatically propounds that "The percept taken in its entirety with the world horizon *which announces both its possible disjunction and its possible replacement by another perception*, certainly does not mislead us" (PhP, 344).

161. We must not succumb to "the temptation to construct perception out of the perceived, to construct our contact with the world out of what it has taught us about the world . . ." (VI, 156). Lévinas speaks in this connection of "Husserlian analyses, which themselves are always more surprising than the 'system' and programmatic discourse." Emmanuel Lévinas, "Philosophy and Awakening" (WCAS, 209).

162. In a small sentence that casts a dramatically distinctive light on the preface to *Being and Nothingness*, Sartre adds that "consciousness is an abstraction since it con-

ceals within itself an ontological source in the region of the in-itself, and conversely the phenomenon is likewise an abstraction since it must 'appear' to consciousness" (BN, 34). Indeed, in its concrete setting, that of being-in-the-world, and as the event of "decompression," the for-itself is the very activity of abstracting or noticing—not, we must say, an ectoplasmic abstraction.

163. This should be complemented with Merleau-Ponty's congruent observation, "In the primary field we have not a mosaic of qualities, but a total configuration which distributes functional values according to the demands of the whole. . . ." (PhP, 241).

164. André de Muralt, *The Idea of Phenomenology: Husserlian Exemplarism*, trans. Garry L. Breckon (Evanston, Ill.: Northwestern University Press, 1973), p. 320.

165. Merleau-Ponty amplifies: "Every ideation, because it is an ideation, is formed in a space of existence, under the guarantee of my duration, which must turn back into itself in order to find there again the same idea I thought an instant ago and must pass into the others in order to rejoin it also in them. Every ideation is borne by this tree of my duration and other durations, this unknown sap nourishes the transparency of the idea; behind the idea, there is the unity, the simultaneity of all the real and possible durations, the cohesion of one sole Being from one end to the other. Under the solidity of the essence and of the idea there is the fabric of experience, this flesh of time. . . ." (VI, 111).

166. In Derrida's explication, "In order that the possibility of . . . repetition may be open, *ideally* to infinity, one ideal form must assure this unity of the *indefinite* and the *ideal*: this is the present, or rather the ideality of ideality, that in which in the last instance one may anticipate or recall all repetition, is the *living present*, the self-presence of transcendental life. . . ." Jacques Derrida, *Speech and Phenomena and Other Essays on Husserl's Theory of Signs*, David B. Allison, trans (Evanston, Ill.: Northwestern University Press, 1973), p. 6. Again: "Ideality is the preservation or mastery of presence in repetition. In its pure form this presence is the presence of nothing existing in the world; it is a correlation with the acts of repetition, themselves ideal . . . the relation with infinity can be instituted only in the opening of the form of presence upon ideality, as the possibility of a return ad infinitum." Derrida, *Speech and Phenomena*, pp. 9–10, 54.

167. Sartre tells us that "Leibniz' effort to define necessity in terms of possibility . . . is undertaken from the point of view of knowledge and not from the point of view of being. The passage from possibility to being such as Leibniz conceives it (the necessary is a being whose possibility implies its existence) marks the passage from our ignorance to knowledge. In fact, since possibility precedes existence, it can be possibility only with respect to our thought" (BN, 128–29).

168. Aron Gurwitsch, *Studies in Phenomenology and Psychology* (Evanston, Ill.: Northwestern University Press, 1966), p. 383.

169. And as Merleau-Ponty tells us, "The myth holds the essence *within* the appearance; the mythical phenomenon is not a representation, but a genuine presence" (PhP, 290).

170. Lacan sees that "There is only one gesture, known since Augustine, which corresponds to nomination: that of the index-finger which shows, but . . . by itself this gesture is not even adequate to designate what is named in the object indicated." Jacques Lacan, "Merleau-Ponty," in *Le Problème du Style, suivi de Merleau-Ponty*, pirate edition (Paris: n.d.), p. 13.

171. In Kohák's entertaining illustration: "When I try, unsuccessfully, to squeeze a tennis ball into a wine bottle, I need not try several wine bottles and several tennis balls

before, using Mill's canons of induction, I arrive inductively at the hypothesis that tennis balls do not fit into wine bottles. One instance is enough. I *see* not only that this tennis ball won't fit into this wine bottle but that, in principle, tennis balls do not fit into wine bottles, and, for that matter, I *see* that large objects do not fit into small openings." Erazim Kohák, *Idea and Experience: Edmund Husserl's Project of Phenomenology in IDEAS I* (Chicago: University of Chicago Press, 1978), p. 16. Again: "[W]hen you have seen one parallelogram, you have seen them all." Idem, p. 17.

172. Merleau-Ponty understands eternity as "the power to embrace and anticipate temporal developments in a single intention. . . ." (PhP, 372). For him, "an eternal subject perceiving itself in absolute transparency" is "utterly incapable of making its descent into time. . . ." (PhP, 424).

173. "Style," in Kristeva's pronouncement, "is a certain way of doing violence to sentences . . . of having them slightly fly off the handle, so the speak, displacing them, and thus making the reader himself displace his meaning. But ever so slightly! Oh, ever so slightly!" Julia Kristeva, *Powers of Horror: An Essay on Abjection*, trans. L. S. Roudiez (New York: Columbia University Press, 1982), p. 203. Consider, in this connection, Arikha's alternative persuasion: "[S]tyle is a way of protecting oneself from that which is untrue." Michael Heller, "Notes" (BSM, 135).

174. Merleau-Ponty remarks that "the essence is . . . not the end, but a means " (PhP, xiv).

175. Fittingly, Streng advances that "'becoming' and knowledge are coextensive" (E, 38).

176. We must burst "the solipsist illusion that consists in thinking that every going beyond is a surpassing accomplished by oneself" (VI, 143).

177. For Sartre, "there exists no 'synthesis of recognition' if we mean by that a progressive operation of identification which by successive organization of the 'nows' would confer a *duration* on the thing perceived" (BN, 280).

178. Kakuan propounds that "As soon as the six senses merge, the gate is entered. . . . This unity is like salt in water, like color in dyestuff. The slightest thing is not apart from self" (ZFZB, 140).

179. Nietzsche hammers: "That which is last, thinnest, and emptiest is put first, as *the* cause, as *ens realissimum*." Friedrich Nietzsche, *The Twilight of the Idols*, in Walter Kaufmann, trans. and ed., *The Portable Nietzsche* (New York: Viking, 1968), p. 483.

180. "Mercury, when divided, becomes small pearl-like droplets, each separate and whole in and of itself. But when the mercury is allowed to run together, it forms one totality in which the separate parts are indistinguishable from the whole" (OT, 88).

181. Quoted in Keiji Nishitani, "What is Religion?" *Philosophical Studies of Japan* 2 (1960): 40.

182. Søren Kierkegaard, *The Concept of Dread* (Princeton: Princeton University Press, 1954), p. 55.

183. However, in Merleau-Ponty's estimation, the phenomenological reduction decidedly is afflicted with "the Cartesian defect of being a *hypothesis of the Nichtigkeit of the world. . . .*" (VI, 172).

184. As Bourdieu insists, "*Esse est interesse. . . .*" Pierre Bourdieu, "The Philosophical Institution" (PFT, 1).

185. For Lévinas, "To accede to the rational is to grasp." Emmanuel Lévinas, "Philosophy and Awakening" (WCAS, 208).

186. From Hakuin's *Orategama*, as translated by Dumoulin, in Heinrich Doumoulin, *A History of Zen Buddhism* (New York: Random House, 1963), p. 257f.

187. Maurice Merleau-Ponty, *Signs*, trans. R. C. McCleary (Evanston, Ill.: Northwestern University Press, 1964), p. 21.

188. "Der Grund hat sein Un-wesen, weil er der endlichen Freiheit entspringt. Diese selbst kann sich dem, was ihr so entspringt, nicht entziehen. Der transzendierend entspringende Grund legt sich auf die Freiheit selbst zurück, und sie wird *als Urspring* selbst zum «Grund». *Die Freiheit ist der Grund des Grundes*. . . . Als *dieser* Grund aber ist die Freiheit der *Ab-grund* des Daseins." Martin Heidegger, *The Essence of Reasons/Vom Wesen des Grundes* (bilingual edition), trans. Terrence Malick (Evanston, Ill.: Northwestern University Press, 1969), pp. 126–29; translation modified.

189. Heidegger, *Being and Time*, pp. 193–94.

190. It should be remarked from the outset that the "emptiness" illustrated in Heidegger's poetic musing is to the *śūnyatā* of Buddhism as *place* is to *space:* "When we fill the jug with wine, do we pour the wine between the sides and the bottom? At most, we pour the wine between the sides and over the bottom. Sides and bottom are, to be sure, what is impermeable in the vessel. But what is impermeable is not yet what does the holding. When we fill the jug, the pouring that fills it flows into the empty jug. The emptiness, the void *[die Leere]*, is what does the vessel's holding. The emptiness, the void, this nothingness *[dieses Nichtes]* of the jug, is what the jug is as the holding vessel." Martin Heidegger, *Poetry, Language, Thought*, trans. A. Hofstadter (New York: Harper and Row, 1971), p. 169.

191. Hyperreflection is thus "The science of pre-science, as the expression of what is before expression. . . ." (VI, 167).

192. As Corless conveys: "It is not that there is suffering *in* samsara, along with no suffering, but that samsara *is* suffering, through and through. Samsara and duhkha are synonymous." Corless, *The Vision of Buddhism*, p. 207.

193. As Guenther imparts, "Saṁsāra is basically a descriptive term for the observable fact that man in ignorance of his real being is driven by his actions and emotions, while Nirvāṇa refers to the experienceable passage beyond suffering." Herbert V. Guenther, "Indian Buddhist Thought in Tibetan Perspective," in *Tibetan Buddhism in Western Perspective* (Berkeley, Calif.: Dharma Publishing, 1977), p. 134.

194. Richard Schmitt, "Husserl's Transcendental-Phenomenological Reduction," *Philosophy and Phenomenological Research* 20 (1959–60): 61.

195. Corless corroborates: "[I]f nirvana really were a condition of final rest, it could be distinguished from samsara, and so could not really be nirvana." Corless, *The Vision of Buddhism*, p. 255.

196. *Nirvāṇa*, remarks Levin, "may be said to 'begin' when our motility is *deeply in touch* with the five senses and their respective fields and zones (vision, hearing, tactility, taste, and smell); for, at the level of synaesthesia, the stratum of 'intertwining,' there arises a 'great transcending awareness'. . . ." David Michael Levin, *The Body's Recollection of Being* (Boston: Routledge, 1985), p. 112.

197. Corless's device of crossing out the words "continual" and "freshness" in the succeeding sentence may have somewhat the same effect: "Nirvana . . . is continual [crossed out] freshness [crossed out]." He continues: "Zen calls it *shoshin*, 'beginner's mind', the innocent heart constantly awakening to the shock of wonder, like a child on Christmas morning. In the nirvanic mode, the mind does not plan or work. It marries each

moment flawlessly. It is spontaneous, it plays, it does not have an end in view nor a sense of time passing or space being passed through so as to get from here to there." Corless, *The Vision of Buddhism*, p. 281. In Candrakīrti's illuminating explication of Nāgārjuna (MK, 25:24), nirvāṇa is seen as "the utter dissipation of ontologizing thought," and indeed "the non-functioning of perceptions as signs of all named things." Quoted in David Loy, *Nonduality: A Study in Comparative Philosophy* (New Haven: Yale University Press, 1988), p. 250.

198. Wagner, "Critical Observations Concerning Husserl's Posthumous Writings," p. 221.

199. Kohák, *Idea and Experience* pp. 36–37.

200. Conze explains that "Nirvana is in no relation at all to his personal self, either positive or negative. Access to Nirvana is contingent on the extinction of his personal self and is possible only where his 'self' is not" (BTI, 71). Again: "Nirvana and I are absolutely different. I cannot get it, and it cannot get me. I can never find it, because I am no longer there when it is found. It cannot find me, because I am not there to be found. But Nirvana, the everlasting, is there all the time. . . . What keeps me apart from it, now, in me? Nothing real at all, since the self is a mere invention. So even now, in truth, there is no real difference at all between me and Nirvana. The two are identical" (BTI, 264).

201. Sangharakshita, *A Survey of Buddhism: Its Doctrines and Methods through the Ages* (London: Tharpa Publications, 1987), p. 145.

202. The *Kevaddhasutta* depicts *nirvāṇa* as "signless, boundless, all-luminous." *Dīgha Nikāya*, xi 85, in Maurice Walsche, trans., *Thus Have I Heard: The Long Discourses of the Buddha* (London: Wisdom Publications, 1987), p. 179. An alternative translation admonishes: "Do not think that this *[nirvāṇa]* is an empty or void state. There is this consciousness, without a distinguishing mark, infinite and shining everywhere . . . ; it is untouched by the material elements and not subject to any power." Cf. Loy, *Nonduality*, p. 193. In Conze's summation, "Nirvana = an invisible infinite consciousness, which shines everywhere" (BTI, 196).

203. In Corless's phenomenological elucidation: "The nama-rupa distinction is *not* a division into *mental and physical but into mental components as I perceive them and physical components as I perceive them.*" Corless, *The Vision of Buddhism*, p. 123.

204. Conze explains that "Nirvana is 'unthinkable', or 'inconceivable', if only because there is nothing general about it. . . ." (BTI, 57). Thus, "All conceptions of Nirvana are misconceptions" (BTI, 57).

205. For Bataille, inner experience "is not beyond expression—one doesn't betray it if one speaks of it—but it steals from the mind the answers it still had to the questions of knowledge. Experience reveals nothing and cannot found belief nor set out from it" (IE, 3–4).

206. Edward Conze, *Buddhism: Its Essence and Development* (New York: Philosophical Library, 1951), p. 40.

207. In Corless's penetrating assertion: "Samsara is repetition." Corless, *The Vision of Buddhism*, p. 281.

208. Quoted in Richard H. Robinson, *The Buddhist Religion: A Historical Introduction* (Belmont, Calif.: Dickenson, 1970), p. 18.

209. Hakuin, *Orategama*, in Dumoulin, *A History of Zen Buddhism*, p. 258.

210. Fink, "Phenomenological Philosophy of Husserl," p. 105. Fink's remark is echoed in that of Landgrebe: "This possibility of . . . self-knowing, which is the presup-

position for man's ability to turn himself critically toward all valuing and everything that is valued and everything that exists, is not derivable from anything else. . . . It is a *transcendental experience* in the following sense: it is the ground on the basis of which there is experience. . . ." Ludwig Landgrebe, "The Problem of the Beginning of Philosophy in Husserl's Phenomenology," in Lester E. Embree, ed., *World and Consciousness: Essays for Aron Gurwitsch* (Evanston, Ill.: Northwestern University Press, 1972), p. 52.

211. For Bataille, "no longer to wish oneself to be everything is to put everything into question" (IE, xxxii).

212. Fink, "Phenomenological Philosophy of Husserl," p. 131.

213. "Experience," Adorno remarks, "lives by consuming the standpoint; not until the standpoint is submerged in it would there be philosophy" (ND, 30).

214. In language arrestingly similar, Adorno writes: "To think non-thinking *(Nicht-denken)* is not a seamless consequence of thought" (AE, 25).

215. Huang-po Hsi-yün proclaims: "This mind is illuminated, and pure as the Void, without form. Any thought deviates from the true source" (OT, 87).

216. Menzan declares: "[I]f you think that *munen* (no-thought) is your real mind and become attached to the condition of no-thought where neither good nor evil arises, it is the same as thinking that where no-reflection exists is the mirror itself, and thus becoming attached to the backside of the mirror. If the mirror reflects nothing, it is the same as if it were a piece of stone or a tile, the function of the light of the mirror is lost." Menzan Zuiho Osho, *Jijuyu-zanmai* [Samādhi of the self] (DZ, 63).

217. "There are changes," as Bergson wisely notes, "but there are underneath the change no things which change: change has no need of a support . . . movement does not imply a mobile." Henri Bergson, "The Perception of Change" in *The Creative Mind* (New York: Philosophical Library, 1946), p. 173.

218. "O good friends, what is there for *wu* (of *wu-nien*, unconsciousness) to negate? And what is there for *nien* to be conscious of? *Wu* is to negate the notion of two forms (dualism), and to get rid of a mind which worries over things, while *nien* means to become conscious of the primary nature of Suchness *(tathatā);* for Suchness is the Body of Consciousness, and Consciousness is the Use of Suchness. It is the self-nature of Suchness to become conscious of itself. . . ." (NM, 59).

219. Stcherbatsky notes that "Instantaneous Being *(kṣaṇikatva),* [is] the fundamental doctrine by which all the Buddhist system is established 'at one stroke.'" F. Th. Stcherbatsky, *Buddhist Logic* (New York: Dover, 1962), 1:554. And in Adorno's remarkably congruent posture, "With the imposition of the persisting *(das Bleibende)* as the true, the onset of truth becomes the onset of deception" (AE, 17).

220. For Nāgārjuna, "'what is impermanent' does not exist in emptiness" (MK, 23:13; E, 211).

221. Hui-hai paradoxically avers: "[T]he 'right' dharma is neither wrong nor right" (HH, 118).

222. "The desire *to have*," Sartre tells us, "is at bottom reducible to the desire to be related to a certain object in a certain *relation of being*" (BN, 751).

223. In Sartre's sobering remark, "the recognition that it is impossible to *possess* an object involves for the for-itself a violent urge to *destroy* it" (BN, 756).

224. Sartre says, "All which I abandon, all which I give, I enjoy in a higher manner through the fact that I give it away. . . ." (BN, 758).

225. Heidegger contends that "The hand is infinitely different from all grasping

organs—paws, claws, or fangs—different by an abyss of essence. Only a being who can speak, that is, think, can have hands and can be handy in achieving works of handicraft. . . ." Martin Heidegger, *What Is Called Thinking?* trans. Fred D. Wieck and J. Glenn Gray (New York: Harper and Row, 1968), pp. 16–17.

226. Findlay discloses presence as a subtle brutality: "[T]he manifestation of bodies to the senses involves a violence." Findlay, *Discipline of the Cave*, p. 85.

227. In Daumal's lyrical expression:

> I am dead because I lack desire;
> I lack desire because I think I possess;
> I think I possess because I do not try to give.
> In trying to give, you see that you have nothing;
> Seeing you have nothing, you try to give of yourself;
> Trying to give of yourself, you see that you are nothing;
> Seeing you are nothing, you desire to become;
> In desiring to become, you begin to live.

René Daumal, *Mount Analogue: A Novel of Symbolically Authentic Non-Euclidean Adventures in Mountain Climbing*, trans. Roger Shattuck (Baltimore: Penguin, 1974), p. 113.

228. Taylor elaborates: "*Begriff, begreifen*, and *erfassen* all carry connotations of grasping and seizing. *Fassen* is to grasp, seize, hold, lay hold of, contain, include, apprehend, comprehend, conceive. The noun *Griff* means grip, grasp, hold, catch, or hand-hold." Mark C. Taylor, *Altarity* (Chicago: University of Chicago Press, 1987), p. 19n.

229. And Husserl is assuredly right in his contention that "experience is not an opening through which a world, existing prior to all experience, shines into a room of consciousness." Edmund Husserl, *Formal and Transcendental Logic*, trans. Dorion Cairns (The Hague: Martinus Nijhoff, 1969), p. 206.

230. "All sudden understanding is in the last analysis the revelation of a clear non-understanding" (GH, 8).

231. Of Heidegger's parallel notion, Levin very helpfully remarks: "The ideal of Gelassenheit calls for a gaze which is relaxed, playful, gentle, caring; a gaze which moves freely, and with good feeling; a gaze which is alive with awareness; a gaze at peace with itself, not moved, at the deepest level of its motivation, by anxiety, phobia, defensiveness and aggression; a gaze which resists falling into patterns of seeing that are rigid, dogmatic, prejudiced, and stereotyping; a gaze which moves into the world bringing with it peace and respect, because it is rooted in, and issues from, a place of integrity and deep self-respect." David Michael Levin, *The Opening of Vision* (London: Routledge and Kegan Paul, 1988), p. 238.

Mindless Minding: Reflections on Intentionality

The haiku by Ryōta is from Harold G. Henderson, *An Introduction to Haiku: An Anthology of Poems and Poets from Bashō to Shiki* (Garden City, N.Y.: Doubleday, 1958), p. 119.

1. Act 1, scene 2 of *The Winter's Tale*, in *The Arden Edition of the Works of William Shakespeare*, ed. J. H. Pafford (Cambridge: Harvard University Press, 1963), p. 18.

2. Merleau-Ponty perceives that "The whole Husserlian analysis is blocked by the framework of *acts* which imposes upon it the philosophy of *consciousness*" (VI, 244).

3. In Sartre's exuberant claim: "To know is to devour with the eyes" (BN, 739).

4. Suzuki voices the obligatory Zen epistemology: "To know the flower is to become the flower, to be the flower, to bloom as the flower, and to enjoy the sunlight as well as the rainfall. When this is done, the flower speaks to me and I know all its secrets, all its joys, all its sufferings; that is, all its life vibrating within itself." D. T. Suzuki, "East and West," in Robert Sohl and Audrey Carr, eds., *The Gospel According to Zen: Beyond the Death of God* (New York: Mentor, 1970), p. 85.

5. Krishnamurti sagely affirms, "If I follow a particular method of knowing myself, then I shall have the result which that system necessitates; but the result will obviously not be the understanding of myself. . . . there is no method for self-knowledge." J. Krishnamurti, "Self-Knowledge," in Sohl and Carr, *The Gospel According to Zen*, p. 101.

6. Retaining the word, but altering its significance, Merleau-Ponty proposes that "Consciousness is . . . not a matter of 'I think that' but of 'I can'" (PhP, 137).

7. Pierre Trotignon, "The End and Time," in A.-T. Tymieniecka, ed., *Analecta Husserliana* 9, p. 302.

8. Phenomenology, according to Merleau-Ponty, is "an ontology that obliges whatever is not nothing to *present* itself to the consciousness across *Abschattungen* and as deriving from an originating donation which is an *act*, i.e., one *Erlebnis* among others. . . ." (VI, 244).

9. Sartre applauds "modern thought" for "reducing the existent to the series of appearances which manifest it" (BN, 3), and seems consistently to confuse "appearance" with both "appearing" and the *object as it appears* (i.e., the phenomenon in the Husserlian sense). Cf. BN, 3–7.

10. We must ask "of our experience of the world what the world is before it is a thing one speaks of and which is taken for granted, before it has been reduced to a set of manageable, disposable significations. . . ." (VI, 102).

11. In Lévinas's exposition, "Intentionality signifies an exteriority in immanence and the immanence of all exteriority." Emmanuel Lévinas, "Beyond Intentionality" (PFT, 106).

12. Jean-Paul Sartre, "Intentionality: A Fundamental Idea of Husserl's Phenomenology," trans. Joseph P. Fell, *Journal of the British Society for Phenomenology* 1 (1970): 4–5.

13. Aron Gurwitsch, "On the Intentionality of Consciousness," in Marvin Farber, ed., *Philosophical Essays in Memory of Edmund Husserl* (Cambridge: Harvard University Press, 1940), and reprinted in Joseph J. Kockelmans, ed., *Phenomenology: The Philosophy of Edmund Husserl and Its Interpretation* (Cambridge: Harvard University Press, 1940), pp. 135–36.

14. What, by the way, will *that* be? The Venerable Somaloka once conveyed to me this very question as a puzzle (not to say *koan*). "What will your very next thought be?" If I "know," I am wrong. For to know my next thought is thereby to entertain it, and in thus entertaining it, it ceases to be *next*. Suppose, moreover, that I believe my next thought will

concern *X*, and want to test the hypothesis. The moment comes. I will not be thinking about *X*, but checking to see whether I am thinking about *X*—thinking about "thinking about *X*." The prediction could be proved correct only if I ceased to care whether it were correct or not. So long as its truth matters, I am wrong. Thus, I cannot deliberately set out to ensure the truth of the prognosis. Thoughts simply "arise." This, I've come to call "Somaloka's paradox." Allen Ginsberg concomitantly queries, "For where does a thought come from? You can't trace it back to a womb, a thought is 'unborn.'" "Meditation and Poetics" (BSM, 97). Indeed, "You can't go back and change the sequence of the thoughts you had; you can't revise the process of thinking or deny what was thought, but thought obliterates itself anyway. You don't have to worry about that, you can go on with the next thought" (BSM, 99). As Agamben says, "*We can repeat that which has been said. But that which has been thought can never be said again*" (PN, 108).

15. Yet, as Brand rightly acknowledges, "True being is not being object; there is, therefore, no truth of one being." Gerd Brand, "Intentionality, Reduction, and Intentional Analysis in Husserl's Later Manuscripts," in *Welt, Ich, und Zeit* (The Hague: Martinus Nijhoff, 1955), and reprinted in Kockelmans, *Philosophy of Edmund Husserl and Its Interpretation*, p. 204.

16. Franz Brentano, *Psychology from an Empirical Standpoint*, ed. Linda L. McAlister; trans. D. B. Terrell, Antos C. Rancurello and Linda L. McAlister (New York: Humanities, 1973), pp. 88–89.

17. See the second chapter of my *Foundations for a Phenomenological Theology* (Lewiston, N.Y.: Edwin Mellen Press, 1988). Chisholm's encyclopedia article is very helpful in this connection. See Roderick M. Chisholm, "Intentionality," in *The Encyclopedia of Philosophy*, ed. Paul Edwards (New York: Macmillan, 1972), 4:201–4.

18. Nietzsche's repudiation of subjectivity is unmistakably Buddhist in its implications: "There is no 'being' behind doing, effecting, becoming; 'the doer' is merely a fiction added to the deed—the deed is everything." Friedrich Nietzsche, *On the Genealogy of Morals*, trans. Walter Kaufmann and R. J. Hollingdale (New York: Vintage, 1968), p. 13. Again: "If I say 'lightning flashes,' I have posited the flash once as an activity and a second time as a subject, and thus added to the event a being that is not one with the event but is rather fixed, *is*, and does not 'become.'" Friedrich Nietzsche, *The Will to Power*, trans. Walter Kaufmann and R. J. Hollingdale (New York: Vintage, 1968), p. 531.

19. In Anthony Piccione's poetic enquiry:

> If this is not the world, why are we here?
> Well, we will call this silence the universe.

Anthony Piccione, "Visit from a Friend," in *Seeing it was So* (Brockport, N.Y.: BOA Editions, Ltd., 1986), p. 78. Used with permission of the author.

20. Stephen Berg, poetically voicing a Buddhist alternative to Plato, writes of "forgetting in which only this moment has meaning." "Oblivion" (BSM, 29).

21. Milton Fisk, *Nature and Necessity: An Essay in Physical Ontology* (Bloomington: Indiana University Press, 1973), p. 183.

22. Yet, according to Nietzsche, once a given conscious activity has terminated, "We separate ourselves, the doers, from the deed, and we make use of this pattern

everywhere—we seek a doer for every event. What is it we have done? We have misunderstood the feeling of strength, tension, resistance, a muscular feeling that is already the beginning of the act, as the cause. . . . A necessary sequence of states does not imply a causal relationship between them. . . . If I think of the muscle apart from its 'effects,' I negate it. . . . A 'thing' is the sum of its effects." Nietzsche, *Will to Power*, p. 551.

23. Merleau-Ponty is clear that "movement is never the successive occupation, by a moving body, of every position between two extremes" (PhP, 269); "The moving object . . . is not identical *beneath* the phases of movement, it is identical *in* them" (PhP, 273).

24. "To reflect," Merleau-Ponty remarks, "is not to coincide with the flux from its source unto its last ramifications; it is to disengage from the things, perceptions, world, and perception of the world, by submitting them to a systematic variation. . . ." (VI, 45–46).

25. This is captured in Lispector's words: "But the instant, the very instant—the right now—*that* is unimaginable, between the right now and the I there is no space: it is just now, inside me" (GH, 70). For Merleau-Ponty, "Consciousness . . . is, though not atomized into instants, at least haunted by the specter of the instant which it is obliged continually to exorcise by a free act" (PhP, 438).

26. Jean-Paul Sartre, *Nausea*, trans. Lloyd Alexander (New York: New Directions, 1964), pp. 96–97.

27. Sartre advances that "There has been no break in continuity within the flux of the temporal development, for that would force us to return to the inadmissible concept of the infinite divisibility of time and of the temporal point or instant as the limit of the division. Neither has there been an abrupt interpolation of an opaque element to separate prior from subsequent in the way that a knife blade cuts a piece of fruit in two. . . . What separates prior from subsequent is exactly *nothing*" (BN, 64).

28. Gurwitsch, "Intentionality of Consciousness," p. 135.

29. Accordingly, "the *intentional* analysis that tries to compose the field with intentional threads does not see that the threads are emanations and idealizations of one fabric, differentiations of the fabric" (VI, 231).

30. Though intentionality is a certain "directedness" of consciousness, "A *direction*," Merleau-Ponty observes, "is not *in* space: it is in filigree across it—It is therefore transposable to thought" (VI, 222).

31. George Berkeley, "Three Dialogues Between Hylas and Philonous," in *The Principles of Human Knowledge and Three Dialogues Between Hylas and Philonous* (Gloucester, Mass.: Peter Smith, 1978), p. 186.

32. In Claudel's vibrant depiction, "We can thus see in the eye a sort of reduced, portable sun, endowed, like its prototype, with the ability to establish a radius from itself to every point on the circumference [Nous pouvons donc voir dans l'oeil une sorte de soleil réduit, portatif, doué, comme son prototype, de la faculté d''établir un *rayon* de lui à tout point de la circonférence]." Paul Claudel, *Art poétique* (Paris: Mercure de France, 1929), p. 106. Heidegger provides the needed complement to Claudel's proposal: "In the Greek language, one is not speaking about the action of seeing, about *vidēre*, but about that which gleams and radiates. But it can radiate only if openness has already been granted. The beam of light does not first create the opening, openness, it only traverses it." Martin Heidegger, "The End of Philosophy and the Task of Thinking," in David Farrell Krell, ed., *Martin Heidegger: Basic Writings* (New York: Harper and Row, 1977), p. 385.

33. We learn from Merton that "For Hui-neng there is no primal 'object' on which to stand, there is no stand, the 'seeing' of Zen is a non-seeing, as Suzuki says, describing Hui-neng's teaching, 'The seeing is the result of having nothing to stand on.' Hence, illumination is not a matter of 'seeing purity' or 'emptiness' as an object which one contemplates or in which one becomes immersed. It is simple 'pure seeing,' beyond subject and object, and therefore 'no-seeing.'" Thomas Merton, *Mystics and Zen Masters* (New York: Farrar, Straus & Giroux, 1967) p. 32.

34. Furthermore, "the unreflected [*irréfléchi*] comes into existence for us only through reflection" (PP, 30).

35. Merleau-Ponty discloses that "if it [depth] were a dimension, it would be the *first* one; there are forms and definite planes only if it is stipulated how far from me their different parts are. But a *first* dimension that contains all the others is no longer a dimension, at least in the ordinary sense of a *certain relationship* according to which we make measurements. Depth thus understood is, rather, the experience of the reversibility of dimensions, of a global 'locality'—every thing in the same place at the same time, a locality from which height, width, and depth are abstracted, of a voluminosity we express in a word when we say that a thing is *there*." Merleau-Ponty, "Eye and Mind" (PP, 180).

36. Dwight Goddard, ed., *A Buddhist Bible* (Boston: Beacon Press, 1970), pp. 110–11.

37. Ibid., p. 127.

38. David Michael Levin, *The Body's Recollection of Being*: *Phenomenological Psychology and the Deconstruction of Nihilism* (Boston: Routledge, 1985), p. 274.

39. In Sartre's depiction, "Consciousness has nothing substantial, it is pure 'appearance' in the sense that it exists only to the degree to which it appears. But it is precisely because consciousness is pure appearance, because it is total emptiness (since the entire world is outside it)—it is because of this identity of appearance and existence within it that it can be considered absolute" (BN, 17). Turning precisely upon the denial this identity, Buddhism discloses consciousness as a "non-substantial relative."

40. Quoted in Robert Denoon Cumming, ed., *The Philosophy of Jean-Paul Sartre* (New York: Vantage, 1965), p. 19. I prefer Cumming's more vivid translation to Fell's paler version: "[W]e have all believed that the spidery mind trapped things in its web, covered them with a white spit and slowly swallowed them, reducing them to its own substance." Jean-Paul Sartre, "Intentionality," p. 4.

41. Sartre explains that "The known is transformed into *me* . . . the known remains in the same place, indefinitely absorbed, devoured, and yet indefinitely intact, wholly digested and yet wholly outside, as indigestible as stone . . . the 'digested indigestible' . . ." (BN, 739); "we are not yet rid of that primitive illusion . . . according to which to know is to eat—that is, to ingest the known object, to fill oneself with it *(Erfüllung),* and to digest it ('assimilation')" (BN, 258–59).

42. Merleau-Ponty notes that "the mobile entity has only a style" (PhP, 274).

43. Levin writes: "Depicted in its archetypal form, i.e., as a circle, the hermeneutical gesture . . . is, of course, a welcoming, gathering into a whole; but the whole it makes is open, not totalized. . . . As a gathering which encircles, the hermeneutical gesture inevitably alludes to a center, something precious and worthy of protection. But the center is only *evoked* by the encircling: the gesture makes no move to point to it *directly* . . . there is 'nothing' in this center—nothing at all. In the center of the hermeneutical circle, 'there

is' only emptiness, the presencing of an absence, the absencing of a presence. No origin. No goal . . . nothing is there to be grasped, nothing to be posited, nothing to be possessed, nothing reached." David Levin, *The Body's Recollection of Being*, pp. 164–65.

44. Cf. David Loy, *Nonduality: A Study in Comparative Philosophy* (New Haven: Yale University Press, 1988), p. 263.

45. Conze is ready with a response: "Just as a weak man gets up and can stand upright by leaning on a stick or hanging on to a rope, so thought and its concomitants arise through having sights, etc., to: mind-objects for their objective support, and through them they also maintain themselves" (BTI, 150).

46. As Merleau-Ponty attests, "The philosopher's manner of question is therefore not that of *cognition*; being and the world are not for the philosopher unknowns such as are to be determined through their relation with known terms, where both known and unknown terms belong in advance to the same order of *variables* which an active thought seeks to approximate as closely as possible. Nor is philosophy an *awakening of consciousness (prise de conscience)*: it is not a matter of philosophy rediscovering in a legislative consciousness the signification it would have given to the world and to being by nominal definition" (VI, 101).

47. "A philosopher," writes Agamben, "is one who, having been surprised by language, having thus abandoned his habitual dwelling place in the word, must now return to where language already happened to him. He must 'surprise the surprise,' be at home in the marvel and in the division" (PN, 93–94).

48. "Perception opens the world to me as the surgeon opens a body, catching sight, through the window he has contrived, of the organs in full functioning, taken *in their activity*, seen sideways" (VI, 218).

49. Yet, as Lévinas proposes, "everything happens as if, in its lucidity, the reason that identifies being were sleepwalking or daydreaming, as if, despite its lucidity as regards objective order, it were sleeping off some mysterious wine in broad daylight." Emmanuel Lévinas, "Philosophy and Awakening" (WCAS, 210).

50. Robert Sokolowski, *The Formation of Husserl's Concept of Constitution* (The Hague: Martinus Nijhoff, 1964), p. 135.

51. J. N. Findlay, *Ascent to the Absolute: Metaphysical Papers and Lectures* (New York: Humanities, 1970), p. 244.

52. Martin Heidegger, *Identity and Difference* (New York: Harper and Row, 1969), p. 47.

53. Merleau-Ponty supplements: "[I]n the absence of all difference, there would be no mediation, movement, transformation; one would remain in full positivity. But there is no self-mediation either if the mediator is the simple or absolute negation of the mediated: the absolute negation would simply annihilate the mediated and, turning against itself, would annihilate itself also, so that there would still be no mediation, but a pure and simple retreat toward positivity. It is therefore ruled out that the mediation have its origin in the positive term, as though it were one of its *properties*—but it is likewise precluded that the mediation come to the positive term from an abyss of exterior negativity, which would have no hold on it and would leave it intact" (VI, 92).

54. Martin Heidegger, *Poetry, Language, Thought* (New York: Harper, 1971), p. 202.

55. In Sartre's portrayal, "*nothingness haunts being*" (BN, 49).

56. "With transcendence I show that the visible is invisible. . . ." (VI, 220).

57. Joseph P. Fell, "Battle of the Giants Over Being," in Paul Arthur Schilpp, ed., *The Philosophy of Jean-Paul Sartre* (La Salle, Ill.: Open Court, 1981), p. 273.

58. Klaus Hartmann, *Sartre's Ontology: A Study of* Being and Nothingness *in the Light of Hegel's Logic* (Evanston, Ill.: Northwestern University Press, 1966), p. 6.

59. In this connection, Merleau-Ponty speaks of "that inner weakness which prevents us from ever achieving the density of an absolute individual" (PhP, 428).

60. In Klee's words, "I cannot be caught in immanence *[Je suis insaissable dans l'immanence].*" Quoted in Merleau-Ponty, "Eye and Mind" (PP, 188).

61. For Adorno: "[T]he conceived world is not its own but a world hostile to the subject.

"All but unrecognizably, this is attested by Husserl's doctrine of essence perception. What this amounts to is totally alien to the consciousness that grasps it." (ND, 167).

62. "The for-itself *is*, in the manner of an event. . . ." (BN, 127).

63. "Nothing said of the subject is false," advises Merleau-Ponty. "[I]t is true that the subject as an absolute presence to itself is rigorously indeclinable, and that nothing could happen to it of which it did not bear within itself the lineaments" (PhP, 426–27).

64. Compare the irony of Sartre's situation: "I want to grasp this being and I no longer find anything but *myself*" (BN, 297).

65. For Merleau-Ponty, "the philosopher is always implicated in the problems he poses. . . ." (VI, 90).

66. "The in-itself," Sartre tells us, "is full of itself, and no more total plenitude can be imagined, no more perfect equivalence of content to container. There is not the slightest emptiness in being, not the tiniest crack through which nothingness might slip in" (BN, 120–21).

67. An adequate phenomenology "must question the world, it must enter into the forest of references that our interrogation arouses in it, it must make it say, finally, what in its silence *it means to say*. . . ." (VI, 39).

68. As Merleau-Ponty affirms, "The only way to ensure my access to the things themselves would be to purify my notion of the subjectivity completely. . . ." (VI, 52).

69. Says Yün-mên Wên-yen: "Even though I tell you that there is nothing lacking within you, this too is deceit" (OT, 284).

70. For Sartre, "the lemon is extended throughout its qualities, and each of its qualities is extended throughout each of the others. It is the sourness of the lemon which is yellow, it is the yellow of the lemon which is sour. We eat the color of a cake, and the taste of this cake is the instrument which reveals its shape and its color to what we may call the alimentary intuition. . . . it is this total interpenetration which we call the *this*" (BN, 257).

71. Heidegger's remark is pertinent: "Nothingness is neither an object nor a being at all. Nothingness neither comes forth by itself alone nor together with beings to which it clings, as it were. Nothingness is the making possible of the openness to beings as such for human Dasein. Nothingness does not first stand as a counter-concept to beings, but belongs originally to their very essence [Das Nichts ist weder ein Gegenstand noch überhaupt ein Seiendes. Das Nichts kommt weder für sich vor noch neben dem Seienden, dem es sich gleichsam anhängt. Das Nicht ist die Ermöglichung der Offenbarkeit des Seienden als eines solchen für das menschliche Dasein. Das Nichts gibt nicht erst den

Gegenbegriff zum Seienden her, sondern gehört ursprünglich zum Wesen selbst].” Martin Heidegger, *Wegmarken* (Frankfurt am Main: Klostermann, 1967), p. 12.

72. Heidegger suggests that “nothingness, as the not-ness of beings, is the sharpest opponent of pure nothing. Nothingness is never nothing; even less is it a something in the sense of an object. It is being itself, to the truth of which man is converted when he has overcome himself as subject, and that means when he no longer posits beings as objects [Aber das Nichts ist als das Nichthafte des Seienden der schärfste Wiederpart des bloß Nichtigen. Das Nichts ist niemals nichts, es ist ebensowenig ein Etwas im Sinne eines Gegenstandes, est ist das Sein selbst, desen Wahrheit der Mensch dann übereignet wird, wenn er sich als Subjekt überwunden hat und d. h., wenn er das Seiend nicht mehr als Objekt vorstellt].” Martin Heidegger, *Holzwege* (Frankfurt am Main: Klostermann, 1950), p. 104. Sartre adds that “this nothing because it is nothingness is impassable” (BN, 296).

73. For Adorno, “Total contradiction is nothing but the manifested untruth of total identification” (ND, 6).

74. For Merleau-Ponty, “It is from this test that the essence emerges—it is therefore not a positive being. It is an in-variant, it is exactly that whose change or absence would alter or destroy the thing; and the solidity, the essentiality of the essence is exactly measured by the power we have to vary the thing” (VI, 111).

75. For Heidegger, “This nothingness which is not a being and which, at the same time, *is* is not a nothing. It belongs to that which is present. Being and nothingness do not exist alongside each other. One uses the other in an affinity whose fullness of essence we have hardly begun to comprehend. . . . Being ‘is’ as little as nothingness. But both ‘exist’ [Dieses Nichts, das nicht das Seiende ist und das *es* gleichwohl *gibt*, ist nicht Nichtiges. Es gehört zum Anwesen. Sein und Nichts gibt es nicht nebeneinander. Eines verwendet sich für das Andere in einer Verwandtschaft, deren Wesensfülle wir noch kaum bedacht haben . . . Das »ist« so wenig wie das Nichts. Aber *es gibt* beides].” Heidegger, *Wegmarken*, p. 247. Yet, in Sartre’s words, “Nothingness is always an *elsewhere*. . . .” (BN, 126).

76. More searchingly, as Nishitani remarks, “true nothingness means that there is no thing that is nothingness, and this is *absolute nothingness*.” Keiji Nishitani, *Religion and Nothingness*, trans. Jan Van Bragt (Berkeley: University of California Press, 1982), p. 70.

77. Donald S. Lopez Jr., *The Heart Sutra Explained: Indian and Tibetan Commentaries* (Albany: SUNY Press, 1988), p. 19. Lopez observes that “There is a critical difference between form being empty and form being emptiness. . . .” Lopez, p. 58. There is the story of a monk reciting the passage in the *Diamond Sutra*, “[I]f one sees that *forms are not forms*, he then sees Buddha.” The Master was passing by and heard it. He then said to the monk, “You recite wrongly. It goes like this: ‘If one sees that *forms are forms*, he then sees Buddha.’” The monk exclaimed, “What you have said is just the opposite to the words of the *Sutra*!” The Master then replied, “How can a blind man read the *Sutra*?” (OT, 11).

78. In Stcherbatsky’s engaging admission, “But, although the conception of an element of existence has given rise to an imposing superstructure in the shape of a consistent system of philosophy, its inmost nature remains a riddle. What is *dharma*? It is inconceivable! It is subtle! No one will ever be able to tell what its real nature *(dharma-svabhāva)* is! It is transcendental!” F. Th. Stcherbatsky, *The Central Conception of Buddhism and the Meaning of the Word “Dharma”* (India: Susil Gupta, 1956), p. 61. In

the Buddha's arresting evocation: "It is just through their essential nature that those *dharmas* are not a something. Their nature is non-nature, and their no-nature is their nature. Because all *dharmas* have one mark only, i.e., no mark. . . . the nature of all *dharmas* is no-nature, and their non-nature is their nature." *Aṣṭasāhasrikā*, viii, 192, in Conze, *Selected Sayings from the Perfection of Wisdom* (London: The Buddhist Society, 1955), p. 51.

79. Accordingly, "if being is wholly in itself, it is itself only in the night of identity, and my look, which draws it therefrom, destroys it as being. . . ." (VI, 75).

80. Dews bears witness to this loss—"the immanence of transcendental consciousness begins to fracture" (LD, 14)—and observes "the fracturing of the immanence of transcendental consciousness, its exposure to its repressed 'outside'" (LD, 17).

81. Compare Streng's translation: "One may not say that there is "emptiness *(śūnytā)*, nor that there is "non-emptiness."

"Nor that both [exist simultaneously], nor that neither exists; the purpose for saying ["emptiness"] is for the purpose of conveying knowledge" (MK, 21:11; E, 210).

82. In Nāgārjuna's words, "The wise men (i.e., enlightened ones) have said that *śūnyatā* or the nature of thusness is the relinquishing of all false views. Yet it is said that those who adhere to the idea or concept of *śūnyatā* are incorrigible" (MK, 13:8; N, 93). Compare: "Emptiness is proclaimed by the victorious one as the refutation of all viewpoints;

"But those who hold "emptiness" as a viewpoint—[the true perceivers] have called those "incurable" *(asādhya)*" (MK, 13:8; E, 198).

Streng explains that "The purpose of Nagarjuna's negations is not to describe *via negativa* an absolute which cannot be expressed, but to deny the illusion that such a self-existent reality exists" (E, 146). Again, N0g0rjuna "is not saying that the true eternal state of reality is a blank; the calmness of *nirv0na* does not refer to an ontological stratum beneath or behind the flux of experienced existence" (E, 146).

83. This equilibrium is imaged in the dance of Bassui's snowflake: "Your end which is endless is as a snowflake dissolving in the pure air" (ZFZB, 79).

84. In the words of Yang-shan Hui-chi, "This is just like fooling a child with an empty hand, for there is nothing real in it at all" (OT, 213).

85. *Śūnyatā*, as Suzuki makes plain, "is neither quiet nor illuminating; it is neither real nor empty; it does not abide in the middle way; it is not-doing, it is no-effect-producing, and yet it functions with the utmost freedom: the Buddha-nature is all-inclusive" (NM, 35).

86. As Suzuki discerns, "Emptiness constantly falls within our reach; it is always with us and in us, and conditions all our knowledge, all our deeds, and is our life itself. It is only when we attempt to pick it up and hold it forth as something before our eyes that it eludes us, frustrates all our efforts, and vanishes like vapour. We are ever lured towards it, but it proves a will-o'-the-wisp" (NM, 60).

87. Edmund Husserl, *Cartesian Meditations: An Introduction to Phenomenology*, trans. Dorion Cairns (The Hague: Martinus Nijhoff, 1960), p. 20.

88. Edmund Husserl, *The Paris Lectures*, trans. Peter Koestenbaum (The Hague: Nijhoff, 1967), p. 9. For Sartre, "the *cogito* never gives out anything other than what we ask of it" (BN, 119).

89. M. C. Dillon, *Merleau-Ponty's Ontology* (Bloomington: Indiana University Press, 1988), p. 10.

90. Husserl, *Cartesian Meditations*, pp. 83–84.

91. "The bad dialectic," which seems to inform Husserl's vision, "is that which does not wish to lose its soul in order to save it, which wishes to be dialectical immediately, becomes autonomous, and ends up at cynicism, at formalism, for having eluded its own double meaning" (VI, 94).

92. In Brown's useful clarification: "*wer* = man, *ald* = age, old. The world may be taken to be the *manifest* properties of the all, its identity with the age of man being evident through the fact that man is a primary animal with a hand ('manifest' coming from *manus* = hand, *festus* = struck). Thus the world is considerably less than the all, which includes the unmanifest, but considerably greater than 'the' universe (more correctly, than *any* universe), which is merely the *formal appearance* of *one* of the possible manifestations which make up the world" (LF, 109n).

93. Husserl, *Cartesian Meditations*, p. 21. "Husserl," as Sartre reminds us, "remained timidly on the plane of functional description. Due to this fact he never passed beyond the pure description of the appearance as such; he has shut himself up inside the *cogito* and deserves . . . to be called a phenomenalist rather than a phenomenologist. . . . Heidegger . . . begins with the existential analytic without going through the *cogito*" (BN, 119).

94. Edmund Husserl, *The Crisis of European Sciences and Transcendental Phenomenology*: *An Introduction to Phenomenological Philosophy*, trans. David Carr (Evanston, Ill.: Northwestern University Press, 1970), p. 181.

95. Brown concludes: "Thus the world, whenever it appears as a physical universe, must always seem to us, its representatives, to be playing a kind of hide-and-seek with itself. What is revealed will be concealed, but what is concealed will again be revealed" (LF, 106).

96. Such a phenomenon would seem to disclose "a world almost demented because it is complete when it is yet only partial." Merleau-Ponty, "Eye and Mind" (PP, 166).

97. In the words of Saint-Exupéry, "Man is but a network of relationships. Only relationships matter to him [L'homme n'est qu'un noeud de relations. Les relations comptent seules pour l'hommes]." Antoine de Saint-Exupéry, *Pilote de Guerre* (New York: Éditions de la Maison Française, 1942), p. 176.

98. Adorno contends that "While philosophy of immanence . . . can only be ruptured immanently, i.e., in confrontation with its own untruth, its immanence itself is untruth" (AE, 25).

99. "What I am trying to translate to you is more mysterious; it is entwined in the very roots of being, in the impalpable source of sensations." J. Gasquet, *Cézanne*, quoted in Merleau-Ponty, "Eye and Mind" (PP, 159).

100. Husserl firmly denies "that there is no *essential difference* between transcendent and immanent," thus repudiating a theory of omniscience which would assert that "in the postulated divine intuition a spatial thing is a real *(reeles)* constituent, and indeed an experience itself, a constituent of the stream of the divine consciousness and the divine experience." Edmund Husserl, *Ideas*: *General Introduction to Pure Phenomenology*, trans. W. R. Gibson (New York: Macmillan, 1931), p. 123.

101. "*Āvidyā*," as Parsons tells us, "is the blindness of all organismic striving; it is the Greek eros, Hobbes' 'appetite' and 'aversion', Spinoza's 'power', Schopenhauer's 'will to live', Nietzsche's 'will to power', and Bergson's *élan vital*." Howard L. Parsons, *The Value of Buddhism for the Modern World,* Wheel Publication no. 232–33 (Kandy: Buddhist Publishing Society, 1976), p. 7.

102. Maurice Merleau-Ponty, *Signs*, trans. Richard C. McLeary (Evanston, Ill.: Northwestern University Press, 1964), p. 20. The same point is made in *The Visible and the Invisible*: "[T]o see is always to see more than one sees. . . ." (VI, 247).

103. J. N. Findlay, *Values and Intentions: A Study in Value-Theory and Philosophy of Mind* (New York: Humanities, 1968), p. 75.

104. Helmut Kuhn, "The Phenomenological Concept of 'Horizon,'" in Farber, *Philosophical Essays in Memory of Edmund Husserl*, p. 115.

105. George Quasha speaks appropriately of "a kind of shift in noetic ecology where the intensification of presence and responsiveness paradoxically extends the periphery of identity beyond the field of sentience. . . . it is here that one begins to assume responsibility for what lies outside the range of (ordinary) direct experience but is somehow still within one's field of resonance. The ability to consciously and articulately work within one's resonant (yet ultimately transient) field is primarily a function of practice." "A Virtual Account" (BSM, 210–11).

106. Cornelius A. Van Peursen, "The Horizon," in Frederick A. Elliston and Peter McCormick, eds., *Husserl: Expositions and Appraisals* (Notre Dame, Ind.: University of Notre Dame Press, 1977), pp. 182–85.

107. Ibid., p. 189.

108. Merleau-Ponty regards the "interior horizon" as "that darkness stuffed with visibility of which their surface is but the limit. . . ." (VI, 148).

109. Husserl, *Ideas*, trans. Gibson, p. 92; Edmund Husserl, *Ideas Pertaining to a Pure Phenomenology and to a Phenomenological Philosophy: First Book: General Introduction to a Pure Phenomenology*, trans. F. Kersten (The Hague: Martinus Nijhoff, 1982), p. 52.

110. In Lévinas's elucidation, "presence is produced as a *hand-holding-now (maintenant)*." Emmanuel Lévinas, "Beyond Intentionality" (PFT, 102).

111. Baudrillard cautions, however, that "We are witnessing the end of perspective and panoptic space. . . ." (SS, 54).

112. Merleau-Ponty explains that "The natural world is the horizon of all horizons, the style of all possible styles. . . ." (PhP, 330).

113. Loy, *Nonduality*, p. 86.

114. In Merleau-Ponty's formula, "A world . . . = an organized ensemble, which is *closed*, but which, strangely, is representative of all the rest, possesses its symbols, its equivalents for everything that is not itself" (VI, 223).

115. "The horizon no longer emits light of itself." Martin Heidegger, *The Question Concerning Technology and Other Essays*, trans. W. Lovitt (New York: Harper and Row, 1977), p. 107.

116. In Hartshorne's words, "objective necessity is merely what all real possibilities have in common. . . ." Charles Hartshorne, *Anselm's Discovery: A Re-Examination of the Ontological Proof for God's Existence* (La Salle, Ill.: Open Court, 1965), p. 43. Consider also Hartshorne's earlier declaration that "Necessary existence is not actuality, plus something, some necessity or other. It is nothing actual at all, but an essence, embodied in any and every total state of contingent actuality." Charles Hartshorne, *The Logic of Perfection and Other Essays in Neoclassical Metaphysics* (La Salle, Ill.: Open Court, 1962), p. 102.

117. Bataille speaks of "this secret" which "is only the inner presence, silent, unfathomable and naked, which an attention forever given to words (to objects) steals from us,

and which it ultimately gives back if we give it to those most transparent among objects. But this attention does not fully give it up unless we know how to detach it, in the end, even from its discontinuous objects, which we can do by choosing for them as a sort of resting place where they will finally disappear, the silence which is no longer anything" (IE, 16).

118. Saul Kripke, *Naming and Necessity* (Cambridge: Harvard University Press, 1972), pp. 113–14.

119. Dōgen, in Kazuaki Tanahashi, ed. and trans., *Moon in a Dewdrop: Writings of Zen Master Dōgen* (San Francisco: North Point Press, 1985), p. 71.

120. Merleau-Ponty believes that "With Husserl, the unicity of the world means not that it is actual and that every other world is imaginary, not that it is in itself and every other world for us only, but that it is at the root of every thought of possibles, that it even is surrounded with a halo of possibilities which are its attributes, which are *Möglichkeit an Wirklichkeit* or *Weltmöglichkeit*, that, taking on the form of the world of itself, this singular and perceived being has a sort of natural destination to be and to embrace every possible one can conceive of, to be *Weltall*" (VI, 228–29).

121. "For this Suchness is something uniform, something beyond going and coming, something eternally abiding *(sthititā)*, above change and separateness and discrimination *(nirvikalpā)*, absolutely one, betraying no traces of conscious striving, etc." *Aṣṭasāhasrikā-prajñāpāramitā*, chapter 26, "Tathatā" (translated in EZB III, 116). In Alan Davies' charmingly simple verse:

> How perfectly simple that this
> is all there is.
>
> (BSM, 55)

122. Robert Magliola, *Derrida on the Mend* (West Lafayette, Ind.: Purdue University Press, 1986), p. 104.

123. Jonathan Bennett, "Thoughtful Brutes," *Proceedings and Addresses of the American Philosophical Association* 62 (1988): 208, supplement. Cf. Robert Epstein, Robert P. Lanza, and B. F. Skinner, "'Self-Awareness' in the Pigeon," *Science* 212 (1980): 695ff.

124. Bennett, "Thoughtful Brutes," 207. Cf. Gordon G. Gallup, Jr., "Chimpanzees and Self-Awareness," in M. A. Roy, ed., *Species Identity and Attachment: A Phylogenetic Evaluation* (Garland: New York, 1980), pp. 223–43.

125. Bennett, "Thoughtful Brutes," p. 208.

126. Ibid., p. 209.

127. Ibid.

128. What Sartre says regarding the picture is of decisive relevance: "[I]t is necessary . . . that it exist *through me*. Evidently in one sense the ideal would be that I should sustain the picture in being by a sort of continuous creation and that consequently it should be *mine* as though by a perpetually renewed emanation. But in another sense it must be radically distinct from myself—in order that it may be *mine* but not *me*. . . . In fact it is this synthesis of self and not-self" (BN, 736–37).

129. We should ask, with Sarah Kofman, "But what is this *you* that you are when you believe that you are something?" Kofman, "Descartes Entrapped" (WCAS, 186).

130. For Sartre, "the for-itself is the foundation of its own nothingness in the form of

the phantom dyad—the reflection-reflecting. The reflecting exists only in order to reflect the reflection, and the reflection is the reflection only in so far as it refers to the reflecting. . . . the two terms of the quasi-dyad support their two nothingnesses on each other, conjointly annihilating themselves. It is necessary that the reflecting reflect *something* in order that the ensemble should not dissolve into nothing" (BN, 240–41).

131. The deep ambiguity of the vision of ourselves in the mirror is suggested in Merleau-Ponty's description: "[S]moking a pipe before a mirror, I feel the sleek, burning surface of the wood not only where my fingers are but also in those ghostlike fingers, those merely visible fingers inside the mirror. The mirror's ghost lies outside my body, and by the same token my own body's 'invisibility' can invest the other bodies I see. . . . The mirror itself is the instrument of a universal magic that changes things into a spectacle, spectacles into things, myself into another, and another into myself." Merleau-Ponty, "Eye and Mind" (PP, 168).

132. Lacan regards as a "false recurrence to infinity of reflexion" representing no "progress in interiority," the situation of an observer standing between two mirrors: "In seeing one's image repeated . . . [the observer] too is seen by the eyes of another when [she] looks at [herself], since without this other that is [her] image, [she] would not see [herself] seeing [herself]." *Écrits*: *A Selection*, trans. Alan Sheridan (New York: Norton, 1977), p. 134. Dews explains that "This is because, however many times it is reduplicated, the image of the observer seeing him- or herself, which appears in the mirror, must always remain the object of an uncaptured *pre-existing gaze*" (LD, 87–88).

133. In Bataille's interesting confession, "[E]verything in me gives itself to others" (IE, 129).

134. *Dhammapāda*, xx, 279, John Ross Carter and Mahinda Palihawadana, *The Dhammapada* (New York: Oxford University Press, 1987), p. 312.

135. In Bataille's striking phrase, "The 'I' embodies currish docility. . . ." (IE, 115).

136. As Descombes instructs us, "The Cartesian argument requires that we do not understand the pronoun *I* (in the cases when it is used by Descartes) and the name *Descartes* as mutually substitutable terms. . . . We should in no way say: Descartes is certain that Descartes thinks, but Descartes is not certain that Descartes exists, nor that Descartes is Descartes. We must say instead: Descartes is certain of a truth that he expresses to himself by saying 'I am, I exist,' but Descartes is not certain that there is, beyond that, a person named Descartes." Vincent Descombes, "Apropos of the 'Critique of the Subject' and of the Critique of this Critique" (WCAS, 124). More starkly, "Descartes is justified in saying 'I am not Descartes.' . . ." (WCAS, 125). Thus, "Descartes is justified in saying that Descartes is not the subject to which we should attribute the thoughts that we attribute, in our prephilosophical manner of speaking, to Descartes . . . Descartes is not the subject or his thoughts. We must not say: *Descartes thinks*. We must say: *it thinks in Descartes*" (WCAS, 125).

137. For Merleau-Ponty, "I can never say 'I' absolutely. . . ." (PhP, 208).

138. Courtine's interesting query "With regard to what unshakable certainty could the Cartesian 'foundation' reveal itself to be uncertain and ill-assured?" (Jean-François Courtine, "Voice of Conscience and Call of Being" [WCAS, 80]) is answered in a Heideggerean vein: *death*. Merleau-Ponty remarks that "The Cogito of Descartes (reflection) is an operation on significations, a statement of relations between them (and the significations themselves sedimented in acts of expression)" (VI, 170).

139. René Descartes, *Discourse on the Method of Rightly Conducting the Reason*, trans. Elizabeth S. Haldane and G. R. T. Ross (Cambridge: Cambridge University Press, 1934), p. 101. Corless cheerfully rejoins: "Descartes said, 'I think therefore I am,' but Buddhism replies, 'Think again.'" Roger J. Corless, *The Vision of Buddhism: The Space Under the Tree* (New York: Paragon House, 1989), p. 125.

140. Descartes, *Meditations on First Philosophy*, 1:150. In Lacoue-Labarthe's hypothetical musing "[I]t is the feeling that I exist that carves the bottomless pit of the experience of pain, to the extent indeed that it is marked indissociably as the revelation of the *né*-ant, of being as the nothing of the being. . . ." Philippe Lacoue-Labarthe, "The Response of Ulysses" (WCAS, 200).

141. Merleau-Ponty says, "Such certitude is limited to my existence and to my pure and completely naked thought. As soon as I make it specific with any particular thought, I fail, because, as Descartes explains, every particular thought uses premises not actually given. Thus the first truth, understood in this way, is the only truth. Or rather it cannot even be formulated as truth; it is experienced in the instant and in silence. The *cogito* understood in this way—in the skeptical way—does not account for our idea of truth" (PP, 21). A common response, and one concordant with Buddhist insight, is that Descartes is entitled to no more than the tautological "Thinking is occurring, therefore it is occurring." But is well to bear in mind that "even the 'it' contains an *interpretation* of the process, and does not belong to the process itself." Friedrich Nietzsche, *Beyond Good and Evil*, trans. Walter Kaufmann (New York: Random House, 1966), sec. 17, p. 24.

142. Descartes, *The Principles of Philosophy*, 2:232.

143. Jean-Paul Sartre, *The War Diaries of Jean-Paul Sartre: November 1939/March 1940*, trans. Quintin Hoare (New York: Pantheon, 1984), p. 36.

144. Notwithstanding, "The history of philosophy," Merleau-Ponty advises us, "is the history of implication" (VI, 198).

145. In Nietzsche's relentless challenge, "Who guarantees us that thanks to the *ergo* we will not gain something from this belief and its opinion, such that there remains something more than this: 'Something is believed, therefore something is believed'—vicious circle! Finally, one would have to know what 'being' is in order to get the *sum* from the *cogito*; one would also have to know what 'knowing' is: one starts from belief in logic—in the *ergo* before all else—and not uniquely from the position of a fact! Is 'certainty' possible in knowledge? Isn't immediate certainty perhaps a *contradictio in adjecto*? What is knowing in relation to being? For whoever brings to all these points a ready-made belief, Cartesian prudence no longer has meaning; it comes too late. Before coming to the problem of 'being,' one would have to have resolved the problem of the value of logic." Friedrich Nietzsche, *Nachgelaßene Fragmente* (1885), following Sarah Kofman, "Descartes Entrapped" (WCAS, 178).

146. The "import" is patent in Merleau-Ponty comment, "I read, let us say, the *Second Meditation*. It has indeed to do with me, but a me in idea, an idea which is, strictly speaking, neither mine nor, for that matter, Descartes', but that of any reflecting man. By following the meaning of the words and the argument, I reach the conclusion that indeed because I think, I am; but this is merely a verbal *cogito*, for I have grasped my thought and my existence only through the medium of language, and the true formula of this *cogito* should be: 'One thinks, therefore one is'" (PhP, 400).

147. Dillon, *Merleau-Ponty's Ontology*, pp. 14–15.

148. "This act grasps itself in its own operation [*à l'oeuvre*] and thus cannot doubt itself" (PP, 22).

149. "This supposes that the subject is perfectly transparent for itself, like an essence, and is incompatible with the idea of the hyperbolic doubt which even reaches to essences" (PP, 22).

150. Bataille remarks that "There is in divine things a transparency so great that one slips into the illuminated depths of laughter beginning even with opaque intentions" (IE, 33).

151. Writes Sartre: "The ideal nothingness in-itself is *quantity*. Quantity in fact is pure exteriority; it does not depend on the terms added but is only the affirmation of their independence" (BN, 263).

152. As Henry expresses it, "'I think' . . . is equal to 'I represent to myself that I think.' Which means that the Being of the subject is classed as the object of a representation, an object that, on the one hand, presupposes this subject and, on the other, never contains by itself, insofar as it is represented, any *reality*—just as to represent to oneself a thaler does not imply that one has one in one's pocket. Thus the foundation of any conceivable Being is stricken with a profound ontological indigence that prevents us from attributing to Being itself any kind of Being." Michel Henry, "The Critique of the Subject" (WCAS, 159).

153. The West is not, of course, devoid of proponents of nonduality. Fichte, for one, insists that "there is a consciousness in which the subjective and the objective are not at all to be separated, but are absolutely one and the very same. It is such a consciousness which we require in order to explain consciousness at all [es gibt ein Bewußtseyn, in welchem das Subjective und das Objective gar nicht zu trennen, sondern absolute Eins, und eben dasselbe sind. Ein solches Bewußtseyn sonach wäre es, dessen wir bedürften, um das Bewußtseyn überhaupt zu erklären]" Johann Gottlieb Fichte, *Versuch einer neuen Darstellung der Wissenschaftslehre*, in *Gesamtausgabe* I, 4, ed. Reinhard Lauth and Hans Gliwitzky (Stuttgart-Bad Cannstatt: Friedrich Frommann Verlag, 1970), p. 275.

154. Derrida provides "A more or less argot translation of the *cogito*," namely: "I am therefore dead." "This," he tells us, "can only be written." Jacques Derrida, *Glas*, trans. J. P. Leavey and R. A. Rand (Lincoln: University of Nebraska Press, 1986), p. 92. Blanchot echoes: "When the Cartesian 'I think, therefore I am' is written it is, in effect, rewritten as 'I think, therefore I am not'" Maurice Blanchot, *Thomas the Obscure*, trans. R. Lamberton (New York: David Lewis, 1973), p. 99.

155. Thus, "[T]o retire into oneself is also to leave oneself" (VI, 49). Elsewhere, and to the same effect: "[T]o retire into oneself is identical to leaving oneself" (VI, 65).

156. As Sartre admits, the immanence of the *cogito* is ruptured by this very self-disclosure: "The *self*. . . represents an ideal distance within the immanence of the subject in relation to himself" (BN, 123–24). Lévinas remarks that "In the identity of self-presence—in the silent tautology of the prereflexive—lies an avowal of difference between the same and the same, a disphasure, a difference at the heart of intimacy." Emmanuel Lévinas, "Philosophy and Awakening" (212–13).

157. Clearly, of course, "if I *desire* to be (an) I, if I *desire* myself, it must, following elementary logic, be because I am not it. Thus, this singular desire, by and large, is the desire of no subject." Mikkel Borch-Jacobsen, "The Freudian Subject, from Politics to Ethics" (WCAS, 66).

158. For Dōgen, "There is a 'who' in beyond-thinking. That 'who' upholds the self." Dōgen, *Shōbōgenzō Zazenshin*, in Menzan Zuiho Osho, *Jijuyu-zanmai* [Samādhi of the self] (DZ, 95).

159. Thus, in Granel's striking depiction, the cogito is seen as "an ontological puppet, whose inventor at the same time sketched a new figure of the philosopher as transcendental-talking ventriloquist. . . ." Gérard Granel, "Who Comes after the Subject?" (WCAS, 148).

160. Perhaps, in Lacoue-Labarthe's questioning proposal, "when Ulysses responds 'No One' (in Greek, *outis*, or *oudeis*), it is his proper name *(Odusseus)* that he only slightly deforms[.] . . . To the question of Polyphemus, 'Who?' Ulysses appears to respond negatively with a 'what'. . . ." Philippe Lacoue-Labarthe, "The Response of Ulysses" (WCAS, 199).

161. For Merleau-Ponty, "reflection reiterated ever anew would give only 'always the same thing'. . . ." (VI, 173).

162. Hui-neng speaks relevantly of "the voidness of non-void" (PS/pw, 26).

163. Adorno also sees that "The human mind is both true and a mirage: it is true because nothing is exempt from the dominance which it has brought into pure form; it is untrue because, interlocked with dominance, it is anything but the mind it believes and claims to be" (ND, 186).

164. Sartre, *War Diaries*, p. 211.

165. Ibid.

166. Suzuki rightly puzzles: "Where is this 'I'? What does it look like?" (NM, 115).

167. Merleau-Ponty speaks concomitantly of "a circle of the touched and the touching" in which "the touched takes hold of the touching." (VI, 143).

168. Explaining Lacan, Dews tells us that "An insistence upon the primacy of inwardness belongs to the illusions of the ego" (LD, 67).

169. Yün-mên Wên-yen relates: "Master Hsüeh-fêng said, 'The entire great earth is nothing but yourself.' . . . Master Lo-p'u said, 'When you hold a grain of dust, you are holding the great earth in your hand'" (OT, 287). It is also said, "I lift a finger and the whole universe moves along with it" (OT, 269).

170. Mu-chou Tao-tsung declares that "When one understands, a drop of water on the tip of a hair contains the great sea, and the great earth is contained in a speck of dust" (OT, 108).

171. Sartre, *War Diaries*, p. 211.

172. Bataille confesses, "This infinite improbability from which I come is beneath me like a void: my presence above this void is like the exercise of a fragile power, as if this void demanded the challenge that I *myself* bring it, I—that is to say the infinite, painful improbability of an irreplaceable being which I am" (IE, 69).

173. In Nāgārjuna's evocation, "We declare that whatever is relational origination is *śūnyatā*" (MK 24:18; N, 148).

174. Yet, as Nietzsche demands, "What does it matter what I am?" (following IE, 20).

175. "And when we ask the question: 'Who was the subject of this experience?' this question is perhaps already an answer, if, for the one who introduced it, it was affirmed in itself in this interrogative form, in substituting for the closed and unique 'I' the openness of a 'Who?' without answer. Not that this means that he simply had to ask

himself: 'What is this me that I am?,' but much more radically he had to seize hold of himself without letting go, no longer as an 'I?' but as a 'Who?,' the unknown and sliding being of a 'Who?' [«Qui fut le sujet de cette expérience?», cette question fait peut-être déjà réponse, si, à celui même qui l'a conduite, c'est sous cette forme interrogative qu'elle s'est affirmée en lui, en substituant au «Je» fermé et unique l'ouverture d'un «Qui?» sans réponse; non que cela signifie qu'il lui ait fallu seulement se demander: «Quel est ce moi que je suis?», mais bien plus radicalement se ressaisir sans relâche, non plus comme «Je», mais comme un «Qui», l'être inconnu et glissant d'un «Qui?» indéfini]." Maurice Blanchot, *L'Amitié* (Paris: Gallimard, 1971), p. 328.

176. In Merleau-Ponty's more accurate claim: "I do not perceive any more than I speak. . . ." (VI, 190).

177. As I have argued in a previous deposition, "How is one to distinguish the genuine 'creative power' of immediate experience from the 'degraded and bastard spontaneity' of the ego? *Phenomenologically*, there is only one course available: 'solar' and 'lunar' illumination must possess different *modes of appearing*. Sartre, in fact, must decide whether the sun/moon or the object/reflected metaphor is the more adequate. Moonlight, of course, is reflected sunlight, and its total effulgence is a 'sun-image.' The difference of appearance, however, is inescapable. Moonlight, as so many would-be poets have intoned, possesses a pale, ghostly luminescence qualitatively different from the bedazzling intensity of the sun. But the reflection of an object formed in a mirror ideally free from distortion is phenomenally indistinguishable from the object. If the ego is, as Sartre has maintained from the beginning, and as Ch'an itself suggests, the 'reflection' of reflecting consciousness, and if consciousness, reflective and prereflective alike, is, as Sartre vigorously insists, utterly vacuous and 'luminescent,' if the 'mind-mirror' is perfectly free from distortion, then it becomes impossible to see how any descriptive discrimination between 'image' and 'original,' formulated on purely phenomenological grounds, could be made." "Sartre and a Chinese Buddhist Theory of No-Self: The Mirroring of Mind," *Buddhist-Christian Studies* 9 (1989): 39.

178. Merleau-Ponty remarks that "This deceiving nature, this opaque something that would shut us up in our lights, is only a phantasm of our rigorism, a perhaps" (VI, 106).

179. The theory which Sartre erects is, of course, altogether too static to effect coherence with the dynamism of the Buddhist view. A psychic state, for example, must be understood not as a perduring abstractum, but more appropriately as "a snowball on the snow, rolling upon itself." Henri Bergson, *Creative Evolution*, trans. Arthur Mitchell (New York: Henry Holt, 1944), p. 2.

180. Like Bergson, Buddhism offers a dispositional analysis of the phenomenal realm *(saṁsāra):* "All reality is, therefore, tendency, if we agree to call tendency a nascent change of direction." Henri Bergson, "The Perception of Change" in *The Creative Mind* (New York: Philosophical Library, 1946), p. 222.

181. Trinh thi Minh-hà, *Woman, Native, Other: Writing, Postcoloniality and Feminism* (Bloomington: Indiana University Press, 1989), p. 22.

182. Ibid., pp. 22–23.

183. And as Bataille well knows, "the foolishness of the wisest is infinite" (IE, 198).

The haiku by Sodō is from Harold G. Henderson, *An Introduction to Haiku: An Anthology of Poems and Poets from Bashō to Shiki* (Garden City, N.Y.: Doubleday, 1958), p. 86.

Bibliography

Frequently Cited Texts

[AE] Adorno, Theodor W. *Against Epistemology: A Metacritique: Studies in Husserl and the Phenomenological Antinomies*. Translated by Willis Domingo. Cambridge: MIT Press, 1983.

[ND] Adorno, Theodor W. *Negative Dialectics*. Translated by E. B. Ashton. New York: Continuum, 1973.

[PN] Agamben, Giorgio. *Language and Death: The Place of Negativity*. Translated by Karen E. Pinkus and Michael Hardt. Minneapolis: University of Minnesota Press, 1991.

[IE] Bataille, George. *Inner Experience*. Translated by Leslie Anne Boldt. Albany: SUNY Press, 1988.

[SS] Baudrillard, Jean. *Simulations*. Translated by Paul Foss, Paul Patton, and Philip Beitchman. New York: Semiotext(e), 1983.

[HH] Blofeld, John, trans. *The Zen Teaching of Hui Hai on Sudden Illumination*. New York: Samuel Weiser, 1972.

[RM] Borradori, Giovanna, ed. *Recoding Metaphysics: The New Italian Philosophy*. Evanston, Ill.: Northwestern University Press, 1988.

[LF] Brown, G. Spencer. *Laws of Form*. New York: Bantam, 1973.

[TCB] Burtt, E. A., ed. *The Teachings of the Compassionate Buddha*. New York: New American Library, 1955.

[WCAS] Cadava, Eduardo, Peter Connor, and Jean-Luc Nancy, eds. *Who Comes After the Subject?* New York: Routledge, 1991.

[OT] Chang Chung-yuan. *Original Teachings of Ch'an Buddhism*. New York: Vintage, 1971.

[BTI] Conze, Edward. *Buddhist Thought in India: Three Phases of Buddhist Philosophy*. London: George Allen & Unwin, 1962.

[LD] Dews, Peter. *Logics of Disintegration: Post-structuralist Thought and the Claims of Critical Theory*. London: Verso, 1988.

[N] Inada, Kenneth K. *Nagarjuna: A Translation of his Mulamadhyamakakarika with an Introductory Essay*. Tokyo: Hokuseido Press, 1970.

[BSM] Johnson, Kent, and Craig Paulenich, eds. *Beneath a Single Moon: Buddhism in Contemporary American Poetry*. Boston: Shambhala, 1991.

[GH] Lispector, Clarice. *The Passion According to G. H.* Translated by Ronald W. Sousa. Minneapolis: University of Minnesota Press, 1988.

[PhP] Merleau-Ponty, Maurice. *Phenomenology of Perception*. Translated by Colin Smith. London: Routledge and Kegan Paul, 1962.

[PP] Merleau-Ponty, Maurice. *The Primacy of Perception and Other Essays on Phenomenological Psychology, and the Philosophy of Art, History and Politics*. Edited by James M. Edie. Evanston, Ill.: Northwestern University Press, 1964.

[VI] Merleau-Ponty, Maurice. *The Visible and the Invisible*. Edited by Claude Lefort and translated by Alphonso Lingis. Evanston, Ill.: Northwestern University Press, 1968.

[PFT] Montefiore, Alan, ed. *Philosophy in France Today*. Cambridge: Cambridge University Press, 1983.

[CPB] Murti, T. R. V. *The Central Philosophy of Buddhism: A Study of the Madhyamika System*. London: Allen & Unwin, 1987.

[DZ] Okumura, Shohaku, and Daitsu Tom Wright, trans. *Dogen Zen*. Kyoto: Kyoto Soto-Zen Center, 1988.

[PS/pw] Price, A. F., and Mou-Lam Wong, trans. *The Sutra of Hui Neng*. Boulder: Shambhala, 1969.

[ZFZB] Reps, Paul, ed. *Zen Flesh, Zen Bones: A Collection of Zen & Pre-Zen Writings*. Garden City: Doubleday, n.d.

[BN] Sartre, Jean-Paul. *Being and Nothingness: An Essay on Phenomenological Ontology*. Translated by Hazel E. Barnes. New York: Washington Square Press, 1971.

[TE] Sartre, Jean-Paul. *La transcendance de l'ego, Esquisse d'une description phénoménologique.* Edited by Sylvia Le Bon. Paris: Librarie philosophique J. Vrin, 1965. Translations by author.

[TI] Solé-Leris, Amadeo. *Tranquility and Insight: An Introduction to the Oldest Form of Buddhist Meditation*. Kandy, Sri Lanka: Buddhist Publication Society, Inc., 1992..

[E] Streng, Fredrick J. *Emptiness: A Study in Religious Meaning*. New York: Abingdon, 1967.

[EZB I] Suzuki, Daisetz Teitaro. *Essays in Zen Buddhism*. First Series. London: Rider, 1970.

[EZB III] Suzuki, Daisetz Teitaro. *Essays in Zen Buddhism*. Third Series. New York: Samuel Weiser, 1971.

[NM] Suzuki, Daisetz Teitaro. *The Zen Doctrine of No-Mind: The Significance of the Sutra of Hui-Neng (Wei-Lang)*. York Beach, Me: Samuel Weiser, 1981.

[PS/y] Yampolsky, Philip B. *The Platform Sutra of the Sixth Patriarch*. New York: Columbia University Press, 1967.

Other Texts Cited

Albrecht, Carl. *Das mystische Erkennen. Gnoseologie und philosophische Relevanz der mystischen Relation*. Bremen: C. Schüneman, 1958.

Alexander, H. G., ed. *The Leibniz-Clarke Correspondence, together with Extracts from Newton's* Principia *and* Optiks. Manchester: Manchester University Press, 1956.

Allen, Reginald E. "Participation and Predication in Plato's Middle Dialogues." In *Plato: A Collection of Critical Essays, I: Metaphysics and Epistemology*, edited by Gregory Vlastos. New York: Doubleday, 1971.

Almaas, A. H. *The Void: A Psychodynamic Investigation of the Relationship between Mind and Space*. Berkeley: Diamond Books, n.d.

Andrade, E. N. da C. *An Approach to Modern Physics*. New York: Doubleday Anchor Books, 1957.

Bachelard, Gaston. *La terre et les rêveries du repos*. Paris: Corti, 1948.

Badiou, Alain. "On a Finally Objectless Subject." In *Who Comes After the Subject?* [WCAS], edited by Eduardo Cadava et al. New York: Routledge, 1991.

Baier, Annette. *Postures of the Mind: Essays on Mind and Morals*. Minneapolis: University of Minnesota Press, 1985.

Beckh, Hermann. *Buddha und seine Lehre*. Stuttgart: Verlag Freies Geistesleben, 1958.

Bennett, Jonathan. "Thoughtful Brutes." *Proceedings and Address of the American Philosophical Association* 62 (1988).

Bergson, Henri. *Creative Evolution*. Translated by A. Mitchell. New York: Modern Library, 1944.

———. *The Creative Mind*. New York: Philosophical Library, 1946.

Berkeley, George. "Three Dialogues Between Hylas and Philonous." In *The Principles of Human Knowledge and Three Dialogues Between Hylas and Philonous*. Gloucester, Mass.: Peter Smith, 1978.

Blake, William. *The Marriage of Heaven and Hell*. London and New York: Oxford University Press, 1975.

Blanchot, Maurice. *L'Amitié*. Paris: Gallimard, 1971.

———. *Le Pas au-delà*. Paris: Gallimard, 1973.

———. *Thomas the Obscure*. Translated by R. Lamberton. New York: David Lewis, 1973.

Blyth, R. H. *Games Zen Masters Play*. New York: New American Library, 1976.

Borch-Jacobsen, Mikkel. "The Freudian Subject, from Politics to Ethics." In *Who Comes After the Subject?* [WCAS], edited by Eduardo Cadava et al. New York: Routledge, 1991.

Borges, Jorge Luis. *A Personal Anthology*. Edited by Anthony Kerrigan. New York: Grove Press, 1967.

Bourdieu, Pierre. "The Philosophical Institution." In *Philosophy in France Today* [PFT], edited by Alan Montefiore. Cambridge: Cambridge University Press, 1983.

Bouwsma, O. K. "Descartes' Evil Genius." *Philosophical Review* 58 (1949).

Brand, Gerd. "Intentionality, Reduction, and Intentional Analysis in Husserl's Later Manuscripts." In *Phenomenology: The Philosophy of Edmund Husserl and Its Interpretation,* by Joseph J. Kockelmans. Garden City, N.Y.: Doubleday, 1967.

———. *Welt, Ich, und Zeit.* The Hague: Martinus Nijhoff, 1955.

Breazeale, Daniel, ed. *Philosophy and Truth: Selections from Nietzsche's Notebooks of the Early 1870s*. Atlantic Highlands, N.J.: Humanities, 1979.

Bresson, François. "Perception et indices perceptifs." In *Logique et perception. Études d'épistémologie génétique*, vol. 6. Edited by Bruner, Bresson, Morf, and Piaget. Paris: Presses Universitaires de France, 1958.

Brumbaugh, Robert S. *The Philosophers of Greece*. Albany: SUNY Press, 1981.

Bruner, Bresson, Morf, and Piaget, eds. *Logique et perception. Études d'épistémologie génétique*, vol. 6. Paris: Presses Universitaires de France, 1958.

Buchler, Justus, ed. *Philosophical Writings of Peirce*. New York: Dover, 1955.

Buddhaghosa, Bhadantācariya. *The Path of Purification* (*Visuddhimagga*). Translated by Bhikkhu Ñaṇamoli. Colombo: Semage, 1956.

———. *The Path of Purification* (*Visuddhimagga*). Translated by Bhikkhu Ñaṇamoli. Berkeley, Calif.: Shambhala, 1976.

Burtt, E. A. "What Can Western Philosophy Learn from India?" *Philosophy East and West* 5 (1955).

Butchvarov, Panayot. *Being Qua Being: A Theory of Identity, Existence and Predication.* Bloomington: Indiana University Press, 1979.

Campbell, Joseph, ed. *Myths, Dreams and Religion*. New York: Dutton, 1970.

Camus, Albert "The Myth of Sisyphus." In *Existentialism: From Dostoevsky to Sartre*, edited by Walter Kaufmann. New York: New American Library, 1975.

Candrakīrti. *Lucid Exposition of the Middle Way: The Essential Chapters from the* Prasannapāda *of Candrakīrti*. Translated by Mervyn Sprung. Boulder, Colo.: Prajñā Press, 1969.

Carr, David. "Intentionality." In *Phenomenology and Philosophical Understanding,* edited by Edo Pivcevic. London: Cambridge University Press, 1975.

Cavell, Stanley. *Must We Mean What We Say? A Book of Essays*. New York: Charles Scribner's Sons, 1969.

Chang Chung-yuan. *Tao: A New Way of Thinking*. New York: Harper and Row, 1975.

Chang, Garma C. C., trans. *The Buddhist Teaching of Totality*. University Park: Pennsylvania State University Press, 1977.

Chisholm, Roderick M. "Intentionality." In *The Encyclopedia of Philosophy*, vol. 4. Edited by Paul Edwards. New York: Macmillan, 1972.

Claudel, Paul. *Art poétique*. Paris: Mercure de France, 1929.

Commins, Saxe, and Robert N. Linscott, eds. *Man and the Universe: The Philosophers of Science*. New York: Washington Square Press, 1969.

Conze, Edward. *Buddhism: Its Essence and Development*. New York: Philosophical Library, 1952.

———, trans. *Selected Sayings from the Perfection of Wisdom*. Boulder, Colo.: Prajñā Press, 1978.

Corless, Roger J. *The Vision of Buddhism: The Space Under the Tree*. New York: Paragon House, 1989.

Cumming, Robert Denoon, ed. *The Philosophy of Jean-Paul Sartre*. New York: Vantage, 1965.

Cusa, Nicholas of. *The Vision of God*. New York: Frederick Ungar, 1960.

Danto, Arthur C. *Mysticism and Morality: Oriental Thought and Moral Philosophy*. New York: Columbia University Press, 1988.

Daumal, René. *Mount Analogue: A Novel of Symbolically Authentic Non-Euclidean Adventures in Mountain Climbing*. Translated by Roger Shattuck. Baltimore: Penguin, 1974.

Deleuze, Gilles. *Nietzsche and Philosophy*. London: Athlone, 1983.

Derrida, Jacques. "'Eating Well,' or the Calculation of the Subject: An Interview with Jacques Derrida." In *Who Comes After the Subject?* [WCAS], edited by Eduardo Cadava et al. New York: Routledge, 1991.

———. *L'écriture et la différance*. Paris: Éditions du Seuil, 1967.

———. *Edmund Husserl's Origin of Geometry: An Introduction*. Translated by John P. Leavey. New York: Nicolas Hays, 1977.

———. *Of Grammatology*. Baltimore: Johns Hopkins University Press, 1976.

———. *Glas*. Translated by J. P. Leavey and R. A. Rand. Lincoln: University of Nebraska Press, 1986.

———. "Limited Inc abc . . ." *Glyph* 2 (1977).

———. *Marges de la philosophie*. Paris: Les Éditions de Minuit, 1972.

———. *Margins of Philosophy*. Chicago: University of Chicago Press, 1982.

———. *Speech and Phenomena and Other Essays on Husserl's Theory of Signs*. Translated by David B. Allison. Evanston, Ill.: Northwestern University Press, 1973.

———. *Writing and Difference*. Translated by Alan Bass. Chicago: University of Chicago Press, 1978.

Descartes, René. *Discourse on the Method of Rightly Conducting the Reason*. Translated by E. S. Haldane and G. R. T. Ross. Cambridge: Cambridge University Press, 1934.

———. *Meditations on First Philosophy*. Translated by John Cottingham. Cambridge: Cambridge University Press, 1986.

———. *The Principles of Philosophy*. Translated by Elizabeth S. Haldane and G. R. T. Ross. Cambridge: Cambridge University Press, 1972.

———. *Rules for the Direction of the Mind*. In *The Philosophical Works of Descartes*. Edited and translated by Elizabeth S. Haldane and G. R. T. Ross. New York: Dover, 1955.

Dillon, M. C. *Merleau-Ponty's Ontology*. Bloomington: Indiana University Press, 1988.

Duméry, Henry. *The Problem of God in Philosophy of Religion*. Translated by Charles Courtney. Evanston, Ill.: Northwestern University Press, 1964.

Dummett, Michael. *Truth and Other Enigmas*. Cambridge: Harvard University Press, 1978.

Dumoulin, Heinrich. *A History of Zen Buddhism*. New York: Random House, 1963.

———. *Östliche Meditation und christliche Mystik*. Freiburg and Munich: Alber, 1966.

———. *Zen Buddhism: A History*, vol. 1: *India and China*. Translated by James W. Heisig and Paul Knitter. New York: Macmillan, 1988.

Eliot, T. S. *The Complete Poems and Plays: 1909–1950*. New York: Harcourt, Brace & World, 1971.

Elliston, Frederick A. and Peter McCormick, eds. *Husserl: Expositions and Appraisals*. Notre Dame, Ind.: University of Notre Dame Press, 1977.

Elveton, R. O., ed. *The Phenomenology of Husserl: Selected Critical Readings*. Chicago: Quadrangle, 1970.

Embree, Lester E., ed. *World and Consciousness: Essays for Aron Gurwitsch*. Evanston, Ill.: Northwestern University Press, 1972.

Emerson, Ralph Waldo. "The Poet." In *Essays: Second Series*. New York: Lovell, Coryell, n. d.

Epstein, Robert, Robert P. Lanza, and B. F. Skinner, "'Self-Awareness' in the Pigeon." *Science* 212 (1980).

Fallico, Arturo B. *Art and Existentialism*. Englewood Cliffs, N.J.: Prentice-Hall, 1962.

Farber, Marvin ed. *Philosophical Essays in Memory of Edmund Husserl*. New York: Greenwood, 1968.

Fell, Joseph P. "Battle of the Giants Over Being." In Paul Arthur Schilpp, ed., *The Philosophy of Jean-Paul Sartre*. La Salle, Ill.: Open Court, 1981.

Fichte, Johann Gottlieb. *Die Wissenschaftslehre—Zweiter Vortrag im Jahre 1804*. Hamburg: Felix Meiner Verlag, 1975.

Findlay, J. N. *Ascent to the Absolute: Metaphysical Papers and Lectures*. New York: Humanities, 1970.

———. *The Discipline of the Cave*. New York: Humanities, 1966.

———. *Values and Intentions: A Study in Value-Theory and Philosophy of Mind*. New York: Humanities, 1968.

Fink, Eugen. "The Phenomenological Philosophy of Edmund Husserl and Contemporary Criticism." In *The Phenomenology of Husserl: Selected Critical Readings*, edited by R. O. Elveton. Chicago: Quadrangle, 1970.

Fisk, Milton. *Nature and Necessity: An Essay in Physical Ontology*. Bloomington: Indiana University Press, 1973.

Føllesdal, Dagfin. "Husserl's Notion of Noema." *The Journal of Philosophy* 66 (1969).

Foucault, Michael. *The Birth of the Clinic: An Archaeology of Medical Perception.* Translated by A. M. Sheridan Smith. New York: Pantheon, 1973.

———. *Language, Counter-Memory, Practice: Selected Essays and Interviews.* Edited by Donald F. Bouchard. Ithaca, N.Y.: Cornell University Press, 1977.

———. "The Order of Discourse." In *Untying the Text: A Post-Structuralist Reader,* edited by Robert Young. Boston: Routledge and Kegan Paul, 1981.

Frauwallner, Erich. *History of Indian Philosophy,* vol. 1. Translated by M. Bedekar. Delhi: Motilal Banaridass, 1973.

———. *Die Philosophie des Buddhismus.* Berlin: Akademie-Verlag, 1956.

Freeman, Kathleen. *Ancilla to the Pre-Socratic Philosophers: A Complete Translation of the Fragments in Diels'* Fragmente der Vorsokratiker. Cambridge: Harvard University Press, 1983.

Furley, David J., and R. E. Allen, eds. *Studies in Presocratic Philosophy,* vol. 2. New York: Humanities, 1975.

———. *Two Studies in the Greek Atomists.* Princeton: Princeton University Press, 1967.

Gadamer, Hans Georg. *Truth and Method.* New York: Seabury Press, 1975.

Gallup, Gordon G., Jr. "Chimpanzees and Self-Awareness." In *Species Identity and Attachment: A Phylogenetic Evaluation,* edited by M. A. Roy. New York: Garland, 1980.

Gargani, Aldo G. "Friction of Thought." In *Recoding Metaphysics* [RM], edited by Giovanna Borradori. Evanston, Ill.: Northwestern University Press, 1988.

Gasché, Rodolphe. "God, For Example." In *Phenomenology and the Numinous,* edited by André Schuwer. Pittsburgh: Simon Silverman Phenomenology Center, 1988.

———. *The Tain of the Mirror: Derrida and the Philosophy of Reflection.* Cambridge: Harvard University Press, 1986.

Gassiot-Talabot, Gérald, et al. *Figurations 1960-1973.* Paris: Klincksieck, 1973.

Goddard, Dwight, ed. *A Buddhist Bible.* Boston: Beacon Press, 1970.

Gordon, Jeffrey. "Dream-World or Life-World? A Phenomenological Solution to an Ancient Puzzle." *Husserl Studies* 2 (1985).

Graham, Dom Aelred. *The End of Religion.* New York: Harcourt Brace Jovanovich, 1971.

Granel, Gérard. "Who Comes After the Subject?" In *Who Comes After the Subject?* [WCAS], edited by Eduardo Cadava et al. New York: Routledge, 1991.

Grossman, Reinhardt. *Ontological Reduction.* Bloomington: Indiana University Press, 1973.

Guenther, Herbert V. *From Reductionism to Creativity: rDzogs-chen and the New Sciences of Mind.* Boston: Shambhala, 1989.

———. "Indian Buddhist Thought in Tibetan Perspective." In *Tibetan Buddhism in Western Perspective.* Berkeley, Calif.: Dharma Publishing, 1977.

Gurwitsch, Aron. *The Field of Consciousness.* Pittsburgh: Duquesne University Press, 1964.

———. "On the Intentionality of Consciousness." In *Philosophical Essays in Memory of Edmund Husserl,* edited by Marvin Farber. Cambridge: Harvard University Press, 1940.

———. *Studies in Phenomenology and Psychology.* Evanston, Ill.: Northwestern University Press, 1966.

Hanson, Norwood Russell. *Patterns of Discovery: An Inquiry into the Conceptual Foundations of Science.* Cambridge: Cambridge University Press, 1958.

Harding, D. E. "On Having No Head." In *The Mind's I: Fantasies and Reflections on Self and Soul,* edited by Douglas R. Hofstadter and Daniel C. Dennet. New York: Basic Books, 1981.

Hart, James G. "A Précis of an Husserlian Philosophical Theology." In *Essays in Phenomenological Theology,* edited by Steven W. Laycock and James G. Hart. Albany: SUNY Press, 1986.

Hartmann, Klaus. *Sartre's Ontology: A Study of* Being and Nothingness *in the Light of Hegel's Logic.* Evanston, Ill.: Northwestern University Press, 1966.

Hartshorne, Charles. *Anselm's Discovery: A Re-Examination of the Ontological Proof for God's Existence.* La Salle, Ill.: Open Court, 1965.

———. *The Logic of Perfection and Other Essays in Neoclassical Metaphysics.* La Salle, Ill.: Open Court, 1962.

Heidegger, Martin. *Martin Heidegger: Basic Writings.* Edited and translated by David Farrell Krell. New York: Harper and Row, 1977.

———. *Being and Time.* Translated by John Macquarrie and Edward Robinson. New York: Harper and Row, 1962.

———. *The Essence of Reasons/Vom Wesen des Grundes.* Bilingual edition. Translated by Terrence Malick. Evanston, Ill.: Northwestern University Press, 1969.

———. *Holzwege.* Frankfurt am Main: Klostermann, 1950.

———. *Identity and Difference.* New York: Harper and Row, 1969.

———. "Letter on Humanism." Translated by Frank A. Capuzzi. In *Martin Heidegger: Basic Writings,* edited by David Farrell Krell. New York: Harper and Row, 1977.

———. *Nietzsche,* vol. 1: *The Will to Power as Art.* Translated by David Ferrell Krell. New York: Harper and Row, 1979.

———. *On the Way to Language.* Translated by Peter D. Hertz. New York: Harper and Row, 1971.

———. "Overcoming Metaphysics." *The End of Philosophy.* New York: Harper and Row, 1973.

———. *Poetry, Language, Thought.* Translated by Albert Hofstadter. New York: Harper and Row, 1971.

———. *The Question Concerning Technology and Other Essays.* Translated by W. Lovitt. New York: Harper and Row, 1977.

———. *Wegmarken.* Frankfurt am Main: Klostermann, 1967.

———. *What Is Called Thinking?* Translated by Fred D. Wieck and J. Glenn Gray. New York: Harper and Row, 1968.

Heiler, Friedrich. *Die buddhistische Versenkung: Eine religionsgeschichtliche Untersuchung.* Munich: Verlag von Ernst Reinhardt, 1922.

Heisenberg, Werner. *The Physicist's Conception of Nature*. 1958: Harcourt, Brace, 1958.

Henderson, Harold G. *An Introduction to Haiku: An Anthology of Poems and Poets from Bashō to Shiki*. Garden City, N.Y.: Doubleday, 1958.

Henry, Michel. "The Critique of the Subject." In *Who Comes After the Subject?* [WCAS], edited by Eduardo Cadava et al. New York: Routledge, 1991..

Hofstadter, Douglas R., and Dennet, Daniel C., eds. *The Mind's I: Fantasies and Reflections on Self and Soul*. New York: Basic Books, 1981.

Hughes, P., and G. Brecht. *Vicious Circles and Infinity*. New York: Penguin, 1979.

Hume, David. *Dialogues Concerning Natural Religion*. Edited by Norman Kemp Smith. Indianapolis: Bobbs-Merrill, 1980.

Husserl, Edmund. *Cartesian Meditations: An Introduction to Phenomenology*. Translated by Dorion Cairns. The Hague: Martinus Nijhoff, 1960.

———. *The Crisis of European Sciences and Transcendental Phenomenology: An Introduction to Phenomenological Philosophy*. Translated by David Carr. Evanston, Ill.: Northwestern University Press, 1970.

———. *Formal and Transcendental Logic*. Translated by Dorion Cairns. The Hague: Martinus Nijhoff, 1969.

———. *Ideas: General Introduction to Pure Phenomenology*. Translated by W. R. Gibson. New York: Macmillan, 1931.

———. *Ideas Pertaining to a Pure Phenomenology and to a Phenomenological Philosophy: First Book: General Introduction to a Pure Phenomenology*. Translated by F. Kersten. The Hague: Martinus Nijhoff, 1982.

———. *The Paris Lectures*. Translated by Peter Koestenbaum. The Hague: Nijhoff, 1967.

———. *Phänomenologische Psychologie*. Edited by Walter Biemel. Husserliana IX. The Hague: Martinus Nijhoff, 1968.

———. *Phenomenological Psychology*. Translated by John Scanlon. The Hague: Martinus Nijhoff, 1977.

Hwa Yol Jung. "Heidegger's Way with Sinitic Thinking." In *Heidegger and Asian Thought*, edited by Graham Parkes. Honolulu: University of Hawaii Press, 1987.

Inada, Kenneth K., and Nolan P. Jacobson, eds. *Buddhism and American Thinkers*. Albany: SUNY Press, 1984.

Ingarden, Roman. *The Literary Work of Art*. Translated by George G. Grabowicz. Evanston, Ill.: Northwestern University Press, 1973.

Kant, Immanuel. *Critique of Practical Reason*. Translated by Lewis White Beck. New York: Liberal Arts Press, 1956.

Katsuki Sekida. *Two Zen Classics: Mumonkan and Hekiganroku*. New York: John Weatherhill, 1977.

Kaufmann, Walter, ed. *Existentialism: From Dostoevsky to Sartre*. New York: New American Library, 1975.

———. *The Portable Nietzsche*. New York: Viking, 1954.

Kierkegaard, Søren. *The Concept of Dread*. Princeton: Princeton University Press, 1954.

———. *Philosophical Fragments*. Translated by D. F. Swenson and H. V. Hong. Princeton: Princeton University Press, 1971.

Kirk, G. S., J. E. Raven, and M. Schofield. *The Presocratic Philosophers: A Critical History with a Selection of Texts*. Cambridge: Cambridge University Press, 1985.

Knipe, Rita. *The Water of Life: A Jungian Journey through Hawaiian Myth*. Honolulu: University of Hawaii Press, 1989.

Kofman, Sarah. "Descartes Entrapped." In *Who Comes After the Subject?* [WCAS], edited by Eduardo Cadava et al. New York: Routledge, 1991.

Kohák, Erazim. *Idea and Experience: Edmund Husserl's Project of Phenomenology in IDEAS I*. Chicago: University of Chicago Press, 1978.

Kripke, Saul. *Naming and Necessity*. Cambridge: Harvard University Press, 1972.

Kristeva, Julia. *Powers of Horror: An Essay on Abjection*. Translated by S. Roudiez. New York: Columbia University Press, 1982.

Kuhn, Helmut. "The Phenomenological Concept of 'Horizon'." In *Philosophical Essays in Memory of Edmund Husserl,* edited by Marvin Farber. New York: Greenwood, 1968.

Lacan, Jacques. *Écrits*. Paris: Éditions du Seuil, 1966.

———. *Écrits: A Selection*. Translated by Alan Sheridan. New York: Norton, 1977.

———. *The Four Fundamental Concepts of Psycho-Analysis*. London: Hogarth Press, 1977.

———. "Of Structure as an Inmixing of an Otherness Prerequisite to any Subject Whatever." In *The Languages of Criticism and the Sciences of Man: The Structuralist Controversy*. Edited by Richard Macksey and Eugenio Donato. Baltimore: Johns Hopkins University Press, 1970.

———. "Merleau-Ponty." In *Le Problème du Style, suivi de Merleau-Ponty*. Pirate edition. Paris: n.d.

Lacoue-Labarthe, Philippe. "The Response of Ulysses." In *Who Comes After the Subject?* [WCAS], edited by Eduardo Cadava, Peter Connor, and Jean-Luc Nancy. New York: Routledge, 1991.

Lamotte, Étienne. *Histoire du bouddhism indien*. Louvain: Institut orientaliste, Bibliothèque de l'Université, 1967.

Landgrebe, Ludwig. "The Problem of the Beginning of Philosophy in Husserl's Phenomenology." In *World and Consciousness: Essays for Aron Gurwitsch,* edited by Lester E. Embree. Evanston, Ill.: Northwestern University Press, 1972.

Laycock, Steven W., and James G. Hart. *Essays in Phenomenological Theology*. Albany: SUNY Press, 1986.

Laycock, Steven W. "Actual and Potential Omniscience." *International Journal of Philosophy of Religion* 26 (1989).

———. *Foundations for a Phenomenological Theology*. Lewiston, N.Y.: Edwin Mellen Press, 1988.

———. "Harmony as Transcendence: A Phenomenological View." *The Journal of Chinese Philosophy* 16 (1988).

———. "Hui-Neng and the Transcendental Standpoint." *The Journal of Chinese Philosophy* 12 (1985).

———. "Nothingness and Emptiness: Exorcizing the Shadow of God in Sartre." *Man and World* 24 (1991).

———. Review of Reinhardt Grossmann's *Ontological Reduction. Husserl Studies* 4 (1987).

———. "Sartre and a Chinese Buddhist Theory of No-Self: The Mirroring of Mind." *Buddhist-Christian Studies* 9 (1989).

Lee, Pali Jae, and Koko Willis. *Tales from the Night Rainbow: Mo'oleloo na Pō Mā-kole: The Story of a Woman, a People, and an Island.* Honolulu: Night Rainbow, 1990.

Leibrecht, Walter, ed. *Religion and Culture: Essays in Honor of Paul Tillich.* Freeport, N.Y.: Books for Libraries Press, 1972.

Levin, David Michael. *The Body's Recollection of Being: Phenomenological Psychology and the Deconstruction of Nihilism.* Boston: Routledge, 1985.

———. "Husserl's Notion of Self-Evidence." In *Phenomenology and Philosophical Understanding,* edited by Edo Pivcevic. London: Cambridge University Press, 1975.

———. *The Opening of Vision.* London: Routledge and Kegan Paul, 1988.

———. *Reason and Evidence in Husserl's Phenomenology.* Evanston, Ill.: Northwestern University Press, 1970.

Lévinas, Emmanuel. "Beyond Intentionality." In *Philosophy in France Today* [PFT], edited by Alan Montefiore. Cambridge: Cambridge University Press, 1983.

———. "Philosophy and Awakening." In *Who Comes After the Subject?* [WCAS], edited by Eduardo Cadava et al. New York: Routledge, 1991.

Loewenberg, Jacob. *Hegel's* Phenomenology: *Dialogues on the Life of Mind.* La Salle., Ill.: Open Court, 1965.

Lopez, Donald S. Jr. *The Heart Sutra Explained: Indian and Tibetan Commentaries.* Albany: SUNY Press, 1988.

Loy, David. *Nonduality: A Study in Comparative Philosophy.* New Haven: Yale University Press, 1988

Lyotard, Jean-François. "Contributions des tableaux de Jacques Monore." In *Figurations 1960–1973,* by Gérald Gassiot-Talabot et al. Paris: Klincksieck, 1973.

———. *Discours, Figure.* Paris: Klincksieck, 1971.

———. *Économie libidinale.* Paris: Editions de minuit, 1974.

———. *Phenomenology.* Translated by Brian Beakley. Albany: SUNY Press, 1991.

———. "Presentations." In *Philosophy in France Today* [PFT], edited by Alan Montefiore. Cambridge: Cambridge University Press, 1983.

———. *Rudiments païens.* Paris: Union Générale d'Éditions, 1977.

Magee, Bryan, ed. *Men of Ideas.* New York: Viking, 1978.

Magliola, Robert. *Derrida on the Mend.* West Lafayette, Ind.: Purdue University Press, 1986.

Maimonides. *The Guide to the Perplexed*. Translated by Schlomo Pines. Chicago: University of Chicago Press, 1963.

Margolis, Joseph. "Deconstruction; or, The Mystery of the Mystery of the Text." In *Hermeneutics & Deconstruction,* edited by Hugh J. Silverman and Don Ihde. Albany: SUNY Press, 1985.

McDaniel, Jay. "Mahayana Enlightenment in Process Perspective." In *Buddhism and American Thinkers,* edited by Kenneth K. Inada and Nolan P. Jacobson. Albany: SUNY Press, 1984.

McKeon, Richard, ed. *The Basic Works of Aristotle*. New York: Random House, 1941.

Mehta, J. L. "Heidegger and Vedanta: Reflections on a Questionable Theme," in *Heidegger and Asian Thought,* edited by Graham Parkes. Honolulu: University of Hawaii Press, 1987.

Menzan Zuiho Osho. *Jijuyu-zanmai* [Samadhi of the self]. In *Dogen Zen* [DZ], translated by Okumura and Wright. Kyoto: Kyoto Soto-Zen Center, 1988.

Merleau-Ponty, Maurice. "Eye and Mind." In *The Primacy of Perception and Other Essays on Phenomenological Psychology, and the Philosophy of Art, History and Politics* [PP], edited by James M. Edie. Evanston, Ill.: Northwestern University Press, 1964.

———. "The Philosopher and Sociology." In *Phenomenology, Language, and Sociology: Selected Essays of Maurice Merleau-Ponty,* edited by John O'Neill. London: Heinemann, 1974.

———. *Signs*. Translated by Richard C. McLeary. Evanston, Ill.: Northwestern University Press, 1964.

Merton, Thomas. *Mysticism and Zen Masters*. New York: Farrar, Straus, & Giroux, 1967.

Misra, R. S. Interview with Dom Aelred Graham. In *The End of Religion,* by Dom Aelred Graham. New York: Harcourt Brace Jovanovich, 1971.

Morris, Phyllis Sutton. "Sartre on the Self-Deceiver's Translucent Consciousness." *Journal of the British Society for Phenomenology* 23 (1992).

Muralt, André de. *The Idea of Phenomenology: Husserlian Exemplarism*. Translated by Garry L. Breckon. Evanston, Ill.: Northwestern University Press, 1973.

Ñaṇajivako, Bhikkhu. "Karma—The Ripening Fruit." In *Kamma and its Fruit*. Wheel Publication no. 221–24. Kandy: Buddhist Publication Society, 1975.

Ñaṇamoli, Bhikkhu. *The Life of the Buddha*. Kandy: Buddhist Publication Society, 1972.

Nancy, Jean-Luc. Introduction to *Who Comes After the Subject?* [WCAS], edited by Eduardo Cadava et al. New York: Routledge, 1991..

Natanson, Maurice. *Edmund Husserl: Philosopher of Infinite Tasks*. Evanston, Ill.: Northwestern University Press, 1973.

Nietzsche, Friedrich. *Beyond Good and Evil*. Translated by Walter Kaufmann. New York: Random House, 1966.

———. *The Gay Science: With a Prelude in Rhymes and an Appendix of Songs*. Translated by Walter Kaufmann. New York: Vintage, 1974.

———. *On the Genealogy of Morals*. Translated by Walter Kaufmann and R. J. Hollingdale. New York: Vintage, 1968.

——. *Gesammelte Werke*, vol. 12. Munich: Musarion Verlag, 1924.

——. *Human, All-Too-Human*. Translated by Paul V. Cohn and edited by Oscar Levy. New York: Russell & Russell, 1964.

———. *The Portable Nietzsche*. Edited by Walter Kaufmann. New York: Penguin, 1980.

———. *Thus Spake Zarathustra: A Book for All and None*. Translated by Thomas Common. Edinburgh: Darien Press, 1909.

———. *Thus Spake Zarathustra*. In *The Portable Nietzsche,* edited by Walter Kaufmann. New York: Viking, 1954.

———. *The Twilight of the Idols*. Translated by Walter Kaufmann. In *The Portable Nietzsche,* edited by Walter Kaufmann. New York: Viking, 1968.

———. *The Will to Power*. Translated by Walter Kaufmann and R. J. Hollingdale. New York: Vintage, 1968.

Nishida, Kitaro. *A Study of Good*. Translated by V. H. Viglielmo. Tokyo: Japanese Government Printing Office, 1960.

Nishitani, Keiji. "What is Religion." *Philosophical Studies of Japan* 2 (1960).

———. *Religion and Nothingness*. Translated by Jan Van Bragt. Berkeley: University of California Press, 1982.

Nott, Kathleen. *The Emperor's Clothes*. London: Heinemann, 1953.

O'Neill, John, ed. *Phenomenology, Language, and Sociology: Selected Essays of Maurice Merleau-Ponty*. London: Heinemann, 1974.

Parkes, Graham, ed. *Heidegger and Asian Thought*. Honolulu: University of Hawaii Press, 1987.

Parsons, Howard L. *The Value of Buddhism for the Modern World*. Wheel Publication no. 232–33. Kandy: Buddhist Publishing Society, 1976.

Paz, Octavio. *Conjunctions and Disjunctions*. Translated by Helen R. Lane. New York: Viking, 1969.

Peirce, Charles Sanders. "Critical Common-Sensism." In *Philosophical Writings of Peirce,* edited by Justus Buchler. New York: Dover, 1955.

———. "Some Consequences of Four Incapacities." In *Philosophical Writings of Peirce,* edited by Justus Buchler. New York: Dover, 1955.

Pivcevic, Edo, ed. *Phenomenology and Philosophical Understanding*. London: Cambridge University Press, 1975.

Plotinus. *The Enneads*. Translated by Stephen MacKenna. London: Faber and Faber, 1969.

Polheim, K. K. *Die Arabeske, Ansichten und Ideen aus Friedrich Schlegels Poetik*. Paderborn: Schöningh, 1966.

Poundstone, William. *Labyrinths of Reason: Paradox, Puzzles, and the Frailty of Knowledge*. New York: Anchor, 1988.

Prufer, Thomas. "Welt, Ich und Zeit in der Sprache." *Philosophische Rundschau* 20 (1973).

Quine, W. V. *Philosophy of Logic*. Englewood Cliffs, N.J.: Prentice-Hall, 1970.

Rancière, Jacques. "After What." In *Who Comes After the Subject?* [WCAS], edited by Eduardo Cadava et al. New York: Routledge, 1991.

Raven, J. E. *Pythagoreans and Eleatics*. Cambridge: Cambridge University Press, 1948.

Rella, Franco. "Fabula." In *Recoding Metaphysics* [RM], edited by Giovanna Borradori. Evanston, Ill.: Northwestern University Press, 1988.

Ricoeur, Paul. *Fallible Man*. Translated by Charles Kelbley. Chicago: Henry Regnery, n.d.

———. "Philosophy of Will and Action." In *Phenomenology of Will and Action*, edited by Erwin W. Strauss and Richard M. Griffith. Pittsburgh: Duquesne University Press, 1967.

Robinson, Richard H. *The Buddhist Religion: A Historical Introduction*. Belmont: Dickenson, 1970.

Rorty, Richard. *Consequences of Pragmatism*. Minneapolis: University of Minnesota Press, 1982.

———. *Essays on Heidegger and Others: Philosophical Papers*, vol. 2. New York: Cambridge University Press, 1991.

———. *Philosophy and the Mirror of Nature*. Princeton: Princeton University Press, 1980.

Roy, M. A., ed. *Species Identity and Attachment: A Phylogenetic Evaluation*. New York: Garland, 1980.

Royce, Josiah. *The World and the Individual*, 2d ser.: *Nature, Man, and the Moral Order*. Gloucester, Mass.: Peter Smith, 1976.

Saint-Exupéry, Antoine de. *Pilote de Guerre*. New York: Éditions de la Maison Française, 1942.

Salmon, Wesley C., ed. *Zeno's Paradoxes*. Indianapolis: Bobbs-Merrill, 1970.

Sangharakshita. *A Survey of Buddhism: Its Doctrines and Methods through the Ages*. London: Tharpa Publications, 1987.

Sartre, Jean-Paul. "Intentionality: A Fundamental Idea of Husserl's Phenomenology." Translated by Joseph P. Fell. *Journal of the British Society for Phenomenology* 1 (1970).

———. *Nausea*. Translated by Lloyd Alexander. New York: New Directions, 1964.

——— *The War Diaries of Jean-Paul Sartre: November 1939/March 1940*. Translated by Quintin Hoare. New York: Pantheon, 1984.

Schilpp, Paul Arthur, ed. *The Philosophy of Jean-Paul Sartre*. La Salle, Ill.: Open Court, 1981.

Schmitt, Richard. "Husserl's Transcendental-Phenomenological Reduction." *Philosophy and Phenomenological Research* 20 (1959–60).

Schrag, Calvin O. *Radical Reflection and the Origin of the Human Sciences*. West Lafayette, Ind.: Purdue University Press, 1980.

Schrödinger, Erwin. *What is Life? and Mind and Matter*. London: Cambridge University Press, 1969.

Schuwer, André, ed. *Phenomenology and the Numinous*. Pittsburgh: Simon Silverman Phenomenology Center, 1988.

Severino, Emanuele. "The Earth and the Essence of Man." In *Recoding Metaphysics* [RM], edited by Giovanna Borradori. Evanston, Ill.: Northwestern University Press, 1988.

Shakespeare, William. *The Winter's Tale*. In *The Arden Edition of the Works of William Shakespeare*, edited by J. H. Pafford. Cambridge: Harvard University Press, 1963.

Shibayama Zenkei. *Zen Comments on the Mumonkan*. New York: New American Library, 1974.

Silverman, Hugh J., and Don Idhe, eds. *Hermeneutics & Deconstruction*. Albany: SUNY Press, 1985.

Smullyan, Raymond. *5000 B.C. and Other Philosophical Fantasies*. New York: St. Martin's Press, 1983.

Sohl, Robert, and Audrey Carr, eds. *The Gospel According to Zen: Beyond the Death of God*. New York: Mentor, 1970.

Sokolowski, Robert. *The Formation of Husserl's Concept of Constitution*. The Hague: Martinus Nijhoff, 1964.

———. *Husserlian Meditations: How Words Present Things*. Evanston, Ill.: Northwestern University Press, 1974.

———. *Presence and Absence: A Philosophical Investigation of Language and Being*. Bloomington: Indiana University Press, 1978.

Solomon, Robert C., ed. *Phenomenology and Existentialism*. New York: Harper and Row, 1972.

Spiegelberg, Herbert. *The Phenomenological Movement: A Historical Introduction*. The Hague: Martinus Nijhoff, 1982.

Sprung, Mervyn, ed. *The Question of Being*. University Park: Pennsylvania State University Press, 1978.

Stcherbatsky, F. Th. *Buddhist Logic*, vol. 1. New York: Dover, 1962.

———. *The Central Conception of Buddhism and the Meaning of the Word "Dharma."* India: Susil Gupta, 1956.

Strauss, Erwin W., and Richard M. Griffith, eds. *Phenomenology of Will and Action*. Pittsburgh: Duquesne University Press, 1967.

Stryk, Lucien and Ikemoto, Takashi, trans. *Zen: Poems, Prayers, Sermons, Anecdotes, Interviews*. Garden City, N.Y.: Doubleday, 1963.

Sullivan, J. W. N. *The Limitations of Science*. New York: Mentor, 1949.

Suzuki, Daisetz Teitaro. *An Introduction to Zen Buddhism*. Kyoto: Eastern Buddhist Society, 1934.

———. *Mysticism: Christian and Buddhist*. New York: Harper, 1957.

———. *Zen Buddhism*. Edited by William Barrett. Garden City, N.Y.: Doubleday, 1956.

Takeuchi, Yoshinori. "Buddhism and Existentialism: The Dialogue between Oriental and Occidental Thought." In *Religion and Culture: Essays in Honor of Paul Tillich,* edited by Walter Leibrecht. Freeport, N.Y.: Books for Libraries Press, 1972.

Tanahashi, Kazuaki, ed. and trans. *Moon in a Dewdrop: Writings of Zen Master Dōgen.* San Francisco: North Point Press, 1985.

Tarthang Tulku. *Time, Space and Knowledge: A New Vision of Reality.* Emeryville, Calif.: Dharma Publishing, 1977.

Taylor, Mark C. *Altarity.* Chicago: University of Chicago Press, 1987.

Tetsuaki Kotoh. "Language and Silence: Self-Inquiry in Heidegger and Zen." In *Heidegger and Asian Thought,* edited by Graham Parkes. Honolulu: University of Hawaii Press, 1987.

Thomas, Edward Joseph. *The History of Buddhist Thought.* New York: Barnes & Noble, 1951.

Thompson, James. "Tasks and Super-Tasks." In *Zeno's Paradoxes,* edited by Wesley C. Salmon. Indianapolis: Bobbs-Merrill, 1970.

Trinh thi Minh-hà. *Woman, Native, Other: Writing, Postcoloniality and Feminism.* Bloomington: Indiana University Press, 1989.

Uchiyama Kosho Roshi. *Dogen Zen as Religion.* In *Dogen Zen* [DZ], translated by Okumura and Wright. Kyoto: Kyoto Soto-Zen Center, 1988.

Valéry, Paul. *Introduction à la poétique.* Paris: Gallimard, 1938.

Vallée-Poussin, Louis de la. *Nirvâṇa.* Paris: Gabriel Beauchesne, 1925.

Van Peursen, Cornelius A. "The Horizon." In *Husserl: Expositions and Appraisals,* edited by Frederick A. Elliston and Peter McCormick. Notre Dame, Ind.: University of Notre Dame Press, 1977.

Wagner, Hans. "Critical Observations Concerning Husserl's Posthumous Writings" in *The Phenomenology of Husserl: Selected Critical Readings,* edited by R. O. Elveton. Chicago: Quadrangle, 1970.

Waldenfels, Hans. *Absolute Nothingness: Foundations for a Buddhist-Christian Dialogue.* Translated by J. W. Heisig. New York: Paulist Press, 1980.

Waley, Arthur. *The Way and its Power: A Study of the* Tao Tê Ching *and its Place in Chinese Thought.* London: George Allen & Unwin, 1934.

Walsche, Maurice, trans. *Thus Have I Heard: The Long Discourses of the Buddha.* London: Wisdom Publications, 1987.

Watts, Alan W. *Psychotherapy East and West.* New York: Ballantine, 1969.

———. "Western Mythology: Its Dissolution and Transformation." In *Myths, Dreams and Religion,* edited by Joseph Campbell. New York: Dutton, 1970.

Whorf, B. J. *Language, Thought, and Reality.* Cambridge: MIT Press, 1956.

Wittgenstein, Ludwig. *Tractatus Logico-Philosophicus.* London: Routledge and Kegan Paul, 1961.

Wright, Walter E. "Fichte and Philosophical Method." *The Philosophical Forum* 19 (1988).

Young, Robert, ed. *Untying the Text: A Post-Structuralist Reader*. Boston: Routledge and Kegan Paul, 1981.

Zaner, Richard M. "On the Sense of Method in Phenomenology." In *Phenomenology and Philosophical Understanding,* edited by Edo Pivcevic. London: Cambridge University Press, 1975.

Index of Subjects

Page references to the notes are given in italics.

Index of Names